ST ANDREWS
IN PHILOSOPHY AND
Founding and General Editor:
John Haldane, University of St Andrews

Values, Education and the Human World
edited by John Haldane

Philosophy and its Public Role
edited by William Aiken and John Haldane

Relativism and the Foundations of Liberalism
by Graham Long

Human Life, Action and Ethics: Essays by G.E.M. Anscombe
edited by Mary Geach and Luke Gormally

*The Institution of Intellectual Values:
Realism and Idealism in Higher Education*
by Gordon Graham

Life, Liberty and the Pursuit of Utility
by Anthony Kenny and Charles Kenny

Distributing Healthcare: Principles, Practices and Politics
edited by Niall Maclean

Liberalism, Education and Schooling: Essays by T.M. Mclaughlin
edited by David Carr, Mark Halstead and Richard Pring

The Landscape of Humanity: Art, Culture & Society
by Anthony O'Hear

*Faith in a Hard Ground:
Essays on Religion, Philosophy and Ethics by G.E.M. Anscombe*
edited by Mary Geach and Luke Gormally

Subjectivity and Being Somebody
by Grant Gillett

Understanding Faith: Religious Belief and Its Place in Society
by Stephen R.L. Clark

*Profit, Prudence and Virtue:
Essays in Ethics, Business & Management*
edited by Samuel Gregg and James Stoner

Practical Philosophy: Ethics, Society and Culture
by John Haldane

Sensibility and Sense: Aesthetic Transformation of the World
by Arnold Berleant

*Understanding Teaching and Learning:
Classic Texts on Education*
edited by T. Brian Mooney and Mark Nowacki

Truth and Faith in Ethics
edited by Hayden Ramsay

From Plato to Wittgenstein: Essays by G.E.M. Anscombe
edited by Mary Geach and Luke Gormally

*Natural Law, Economics, and the Common Good:
Perspectives from Natural Law*
edited by Samual Gregg and Harold James

The Philosophy of Punishment
by Anthony Ellis

Social Radicalism and Liberal Education
by Lindsay Paterson

Logic, Truth and Meaning: Writings by G.E.M. Anscombe
edited by Mary Geach and Luke Gormally

The Moral Philosophy of Elizabeth Anscombe
edited by Luke Gormally, David Albert Jones and Roger Teichmann

The Moral Philosophy of Elizabeth Anscombe

Edited by
Luke Gormally, David Albert Jones
and Roger Teichmann

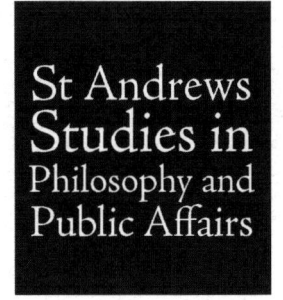

St Andrews
Studies in
Philosophy and
Public Affairs

ia
imprint-academic.com

Copyright © Luke Gormally, David Albert Jones and Roger Teichmann 2016

Individual contributions © the respective authors 2016

The moral rights of the authors have been asserted.
No part of this publication may be reproduced in any form
without permission, except for the quotation of brief passages
in criticism and discussion.

Published in the UK by Imprint Academic
PO Box 200, Exeter EX5 5YX, UK

Distributed in the USA by
Ingram Book Company,
One Ingram Blvd., La Vergne, TN 37086, USA

ISBN 9781845408961 paperback
ISBN 9781845408978 cloth

A CIP catalogue record for this book is available from the
British Library and US Library of Congress

Cover Photograph:
St Salvator's Quadrangle, St Andrews by Peter Adamson
from the University of St Andrews collection

Contents

John Haldane, Preface	vii
Contributors	ix
David Albert Jones, Introduction	1
Anselm Winfried Müller, The Spiritual Nature of Man	10
Duncan Richter, The Conception of the Architectonic Good in Anscombe's Moral Philosophy	33
José M. Torralba, On Morally Neutral Actions, and the Relevance of Practical Truth for Action Theory	51
Matthew B. O'Brien, On Obligation and the Virtues of Law	75
Thomas Pink, Anscombe, Williams and the Positivization of Moral Obligation	98
Candace Vogler, Anscombe on Promising	119
Luke Gormally, On Killing Human Beings	133
David Goodill OP, Elizabeth Anscombe on Just War	154
David Albert Jones, Anscombe on the Human Embryo	172
Kevin L. Flannery SJ, Anscombe on Two Jesuits and Lying	192
Roger Teichmann, Sincerity in Thought	212
Mary Geach, Anscombe on Sexual Ethics	227
Edward Harcourt, Internalized Others, Joint Attention and the Moral Education of the Child	243
John Finnis, Body, Soul and Information: On Anscombe's 'Royal Road' to True Belief	263
Index	289

John Haldane

Preface

Elizabeth Anscombe's article 'Modern Moral Philosophy', published in 1958, is in some respects a characteristic piece of work. It approaches its topic afresh, argues from first to last, introduces many striking ideas (some as asides), but is more concerned to identify fallacies and confusions and refute prevailing dogmas than it is to set out a theory of its own. It is unlike much of her work, however, in having a broadly narrative structure, and offering something of a historical survey. These two features may be attributable to the circumstances that led to its being composed: reading in short order a great many writings in moral philosophy for the purpose of tutoring in the subject, and undertaking to give a non-specialist talk on the theme of the title.

Like much of Anscombe's work its freshness endures; but it also seems to have something of a prophetic character. The latter impression is due in large part to the fact that it gave rise to future developments in British, and later American, moral philosophy, so that looking back at it later it appeared to anticipate them. The main developments came in two phases: first, stalling and then reversing the trend to assume that there is no intrinsic connection between facts, values and practical directives; second, directing attention towards the category of virtues in attempting to say how one ought to act. Although the second is now the more prominent association, it is the first that she was herself more concerned with.

If Anscombe had written nothing else on ethics she would still have been known for 'Modern Moral Philosophy'; and indeed many who know of it may have read little else by her on moral themes. Such is the unsystematic character of her writings that it is not obvious at first or second pass what the connections may be between her investigations of intention, promising, authority, killing and other topics. There is also the fact that much of what she wrote on first-order topics, or ethical questions, appeared in publications that would not easily come to the attention of academic philosophers; and remained uncollected in her lifetime.

Ten years ago St Andrews Studies in Philosophy and Public Affairs published *Human Life, Action and Ethics: Essays by G.E.M. Anscombe* edited by Mary Geach and Luke Gormally. A decade later three further volumes of Anscombe's writings have appeared in the same series. I am very grateful to those editors for their work in making this body of material available. It includes a few essays previously included in earlier collected papers but which are now set in contexts of other hitherto inaccessible or unpublished associated writings thereby allowing readers to get a broader, deeper and more detailed sense of Anscombe's thought.

Given this background it is very fitting that the volume immediately succeeding the last of Anscombe's own writings should be a collection of essays exploring aspects of her moral philosophy. Here we see reflections on themes presented in the 1958 essay, but also on topics from earlier and mostly from later writings. As we proceed towards the centenary of her birth in 1919, thanks to Geach and Gormally and to the editors of the present volume and the authors they have collected, we are in a better position than ever before to understand Elizabeth Anscombe's philosophy and to evaluate it.

As General Editor of the series I am grateful to all concerned, including Jared Brandt and Graham Horswell who were involved in aspects of the production.

Contributors

John Finnis is Biolchini Family Professor of Law, University of Notre Dame, and Emeritus Professor of Law and Legal Philosophy, Oxford University.

Kevin L. Flannery SJ is Professor of Ancient Philosophy, Gregorian University, Rome.

Mary Geach is the literary executor of Elizabeth Anscombe, co-editor of four volumes of her papers, and an independent scholar.

David Goodill OP is a lecturer in moral theology, Blackfriars, Oxford.

Luke Gormally is Director Emeritus of The Linacre Centre for Healthcare Ethics and co-editor of four volumes of Elizabeth Anscombe's papers.

Edward Harcourt is a University Lecturer (CUF) and Official Fellow and Tutor in Philosophy, Keble College, Oxford.

David Albert Jones is the Director of the Anscombe Bioethics Centre, Research Fellow at Blackfriars Hall, Oxford, and Visiting Professor at St Mary's University, Twickenham.

Anselm Winfried Müller is Chicago Moral Philosophy Seminar Visiting Professor, University of Chicago, and Emeritus Professor of Philosophy, University of Trier.

Matthew B. O'Brien works in finance and formerly was a lecturer in philosophy at Rutgers University and a post-doctoral fellow at Villanova University.

Thomas Pink is Professor of Philosophy, King's College, London.

Duncan Richter is Professor of Philosophy, Virginia Military Institute.

Roger Teichmann is Lecturer in Philosophy, St Hilda's College, Oxford.

José M. Torralba is Associate Professor of Philosophy and Director of the Institute of Anthropology and Ethics, University of Navarre.

Candace Vogler is David B. and Clara E. Stern Professor of Philosophy and Professor in the College, University of Chicago.

Reference Abbreviations to Elizabeth Anscombe's publications

CPP1 G.E.M. Anscombe, *Collected Philosophical Papers, Volume 1: From Parmenides to Wittgenstein* (Oxford: Basil Blackwell, 1981).

CPP2 G.E.M. Anscombe, *Collected Philosophical Papers, Volume 2: Metaphysics and the Philosophy of Mind* (Oxford: Basil Blackwell, 1981).

CPP3 G.E.M. Anscombe, *Collected Philosophical Papers, Volume 3: Ethics, Religion and Politics* (Oxford: Basil Blackwell, 1981).

FHG *Faith in a Hard Ground: Essays on Religion, Philosophy and Ethics by G.E.M. Anscombe*, edited by Mary Geach and Luke Gormally (Exeter, UK & Charlottesville, VA, USA: Imprint Academic, 2008).

HLAE *Human Life, Action and Ethics: Essays by G.E.M. Anscombe*, edited by Mary Geach and Luke Gormally (Exeter, UK & Charlottesville, VA, USA: Imprint Academic, 2005).

I G.E.M. Anscombe, *Intention*, second edition (Oxford: Basil Blackwell, 1963).

PtW *From Plato to Wittgenstein: Essays by G.E.M. Anscombe*, edited by Mary Geach and Luke Gormally (Exeter, UK & Charlottesville, VA, USA: Imprint Academic, 2011).

In chapters of this volume the initial reference to a paper by Elizabeth Anscombe gives its location in one or other collection of her papers in the abbreviated format indicated above.

David Albert Jones

Introduction

This collection had as its origin a conference held in September 2013 at St Hugh's College in Oxford, where Elizabeth Anscombe had been an undergraduate seventy five years previously. The centrepiece of the conference was the Anscombe Memorial Lecture given that year by Professor Anselm Müller, and Müller's paper helpfully provides a structure within which the other papers of this collection can be understood.

Müller argues that Anscombe has a distinctive and helpful account of the spiritual character of human nature, not as an immaterial adjunct to an animal nature but as an aspect of the kind of rational-animal nature that humans possess. More specifically, Müller sketches out a set of 'reflexions on Anscombian lines' which lead us to the conclusion that the spiritual nature that distinguishes human beings from the other animals, and that is the basis of specifically human dignity, consists in this: 'Qua human beings, we are all of a kind such as to be guided in our thinking and acting by the norms of truth and goodness.' In this context he quotes Anscombe as saying that, 'The reason for speaking of the spirituality of the soul [...] is not a quasi-physical common property, but that human beings are in for a final orientation towards or away from the good.'

1

From this starting point two sets of questions arise. In the first place we may ask whether Anscombe is correct in stating that human beings all have 'a final orientation towards or away from the good'. Duncan Richter sets up a sceptical challenge to this, not sceptical about the reality of such an orientation but about its demonstrability. He questions whether it is possible to demonstrate by secular ethical reasoning the need or existence of a final, overarching, or architectonic good against which immediate goods can be measured. Taking a concrete example, he doubts that, without appeal to the divine, it could be shown to be more rational from the perspective of practical reason, 'to prefer condemnation to die at the hands of the SS rather than join the SS and do what they have to do'.

Richter's sceptical challenge can be addressed in a variety of ways and subsequent papers seek to do so by appeal to practical truth, practical necessity, appraisal of character or social practices. José M. Torralba reads Anscombe as arguing that the very idea of practical reasoning implies the concept of practical truth and this in turn implies an architectonic good against which actions are judged good or not good. This kind of formal argument may not help the would-be martyr in Richter's example. It will not identify the *content* of the good, but will be more like the saying of St Paul that people have their minds set either on earthly things or heavenly things so that for some 'their god is the belly' (Philippians 3.19). Even if Torralba is judged successful in his attempt to demonstrate that practical reasoning of necessity implies some ultimate end, this would not show that the ultimate end of a particular action is the same for everyone or is the true end of human nature (the end we ought to have). The possibility that one could fail to act for the end one ought to have is indeed implied in the quotation from Anscombe who says that it is a mark of our spiritual nature to have 'a final orientation towards *or away from* the good'.

Richter is, in effect, concerned with the question 'How can one justify the absolute refusal to commit injustice?' Is such an absolute moral obligation even intelligible apart from the context of a divine law? Matthew O'Brien and Thomas Pink both address the concept of 'moral obligation', on which Anscombe famously wrote in her essay 'Modern Moral Philosophy'. O'Brien argues that moral obligation is a species of practical necessity. 'Obligation', he asserts, is 'a normative force of practical reason that is essentially linked with law and authority'. He argues that the obligations of practical reason can be recognized without explicit reference to God. Nevertheless, the importance of 'authority' to this definition leads him to argue that 'someone who recognizes the reality of moral obligation, but lacks this conception of God, is in an epistemically unstable position.' Moral obligation implicitly presupposes divine authority. This account differs from that of Pink who regards obligation as being linked not to moral authority but to negative moral appraisal. Pink argues that the early-modern scholastic tradition already had a sophisticated account of obligation which, in contrast to Anscombe, was not necessarily linked to an idea of law, and certainly not to a divine lawgiver. O'Brien and Pink thus offer divergent explanations for the moral force of obligations, one drawing on Anscombe and the other critical of Anscombe, but both seek to answer the sceptical challenge embodied by positions such as that set out by Richter.

Candace Vogler considers not obligation in general but the specific obligations consequent on promising. She brings Anscombe into dialogue not with high-scholastic philosophy but with contemporary Anglo-analytic accounts which are addressing a problem that troubled David Hume. She reads Anscombe as locating the *intelligibility* of promising-making in a set of practices that are presupposed by the concept. However, she reads Anscombe as relating the *obligatory character* of promises to the human goods served by these practices. Vogler thus returns to the issue of the human good that is served by actions, practices or dispositions.

2

A second set of questions arising from Müller's characterization of human nature is how the contours of this spiritual nature determine the specific ways in which its dignity is respected or violated. These questions are addressed in the second half of this collection, beginning with Luke Gormally's discussion of taking human life. Intentional killing of the innocent is the archetype of failure to respect the dignity of another person. There are many practical reasons that a government might discourage citizens from killing one another, not least the maintenance of a minimal level of public order without which no social life is possible. However, discussion of homicide precisely as *injustice* demands more than pragmatic reasons which hold, not always, but only for the most part. To address this challenge Gormally appeals to an account of dignity similar to that sketched out by Müller. While he acknowledges that Anscombe did not develop a systematic account of dignity in relation to homicide, Gormally shows that such an account is implicitly at work in texts such as the following:

> [...] man is spirit. [Anscombe wrote] He moves in the categories of innocence and answerability and desert—one of the many signs of a leap to another kind of existence from the life of the other ani-

mals. The very question 'Why may we not kill innocent people' asks whether it may not be justified to do so, and this is itself a manifestation of this different life.

As Müller's paper is architectonic for the collection as a whole, Gormally provides the structure for the second half of the collection. After these considerations of the essential injustice of homicide in the central case, David Goodill addresses the concept of the just war, a topic that Anscombe discusses in a number of places. He defends her account against Nicholas Denyer and others who allege that killing in warfare can no longer be justified, if indeed it ever could. As Goodill discusses homicide that may nevertheless be just, my own paper discusses the issue of abortion which Anscombe regarded as unjust but which she thought might not always constitute homicide. Anscombe was not convinced that the early human embryo was a human being in the sense of 'a *Mensch* if we are talking German, an *anthropos* in Greek, a *homo* in Latin', but she was convinced that intentional destruction of the human embryo was murderous, if murder is understood in a non-pedantic sense.

If the dignity of human nature is constituted by an orientation towards truth and goodness then lying will be another archetypal failure to respect that dignity. Kevin Flannery discusses the issue through Anscombe's critique of a Jesuit moralist Vermeersch. Flannery admits her main criticisms of Vermeersch are sound but argues that her alternative raises issues regarding the nature of venial sin, concerning which Thomas Aquinas proves a helpful guide. Flannery provides insights into an argument of Anscombe in relation to lying, but does not address the theme of honesty as a virtuous disposition of character and the need to cultivate discretion as well as seeking to tell the truth and to avoid lying. These broader aspects are considered by Roger Teichmann with reference to Anscombe's article 'On Being in Good Faith'. It seems that, not only someone's statements, but also his or her thoughts are capable of being insincere (or sincere); and this is of importance for the question whether one can be responsible for one's thoughts.

When considering sincerity, honesty or virtue generally, understood as something honourable in itself, the Western moral tradition has given particular place to the virtue of chastity. Indeed there have been periods when the word 'virtue' was used as synonym for this particular virtue. Mary Geach argues that the virtue of chastity is one of the virtues which relates to the final human end in that it prevents disturbances and distortions of the mind that hinder the contemplation of God. This understanding of the virtue of chastity, despite its roots in the classical tradition, in Plato and Aristotle, and its prominence in the early Christian tradition, is rarely defended in modern accounts either secular or religious. Even in Anscombe's thought chastity as a 'shining virtue' is less prominent than the discussion of sexual acts in relation to marriage and procreation. Geach provides an account along Anscombian lines that seeks to recover an appreciation of this aspect of the virtue.

The final paper in this second section concerns not particular aspects of the human good but the way in which children acquire an orientation to truth and goodness. In particular Edward Harcourt argues that moral education necessarily involves a child being taught to attend to 'ends and concerns [by ...] its adults'. Drawing on Anscombe's paper on 'The Moral Environment of the Child', this chapter suggests that the transition from obedience to autonomy can be explained only if the parent's role as moral educator consists in focusing with the child on objects of joint attention.

3

The last paper in the volume, which stands somewhat apart from the others, is a discussion by John Finnis of strands of thought in Anscombe's writings which move beyond what can be known directly on the basis of human reason. Finnis follows Anscombe in making the case for a source of knowledge of human nature in a specific process of historical revelation. A version of Finnis's paper was given as the Anscombe Memorial Lecture for 2014, one year after Müller' lecture, and indeed the starting point of the argument is similar. Both use Anscombe to help defend an understanding of the spiritual character and dignity of human nature that does not consist in the addition of a spiritual or immaterial substance to human nature. It is rather that human beings, by virtue of the kind of beings they are, have an orientation to (or away from) goodness and truth so that 'we can say that this bodily act is an act of a man qua spirit'. However, whereas Müller ends on this point, Finnis moves further to ask what the existence of the human spirit implies about the nature of the world, and of history.

Finnis argues that philosophical reflection on the natural history of the universe and the appearance of life and thence spirit disclose the existence of a transcendent source of being and of information. Furthermore, the existence of spiritual creatures (in the sense in which Anscombe uses that word 'spiritual') brings with it 'the logical and it seems empirical possibility of the intentional communication by the transcendent source of all constitutive information', that is, the possibility of revelation. It is an empirical matter whether such revelation has occurred and, in its favour, Finnis argues that on the topics of divine creation, human freedom and the nature of justice the understanding present in the Jewish Scriptures is superior to that found even in the greatest of the Greek philosophers, thus giving credibility to the former's claims for divine origin.

Finnis is not at this point developing the thoughts that Anscombe articulates 'as she might have developed them', and indeed in her essay on 'faith'[1] Anscombe was highly critical of some forms of rational argument for the credibility of the Catholic faith which were common in the period before the Second Vatican Council. What is believed on faith is precisely believed on trust and not independently on the basis of argument. Nevertheless, it is clear that Anscombe did believe that human beings had received a revelation from the transcendent source of all things. This belief is relevant to her moral philosophy in that it explains how she could entertain scepticism about what could be demonstrated (and especially about what could be demonstrated on the basis of philosophical argument) while having no doubts about the ultimate orientation of human nature in relation to truth and goodness. It is certainly not the case that Anscombe took as a kind of philosophical dogma that certain truths about human nature or about the human good *could not* be demonstrated. It is rather that she was always willing to challenge those arguments that were offered and she did not accept, *a priori*, that philosophy would necessarily be able to furnish an argument which would demonstrate the truth of fundamental moral claims (such as, for example, the claim that it is never morally acceptable to execute an innocent man).

---

[1] 'Faith', in *CPP3*, especially pp. 113–114.

4

Taking the collection as a whole it might be thought that the first six papers concern Anscombe's contributions to meta-ethics and the next seven her writings on normative ethics. However, such a characterization suggests the acceptance of distinctions rejected by Anscombe herself, not least the putative gulf between 'facts' and 'values'. To be sure it is possible to discuss human action at different levels of abstraction so that, for example, in her work on *Intention* Anscombe sought to engage in action-theory prior to discussion of particular moral problems. Nevertheless, Torralba is correct to say that the possibility of analysing actions in abstraction from a final end does not show that there is no final end or that there could be morally neutral actions in the concrete (something denied explicitly by Thomas Aquinas, for example).

Furthermore, there will of necessity be conceptual links between the more abstract and more concrete discussion. If analysis of human action is to be realistic it must be adequate to the reality of concrete actions, to the nature in which they originate and to the end to which they tend.

There are themes that run between these papers and commonalities found in contributions throughout the collection, among both those with a more conceptual emphasis and those with a more practical emphasis. One example is the tension between the sceptical elements of Anscombe's thought, evident in 'Modern Moral Philosophy', and the more creative or synthetic elements, evident in *Intention*. These elements do not map perfectly onto the influence of Wittgenstein and that of Aristotle, but the influence of both thinkers is another reminder of the combination of criticism and constructive argument found in Anscombe. When Richter presents a sceptical challenge almost to the very possibility of moral philosophy this is a sceptical challenge which Anscombe both gave voice to and sought to address.

Related to the elements of scepticism and construction is the relationship of moral philosophy to Christian faith. Hence the relevance of the discussion in the final chapter of this collection, which could be regarded as a coda in relation to that strand of the book. In some places in Anscombe's thought it might seem that Christian faith is invoked to supply what is lacking in philosophical argument (for example in underwriting an architectonic ultimate human good, or in providing the context for a legal conception of moral obligation). In other places it seems that Christian faith reinforces or reframes a conception that can be derived from natural reason. This is how Müller and Gormally understand human dignity, for example. They present a division between a kind of dignity that is based on the human orientation to truth and goodness, and a perfective dignity based on the orientation to knowing and loving God. It may be said that the very concept of dignity, or what is honourable in itself, ultimately relies on some things being 'sacred' and this in turn relies on a concept of the divine. However, if this is true it will also apply to truth, goodness and to all moral concepts and indeed to the existence of anything at all including material consequences of actions — for either there is no God or all things that exist are related to God as their origin and ultimate goal.

Some who read Anscombe have either praised her or criticized her for opening up 'explanatory gaps' that can only be filled by God. However, it should be clear that Anscombe had no need for such gaps in order to accommodate the divine. It is not from theological motive but from philosophical reflection that Anscombe questioned the prejudice, as she once called it, that 'whatever can be said at all can be said clearly'.[2] Her scepticism is simply an acknowledgment of the surfeit within philosophy of poor argument and inadequate justification in relation to firmly held conclusions, some of which are certainly true.

This volume concerns the contribution of Elizabeth Anscombe to moral philosophy, but even to expound her own views critically is something that requires philosophical judgment. For the most part the contributors do not confine themselves only to thoughts thought by Anscombe, but typically move from this to some discussion of the issue with which Anscombe was concerned. How can one distinguish human beings from other animals? Is there an overarching architectonic human good by which we can and should judge the goodness of our more immediate goals? What is the nature of obligation and does it rely on some implicit appeal to a divine lawgiver? Why and when is homicide unjust? How do we understand the virtues of sincerity and chastity and how do we educate children to recognize the good?

The thesis defended by Edward Harcourt has application to the collection itself. For, as Anscombe reminds us, the educator

---

[2] See the Preface to Wittgenstein's *Tractatus Logico-Philosophicus*, echoed by Anscombe in 'Parmenides, Mystery and Contradiction' in *CPP1*, p. 8.

does not seek to be the object of the student's interest but seeks to direct his or her attention to things worth looking at. By this measure, Anscombe's thought merits serious attention because she so often provokes new questions and causes us to think about the issues in a fresh way. Ultimately her thought is worthy of serious study inasmuch as it relates to subjects themselves worthy of serious study, and this is because they relate to the dignity of the human being and his or her final orientation 'towards or away from the good'.

Anselm Winfried Müller

The Spiritual Nature of Man

1. A tale of two birds

In a collection of tales from ancient Persia we read:

> A man went to the shop of a bird dealer in order to offer a parrot for sale. 'How much do you want for the parrot?' the dealer asked. 'A hundred Tômân', he answered. 'What?' exclaimed the dealer, 'how can you ask for a hundred Tômân for such a small bird?'. 'Well', said the owner of the parrot, 'this is a particularly able bird: it talks'. But the dealer still said it was far too expensive and did not want to buy it. During their conversation, the owner of the parrot noticed a turkey sitting in one of the dealer's cages. 'How much do you want for it?' he asked the dealer. 'A hundred Tômân'. 'You really want a hundred Tômân for an ordinary bird like this?' 'Why not?', the dealer said, 'if your bird talks, mine thinks'.[1]

Elizabeth Anscombe would have liked this tale. She was a great lover of funny stories, especially if they had a philosophical point. The point of this one is rather straightforward: nobody would ascribe *thought* to an animal in the absence of relevant behaviour in appropriate circumstances; by the same token, you should not describe as *speech* the vocal performances of a parrot in the absence of relevant behaviour in appropriate circumstances.

What, however, is it that makes us humans unique among animals as thinkers and language users? Anscombe calls this distinctive feature *spirituality*. This Memorial Lecture in her honour is to explore the ramifications of this notion and, in

---

[1] Arthur Christensen (ed.), *Persische Märchen* (München: Diedrichs, 1998), p. 169, my translation.

particular, to pinpoint what she maintains is the centre of our spiritual nature, *viz.* our *orientation towards truth and goodness.*

2. Thought and behaviour

In her article 'Analytical Philosophy and the Spirituality of Man' Anscombe reminds us, *inter alia*, of the kind of *behaviour and circumstances* that go with human thinking. Thoughts are typically expressed in *words*, but words cannot acquire and convey their meanings unless their conventional use is kept in place by the kind of *behaviour and circumstances* that typically go with them. Whence the inappropriateness of ascribing speech to the parrot.

Thoughts can be manifested by behaviour in the absence of verbal articulation. 'One can even see someone thinking something', Anscombe writes. She imagines a piece of behaviour that can be translated into the words: 'This pencil's blunt. Oh well, it'll do.'[2] And she gives the example of 'someone [...] doing a jig-saw puzzle, [where] one wants to say he just had the thought "Perhaps it'll fit in *this* place, but the other way round". The player has been trying the piece in a certain position; then his glance shifts, he gives a slight start, turns the piece round, and tries to fit it...'.[3]

Yet one and the same sort of behaviour, such as handing something over to someone, may mean different things and thus manifest different thoughts. This can be taken as a first indication that there is more to thoughts than patterns of behaviour, and hence behaviourism is wrong — although we have not yet arrived here at a case of thinking that is not embedded in any immediately surrounding behaviour at all.

Anscombe's own example of an 'ambivalent embedding', as we might call it, is taken from Wittgenstein, who considers the thought that is involved in *pointing*. This thought determines 'what is being pointed to: whether to the shape of some object, to the kind of stuff it is made of, its colour, or whatever else may be in question'.[4]

---

[2] 'Analytical Philosophy and the Spirituality of Man', in *HLAE*, pp. 12-13. [Hereafter: 'Analytical Philosophy'.]
[3] 'Analytical Philosophy', p. 14 — As the example shows, Anscombe's primary concern here is with datable thoughts and with what is sometimes labelled 'occurrent thinking' — something one can be engaged in doing — rather than believing and other things that may also be called thinking.
[4] 'Analytical Philosophy', p. 7.

How precisely do these alternative pointings differ from each other? Anscombe notes that no discriminating *experience* needs to go with any particular kind of pointing. 'And even if there was an experience which did happen in all such cases, it would still depend on the circumstances—that is, on what happened before and after the pointing—whether we would say that the pointing was a case of pointing to the shape, not the colour.'[5]

Nonetheless, we are tempted to postulate an inner, or mental, pointing that resolves the ambivalence of the pointing done by a finger, and to ascribe that inner pointing to a spiritual substance, a *spirit*, or 'an immaterial part'[6] —much as we apparently ascribe the outer pointing to a body or bodily part, something material.

Following Wittgenstein, Anscombe rejects an account on these lines. Thought is not an immaterial activity taking place in an immaterial medium, in a sort of 'immaterial matter'.[7]

3. The immateriality of human thought

On the other hand, again like Wittgenstein, she is not a behaviourist, who would want to translate an ascription of thought into an ascription of behaviour. Moreover she also rejects the view that thinking is, at least, of necessity and therefore *always* 'carried' by or embedded in a context made up from behaviour plus circumstances, as it actually is in the case of the jig-saw puzzler. And, more particularly, she denies that thinking typically *consists in* physical occurrences in the way that, for example, *paying* or *winning* do.

According to Anscombe, any attempt on such lines to reduce thought to something else will fail to fit the kind of thinking represented by Auguste Rodin's *Thinker*, viz. 'cases of thinking which have nothing to do with one's surroundings or with any activities in which one is currently engaged'. These are cases in which one says things like this: 'At that moment I had the thought...' In view of such cases we have to accept the possibility of *unembedded*, uncarried thoughts: the possibility of 'assignments by speakers of various thoughts to particular times regardless of there being any

---

[5] 'Analytical Philosophy', p. 8.
[6] 'Analytical Philosophy', p. 10.
[7] 'Analytical Philosophy', p. 9.

events round about those times, the totality of which materially carry the thinking'.[8]

But, in saying this, Anscombe seems to leave us with an unsolved problem, *viz.*: How does Rodin's *Thinker* differ from the dealer's turkey? Why ascribe thoughts to the former but not the latter?

Well, a thinker of flesh and blood is unlikely to maintain the posture recommended by Rodin for very long. What you are thinking right now, but also your very nature as a thinking animal, may indeed not be manifested by any immediate surroundings or behaviour. But the *wider context* of such thinking, including the occasional later report, *shows* you to be a thinker and supplies a background for attributing to you *secret* thoughts *besides* the ones that can be ascribed on evidence.

Anyway, there obviously *are* thoughts that are not carried by, let alone identical with, bodily, and thus material, acts. In this, human thought differs from merely animal thought. Are we then to say that it is those unembedded thoughts that are spiritual acts? 'Surely', Anscombe replies, 'the immaterial nature of thought is there, even when there is a full-blown material occurrence to identify as the occurrence of a thought.'[9] In other words: the absence of a material embodiment is not essential to the immateriality and spirituality of thinking.

What *is* essential to thought is the fact that, even when embodied, it is not tied to the operation of an *organ by which* the thinking is done. In this it differs from functions such as seeing or hearing. 'Thought and understanding are immaterial', Anscombe writes, 'because no act of a bodily part is thought or understanding. Thought is not the activity of any bodily organ.'[10]

---

[8] 'Analytical Philosophy', pp. 13-14.
[9] 'Analytical Philosophy', p. 15.
[10] 'Analytical Philosophy', p. 4. Anscombe would not deny that our thinking is conditioned by certain functions of the brain. But she points out that no brain state can be 'a sufficient condition for [...] say, a belief about banks, [for] a human whose brain might get into that state might never have heard of a bank' ('Causation of Action', in *HLAE*, p. 99), so that the state could be ascribed to him but not the belief. Our notion of (human) thought does not even contain *any* reference to specific operations of a specific part of the body in the way the notions of touching, seeing, hearing, etc. do. In maintaining the spirituality of thinking, Anscombe follows Aristotle (*De Anima* III 4, 429a10-28) and Aquinas (e.g. *Summa theologiae* I, q. 75, a. 2).

4. Thought and what it is of

There is a lot more that Anscombe has to say in clarification of what should and what should not be meant, or fancied, in calling human thinking immaterial and spiritual. I shall have to skip most of this here, but I must mention one point that is of central importance, and one problem that I think she is aware of but does not solve. Both concern what might be called the *purity* of thought.

The assertion that thought is an immaterial, spiritual reality, says Anscombe, does not mean that it takes place in an immaterial *medium*. And she has misgivings about the idea that thinking should be ascribed to a (purely) spiritual *substance* such as an immortal soul.[11] It is the human being that thinks; and if thought has to be ascribed to a spiritual substance, why should not this substance be at the same time a material one, *viz.* the human being?[12]

Anscombe does not try to characterize the spirituality of man and of thinking primarily by what is peculiar to dispositions or occurrences or experiences of thinking in comparison with other mental or physical features we ascribe to human beings. Instead, she characterizes human thought in terms of what it is *of*: 'When I tell you my thought, you are to understand the words I use as having *whatever meaning they would have in context anyway.*'[13] If, e.g., somebody wants to be told about your present thoughts, and you happen to be thinking that there are no chairs in the room, then our specification of your *thought* will be *precisely* the same as a specification of the *situation* described by 'there are no chairs in the room': it will include nothing more and nothing less.[14]

Thus, in order to *characterize* any *particular* thought, we have to do so in terms of what it is *of*. This, we might say, is to characterize it directly or from inside, and to give its essence. When we refer to a thought *indirectly*—as the thought, say, which So-and-so had when entering the room—we are merely locating and identifying

---

[11] Cf. 'The Immortality of the Soul', in *FHG*, p. 71: 'I believe that something does show the spirituality of the soul, but that nothing shows its immaterial substantiality; in fact, that the latter conception—the conception of an *immaterial substance* at all—is a delusive one.'
[12] 'Analytical Philosophy', p. 10.
[13] 'Analytical Philosophy', p. 9.
[14] In the history of Western philosophy, Parmenides seems to have been the first to be struck by this point. At least, it gives a highly plausible sense to his claim that *thinking* and *being* are one.

it from outside, as it were; the specification is accidental to it. To know of any given thought *what it is*, is to know what is being thought in it. Hence, in order to understand the spirituality of human thought *in general* we have to understand that its *essence* consists in its *content*. In this, thoughts differ from perceptions and pictures. What any particular thought *is* and what distinguishes it from any other thought can be specified *only* and *completely* by specifying what it is of, i.e. *what is being thought*. This, I think, is Anscombe's view and the background to what she has in mind when she says that 'the [...] originally Platonic conception is right'[15] — the conception, namely, that the human mind, 'which could grasp [the immaterial Forms] had itself to be immaterial: the soul, Plato said, is *akin to* the forms'.[16]

Perhaps we can add that, on this understanding of the spiritual, the immateriality of thought consists in the fact that nothing material or sensory can *represent* things *in the immediate, non-conventional* and *exclusive way* that thought does;[17] and that the conventions in virtue of which a sentence or signal mean that something is the case are themselves of the nature of thought.[18]

This feature of thought, its being *nothing but* representation, might be called its *purity*. Now, purity often has its price, namely

---

[15] 'Analytical Philosophy', p. 15.
[16] 'Analytical Philosophy', p. 4. Cf. 'Knowledge and Reverence for Human Life', in *HLAE*, p. 60. Plato identified what *thought*, or at least *real knowledge*, is *of*, with the Ideas, or Forms.
[17] I am aware that the idea that thought is a kind of *representation* is controversial. And it is of course true that, as Anscombe insists, there is no medium here by whose modification the representing is done, and that thought is therefore not subject to interpretation or misinterpretation. But this is just part of what I am drawing attention to in saying that the being of a thought is nothing but its *'being of...'*. And it is this very *being of...* that characterizes *as representations* things like pictures or sentences, which represent *not* 'purely' but in virtue of features of a medium.
[18] Even a mental image is not immaterial in the relevant sense. Anscombe says that 'an image has to be particular in the way a given drawing is particular, even if a drawing of a cockroach is not a drawing of a particular cockroach' ('Has Mankind One Soul: An Angel Distributed through Many Bodies?', in *HLAE*, p. 24). Now, this *seems* to be true also of the occurrence of a thought (I'll return to this topic shortly). But a mental image that represents *cockroach* (rather than a particular cockroach) is a) not 'exclusive': it is one from among indefinitely many possible cockroach-images that differ from each other qualitatively, and b) not of *general* import independently of a thought, which it carries, and which *determines* that import.

disconnection. In the case of thought, it creates the problem I announced at the beginning of this section: *How* can any particular thought be *yours*, or anyone else's? For neither the thinker, nor a representation of the thinker, is part of the thought; and in the case of secret thoughts, there are no words or other 'thinking behaviour' that might be taken to tie those thoughts to the person who thinks them. They seem to be free-floating danglers.

This problem is addressed in a lecture, given and published by Anscombe in 1985, with the suggestive title 'Has Mankind One Soul — An Angel distributed through Many Bodies?' Here we read:

> The intellect frames or somehow receives general concepts. If these general concepts are to be found in a lot of particular intellects, then they are not general: one could find particular examples of a general concept in all the particular intellects that had it. The general concept would have a particular instantiation in the individual intellect. But that conflicts with what the intellect is supposed to have; it grasps universals, the content of general terms…[19]

To this, one wants to object: 'But you are confusing two kinds of generality, and two corresponding kinds of instantiation. A concept's *general application* — its instantiation by many things falling under it — is quite compatible with its *individual occurrences* in indefinitely many intellects — i.e. the multiple "instantiation" of that concept *qua* mental item.' This objection, however, presupposes that a thought is a mental item like an image that gets its individuality *from* the individual in whose mind it is. But if a thought, or concept, is *nothing but* representation, there is no reality to it in virtue of which it could be *ascribed* to anything individual.[20]

Anscombe professes not to know how to refute this idea: 'All I can say is that the individuation of intellects and of that by which they think of what they think of cannot after all be an impediment

---

[19] 'Has Mankind One Soul?', p. 24.
[20] The doctrine, found in Aquinas, that human thought requires *conversio ad phantasmata* (e.g. *Summa theologiae* I, q. 84, a. 7 and q. 86, a. 1) may point a way out of this problem. For it implies that the employment of concepts has to rely on materially individuated sensory items, so that your thought that p is different from my thought that p because it latches on to a different perception, memory image, fantasy, sensation, impulse, or the like. In 'The Thought', Frege similarly posits individual *ideas* as required to 'aim at' the objective and shareable Thoughts.

to their understanding of what is general.'[21] — This is where I, too, want to leave the topic, in order now to return to the comparison between human and sub-human thinking.

5. Two rival conceptions of the human mind

'The divide between mind and matter', Anscombe writes, 'was drawn differently by the ancients and medievals from the way it is drawn in modern times.'[22] For an Aristotelian, there were operations of the human as well as the merely animal soul, such as perception, that required bodily organs. Thinking, however, required no such organ and was as such the mark of the mental. Only the *human* soul, or that part of it which was responsible for thinking, the intellect or mind (*mens*), was treated as immaterial, and sometimes as an immaterial substance. From Descartes onwards, by contrast, it was not independence from the operation of bodily organs, but consciousness that was taken to characterize the mind. So now 'the acts of soul, of immaterial substance, are all those psychological states and events given expression in an indubitable first person present indicative: "I feel pain", "I see", "I hear" [...].'[23]

Anscombe holds that an 'idea of the immaterial nature of the soul' that is 'associated exclusively' with such states and events is problematic.[24] And she dissociates her own conception of spirituality from the modern, Cartesian, understanding of the mind.

Note that this means that, along with consciousness, *intentionality* too (the directedness of operations, capacities and dispositions of the soul at characteristic objects) is being disqualified as a mark of the spiritual. At least, the kind of intentionality which Anscombe herself attributes to e.g. sensation, and which she is ready to ascribe to many other animals as well as to humans, does not confer a spiritual nature on the subjects of sensation, desire, etc. This is important, as it also applies to the intentionality of the

---

[21] 'Has Mankind One Soul?', p. 25. This paper picks up a topic treated by Aquinas in his *De unitate intellectus contra Averroistas*. Aquinas here argues against the doctrine of Averroes that the intellect is a substance not united to the human organism and shared by all human beings.
[22] 'Analytical Philosophy', p. 5.
[23] 'Analytical Philosophy', p. 6.
[24] 'Analytical Philosophy', p. 6.

sort of cognition and communication that I wish to consider in sections 7–9. Only the intentionality that goes with a conception of *reality* is distinctive of a mind as spirit.

6. Meaning, thought and truth

So far, we have not been given much of a positive account of our spiritual nature—except that it is something to do with thought and what this is of. A further hint in this direction is contained in the following passage:

> When someone points to the colour (as opposed to the shape) there is a material happening with a meaning. [...] And meanings are sometimes referred to points of time when only the scantiest material happenings were relevant or even when there were no material happenings for them to be the meanings of.[25]

Here it appears that *meaning* is what sets the spiritual apart from the material. But just as many non-human kinds of animal can be said to *think* this or that, there are ones, also, that seem to be able to *mean* things, even though we would not ascribe a spiritual nature to them. When a dog barks, e.g., we may wonder what he means by it—aggression, or thrill, or a greeting? This is not just the question what *it*—the barking—means, i.e. what it is a sign of. We want to know, rather, what the dog means, or wants to indicate, by that barking.

And we don't want *just* to say: Yes, but the dog's meaning, like his thought that such-and-such, is necessarily carried by behaviour, while that of a human being is not. For, *why* is this a *relevant* difference? What peculiarity of human thought does it point to? As Anscombe has made clear, the spiritual nature of human thought, and meaning, does not, after all, depend on *its not* being embedded in behaviour.

Man's spirituality thus seems to be characterized by the *possibility* of being actualized in meanings in the absence of 'material happenings for them to be the meanings of'. Brute animals would accordingly be characterized as such by being capable only of meanings and thoughts, if any, for which a 'pure' occurrence of this sort is *impossible*. How is this difference to be accounted for? Anscombe does not explicitly address this issue. But I think

---

[25] 'Analytical Philosophy', p. 13.

reflection on it can actually lead us to a deeper understanding of what she does say. Let us then look at an example.

It is possible to say of a cat that it thinks there is a mouse underneath the cupboard. Now, you, too, may on that occasion think there is a mouse underneath the cupboard. Admittedly, while the *cat's* thought *has to be* manifested by *behaviour in context*, yours may be manifested by behaviour, *or* by words, *or* not at all. Nonetheless, it appears that *what* the cat thinks is the same as what you think.

Now, this appearance, I want to say, is wrong. What the cat thinks is, in a decisive sense, not what you think. The appearance to the contrary is due to the fact that we have to render the feline thought by verbalizing a human variant of it: we put it in words — in the words of human language.

You can of course join the cat in crawling and prying in front of the cupboard. But this possibility does not show that this behaviour of yours would express the same thought as that of the cat, rather than (let us assume) the same thought as *you* could express less dramatically in the *words* 'There is a mouse underneath the cupboard'. That behaviour of yours, however accomplished, *cannot* even reveal exactly what you are thinking (i.e. what your words would express, if uttered at the time). For it could equally mean 'The mouse that is hiding underneath the cupboard must soon appear' and an indefinite range of further alternatives to 'There is a mouse underneath the cupboard'. *Your* thought excludes these alternatives;[26] for the cat's thought there is no range of alternatives to exclude. The cat's behaviour determines its thought exhaustively; yours at best points to a range of thoughts you are likely to be entertaining.

That there is a difference between your thought and the cat's is indicated by the fact that we are ready to say: 'The cat thinks there is a mouse under the cupboard', but not: 'The cat thinks that it is true that there is a mouse under the cupboard.'[27] Is this because

---

[26] This is not quite true. For there are, in particular, spontaneous reactions to unexpected happenings that reveal what I have called, in an unpublished paper, 'practical beliefs' — 'thoughts' that *are*, by definition, exhaustively determined by the behaviour in which they manifest themselves and often conflict with the same subject's considered beliefs. Cf. Tamar Szabó Gendler, 'Alief and Belief', *Journal of Philosophy* 105(10) 2008:634–663.

[27] This point is at the bottom also of the considerations advanced in the previous paragraph. For it is different *truth*-conditions that discriminate between

we assume that the cat is unaware of the redundancy theory—that it is too dim to realize the equivalence between 'such-and-such' and 'It is true that such-and-such'? I suggest it is because the cat is too dim to think *what* you think, in the first place—even though both you and the cat can be *described* as thinking that 'there is a mouse under the cupboard'. The question is how this can be.

7. Cave language

Can I prove that what you think differs from what the cat thinks? I'll try. To do it, however, I have to introduce to you, in addition to the parrot, turkey and cat that you have already met, yet another kind of animal, this time an imaginary mammal, called *caveman*.[28]

Unlike those other creatures, caveman is a language-using species—or so it seems. Are cavemen *rational*? Well, again: so it seems.[29] What, then, are they like? Well, here is what you must know about them for the purpose of my argument:

In some kind of public place that borders on their dwellings they draw marks in the sand that covers that place. We manage to

---

alternative possibilities when *human* behaviour is taken to reveal this, *or* that, *or* that other thought. We cannot take the *cat's* behaviour to express a true thought without associating it, arbitrarily and unjustifiably, with just one of these alternatives.

[28] I find cavemen a philosophically interesting species in their own right. If you don't, just view them as an auxiliary construction useful for clarifying the relationship between human and animal thinking, much as auxiliary lines are of use in geometry for proving properties of a figure of which these lines themselves are no part. The idea is that, allowing ourselves to be struck by the possibility, intelligibility and even plausibility of the cavemen's primitive procedure, we might be in a better position to appreciate, by attending to the contrast, *our own cognitive equipment.*—When I gave the lecture, I was asked in discussion whether Cavemanese is not much the same as the honey-bees' dance. The similarity had not occurred to me. There is, however, as I have conceived of the former, an important difference between them: the cavemen's employment of marks is conventional. Unlike the bees, they have to learn the significance of the relevant promptings from teaching by example and correction. As we are going to see, however, correction is not—as it is in the human acquisition of assertoric language—governed by a standard of *truth*; it merely rectifies divergence from the practices indicated under (1) and (2) in section 7.

[29] Interestingly, Anscombe does not explicitly identify the spiritual nature of man with rationality. And, in order to serve my argument, cavemen will have to turn out to be creatures that lack *spirituality*, whether we ought to ascribe *rationality* to them or not. Cf. also footnotes 35 and 4.

establish a strong correlation between the shapes of the marks and the behaviour of their users, which we are inclined to describe as follows:

1) An individual who has observed the presence of firewood, fruit or wholesome plants in the surroundings tends to produce a mark whose components correlate with a) the kind of good that he or she has observed, b) the direction, as from the public place, in which it was to be found, and c) the number of steps that it took to get back to this place as directly as possible.
2) Individuals who have looked at a particular mark will often walk away in the direction correlated with it, and, in accordance with the other two correlations, take a certain number of steps, then look around for a certain kind of good, often find it and take it or some of it back home.

The practice thus described appears to represent a sort of communication in the service of the cavemen's purposes, with the marks functioning as *symbols indicating* the whereabouts of kinds of good. We shall be inclined to say that, by means of the marks, they tell each other where to find them. And, that such a mark is taken to express *the thought, or judgment, that* food or whatever is to be found at such-and-such a distance in such-and-such a direction from the public place.

There are, however, problems about this assessment. Are we really entitled to describe their procedure in this way, in advance of knowing quite a lot about whatever *further* aspects characterize it? — Obviously, the story can be developed in a number of *different* ways. Here is one such way, which I invite you to consider.

8. Failure as disappointment

It sometimes happens that a caveman, ostensibly guided by his inspection of one of the marks, walks a certain distance, and then looks around, but returns empty-handed. Assuming that such a walk is undertaken for the usual sort of purpose, we shall look for an explanation of that kind of unexpected behaviour.

Upon examination of and reflexion on a good many cases, we find that a number of explanations, matching different types of case, must be taken into account, and in particular the following:

1) After discovering the kind of good that was signified by the mark he has inspected, our caveman loses interest, or gets distracted.

2) He fails to see the kind of good in question; or he sees it alright, but it does not suit his needs, or tastes.
3) What was indicated by the mark has, for whatever reasons, disappeared.
4) Our caveman has failed to walk in the direction correlated with the mark.
5) He has failed to walk the right number of steps.
6) The steps he has taken were too small or too big.
7) He has misread the mark.
8) No goods ever corresponded to this particular mark. I.e. the caveman who produced it did not, in doing so, act in accordance with the standard associations. — There may be any number of reasons for this, which we might classify as 'spelling' error, misremembering, wishful thinking, deceit...
9) After having been produced, the mark was disfigured in a way such as to change *significance*. (Something comparable, for instance, to this: where it originally said *9000 steps* it now says *900 steps*.) — Again, there may be different ways of accounting for the disfigurement: sometimes the rain or strong winds have that effect, or the activities of giant ants or of cave-children.

Given my description of the practice, we can say: the cavemen typically *rely on* those marks, but the marks sometimes *fail* them. Or: application of a mark sometimes succeeds, and sometimes fails to succeed.

Can we also say that the marks in the sand amount to *information*, or statements, that can be *true or false*? — My list of distinguishable sources of failure does not yet enable us to answer this question. Whether Cavemanese can count as assertoric language depends on yet further details of the story; and, in particular, on how the cavemen are represented as *responding to failure*. Let us then look at what happens when one of them has been let down in connexion with the use of one of those marks.

9. No distinction between grounds of failure

As it turns out, the cavemen react with one and the *same* kind of disappointment to every abortive use of a mark — i.e. in any of the cases that *we* should differentiate in terms of explanations (2-9). They do not show any tendency to discriminate between these different ways of accounting for failure of a mark's leading to success.

In particular, nothing indicates that the cavemen distinguish between cases in which

a) the mark that has failed to bring success has, *from the beginning*, been a bad guide because its producer somehow bungled;
b) the mark, although indicative of goods when originally created in the sand, has been *disfigured* by the time of inspection in a way such as to give a wrong orientation;
c) the mark, although produced by one of them in accordance with (correct) observations made by him, is *now* misleading because the goods in question have subsequently *disappeared*;
d) the mark fits the existence of goods alright, but the individual *relying* on it has *failed* to walk as indicated or has not managed to perceive those goods.

The differences between these situations are not matched by any differences between the ways in which the cavemen handle them. In other words: the cavemen take no notice of *grounds* of failure, and even less do they consider *alternative* possibilities of accounting for it. We may assume that a frustrated individual furiously swears, or perhaps expresses dissatisfaction in more sedate ways, and ignores the mark that has misled him. But nothing indicates that he tries to discover *what kind* of misfortune, e.g. from among (a–d), his particular lack of success is an instance of.

10. Falsehood *versus* failure

As far as I can see, the cavemen's *undiscriminating disappointment* at a mark's failure to guide them to the satisfaction which it promises means that they do *not* treat their marks as *assertions*. When an English sentence that you are treating as an *assertion* lets you down, you will in principle allow for a number of *different* reasons why you do not find it confirmed. These will (assuming that tense is involved) include the following:

a) The sentence was never a true assertion (cf. (8) above).
b) It was once true (or false), but is now obsolete, since the situation it was about no longer obtains (cf. (3)).
c) You have not done what you have to do in order to find the assertion confirmed (cf. (4–6)).
d) You have misunderstood the words (cf. (7)).
e) The words in which the assertion was expressed have undergone a physical change that affects their meanings (cf. 9).

If you are unable to envisage these (and other) different possibilities you lack the full notion of an assertion.

This notion involves a number of aspects relevant to the question whether Cavemanese is a language of assertions. Here are some of these aspects: we distinguish between the falsehood of an assertion, on the one hand, and a user's unawareness of the assertion's truth on the other; the assertoric meaning of a sentence is not independent of the speaker's intention in uttering it; merely physical causes (causes not due to human intention) do not count as having an influence on an assertion's meaning. — Unless you are aware of these (and other) aspects of the notion, you cannot be said to make *assertions* or to understand and believe or disbelieve them.

The kind of standard by which an assertion is judged to be true or false is *more complex* and *more specific* than the standard of success and failure, or match and mismatch, that guides the kind of reaction our cavemen show when their use of a mark results in disappointment and frustration rather than satisfaction.

The most glaring deviation of the cavemen's practice from the use of assertions seems to be due to the fact that their practice does not provide for a distinction between physical interference (as from children and ants) and other sources of failure. In *this* respect, the way in which they base their behaviour on the perception of marks in the sand is more reminiscent of our reliance on *the look of the sky* for predicting the weather than our reliance on *the Local Weather Forecast* for the same purpose. (I don't mean to suggest the weather forecast is more reliable. Only, it *signifies* in a different way, *viz.* by virtue of linguistic conventions.)

11. The teleology of assertion and judgment

In view of these observations, we may say that assertions, judgments and beliefs differ from the cavemen's use of marks in their inherent *teleology*. Quite apart from any *further* purposiveness, they are conceptually tied to standards which they are directed at satisfying — standards of assessment that have no application to the cavemen's practice. Assertions, judgments and beliefs are assessed as *true or false*, while the marks succeed or fail to succeed in *procuring satisfaction*. Use of the *marks* is essentially directed at some kind of *non-theoretical success*, and cave beliefs are disqualified by *disappointment* of expectation; whereas *assertions* are, as such, directed at *true* representation, and genuine beliefs are disqualified *only* by being *false*, or, more accurately: the standard of truth is the only standard to which something *has to* be answerable in order to count as belief.

Unlike e.g. guesses, judgments, assertions and beliefs aim not only at truth but at *knowledge*. The marks of the cavemen obviously don't. To do that, their use would have to involve the consciousness that *error* is, at least in principle, possible. But the cavemen react to failure in a way that does not *distinguish* what we would identify as *error*, on the part of either the producer or the user of a mark, from other ways in which production of, or reliance on, that mark leads to *disappointment*.

The profound disparity between human language and Cavemanese can also be brought out by the following observation. The use of cave marks does not imply discrimination between what is called 'directions of fit'. The cavemen's response to failure does not allow us to say *either* that they take the marks to come about in order to match circumstances, *or* that they expect circumstances to match the marks (as people might expect the outcome of an election to match their votes — or their prayers).

12. Cave-assertions and cave-beliefs

Does all this mean that we cannot say of a caveman, for instance: 'He believed that some firewood was located 900 steps north of the public place'? No, we can ascribe beliefs to cavemen on the basis of, roughly, their production of and reliance on marks in the sand, with at least as much justification as we can ascribe beliefs to many other animals on the basis of *their* behaviour. But we should concede, and then remember, that cave-assertions, cave-judgments and cave-beliefs are called assertion, judgment and belief *by courtesy*. It would be more appropriate to call them quasi-assertions, etc. For although they overlap to a considerable extent with their human cousins in formation condition and function, they differ from them in essential respects, and especially in not admitting of truth or falsehood.

Human judgment essentially includes awareness of the characteristic *dimension* of its assessment as *true or false*. You are not judging, or even entertaining the thought, that such-and-such, unless in doing so you are conscious that your thought is subject to the standard of truth and that in judging that such-and-such you are aiming at knowledge.

13. The truthlessness of cats and cavemen

The point of my story is of course to suggest that what is at the bottom of our spiritual nature is the human *capacity for truth*, and to give some flesh to this suggestion. I have introduced the cavemen and their quasi-judgments in order to elucidate, by means of a *contrast*, the notion of a human *thought* as something that can be, and 'wants' to be, *true*.

And here is the proof I promised I would try to give, that *what* the cat thinks about the mouse is never what you think about it: like cave-beliefs, the thoughts we ascribe to cats and dogs and many other animals are no more than quasi-thoughts. With respect to the cavemen, who use conventional signs, we were able to articulate the difference between thought and quasi-thought in terms of the difference between falsehood on the one hand, and indeterminate disappointment of reliance on cave-marks on the other. It seems clear that, *a fortiori*, animal behaviour of a totally non-symbolic, non-linguistic kind is incapable of manifesting thoughts as opposed to quasi-thoughts.

14. Assertion, truth, reality

Though comparable in terms of practical function, Cavemanese is sufficiently dissimilar from the human employment of statements to be instructive, as it were, *ex negativo*, *viz*.: to provide us with a background against which we get a sharper view of the very special nature of our actual assertoric practice and of its relevance to the idea of *reality*. For this idea imports a contrast that is tied to the dichotomy between true and false propositions. Our primary notion of what is real, as opposed to unreal and merely apparent, is inseparable from that of things being as a true proposition states them to be. There is thus, strictly speaking, no reality for cats and cavemen: *what* their cognitions (and quasi-intentions, etc.) relate to is not reality. And what makes us spiritual beings is, ultimately, our ability to frame the notion of reality as something of which we are part, and which is, at the same time, the measure of assessment to which our thinking is accountable by its very nature and inherent teleology.

My argument comes down to this: we grasp what reality is by grasping what truth is, we grasp what truth is by understanding its connexion with falsehood, and this connexion can be elucidated by comparing the way we fault assertions for being false with the way my cavemen recognize failure when expectations created by their marks are not matched by circumstances (a failure that *we* make intelligible to ourselves in terms of a *range* of possible sources, only one of which we classify as falsehood). Reality is what we treat as grounding the verification—or falsification—of assertions. Since nothing stands in this relation to cave marks, the language and the quasi-thought of cavemen cannot be said to involve consciousness of reality. And the same holds of the quasi-thought of actual brute animals. They are not conscious of reality.[30] This is why I said not only is the cat's thinking different from yours: *what* it thinks is also different from what you think.

These reflections may help us to appreciate some of Anscombe's seemingly strange remarks in her paper 'On Wisdom', where she characterizes our cognitive equipment, and thereby human spirituality, as the capacity to think and say 'that something is so'. 'The "saying that ... by many propositions"', she says with reference to quite ordinary statements, 'is what gives them their enormous importance. This lies in the extremely usual peculiar connexion between a saying that ... and a reality. [...] Where there is this connexion, it exists whether the proposition is true or false, for a false proposition is converted into a true one by negating it, and negation introduces no new feature.'[31] And: 'The power of thinking *what is so*, even wrongly, is created in men, giving them language that can express it. "Being so" is the first thing to get into the nascent human intellect, the beginning of knowledge [...].'[32]

15. Conscious normativity: truth and goodness

In judging that such-and-such, you are conscious of subjecting your judgment and yourself, as judger, to an assessment that is not of your choosing or any human choosing at all. Indeed, assertoric thought can be viewed as a paradigm of something that is not only subject, and accountable, to a standard but inevitably contains the consciousness of that subjection and accountability. Not only can your judgment be assessed as true or false: you are

---

[30] Nor, therefore, of mere appearance. It won't do to imagine, e.g., a bear scratching its head in front of a deserted bee-hive. Nothing short of *linguistic* behaviour can express the thought 'I was wrong'.
[31] 'On Wisdom', in *FHG*, p. 265; cf. p. 263.
[32] 'On Wisdom', p. 266.

not even *judging* unless you are aware of this standard and attempting to comply with it.

In a similar way, the practical thought of a *purpose*, and the will and intention to attain it, involve the consciousness and endorsement of a standard. Anscombe certainly holds this view.[33] It coincides with the doctrine, put forward by Aristotle and Aquinas, and nowadays debated under the heading 'the guise of the good', that human action is as such directed at goodness, and at particular objects *qua* ostensibly good. The view implies that your acting is not a matter of the will and not ethically relevant unless 1) it manifests a thought and intention that, at least implicitly, relates that acting to an ultimate end, or an order of practical values, whose implementation appears to be unconditionally good to you, and 2) you are, in acting, conscious of the possibility of failing in this orientation, i.e. of acting wrongly.

Now, just as cavemen, and *a fortiori* speechless animals, manifest bland indifference to the norm of truth by manifesting a kind of cognition in which the consciousness of (possibly) *erroneous belief* has no place, they also exhibit free-thinking nihilism when it comes to questions of good and bad in the realm of behaviour. Their behaviour is indeed directed at what is good — *viz.*, roughly, at an unimpeded life in accordance with their species — by implementing the inclinations of their respective natures. But when that behaviour fails to succeed or to match that standard, there is no way they would respond with regret, let alone remorse. And, even more obviously, they would not exhibit, as a human adult would, regret of *purpose intended* as opposed to regret of *means employed*, nor either of these as opposed to regret regarding *uncomplying circumstances*.

16. Morality as spirituality

The conscious normativity of goodness is the basis of morality. As we have seen, it is an essential aspect of *human* nature that we choose ways of acting, and give relative weight to our various ends, in light of a more or less explicit overall conception of how to live: a conception that directs us, e.g., to give preference to

---

[33] She explicitly endorses Aristotle's view concerning *eupraxia* that 'anyone who acts (*prattei*) has that objective [...]. Acting well [...] is the actual end of any action' ('How Can a Man be Free?', in *PtW*, p. 92). 'Truth is the object of judgement', we read, 'and good the object of wanting' (*I*, §40).

family concerns over hobbies—or *vice versa*! Now, this possibility of '*vice versa*' points to a feature which radically distinguishes specifically human from merely animal striving: the system of ends that directs our life can be *bad* because our overall *conception* of how to live can be bad, and can be *assessed* by ourselves as bad and subjected to criticism and revision.[34] Human action, intention *and even ultimate purpose* involve the consciousness of the possibility of badness. Where, and only where, this is present in a creature, can its striving be said to be (or fail to be) oriented and guided by the good, and thus to be of a spiritual nature.[35]

Here, then, we have the roots of morality. Anscombe certainly thought morality central to our spiritual nature: 'The reason for speaking of the spirituality of the soul [...] is not a quasi-physical common property, but that human beings are in for a final orientation towards or away from the good.'[36]

Unfortunately, I cannot pursue this topic here. The following must suffice as a summary: whatever you do in the everyday sense of *acting* is done in (implicit) awareness and acceptance of a norm. In acting, you are conscious not only of what you are doing but also that, by acting, you are placing this very acting, and, indeed, your will, your life, yourself under a norm of goodness that is not of your choosing. Any choice is itself under that norm. And it is in virtue of the consciousness of that practical normativity that morality is an aspect of your spiritual nature.

17. Human dignity and its basis

Reflexions on Anscombian lines thus lead us to the conclusion that the spiritual nature that distinguishes us from the other animals consists in this: *qua* human beings, we are all of a kind such as to be guided in our thinking and acting by the norms of truth and goodness.—Is that all?

---

[34] Cf. 'Practical Inference', in *HLAE*, p. 147.—If your overall end can be bad, what is the standard by which it is thus assessed? Human nature? The good as formal object of the will? And how would these two suggestions answer that question? Are they mutually exclusive alternatives?

[35] This *may* be the reason why Anscombe does not identify spirituality with rationality (cf. fn. 29). If practical rationality is taken to require only the ability to figure out means to ends, it might occur—perhaps in Köhler's clever apes—without the conception of an overall end, let alone the consciousness of its being subject to, as well as supplying, a standard of assessment.

[36] 'Immortality', p. 83.

Well, is it not enough? I should have thought that the values of truth and goodness are not in need of philosophical propaganda in order to play a central role in human life as well as in our conception of it.[37]

You may of course associate with the expression 'spiritual', if not: *esoterica*, at least exalted things such as care of the inner life, religious attitudes, meditation, or the like. And this association is not altogether alien to Anscombe's treatment of the topic. She says that our *attitude towards* the spiritual nature of man has to be a 'religious' one, an attitude 'of respect before the mystery of human life';[38] she speaks of 'concern with the immaterial part',[39] and of man's 'mystical value';[40] and she says that 'perception of what a human being is [!] makes one perceive human death as awesome'.[41]

But such expressions typically occur in passages concerned with the special *dignity* that attaches to human nature. They are not meant to characterize that dignity's basis, spirituality itself. The dignity of human life that is consequent upon its spiritual nature is in fact of the greatest importance to Anscombe — and ought to be so to anyone, because of the far-reaching practical implications of this dignity. Indeed, what is here *meant* by 'dignity' must be grasped and explained in terms of what we perceive as *acknowledging* and as *violating* it in the many ways that human beings can be and have been treated respectfully, and degradingly.

Now, the care of one's inner life by meditation and the like may well be part of the appropriate acknowledgment of one's own human dignity. But Anscombe draws our attention to other, less 'spiritual', ways of respecting our spiritual nature that are at least as important and probably more in need of being called to mind — respect for human life in the dying and the unborn, rejection of degrading forms of sexuality and reproduction, rejection of cruel

---

[37] Anscombe herself seems to treat our capacity to think and say what is the case almost as the apex of human nature. Cf. 'On Wisdom', p. 265.
[38] 'Murder and the Morality of Euthanasia', in *HLAE*, pp. 269–270.
[39] 'Immortality', p. 70. Cf. Aristotle, *Eudemian Ethics*, VIII 3, 1249b21–23; *Nichomachean Ethics* X 7.
[40] 'Prolegomenon to a Pursuit of the Definition of Murder', in *HLAE*, p. 260.
[41] 'Murder', p. 270.

kinds of punishment, respect for the freedom and self-determination of people especially dependent on others' support.[42]

All these things manifest recognition of man's dignity. And, lacking respect for it, Anscombe says, 'you cannot revere the dignity of your own human-ness'.[43] The *basis* of this dignity, however, is man's spiritual *nature*.

Now, to be sure, this spiritual nature is at work not only in the orientation of judgment and action by the norms of truth and goodness. Anscombe herself mentions, as dependent on our spirituality, 'aesthetic feelings'.[44] And we may add aspects of the moral life such as freedom, conscience, virtue and vice, strength and weakness of will, shame, guilt, repentance, punishment, self-correction; but also things such as culture and education, the tragic and the comic, etc. We may also think of the whole plethora of emotions not displayed by non-human animals, of the creation of institutions, and, finally, of the worship of deities, or the true God.[45]

It is plausible, however, to maintain that all of these aspects of human life have their source in the natural capacity and inclination to *judge* and to *act*, and that this constitutes the *essence* of man's spirituality, which manifests itself in the most humdrum thoughts, intentions and utterances. Judging and acting no doubt have, in general, what Anscombe calls a 'utilitarian' value. But besides this they inevitably exhibit a characteristic 'non-utilitarian' normative teleology. And this seems to be what she takes to give

---

[42] Cf. 'The Dignity of the Human Being', in *HLAE*, pp. 68–73. What Anscombe calls mystical isn't as such exalted or lofty. 'Sexual acts are not sacred acts. But the perception of the dishonour done to the body in treating them as the casual satisfaction of desire is certainly a mystical perception. I don't mean, in calling it a mystical perception, that it's out of the ordinary. It's as ordinary as the feeling for the respect due to a man's dead body: the knowledge that a dead body isn't something to be put out for the collectors of refuse to pick up. This, too, is mystical though it's as common as humanity.' The point of a virtue can be 'supra-utilitarian and hence mystical' ('Contraception and Chastity', in *FHG*, p. 187. Cf. 'Dignity', p. 68).

[43] 'Dignity', p. 72.

[44] 'Dignity', p. 71; cf. 'Immortality', p. 74; p. 77.

[45] The relatively early paper on 'The Immortality of the Soul' treats concern 'with the eternal as an objective' as the core of human spirituality (pp. 74–77). Here, 'spirituality does not seem [...] to be demonstrated by capacity to think, reason, and understand as such' (p. 75).

human life a 'mystical' orientation, and thereby a 'mystical' value.[46]

Even if we think, as Anscombe does, that our spiritual nature rests on our being created by God in his image,[47] it is plausible to hold that what *makes* us resemble God is our orientation towards truth and goodness. And if, again with Anscombe, we think that the claims of truth and goodness whose perception grounds our spirituality are, in the last resort, claims of God himself: even then the *notion of a spiritual nature* seems to involve a reference to truth and goodness rather than to God.

From this point of view, then, it seems right to say that the basis of our dignity is a nature that directs us towards the ends of *truth and goodness* by providing us with a consciousness of being subject to these ends as norms. This consciousness cannot find expression in the manifestations of a purely animal form of life; it characterizes the spiritual nature of man. One of the things that remain to be investigated is the question: How do the contours of this nature determine the specific ways in which its dignity is respected or violated?

---

[46] Cf. 'Contraception and Chastity', p. 187; 'Dignity', p. 68. — That the spirituality of man originally resides in his non-utilitarian orientation towards (theoretical and practical) truth is suggested also by Anscombe's characterization of 'the peculiar character of the human soul. This soul is not merely the life of the animal body whose form it is; it is intellectual' ('Has Mankind One Soul?', p. 21).

[47] 'Human Essence', in *HLAE*, pp. 37–38.

Duncan Richter

The Conception of the Architectonic Good in Anscombe's Moral Philosophy

> Dear parents: I must give you bad news—I have been condemned to death. I and Gustave G. We did not sign up for the SS, and so they condemned us to death [...] Both of us would rather die than stain our consciences with such deeds of horror. I know what the SS have to do.[1]

Philippa Foot quotes this letter (written by someone identified only as a Farm Boy from the Sudetenland) and asks whether its author made a rational choice. Echoing Elizabeth Anscombe, she also asks on what theory of practical rationality we can make out a defence of the claim that his decision was rational. The echo is of the following passage from 'Practical Inference', in which Anscombe asks:

> [M]ay not someone be criticizable for pursuing a certain end, thus characterizable as a certain good of his, where and when it is quite inappropriate for him to do so, or by means inimical to other ends which he ought to have?
> This can be made out only if man has a last end which governs all. Only on this condition can that illusory 'moral ought' be

---

[1] Philippa Foot, 'Rationality and Goodness', in Anthony O'Hear (ed.), *Modern Moral Philosophy* (Cambridge: Cambridge University Press, 2004), pp. 1-13, p 2. The Farm Boy's story comes from H. Gollwitzer, K. Kuhn and R. Schneider (eds.), *Dying We Live* (London: The Harvill Press, 1956), p. 11.

exorcised, while leaving open the possibility of criticizing a piece of practical reasoning, valid in the strict and narrow sense in which theoretical contexts validity contrasts with truth. The criticism will be of the practical reasoning as not leading to the doing of good action. An action of course is good if it is not bad, but being inimical to the last architectonic end would prove that it was not good.[2]

What Foot wants to do is to make out, that is, to see, what theory of practical rationality will allow us to call the decision to be killed rather than join the SS rational. What Anscombe says is that it cannot be made out, i.e. seen, how a man can be criticizable for making the opposite kind of decision unless man has a last end which governs all. The language of making out here is somewhat obscure, so I will try to clarify it. To make something out is to succeed in perceiving it despite some difficulty. This requires both clarification, or the overcoming of the difficulty that stands in the way of perception, and the existence of the thing to be perceived. We cannot see what is not there. I will argue that Anscombe's position is not only that there must be a last architectonic end if actions inimical to it are to be criticizable but also that we must refer to this end in any proof of the badness of such actions. Their badness cannot be made out, cannot be perceived clearly or properly demonstrated, without reference to this end.

It might be thought that Anscombe is saying in the passage I just quoted that if we can criticize a bit of practical reasoning as not leading to the doing of good action, as we surely can (rightly or wrongly), then we are committed to the postulation of an architectonic good. I take it, though, that this is not what she means. What she says is that our having such an end is the only thing that would allow us to achieve two things simultaneously: 1) leaving open the possibility of the kind of criticism we have just described and 2) exorcising the illusory 'moral ought'. Indeed the latter is more significant, given the apparent obviousness of the possibility of saying that some practical reasoning was bad because it led to bad action. If we take the criticism mentioned in 1 to be *justified* criticism then 1 and 2 merge into one point. Criticism of action as bad is justified if we can prove that some things are appropriate and others not, or that there are some ends that we ought to have

---

[2] 'Practical Inference', in *HLAE*, p. 147.

The Conception of the Architectonic Good

and others that we ought not to have. And if we can do this then we do not need any special moral sense of 'ought'.

Why does this sense of 'ought' need to be exorcised? The exorcism in question relates to the second thesis in 'Modern Moral Philosophy':

> the concepts of obligation, and duty—*moral* obligation and *moral* duty, that is to say—and of what is *morally* right and wrong, and of the *moral* sense of 'ought,' ought to be jettisoned if this is psychologically possible; because they are survivals, or derivatives from survivals, from an earlier conception of ethics which no longer generally survives, and are only harmful without it.[3]

Anscombe does not say, and I do not know, what possible ways she might have in mind of exorcising the illusory, vestigial concepts of obligation and duty, etc., that would not leave open the possibility of criticizing practical reasoning in the desired way, so I will concentrate on the way that she does consider: the postulation of an architectonic good. If she had in mind a question merely of empirical psychology then her confidence in the hypothesis that only such postulation will have the required effect would seem unjustifiably high. So I take it that she sees a conceptual connection between the architectonic good and the moral 'ought', or rather the role that the moral 'ought' is taken to have by those who think, or try to think, in such terms. One of the aims of this chapter is to explore and clarify this connection. In what follows I will first describe the role of the moral 'ought', as Anscombe sees it, and then describe the work that the architectonic good might do. I will then consider whether there is such a good, and where this leaves us.

1. The role of the moral 'ought'

Anscombe's objection to the concepts of moral obligation, moral duty, what is morally right and wrong, and the moral sense of 'duty' is that they are harmful without the conception of ethics in which they originally had their home and in which they belong. This is a law conception of ethics. It no longer generally survives, she believes, because there is no longer general belief in a giver, judge and enforcer of the moral law. The only reasonable belief available today about the identity of the giver of such a law is that

---

[3] 'Modern Moral Philosophy', in *HLAE*, p. 169.

it is God. Other candidates are either immoral or incoherent. One might, for instance, take society's norms as the law, but we know that societies can have bad norms. Or it might be suggested that one could legislate a moral law for oneself but, as Anscombe says, 'whatever you do "for yourself" may be admirable; but it is not legislating'.[4] One cannot really be bound by a self-imposed law. Secular ethics, then, cannot be of the law-based kind, on pain of unreasonableness.[5] If we continue to use the vocabulary of law for secular ethics then confusion will inevitably ensue, and confused thinking in ethics can only be harmful. The prohibitions of the law will seem unreal, for instance, because the law in question is unreal. It is metaphorical at most.[6]

Our reasonable options, then, that is the options that are both coherent and decent, seem to be to reject secular ethics in favour of theistic ethics or to reject current (or approximately mid-20th-century) secular ethics in favour of a version that postulates an architectonic good for human beings. This, it seems universally agreed, would be something like *eudaimonia*, but there are some problems with this notion. Before getting to these, let me first say some more about the desirability of an architectonic good as an alternative to the moral 'ought'.

2. The role of the architectonic good

In the *Tractatus Logico-Philosophicus* proposition 6.422 Wittgenstein writes: 'The first thought at the setting up of an ethical law of the form "thou shalt…" is: And what then, if I don't do it?'[7]

---

[4] 'Modern Moral Philosophy', p. 186.
[5] By 'secular' I mean simply non-religious, not rational-as-opposed-to-religious or anything else that implies an anti-religious bias.
[6] Unless it is what Wittgenstein calls a secondary use of words, but in that case Anscombe is not committed to the view that we ought to get rid of it, although she does still seem to think that it is harmful. That is, she says that we should stop using the concepts in question if this is psychologically possible. If they are uses of words in a secondary sense then this will probably not be possible, because such use is not full-blown nonsense and essentially involves the impossibility of saying the same thing by other means. I think that what Anscombe says allows for this possibility, but it does not appear to interest her very much so I will leave the issue there. See Ludwig Wittgenstein, *Philosophical Investigations*, trans. G.E.M. Anscombe, P.M.S. Hacker, and Joachim Schulte (Oxford: Wiley-Blackwell, 2009), pp. 227–228 for the concept of secondary meaning.
[7] My translation.

This is where the architectonic good could come in. The moral 'ought' would be replaced by an ordinary 'ought', and the answer to the question 'What then, if I don't?' would be that in that case you will not reach your goal, the last end that governs all. This goal would have to be something that every human being inescapably wanted. Otherwise they could respond to this answer with a 'So what?'. Wittgenstein himself is sceptical about there being any such goal or end. In his 'Lecture on Ethics' he writes that:

> the *absolute good*, if it is a describable state of affairs, would be one which everybody, independent of his tastes and inclinations, would *necessarily* bring about or feel guilty for not bringing about. And I want to say that such a state of affairs is a chimera. No state of affairs has, in itself, what I would like to call the coercive power of an absolute judge.[8]

Another analogy he gives is with a certain road or path through life, 'the road which *everybody* on seeing it would, *with logical necessity*, have to go, or be ashamed for not going.'[9] He thinks it makes no sense to talk about such a road. I will not argue from Wittgenstein's authority, but I do share some of his sense that the non-existence of an absolutely coercive state of affairs goes without saying and that if there is such a state of affairs then it must be supernatural. If, contrary to this view, there is a non-supernatural last end, then by far the most plausible candidate for what it might be is flourishing or doing well. Surely everybody would do well or regret it. The reasonableness of this thought explains the humour in the quip by Anscombe when, in 'Practical Inference', she writes: 'Aristotle, we may say, assumes a preference for health and the wholesome, for life, for doing what one should do or needs to do as a certain kind of being. Very arbitrary of him.'[10]

Aristotle's preference hardly seems arbitrary, but it is so from a neo-Humean point of view. I follow Warren Quinn here, who writes: 'By a *neo-Humean* conception of rationality I mean one that makes the goal of practical reason the maximal satisfaction of an agent's desires and preferences, suitably corrected for the effects

---

[8] Ludwig Wittgenstein, *Philosophical Occasions 1912–1951*, edited by James Klagge and Alfred Nordmann (Indianapolis: Hackett Publishing Company, 1993), p. 40. Hereafter *Philosophical Occasions*.
[9] *Philosophical Occasions*, p. 40.
[10] 'Practical Inference', p. 116.

of misinformation, wishful thinking, and the like.'[11] Contrary to the preference assumed by Aristotle, there are people who choose sickness, death and inhuman behaviour. It is tempting to classify such behaviour as irrational, but of course there is a well-known and widespread conception of rationality according to which it is no more contrary to reason to prefer the destruction of the world to the scratching of one's finger.[12] Perhaps this conception will become less plausible, but it has not been disposed of yet.

One person who has challenged it is Quinn. In 'Rationality and the Human Good' Quinn argues that there is a 'great deal of plausibility' in the argument that 'the willingness to gain the good by the wrongful means makes it impossible to get what is *really* wanted in the end.'[13] For instance, a conscientious Nazi wants a loving relationship with his family and yet would murder any of them if they turned out to be Jewish, Gypsy or gay. So how much love can he really have for his family? And how much can they love him, knowing the limits of his affection for them? In other words, the Nazi's desires and preferences *corrected for misinformation, wishful thinking and the like* do not include the evils that define Nazism. There is a volitional incoherence in Nazi ideology. It would be nice to be able to argue in this way against all evil, but this kind of argument has limits. As Quinn points out, 'It seems hard to deny that someone might strongly desire [knowledge of the basic physical structure of the universe] even though it could, in the circumstances, be gotten only by shameful means.'[14]

Quinn finds it doubtful that practical rationality, the 'excellence of that part of reason in virtue of which an agent is practically rational as opposed to irrational', can be contemptible or shameful, as it would be if it recommended shameful means.[15] But his conclusion is tentative. One might instead conclude that there is no such thing as practical rationality (as Hume thinks,

---

[11] Warren Quinn, *Morality and Action* (Cambridge: Cambridge University Press, 1993), p. 210. Foot analyses Quinn's neo-Humean theory into two distinct theories (in 'Rationality and Goodness', p. 3), but this is unnecessary for my purposes.
[12] See David Hume, *A Treatise of Human Nature*, edited by L.A. Selby-Bigge, 2nd ed. revised by P.H. Nidditch (Oxford: Oxford University Press, 1978), p. 416.
[13] Quinn, *Morality and Action*, p. 217.
[14] Quinn, *Morality and Action*, p. 218.
[15] Quinn, *Morality and Action*, p. 210.

according to Quinn[16]) or that words such as 'shameful' and 'contemptible' have only emotive meaning. In another paper ('Putting Rationality in Its Place') Quinn tackles emotivism, but even if we agree with him and reject emotivism we might still find other ways to avoid the objectivism and cognitivism in which Quinn believes. Indeed, even if we believe in objective human goods we might believe in a plurality of such goods, with no clear way to choose between them. Hence we might not believe in the existence of *the thing* that we ought to do, all things considered. And if happiness as utilitarians understand it is one of the objective goods that we recognize, then we might still support such actions as the judicial condemnation of the innocent, an example that Anscombe emphasizes.

Near the end of 'Modern Moral Philosophy' she says that, 'It may be possible, if we are resolute, to discard the notion "morally ought," and simply return to the ordinary "ought"', but she does not insist that it is possible. *If* we are sufficiently resolute, she continues, *then* it will be possible to ask whether we ought to commit an injustice, such as procuring the judicial condemnation of the innocent.

She imagines four kinds of answer to such a question:

1) The roughly Aristotelian, virtue theory kind of answer;
2) The consequentialist answer;
3) What I will call the plain man's answer; and
4) The divine law answer.

The third of these has received little attention from philosophers. It is this: 'I know it is in any case a disgraceful thing to say that one had better commit this unjust action.'[17] This is an explicitly unphilosophical response, which is perhaps why it does not appeal to philosophers, and why it might not work as an alternative to the kind of secular ethics, that is, consequentialism, that Anscombe primarily opposes. It is an answer that I find attractive, but it will no doubt strike others as quaint or in need of a kind of support that it can never have. Being unphilosophical it naturally lacks philosophical justification. We might call it the bedrock response, or a kind of moral anti-foundationalism. I will return to it below.

---

[16] See Quinn, *Morality and Action*, p. 227.
[17] 'Modern Moral Philosophy', p. 193.

Anscombe raises several objections to the virtue theory response. Let me first say what this response is and then set out her criticisms of it. Here it is:

> [S]ince justice is a virtue, and injustice a vice, and virtues and vices are built up by the performances of the action in which they are instanced, an act of injustice will tend to make a man bad; and essentially the flourishing of a man *qua* man consists in his being good (e.g. in virtues); but for any X to which such terms apply, X needs what makes it flourish, so a man needs, or ought to perform, only virtuous actions; and even if, as it must be admitted may happen, he flourishes less, or not at all, in inessentials, by avoiding injustice, his life is spoiled in essentials by not avoiding injustice — so he still needs to perform only just actions.[18]

And here is her response:

> [I]t can be seen that philosophically there is a huge gap, at present unfillable as far as we are concerned, which needs to be filled by an account of human nature, human action, the type of characteristic a virtue is, and above all of human 'flourishing.' And it is the last concept that appears the most doubtful. For it is a bit much to swallow that a man in pain and hunger and poor and friendless is flourishing, as Aristotle himself admitted. Further, someone might say that one at least needed to stay alive to flourish.[19]

This brings me back to Quinn and the plain man's bedrockism. Imagine that I am told to do something shameful or disgraceful, and that I will be tortured, starved, robbed and my family murdered (echoing Anscombe's 'in pain and hunger and poor and friendless') unless I do it. Here we are back also to Wittgenstein's question: 'And what then, if I don't do it?' It looks as though I ought to perform the disgraceful act in such a case unless some reason can be given me why not, or unless we simply stop at 'disgraceful' (or 'shameful' or 'mass murder' or whatever it may be) and draw a line in the sand there. Reasons come to an end somewhere, after all. That is, given a choice between disgraceful action (where this is understood as meaning something like intrinsically bad action, not action that will necessarily bring any public disapproval) and death (or hell on earth), one can offer a seemingly sophistical argument to the effect that somehow death is the self-interested option (this is answer number 1), or accept

---

[18] 'Modern Moral Philosophy', p. 193.
[19] 'Modern Moral Philosophy', p. 193.

the disgraceful consequentialist view (answer number 2), or naïvely refuse to do what is disgraceful no matter what (answer 3), or else trust in God and follow his law (answer number 4). Of the secular options, the best might be the naïve one, especially if we can argue successfully that it can never be rational to choose disgrace. But this is a view that, as Anscombe says, is hard to make out. Indeed, if it is a *bedrock* principle then there is *no* explaining it. This is simply what I do, as Wittgenstein puts it.[20] Except, of course, that it *is not* what most of us do.

Probably few of us are so concerned to avoid disgrace that we would sacrifice our friends and family to avoid it without some further reason to do so. One reason that it might be tempting to suggest is that performing a disgraceful act will ruin our lives. I doubt one would have much fun after committing a coerced mass murder, for instance. But this is an empirical question, and the rational thing to do under coercion, on a standard understanding of what it means to be rational, might be thought to be to commit the crime and then see how it goes. Suicide (on this view) is always an option if it does not work out. One might not flourish with this kind of personal history, but it is surely better than being dead. Even a ruined life seems preferable to death (again, bearing in mind that suicide is always likely to be an option if the pain of the ruined life turns out to be unbearable, or merely to outweigh its pleasure).

Unless one has a bedrock commitment to avoid the disgraceful. If one can say and mean that one would rather die than do something disgraceful, then one already has an answer to the question regarding the essentials and inessentials of a good life. The question then would be whether this answer is true. Is it demonstrably irrational not to choose death before dishonour? One way, and perhaps the only way, that it could be shown that choosing death before doing something shameful or disgraceful would be rational would be to show that we have a last end with which shameful acts are incompatible.[21]

Another way in which we might try to prove that one should choose death before disgrace is more aesthetic. We might, for

---

[20] Wittgenstein, *Philosophical Investigations*, §217.
[21] Not that demonstrating the rationality of choosing death before dishonour is the same thing as demonstrating the irrationality of not choosing death before dishonour.

instance, value narrative unity in a life as a way to give it meaning in a secular way.[22] Betraying one's principles in order to avoid suffering, however great, might destroy this unity. It will matter what one's principles are, of course, but for most people joining a death squad would be a significant betrayal of principle. Unless we are unusually virtuous, though, it might contrast with the rest of our lives no more starkly than would heroically preferring death. Another problem with this way of defending self-sacrifice is that the very idea of meaning, or the value of narrative unity, is not all that clear. Why *ought* I to care whether my life has meaning? The value of such a life seems to be aesthetic, a matter of taste, and the same might be said about the value of dying a beautiful death rather than living an ugly life. If someone does not much care whether his life is meaningful or beautiful then it is hard to imagine an argument that could persuade him otherwise. Certainly many of us do care about narrative unity and are moved by the examples set by people such as Sophie Scholl, Gustave G. and the Sudeten Farm Boy who died rather than staining their consciences. What is not certain is whether the rightness of such caring can be demonstrated clearly.

Indeed it seems as though a kind of unclarity might even be essential to the non-cynical view. A beautiful death is not beautiful to look at but to contemplate. When we contemplate this kind of death and its alternative we reach for metaphorical expressions such as the good will's shining like a jewel or the stain on the conscience that would be caused by deeds of horror. It can be easy to see such things but hard to explain them to those who do not see. Without this kind of metaphor it might even be impossible to do so. Perhaps we can call this a case of mystical perception, as Anscombe calls the perception of dishonour done to the body in casual sexual acts.[23] After all, as she says, 'the objection to murder is supra-utilitarian', and hence mystical in her sense of the word, given that what is primarily wrong with murder is not that it makes life less pleasant but that it destroys life.[24] The goodness of self-sacrifice does not seem merely utilitarian either, and hence

---

[22] For more on the idea of narrative unity see Alasdair MacIntyre, *After Virtue* (Notre Dame: University of Notre Dame Press, 1984), especially chapter 15.
[23] See 'Contraception and Chastity', in *FHG*, p. 187.
[24] See 'Contraception and Chastity', p. 187.

cannot easily be made out or articulated. It is not a worldly good fully capturable in worldly terms.[25]

On the kind of neo-Humean view according to which one wants or values what one happens to want or value, and reason is merely a guide to attaining whatever ends one happens to have, the plain man who chooses death before disgrace is no less rational than the man who prefers to join the SS. He is no more rational either. On a different view of rationality, according to which only what is good is rightly called rational, the plain man might be far more rational than the other. Showing that one conception of rationality is better than the other is no easy matter, however, and showing that it is good to prefer death to disgrace is no easier. To someone who already sees these things no showing, proof or making out is necessary. But if someone does not see things as the plain man does, or does not see them clearly, then it appears that Anscombe is right. We can make out the badness of joining the SS in order to save one's life only if there is, and only if we can prove that there is, a last end to which such action is inimical.

3. Is there an architectonic good?

The only serious candidate for what this end might be is flourishing, but what this is and how dying could contribute to it are obscure. Flourishing *can* be regarded as an end for the religious man, Anscombe believes, because:

> if he is a Jew or Christian, he need not have any very distinct notion [of what flourishing is]: the way it will profit him to abstain from injustice is something that he leaves it to God to determine, himself only saying 'It can't do me any good to go against his law'. (He also hopes for a great reward in a new life later on, e.g. at the coming of Messiah; but in this he is relying on special promises.)[26]

There is faith here, of course, and it seems to be of two kinds. Reliance on special promises is a form of trust, but there is also faith regarding the meaning of these promises. The Jew or Christian has faith, rather than knowledge, that he or she will be

---

[25] If we cannot say what we mean without resorting to metaphors whose literal meaning we can never adequately explain in other terms then what Wittgenstein calls secondary uses of words are relevant after all. See the parenthetical discussion at note 6 above.
[26] 'Modern Moral Philosophy', p. 194.

rewarded or will profit by abstaining from injustice. He or she also has no knowledge of exactly what this reward or profit will be. Whether such faith is rational is another question, but without such promises or faith in God it is hard to see how any secular conception of flourishing that requires great self-sacrifice could be significantly less strained than that of the Stoic who believes that one can flourish on the rack.

Christians believe that human beings have a single purpose, memorably described by Anscombe in her essay 'Contraception and Chastity':

> What people are for is, we believe, like guided missiles, to home in on God, God who is the one truth it is infinitely worth knowing, the possession of which you could never get tired of, like the water which if you have you can never thirst again, because your thirst is slaked forever and always.[27]

If God is real and his promises true then it makes sense to prefer death to a violation of the divine law. But it is doubtful that any such purpose could be identified in secular form, and doubtful that Anscombe believed in such an end.

The least bad option if we are looking for a secular last end will be the living of a good life, or something closely related to this. John Finnis argues that, 'Any state which could count as the "one ultimate good for all humans" must involve a plurality of goods' and that practical reasonableness is the architectonic good which provides the standards for the good realization of those basic human goods.[28] Being reasonable means promoting and respecting 'the basic aspects of human flourishing'.[29]

This sounds right, but the idea of reasonableness is a contentious one. Is it reasonable to expect someone to die rather than commit an atrocity? Is it reasonable to choose death for oneself in such circumstances? Of course we might say yes, but others will disagree. The question that Anscombe raises is whether this can be proved. I suggested earlier that what is reasonable is what is coherent and decent, but making out what is decent and what is

---

[27] 'Contraception and Chastity', p. 173.
[28] John Finnis, *Reason in Action: Collected Essays Volume I* (Oxford: Oxford University Press, 2011), p. 172. He is quoting Vernon Bourke, 'Justice as Equitable Reciprocity: Aquinas Updated', *The American Journal of Jurisprudence* 27, 1982:17–31, at p. 25.
[29] Finnis, *Reason in Action*, p. 5.

not can be difficult. Not everyone agrees that the bombing of Hiroshima was unreasonable or indecent, for instance.

As Roger Teichmann notes, according to Anscombe: 'The question whether there is […] an architectonic end "would belong to ethics, if there is such a science"' (*I*, 76).[30] This suggests another problem, that perhaps we cannot even ask the question—it belongs to a science that might not exist. But it does not rule out the possibility that such a science exists, and we might try asking the question in order to find out whether it does. Teichmann takes up the question whether there is an architectonic end, both expressing scepticism and holding out some hope. There seems, he says, no reason to suppose that in 'giving reasons why honesty should come before short-term monetary gain' we should 'at any point reach a single rock-bottom reason, concerning an architectonic end for man'.[31] And he goes further than this tentative 'seems'. Any bedrock that we might reach will be, he says, at the level of what Wittgenstein calls framework propositions. Teichmann accepts that such propositions might exist in ethics, and suggests as examples the propositions 'Human beings are more important than stones' and 'Knowledge is as such better than ignorance.'[32] However, propositions such as these do not identify a final end for the lives and actions of human beings. These framework propositions are presuppositions of ethical discourse, propositions rarely articulated because when put into words they seem so undeniable as to go without saying. Anyone who denied these propositions would be, or at the very least appear to be, crazy or just quite alien to the rest of us. The denial that we have a last end, whether false or not, does not seem to involve this kind of irrationality or unreasonableness.

Teichmann is still somewhat tentative on this point, however, and rightly so. For one thing, he has not yet considered the possibility that flourishing or *eudaimonia* might be this ultimate end. When he does so, he suggests that there is nothing more to *eudaimonia* than 'the sum of all the many and various human goods at which we can aim'.[33] And if this is the case, he continues,

---

[30] Roger Teichmann, *The Philosophy of Elizabeth Anscombe* (Oxford: Oxford University Press, 2008), p. 75, quoting *Intention*, p. 76.
[31] Teichmann, *The Philosophy of Elizabeth Anscombe*, p. 77.
[32] Teichmann, *The Philosophy of Elizabeth Anscombe*, pp. 77–78.
[33] Teichmann, *The Philosophy of Elizabeth Anscombe*, p. 78.

then 'its status as a single end for human life would appear specious'.[34]

But there is hope. As he points out, physical health involves a great variety of things and yet counts as something unitary because its subject is a unitary thing. The processes, activities and functions of the human body are varied, but they all belong to what we recognize as one body. When they go well the person in question is physically healthy. It might be that human lives can be evaluated in a similar way, by looking at how their various projects and activities go, and seeing these as interconnected in the way that the factors that make up good health are interconnected. If this can be done then there will be a close parallel between health and *eudaimonia*. If it cannot be done, then there will not be such a parallel.[35]

The attempt to present human life in this way is an ongoing project, which might yet succeed, but until it succeeds it will be hard to say that it is possible to see a human life as unitary in the relevant sense. From a secular perspective there is no reason to suppose that there is any interconnectedness to find. And as far as I know the project of searching for it is a long way from claiming to have found it. No one has come closer than Philippa Foot, and she regarded the case of the Farm Boy from the Sudetenland as a problem.

Following Michael Thompson (who follows Anscombe, who follows Aristotle), Foot argues that it is possible to identify the natural history of the human race, or any other species, and from it derive behavioural norms that should be followed by members of that species if they are to flourish. For example, when in danger a hedgehog should roll itself into a ball.[36] Similarly there is species-based goodness, natural goodness, in human life. Because of the kind of beings we are, the kind of lives we naturally lead, we need institutions such as promising, we need virtues such as justice, and we need to avoid practices such as slavery. Human beings have far richer emotional and intellectual lives than hedgehogs though. Unlike other animals, we act on reasons. Our mental lives complicate enormously any attempt to work out or discover in what our good ultimately consists. Our forms of practical

---

[34] Teichmann, *The Philosophy of Elizabeth Anscombe*, p. 78.
[35] See Teichmann, *The Philosophy of Elizabeth Anscombe*, p. 79.
[36] See Foot, 'Rationality and Goodness', p. 10.

reasoning are diverse, as Foot notes. We recognize self-interested actions as rational, but also actions that favour one's family or friends, and actions that serve institutions necessary for the general good, such as promise-keeping. Self-sacrifice, even of one's own life, can be rational, according to Foot, but she makes no claim that it can be proved to be so. The question which arguments we should prefer, those defending self-interest or those defending virtuous action, is one on which we can take a stand but not one whose answer can be clearly made out.

This is relevant to Finnis's idea that practical reasonableness is the architectonic good we need. Teichmann points out that 'at the bottom of a wrong ordering of goods there may be, if not unintelligibility, then at any rate confusion or less than total rationality.'[37] When someone chooses to die rather than join the SS we surely do not want to label him unreasonable or even irrational. If he makes the opposite choice, though, is he necessarily confused or irrational? He is probably in some despair, which might be regarded as a form of confusion. He opposes his own choice and actions, but sees no way out that he can accept. Or he might not be like this at all. He might be far more comfortable inflicting death on others than accepting it himself, even without getting any sadistic pleasure or anti-Semitic satisfaction from his work. What to say about such a man's rationality or reasonableness is hard to know, but proving him to be unreasonable would surely be quite a challenge. I would not know where to begin. Is his purportedly self-serving decision actually good for him? Is it good for him as a human being, for instance? Well, no one knows in any factual sense. As far as can be proved he has not lost his humanity in any literal way. If the decision to die rather than join the SS is motivated in part by a perception of the mystical value of human life then we are never likely to make out clearly why this is the right decision. Mystical perception, while as common as the recognition that dead bodies are not to be put out with the rubbish, is not clear in the relevant way. (*Why* would this be so wrong? That is what I claim cannot be made out. *That* it would be bad is as clear as day.) Unless our end lies beyond this world it is hard to see how losing one's life could ever be (rationally, reasonably) preferable to any course of action that does not leave one in unbearable pain.

---

[37] Teichmann, *The Philosophy of Elizabeth Anscombe*, p. 102.

It is different if God and his law are real. Anscombe says that divine law obliges as rules oblige in a game.[38] This kind of obligation is not what she calls Aristotelian necessity, which is the necessity of a hypothetical imperative. It is more absolute than that. If my life is at stake then I might wonder what reason I have to play the game that calls on me to give it up, and various answers might be imagined in this case. One would be from within the perspective of the game itself: *because you promised!, because that would be murder!, because God has forbidden it!*, and so on. Such an answer implies that there is nothing more to be said, that any further question would be illegitimate. This is close to the plain man's position: I don't know everything, but I do know that it would be disgraceful to commit such an injustice. The plain man does not ask further questions, such as why one should care about what is disgraceful. He has, we might say, internalized the relevant norms. It might only be such a person that we would call reasonable. But if others disagree we cannot prove them wrong. Another kind of reason that one might give for obeying the divine law would refer to God's promises, or to the gratitude we owe to God, or other factors external to the game of obeying divine law itself. But there is no secular version of these reasons, of course. They all refer to God.

4. So what?

It follows that we cannot prove that some actions are bad, according to Anscombe. Unless, that is, we can prove that man has a last end which governs all, which she does not claim to be able to prove. This point is worth pausing to consider. In the first of her four McGivney Lectures on sin, Anscombe announces that she assumes 'that reason dictates the worship of the one true deity'.[39] Someone who believes that reason dictates such worship might be said to claim to be able to prove that God exists, but Anscombe's repeated description of this belief of hers as an assumption suggests otherwise. It seems that she believes such a proof to be possible, but she does not claim to be able to provide it herself. She also cites Aristotle as an example of someone who holds 'that reason demands the worship and contemplation of God' but she

---

[38] See 'Modern Moral Philosophy', p. 192.
[39] 'Sin', in *FHG*, pp. 117–156, at p. 119. She refers to this belief as an assumption on p. 118 and again on p. 120.

does not endorse Aristotle's conception of God.[40] In particular she points out that Aristotle does not conceive of God as a giver of moral laws. So while reason might be capable of showing that God exists, Anscombe does not claim to be able to do so. Even Aristotle's reasoning did not lead him to a wholly correct understanding of God or of ethics, at least as Anscombe sees it. It is hard to make out on an Aristotelian conception of ethics why one ought to sacrifice one's life rather than commit injustice. Perhaps a just person would make this refusal, but if the rationality of such refusal is in question then so too is part of the virtue of justice, as Foot points out.[41] If we cannot show or see why it is rational to behave this way then we cannot show or see that a virtuous person would do so.

I began with a question about the rationality of a specific decision, the decision to prefer condemnation to die at the hands of the SS rather than join the SS and do what they have to do. I do not mean at all to suggest that this was not a rational decision. Rather my question has been whether it can be *made out* that this was rational, whether, that is, it can be proved that it was a rational decision, or clearly explained *why* it was a rational decision. This question is relevant to Anscombe because she holds that this is not possible unless human beings have, and can be shown to have, a last end that governs all with which any other decision would have been incompatible. This, I have tried to argue, is difficult, perhaps even impossible, to show. Not only are there different ideas about what is good for human beings to do, there are also competing conceptions of rationality. If we show that the decision was rational according to one conception, it is still open to someone to reject that conception of rationality. If we can show that the rational must be good, it is still open to someone to disagree about what it is genuinely good to do. A solution to this dilemma may yet be found, but in the meantime there are no clear grounds on which to expect this to happen.

This is as much as I mean to claim about what can or cannot be proved. Of course there can be arguments to the effect that it is or is not rational to prefer death to joining the SS. In any debate about this, however, much will depend on what counts as rational. On one conception of rationality it can never be rational to choose

---

[40] 'Sin', p. 121.
[41] See Foot, 'Rationality and Goodness', p. 12.

to join such an evil organization. On the neo-Humean conception, though, doing so might be perfectly rational. So we might also want to consider arguments for and against various conceptions of rationality. I deny neither that such arguments could exist nor that they could be successful, and successful both in the sense of actually persuading people and in the sense of doing so in accordance with right reason. What I do deny is that it is easy to see how to establish which, if any, conception of reason is the right one to use in this case. Moreover, all that I really need to deny in order to make my case is that it is easy to see how to establish that the neo-Humean view is wrong. I am not denying that it is wrong, nor even that this can be demonstrated. My claim is simply that it is not clear that this will be demonstrated, nor what such a demonstration would look like.

This is not to say, of course, that we do not have an ultimate end. Indeed, Anscombe says in the same lecture on sin that I quoted above that an imperative for human beings is to 'Aim at what human life is for attaining'.[42] She adds that it 'can well be argued' that 'there is such a true end'.[43] Unfortunately she does not say how such an argument would go, and what she says is ambiguous. Does the argument amount to proof? If so, what does it prove? Simply that we have a true end? Or that this end involves obedience to God who has promulgated such-and-such laws? I do not know what she meant. But it is clear enough that it would be difficult to prove that we have such an end, and difficult to see how any such end could be suitable for *secular* ethics. Which means that we might never be able to exorcise the moral 'ought', unless the ethics of the plain man make an unexpected return.[44]

---

[42] 'Sin', p. 120.
[43] 'Sin', p. 120.
[44] I am grateful to Mary Geach, Luke Gormally, David Albert Jones, Robert C.B. Miller, Matthew O'Brien, Matthew Pianalto and Roger Teichmann for questions and comments that helped me to improve this chapter.

José M. Torralba

On Morally Neutral Actions, and the Relevance of Practical Truth for Action Theory

Aristotle uses the notion of practical truth only once, but it appears in the central passage of the central book of the *Nichomachean Ethics*, as part of the discussion of *phronesis* (practical wisdom).[1] However, most commentators have given little attention to it.[2] Anscombe, on the contrary, treats practical truth as a key notion in the understanding of human action. And she does this not only for the sake of proper exegesis, but also for systematic, philosophical reasons. She herself adopts the Aristotelian doctrine because she thinks it provides a better understanding of essential aspects of human action: namely, practical knowledge and practical reasoning.

The basic assumption in this discussion is the Aristotelian doctrine that truth is the *ergon* (the work) of knowledge.[3] Since

---

[1] Aristotle, *Nichomachean Ethics*, 1139a25–26.
[2] Some exceptions can be found in Anselm Müller, *Praktisches Folgern und Selbstgestaltung nach Aristoteles* (München: Alber, 1982), pp. 231–294; Fernando Inciarte, *First Principles, Substance and Action. Studies in Aristotle and Aristotelianism*, edited by L. Flamarique (Hildesheim, New York: Olms, 2005), pp. 297–357; Alejandro G Vido, *Zeit und Praxis bei Aristoteles. Die Nikomachische Ethik und die zeit-ontologischen Voraussetzungen des vernunftgesteuerten Handelns* (München: Alber, 1996) and 'Practical Truth and the Intellectual Virtues', *Graduate Faculty Philosophy Journal* 29(1) 2008:73–115.
[3] See Aristotle, *Nichomachean Ethics*, 1139b12–14.

there are two distinct forms of knowledge (theoretical and practical), it can be assumed that each must have its corresponding form of truth. At the very least, it seems that we cannot take practical truth to be a species of theoretical truth, because the latter consists in the correspondence to the thing, and such a relation is impossible in the former, since practical knowledge produces the 'thing' (the action) of which it is knowledge. As Anscombe (quoting Aquinas) famously put it, practical knowledge is 'the cause of what it understands'.[4] This is why — as I hope will become clear as my argument proceeds — the truth of practical knowledge, properly speaking, is the action itself. Practical knowledge achieves its truth (its aim) *in* the action and not, for instance, in a proposition or judgment *about* the action.

Aristotle argued that there is practical knowledge because the realm of human action (*praxis*) cannot be accounted for by means of theoretical knowledge, nor *just* by means of technical knowledge (*techne*).[5] In fact, this is one of the great contributions of Aristotle to the history of philosophy. And Anscombe can certainly be credited for reintroducing this idea to twentieth-century philosophical debates in the English-speaking world.[6] As is well known, Anscombe located the difficulties in understanding the nature of practical knowledge in the 'incorrigibly contemplative conception of knowledge' that is characteristic of modern philosophy.[7] Recently, however, there has been a growing interest in the notion of practical knowledge and a good number of works have been published, which are helping to revitalize contemporary discussion of knowledge and action.[8] In a sense, these works are achieving what Anscombe aimed for, but had not fully

---

[4] See *I*, §48 quoting Aquinas, *Summa theologiae* I–II, q. 3, a. 5.
[5] See *Nichomachean Ethics*, chapter 6, and *De Anima*, chapter 3.
[6] See Georg Henrik von Wright, *Explanation and Understanding* (New York: Cornell University Press, 1971), pp. 25–30; Richard J Bernstein, *Praxis and Action: Contemporary Philosophies of Human Activity* (Philadelphia: University of Pennsylvania Press, 1971), p. 6. For the debate in the German-speaking world, see Manfred Riedel (ed.), *Rehabilitierung der praktischen Philosophie* (Freiburg: Rombach, 1972). See José M Torralba, *Acción intencional y razonamiento práctico según G.E.M. Anscombe* (Pamplona: Eunsa, 2005), pp. 103–107.
[7] See *I*, §32.
[8] See Michael Thompson, *Life and Action: Elementary Structures of Practice and Practical Thought* (Cambridge: Harvard University Press, 2008); Anton Ford, Jennifer Hornsby, Frederick Stoutland (eds.), *Essays on Anscombe's Intention* (Cambridge: Harvard University Press, 2011).

succeeded in doing. For instance, one of the main critiques of the 'standard approach' in contemporary action theory is that it analyses action *just* from a theoretical perspective, by means of the notion of natural causality.

However, despite this recent wave of interest in practical knowledge, very little (if any) attention has been given to the notion of practical truth (and falsehood). In my opinion, two reasons explain this. First, Anscombe does not explicitly discuss practical truth in *Intention*, and says little elsewhere about how it is related to her project in that book. Second, and more importantly, practical truth is a moral concept—since it *is* the morally good action—and, thus, not usually considered necessary for the study of human action as such. However, at the same time practical truth is the truth *of* practical knowledge, which is the kind of knowledge the agent has in the moment of acting. Therefore, action theory proper cannot exclude the study of practical truth. Or so I will argue.

In principle, this might appear to contradict Anscombe's original project, because all moral considerations are expressly banned from *Intention*; even the possibility of a science such as ethics is—rhetorically, anyway—put in question.[9] However, it seems to me that Anscombe's division between action theory and ethics is *only* methodological. It has certainly been a very necessary and, particularly for Anscombe, fruitful division, but to analyse human actions independently of their moral value is, so to speak, a mere abstraction. As the opening lines of 'Modern Moral Philosophy' indicate, Anscombe did it because she wanted to avoid an illusory idea of the 'moral ought' and that a particular moral theory—consequentialism—would determine the understanding of human action.[10] This could be the reason why, despite

---

[9] See *I*, §39.
[10] 'It is not profitable for us *at present* to do moral philosophy; that should be laid aside at any rate *until* we have an adequate philosophy of psychology, in which we are conspicuously *lacking*' ('Modern Moral Philosophy', in *HLAE*, p. 169, emphasis added). By 'philosophy of psychology' she is almost obviously referring to the kind of work done by Wittgenstein in the *Philosophical Investigations*. Anscombe considers that one of the notions that are in need of clarification is precisely 'intention', because after Sidgwick 'intention' has been uniformly understood in a consequentialist fashion: 'From the point of view of the present enquiry, the most important thing about Sidgwick was his definition of intention. He defines intention in such a way that one must be said to intend

the fact that *Intention* contains an extensive discussion of practical reasoning, practical truth is not even mentioned.

In any case, at the end of her 1965 article 'Thought and Action in Aristotle: What is "Practical Truth"?' Anscombe gives an indication of what she takes the connection between practical truth and the project of *Intention* to be when she writes as follows:

> The notion of *truth or falsehood in action* would quite generally be countered by the objection that 'true' and 'false' are senseless predicates as applied to what is done. If I am right there is philosophy to the contrary in Aristotle. And if, as I should maintain, the idea of *descriptions under which* what is done is voluntary is integral to his notion of action (*praxis*), then these predicates apply to actions (*praxeis*) strictly and properly, and not merely by an extension and in a way that ought to be explained.[11]

Practical truth is defined by Aristotle as 'truth in agreement with right desire'.[12] As I will show later, the elements of this definition ('truth' and 'desire') are better understood when considered within the framework of the practical syllogism, since 'truth' refers to the second premise (premise of the possible) and 'desire' to the first (premise of the good).[13] It is in this context that in her 1974 paper 'Practical Inference' Anscombe distinguishes between 'truth in agreement with desire' and 'truth in agreement with *right* desire' as two different ways of understanding the business of practical reasoning: either getting things just the way *one wants them to be* or getting things in a way *it is all right to want them to be*. She considers that only the second characterization provides a complete understanding of practical reasoning. I take this remark to indicate that for Anscombe the consideration of the moral value

---

any foreseen consequences of one's voluntary action' ('Modern Moral Philosophy', p. 183). This is a clear reference to the notion of 'voluntary, but non intentional', which lies at the core of *Intention*. Moreover, Anscombe describes her discussion of practical reasoning in *Intention* (which is necessary for the understanding of practical knowledge) in the following terms: 'So what can the practical syllogism have to do with ethics? It can only come into ethical studies if a correct philosophical psychology is requisite for a philosophical system of ethics' (*I*, §41).

[11] 'Thought and Action in Aristotle: What is "Practical Truth"?', in *CPP1*, p. 77.

[12] *Nichomachean Ethics*, 1139a31.

[13] Alejandro Vigo makes the case for this interpretation in 'Die aristotelische Auffassung der praktischen Wahrheit', *Internationale Zeitschrift für Philosophie* 2, 1998:285–308 (an English translation is forthcoming).

of the action is not (completely) external to the understanding of practical rationality.[14]

In my opinion, the notion of practical truth is relevant to action theory for two reasons. First, because it helps in understanding what is specifically practical in human action (the 'practicality' of action). Second, because it is at the core of the structural connection between action theory and ethics. The proper place to study both aspects is the practical syllogism (or practical reasoning), for the same reason that it is the place to adequately understand the notion of practical knowledge.[15]

With regard to the first reason, I will argue that Anscombe endorses the Aristotelian thesis according to which, properly speaking, the conclusion of a practical syllogism *is* an action and not a proposition *about* an action. Precisely this is what distinguishes a piece of practical reasoning *proper* from an *idle* piece of practical reasoning. The latter is not an instance of practical reasoning or knowledge properly speaking, because it is reasoning towards the truth of a proposition, whereas in practical reasoning proper 'the conclusion is an action'.[16] It can be said that what appears in the conclusion of a piece of practical reasoning is the action under a description, because that description is what the agent's practical knowledge consists in.

With regard to the second reason, since the practical syllogism is a piece of reasoning truth is its aim. For the conclusion to be true, both premises must be true. The truth achieved in the conclusion is what is called practical truth which, in turn, *is* an action itself.[17] The truth of the minor premise (premise of the possible) depends on the *efficacy* of the means in achieving the end and is thus a matter of technical knowledge. For its part, the truth of the major premise (premise of the good, which refers to the desired

---

[14] See 'Practical Inference', in *HLAE*, pp. 144-146.
[15] See *I*, §33.
[16] *I*, §33. See 'Thought and Action in Aristotle', pp. 74-75. In this paper Anscombe refers to Aquinas's notion of 'theoretical *de practicis*' (*Summa theologiae* I, q. 14, a. 16) as equivalent to her notion of the *idle* practical.
[17] In 'Die aristotelische Auffassung der praktischen Wahrheit' Vigo explains that, for Aristotle, practical truth is not — properly speaking — the truth of the conclusion, but the *link* of knowledge and right desire that results in the good action. However, that link is a constitutive element of the action, not something previous to and independent of it.

object) depends on the end of the action being morally right, and only ethics can determine that.

Any piece of practical reasoning presupposes that the agent *already* desires something (object, state of affairs, etc.) and that she desires it under the guise of the good (that is what makes it desirable). That what is desired is *considered* by the agent to be good is a necessary condition for the reasoning to be practical. The conclusion of the syllogism will be true (i.e. a good action) only if what the agent desires is *truly* good. However, the agent always takes her action to be, not only apparently, but truly good, even though she might be wrong.

Where does the connection between action theory and ethics lie? In the fact that the agent necessarily aims to do what is (truly) good and, thus, the question regarding the moral value of her actions is (implicitly) included in any instance of practical reasoning. There is an internal incoherence in a stance of the following kind: 'I do not care if what I do is good or evil.' Even if someone would nominally adopt it (taking morality to be a *particular* set of values or the law conception of ethics or you name it), it would turn out to be a form of caring about what is morally better, of what is the right attitude toward one's life. The reason is that our actions are not isolated events, but parts of wider courses of action and, as such, they refer to our life as a whole. In each of our actions we aim to actualize the form of life which we (somehow) choose to lead. Just as in each particular action the means are the end *here and now*, it can be said that each of our actions is our whole life *here and now*.

These two reasons, it seems to me, situate the notion of practical truth at the core of Anscombe's project. If I am right, Anscombe closely follows Aristotle in his interpretation of that notion and uses the conceptual apparatus developed in *Intention* to better explain it. However—as becomes particularly clear in her papers 'Practical Inference', 'Practical Truth', and 'Vérité et raisonnement pratique'[18]—she considered that, apart from its exegetical interest, the notion of practical truth plays an essential role in the understanding of human action and practical

---

[18] 'Practical Truth', in *HLAE*, pp. 149–158; 'Practical Inference', pp. 109–148; 'Verité et raisonnement pratique', in Barbara Cassin (ed.), *Nos Grecs et leurs moderne. Les stratégies contemporaines d'appropriation de l'Antiquité* (Paris: Éditions du Seuil, 1992), pp. 393–401.

rationality, at least in her understanding of those topics. My aim in this paper is to show how Anscombe appropriated the Aristotelian notion and the consequences it had for her understanding of the relationship between action theory and ethics or, in other words, the moral character of human action. I am not myself interested in the exegetical question of whether at the time of writing *Intention* Anscombe had already a determined understanding of the notion of practical truth (I think this is unclear). It will suffice to show how, in her later writings, Anscombe employed the sound 'philosophy of psychology' developed in *Intention* to make sense of that notion and thus of the moral character of human action.

In this paper I am trying to interpret Anscombe's thought, even though the structure and some of the arguments cannot be found in her writings. The paper is divided into two parts. In section 1 I consider the *possibility* of practical truth. Practical truth is possible if the conclusion of the practical syllogism *is* an action (and not a proposition *about* an action). Section 2 is devoted to the *necessity* of practical truth for action theory. Here I argue that practical truth is a necessary notion because all actions have a truth-value or, what I will call, a goodness-value (are either good or bad). In order to show this the following topics are examined: (2.1.) in what sense Anscombe claims that practical reasoning has no moral content; (2.2.) the role of the notion of '*sub ratione boni*' in practical reasoning; (2.3.) why any piece of practical reasoning aims at good action; (2.4.) the parallelism between the validity/soundness of a syllogism and 'truth in agreement with desire'/'truth in agreement with *right* desire'; and (2.5.) how to determine the truth of the first premise, i.e. the goodness of the desire.

1. The possibility of practical truth.
The conclusion of the practical syllogism is an action

The novelty and interest of the notion of practical truth lies in the fact that it is the truth *of* an action and not of a proposition or judgment about an action. This is probably the most obscure aspect of the notion.[19] If the action is said to be true (or false) only in a secondary or metaphorical sense, the Aristotelian doctrine

---

[19] For instance, Teichmann holds a different interpretation: 'In the end, the question whether "true" and "false" apply to actions "strictly and properly" may not be so important.' Roger Teichmann, *The Philosophy of Elizabeth Anscombe* (Oxford: Oxford University Press, 2008), p. 82.

would lose both its originality and appeal, since actions would be 'true' only because they are in accordance with a right moral judgment and that truth would be the truth *of* the judgment.[20] Even if the judgment in question were not a universal moral judgment (taken from an ethical textbook, for instance), but a particular judgment of the agent at the time of acting (regarding what it is good to do here and now), there would still be something lacking: the *identity* between judgment and action, because the action is not something that exists independently of the practical judgment, since the judgment includes the description of the action: the practical judgment says that doing X is good. For now, we can leave aside the predicate 'is good' and focus on 'doing X', which is the description of the action under which the agent has knowledge of what she is doing. This knowledge has the structure of a bit of practical reasoning, where 'doing X' is its conclusion. Let us take the following example:

Healing this sick person (is what I want to do)
This drug is a way to treat her illness
(The action of) giving her this drug

In this example, the conclusion is an action under a description. Certainly, as is well known, that description includes (implicitly or explicitly) both premises, in the sense that giving this drug *is* healing this person.

Why is it so important for the notion of practical truth that the conclusion of the practical syllogism be the action itself? Because what is said to be true (or false) is the action and — as will be explained later — practical truth is the truth of the conclusion. And why is it so difficult to accept that the conclusion is an action (and not a proposition)? Because, as Anscombe regrets, the 'true character' of practical reasoning 'has been obscured', precisely because it is supposed to be 'ordinary reasoning', i.e. 'reasoning towards the truth of a proposition', so that it leads to 'such a conclusion as: "I ought to do such-and-such"'.[21] The problem is

---

[20] Certainly, truth can be predicated of any good action, but that is not an instance of practical truth. As Anscombe puts it: 'It is practical truth when the judgements involved in the formation of the "choice" leading to the action are all true; but the practical truth is not the truth of those *judgements*' ('Thought and Action in Aristotle', p. 77).

[21] *I*, §33.

that no action follows from an instance of ordinary reasoning, and precisely in the case of practical reasoning, Aristotle claims that an action follows.

Anscombe partly blames Aristotle himself for that mischief. From the point of view of its subject matter, scientific (i.e. ordinary) reasoning concerns what is invariable, whereas practical reasoning concerns non-necessary things. Such criteria seemed to be enough to distinguish ordinary from practical reasoning. However, reasoning about 'what is capable of turning out variously' is not enough 'to make reasoning about it practical'.[22] The difference lies not only in the subject but also in the form: reasoning leading to action as opposed to reasoning for the truth of a conclusion. In fact, Anscombe criticizes Aristotle for saying that 'what "happens" is the same in both'.[23]

At this point, Anscombe introduces her classification of syllogisms: theoretical, *idle* practical and practical *proper*.[24] In the first two, 'the conclusion is "said" by the mind which infers it', whereas in the third 'the conclusion is an action whose point is shewn by the premises, which are now, so to speak, on active service'.[25] Anscombe's distinction between *idle* practical and practical syllogisms *proper* becomes crucial for our topic. In order to determine the kind of practical reasoning one must look to the conclusion, precisely because only the practical syllogism *proper* concludes in an action. The conclusion is the action and not merely

---

[22] *I*, §33.

[23] *I*, §33.

[24] It seems relevant that, even though Anscombe is here mostly following Aristotle, the terminology of this classification is introduced by her. I take this to be a sign that she is not just expounding Aristotle's position, but appropriating it. For instance, in the same passage she says that 'we may accept from Aristotle that practical reasoning is essentially concerned with "what is capable of turning out variously" […]', and then goes on to make some criticism of the deficiencies in the Aristotelian classification of syllogisms. In this regard, what Anscombe wrote in the final paragraph of her 1992 paper on 'Truth and Practical Reasoning' at the conference 'Nos grecs et leurs modernes. Les stratégies contemporaines d'appropriation de l'Antiquité' looks like a clear declaration of intention: '*J'espère que je n'ai pas trahi l'intention de ce congrès. Je n'ai décrit aucune appropriation moderne de la pensée d'Aristote sur l'action et la pensée. J'ai seulement offert mes pensées comme exemple d'une telle appropriation*' ('Verité et raisonnement pratique', p. 401). Anscombe appropriated the Aristotelian notion of practical truth for her understanding of human action.

[25] *I*, §33. See also *I*, §42, 'Thought and Action in Aristotle', p. 73.

a proposition when the premises are in 'active service', that is, when the subject of the reasoning is the agent that finds herself involved in the performance of an action. On the contrary, *idle* practical reasoning is, for Anscombe, a kind of 'classroom example', that is, a piece of reasoning where the agent does not *actually* want what is described in the first premise.[26] She might be considering what she *would* do in such a situation or which is the best way to achieve such an end (e.g. healing the sick person). Thus, the aim of such reasoning is the truth of a proposition: e.g. that such-and-such a drug should be given to such a sick person *in case* one wants or has to heal her.

But, we may ask now, are not there other options for the conclusion of a practical syllogism *proper*, i.e. do we have an instance of such a syllogism only provided that its conclusion is an action? As Anscombe herself acknowledges, in the examples of practical syllogisms given by Aristotle the conclusion is seldom stated. In addition, some interpreters hold that the conclusion of such syllogisms is an imperative, a fiat.[27] Puzzlingly enough, in §42 of *Intention* Anscombe, after making again the point that practical reasonings (proper) are 'reasonings running from an objective through many steps to the performance of a particular action here and now', she provides an example that concludes with 'here is some of that medicine — give it',[28] that is, with an imperative and not, as one might have expected, with '(the action of) giving that medicine'.[29] Let us consider these objections.

With regard to the interpretation of Aristotle's understanding of the conclusion of the practical syllogism, Anscombe as well as other interpreters clearly consider that it is an action.[30] Certainly, sometimes Aristotle does not mention the conclusion, but when he does, he speaks of it as an action.[31] For instance, in 'Thought and Action in Aristotle' Anscombe wrote that 'the conclusion, that a

---

[26] In this regard, Anscombe points out that 'the role of "wanting" in the practical syllogism is quite different from that of a premise. It is that whatever is described in the proposition that is the starting-point of the argument must be wanted in order for the reasoning to lead to any action' (*I*, § 35).
[27] See Anthony Kenny, *Aristotle's Theory of the Will* (London: Duckworth, 1979), p. 142, see also pp. 122–123.
[28] *I*, 42.
[29] I thank Roger Teichmann for pointing this out to me.
[30] See note 2.
[31] *I*, §33.

cloak must be made, Aristotle says, is an action'.[32] And it is also argued that Aristotle 'wants a "must" in the conclusion in the verbalized form in which he gives it in the *Movement of Animals*, though each time he gives the conclusion he adds—"and that's an action"'.[33] This brings us to the second question: whether the conclusion can be an imperative (instead of an action).

Anscombe seems to think that Aristotle seldom states the conclusion of the syllogism precisely because it is an action and not a proposition. However, she claims that 'there is of course no objection to inventing a form of words by which he [the agent] *accompanies* this action, which we may call the conclusion in a verbalized form'.[34] My interpretation is that the imperative is a way of verbalizing the action that appears in the conclusion and not an alternative conclusion for a practical syllogism *proper*.

Anscombe was acquainted with the notion of imperative inference, as discussed by Hare and von Wright.[35] I do not think we need here to get into the whole topic, but only to show what was Anscombe's position in that regard and, particularly, how it affected the understanding of the conclusion of the practical syllogism. She gives two different but complementary accounts, in *Intention* and in 'Practical Inference'.

In *Intention*, the imperative syllogism is described as a kind of practical syllogism from which an action can follow, since its conclusion is a fiat. Thus, 'someone professing to accept the premises will be inconsistent if, when nothing intervenes to prevent him, he fails to act on the particular order with which the argument ends.'[36] In this sense, it is not a species of the scientific syllogism. However, the problem is that, according to Anscombe, its first premise may have to be 'an insane one', because general positive premises such as 'Do everything conductive to not having a car crash' may lead to 'a hundred different and incompatible things'.[37]

In her paper 'Practical Inference' Anscombe gives a different account, since there she is interested in the question whether there

---

[32] 'Thought and Action in Aristotle', p. 73. See Aristotle, *De Motu Animalium*, 701a17-22.
[33] 'Thought and Action in Aristotle', p. 74.
[34] *I*, §33.
[35] See Richard M. Hare, *The Language of Morals* (Oxford: Oxford University Press, 1952), pp. 27-38; G.H. von Wright, 'Deontic Logic', *Mind* 60, 1951:1-15.
[36] *I*, §33.
[37] *I*, §33.

is a special form of practical inference. Imperative inferences have a bearing on the topic of practical inference, since 'the one seeking to obey [an] order has a goal, expressed by what the order requires should become the case'.[38] But the point here is whether the agent *actually* wants to obey the order. In *Intention*, Anscombe dismissed the possibility of *general* imperative premises as insane. Here, in 'Practical Inference' she is considering cases like 'Fiat: some committee is brought before X', that is, *particular* imperatives. In such cases, the conclusion would move one to act (or be an action) depending on the 'service' to which the premises are put.[39] For instance, an agent may begin reasoning how to bring a committee before X, but that will only end up in action provided that the agent actually wants to obey the order. In case she did not, the imperative inference would just be a kind of classroom example. It all depends on whether the premises are in *active* service or not.

Why, then, do we find in §42 of *Intention* a fiat as the conclusion of a practical syllogism *proper*? Because a piece of practical reasoning can be rendered either in the indicative, the optative or the imperative form. What makes a piece of reasoning practical is not its formulation in the imperative, but the desire of the end by the agent. It seems to me that in that passage, Anscombe was just giving a verbalization of the conclusion (which is an action) and such verbalization can equally be given in the imperative: give the drug, or in the indicative, as a description: (the action of) giving the drug.[40]

At this point, someone might add a final objection: in reality, the content of the conclusion of a piece of practical reasoning proper is not the action that is taking place, but rather the choice of the agent, that is, the description of what she is up to or about to do. In a certain sense, this is true and that is why we speak of the *conclusion* of a piece of reasoning, which can be linguistically formulated in a proposition. Of course, saying that the conclusion is an action does not mean that, in order to know what is the content of that conclusion, one could do nothing but *point* to what the agent is doing. However, if by choice one means a distinct,

---

[38] 'Practical Inference', p. 124.
[39] 'Practical Inference', p. 128.
[40] Anscombe makes a reference to the verbalization of 'actions' in speaking of the imperative inference in 'Practical Inference', pp. 125–126. See also pp. 120 and 144 of this paper where she equates the conclusion with an action.

previous act to the action, that might (or not) result in the performance of the action, then what one has in mind is a case of idle practical reasoning or of theoretical reasoning about practical matters. The link between the conclusion and the action is an *internal* one, in the sense that only *accidentally* is it possible for the action not to follow from the conclusion.[41]

What it is necessary to underscore here is that the practical syllogism *proper* is the one that the agent goes by at the time of acting. Such a syllogism is the formalization of the knowledge that is part of the performed action. Practical knowledge is a constitutive element of the action in the sense that, properly speaking, the action performed cannot be separated from the knowledge the agent has of it (i.e. it cannot be separated from the practical syllogism). This is the very well known and, arguably, central thesis of *Intention*: the description of the action determines the 'what' of the action, because there is no way of identifying or specifying actions apart from their descriptions. The thesis that the conclusion of the practical syllogism proper is an action (either verbalized or not, in the indicative, the optative or the imperative form) helps understand the inseparability between practical knowledge and intentional action.

Practical knowledge is a constitutive component of the action. In my opinion, if practical truth — as Anscombe insists — must be the truth *of* action it is necessary to explain in what (non-accidental) sense the action is knowledge (although not *only* knowledge). Such explanation can be found in the distinction between idle and proper practical syllogisms. The latter is the kind of reasoning involved in the performance of an action by an agent that actually desires to achieve the end mentioned in the first premise. The action is not something independent of or isolated from such reasoning.[42] Anscombe's claim — following Aristotle — that the conclusion of a practical syllogism is the action itself, indicates both that the action *belongs to* such a piece of reasoning and

---

[41] See *I*, §48. Even though the word 'idle' has some negative connotations in English, in the context of action theory it is neutral.

[42] For a more detailed discussion of this point, see Alejandro Llano, José M. Torralba,'Rappresentazione e conoscenza pratica. Sull'intenzione come forma dell'azione', in Juan A. Mercado (ed.), *Elizabeth Anscombe e il rinnovamento della psicologia morale* (Roma: Armando Editore, 2010) pp. 173-202.

that the syllogism is *incomplete* until the action is performed (or, at least, begins to be performed).

2. The necessity of practical truth.
Validity and soundness of practical reasoning

In the previous section we have considered why it is *possible* to say that actions are true/false. In this section we will explore why *necessarily* they are true/false or, in other words, why any action is (morally) good/bad. I begin (2.1) by trying to explain in what sense Anscombe denies that the practical syllogism has moral content.[43] In my opinion, that an action has no moral *content* does not amount to it being morally *neutral*. In the next two sections (2.2 and 2.3) I provide two reasons—that can be found in Anscombe—for this interpretation. In section 2.2 I discuss the *'sub ratione boni'* principle and suggest that, just as propositions have 'truth value', it could also be said that actions have 'goodness value'. Following this suggestion, in section 2.3 I argue that good action is the aim of any piece of practical reasoning, just as truth is the aim of theoretical reasoning. In section 2.4 I argue that a parallelism can be traced between the validity and soundness of a piece of practical reasoning and Anscombe's distinction between 'truth in agreement with desire' and 'truth in agreement with *right* desire'. This parallelism helps to understand why practical reasoning, despite not having moral *content*, can only be said to be sound when its conclusion is a (morally) good action. Finally, (2.5) we will consider how the goodness of the end of the action is determined, since that goodness is a necessary condition for the reasoning to be sound.

2.1. Practical reasoning and moral content

Anscombe denies that practical syllogisms as such have moral content. They would have moral content if they involved an inference from universal moral principles leading to the *necessity* of a particular choice or action, by means of the normative force of such principles. Instead, the practical syllogism as such deals only with the means towards the end that the agent *already* desires, regardless of the value or moral content of that end. Practical

---

[43] In the entire section 2, unless otherwise indicated, by practical syllogism is always meant practical syllogism *proper*.

reasoning does not trigger the desire of the end, nor does it conclude what the agent should/ought to desire, but merely connects the end with the means.[44] Accordingly, Anscombe insisted that 'the first premise mentions, not *that* one wants something, but something that one wants'.[45]

Practical reasoning is about the means, not the end.[46] For instance, even in the case where a syllogism included a moral premise such as 'One ought to pay taxes', it would only lead to the action of paying them if the agent *desired* to fulfil her obligations. And a desire to fulfil one's obligations is of the same kind as the desire not to fulfil them or the desire to rest, to heal the sick person, etc.[47]

Practical reasoning determines what the appropriate means to the desired end are. This does not mean that it is not possible (or, even, necessary) to determine which ends are appropriate for a human being. It only means that such a question does not belong to the sphere of practical reasoning (and action theory), but to a different one: ethics. As is well known, this distinction of spheres is crucial for Anscombe's project. However, I would argue that just as important as the distinction itself is the adequate determination of the proper relation between them.

I would like to suggest that the relation between the desire of the end and the choosing of the means toward it can illuminate the relation between action theory and ethics. Just as the desire of the end is *presupposed* in any piece of practical reasoning, it could be said that the moral assessment or consideration of an action is *presupposed* in any instance of practically rational agency. At least two reasons can be provided to explain and support this claim: (1) the

---

[44] This connection is not external but internal because the means are the end *here and now*. In saying that the practical syllogism merely connects the end with the means I do not rule out other forms of practical reasoning, such as what might be called deliberative reasoning regarding what is the good life or what is the morally right action in a given circumstance. The point is only to distinguish those forms from the practical syllogism in the Aristotelian (and Anscombian) sense. For instance, a piece of deliberative reasoning may influence what someone takes as the object of her desire, but such object is the *starting point* of a piece of practical reasoning.
[45] 'Practical Inference', p. 119; see also *I*, §35.
[46] However, given the internal means-end connection, in choosing the means the agent is willing the end. See 'Practical Truth', p. 154.
[47] Thus, the '*moral* ought' does not have any especial normative force. See *I*, §41.

agent always acts 'under the guise of the good' and (2) despite the fact that the practical syllogism does not have moral content (and, thus, its *validity* is independent of the truth of the conclusion), it aims at the (morally) good action, just as theoretical reasoning aims at truth; that is, practical reasoning, *as* an exercise of practical knowledge (the knowledge of the agent) aims at what is (morally) good. I will deal with each of these reasons separately, in the following two sections (2.2 and 2.3).

2.2. Under the guise of the good

The agent acts under the guise of the good. In *Intention*, §§39–40 Anscombe claims that there is a conceptual link between 'wanting' and 'good', parallel to the link between 'judging' and 'truth'. Just as truth is the object of knowing, good is the object of wanting. However, the parallelism is not complete, because 'good' has different meanings (utility, pleasure, perfection, etc.) and any of them is adequate to make sense of the notion of 'wanting'. In order to account for human willing and acting, it is only required that the agent desire something because it *seems* good to her, i.e. that it is good in any of the different meanings of goodness. The question whether it is *really* good or not (i.e. *morally* good) for the agent belongs to ethics and does not *directly* affect the structure just described.

I think that, based on the guise of the good thesis, one could claim the following: similarly to the truth-value of propositions (they are either true or false), it is possible to talk about the goodness-value of actions (they are either good or bad). Whatever action the agent chooses, it is necessarily regarded by her as good, as opposed to bad. No one *can* desire something that *seems* bad to her.[48] As Anscombe explains, even if someone would adopt the principle 'Evil be thou my good', she would do it because she sees something good in doing so, for instance: 'The good of making evil my good is my intact liberty in the unsubmissiveness of my will.'[49]

The kind of good that is needed to account for practical reasoning is the *apparent* good, because it provides a 'desirability

---

[48] This is precisely the first principle of practical reason, according to Aquinas: *bonum est faciendum et prosequendum, et malum vitandum* (good is to be done, and evil avoided). See *Summa theologiae*, I–II, q. 94, a. 2.

[49] *I*, §39.

characterization' and, thus, puts an end to iteration of the question 'What do you want if for?'.[50] The end as desired by the agent is what appears in the first premise. However, it is necessary to go a step further. At first glance, it might seem that in order to qualify an action as (apparently) good it suffices to consider it as a suitable means towards the desired end. But, in reality, our actions are not compartmentalized or isolated. An agent simultaneously pursues different ends (even though she does not necessarily want to achieve all at the same time) and, thus, it might not be *enough* to consider the relation of a particular means to a particular end in order to qualify the action as good. For example, in the case of treating a sick person, providing treatment seems good because it is a way of healing, but if the doctor takes into account other ends she also has (such as improving family life by picking up her children from school), what initially seemed good (spending the time to provide the treatment) might turn out to be bad, because it becomes working too many hours, for instance. Therefore, the notion of goodness-value is not confined to each particular course of action. It also includes the reference of a particular means to other ends.

Moreover, there is a third step, which is the relationship among the different ends. Just as the relation between a particular means and the other ends might change its goodness-value, there has to be also a relationship (or order) among the different ends that makes some means better or worse depending on which end you take into account. In the given situation, for instance, the doctor might consider it good to stay with her patient and make her children wait, because the patient is in a life-threatening situation, and, thus, her end of doing her job or saving lives overrides the end of improving family life. At this level of reflection the question regarding the *real* good (the moral good) becomes salient, because—as we shall explain in section 2.5—the comparison of ends is only possible by reference to an ultimate end or a conception of what a good life amounts to (usually called *eudaimonia*).[51] For now, the provisional conclusion of my argument

---

[50] See *I*, §38. In cases like 'I just did, for no particular reason' there is no calculation or 'desirability characterization'. We can leave these cases aside here.

[51] The desirability characterization that appears in the first premise is, so to speak, the final station of practical reasoning *as such*, but Anscombe added: 'In

is that the action's goodness-value is—ultimately—linked to the question about the goodness of the end, that is, the *apparent* good is not independent of the *real* good (in a sense, this is a trivial claim). Acting under the guise of the good entails taking what one is doing to be the real good. I will return to this topic in section 2.5.

2.3. In what sense is goodness external to practical reasoning?

In the previous pages I have claimed that (a) practical knowledge is of practical truth (the good action) and (b) practical reasoning does not have moral *content*. At the same time, strictly speaking, practical knowledge is exercised *in* practical reasoning and not, for instance, in the moral study of what a good life consists in. So, it seems that practical knowledge is independent of morality or ethics. How is it possible to combine both claims? The following answer is found in Anscombe:

> [...] the goodness of the end of the action is as much of an extra, as external to the validity of the reasoning, as truth of the premises and of the conclusion is an extra, is external to the validity of theoretical reasoning. *As* external, but not *more* external.
>
> We know that the externality is not total. For truth is the object of belief, and truth-preservingness is an essential associate of validity in theoretical reasoning. The parallel will hold for practical reasoning.[52]

The key is to distinguish between the validity and the soundness of a syllogism. A practical syllogism can be valid even though it does not lead to a (morally) good action, but rather to an action that only seems good in some respect. Nonetheless, the validity is not an 'end in itself', but a necessary condition to preserve truth, from the premises to the conclusion. And, similarly, it could be said that the work (*ergon*) of practical reasoning is to preserve the goodness of the end, in the first premise, to the action, in the conclusion. Goodness is, thus, external *only* to the validity of the syllogism, but not to the syllogism *as* an exercise of practical reasoning (or practical knowledge). Let us explore in the next

---

saying this, I do not at all mean to suggest that there is no such thing as taking exception to, or arguing against, the first premise, or its being made the first premise. Nor am I thinking of moral dissent from it; I prefer to leave that out of account' (*I*, §38).

[52] 'Practical Inference', p. 146.

section the distinction between the validity and the soundness of a practical syllogism.

2.4. 'Truth in agreement with desire' and 'truth in agreement with right desire', or the validity and the soundness of a practical syllogism

In section 1 I offered an explanation of the sense in which an action can be said to be true (or false), that is, to have truth-value. And in the preceding paragraphs of section 2 I introduced the notion of goodness-value to underscore that practical reasoning operates under the *assumption* that the conclusion inferred is a (morally) good action: the agent takes her action to be good and not just to seem good. At this point, I would like to explore the connection between the truth-value and the goodness-value of an action. There is a pretty straightforward way of explaining it: an action is true when it is (morally) good, and *vice versa*. Actions are necessarily true or false, because they are necessarily good or bad.

Practical truth is defined as truth in agreement with right desire. In this definition, 'truth' refers to the minor premise (the premise of the possible) and 'right' to the major premise (the premise of the good), where the object of desire is mentioned. Practical truth occurs in the conclusion. At this point, we need to consider the distinction introduced by Anscombe between 'truth in agreement with desire' and 'truth in agreement with *right* desire', precisely to shed light on the distinction between the *mere* validity and the soundness of a practical syllogism.[53] In both cases the conclusion is an action, because the presence of the desire makes them cases of practical reasoning *proper*. The *mere* validity depends on 'correctness of calculation' and produces 'things as one wants them to be'.[54] By contrast, the soundness of the syllogism *also* requires that 'things (i.e. whatever it is proposed to bring about) be rightly desired'.[55] If the inference is not valid, then we have cases of involuntary, unintentional or irrational action.

---

[53] See 'Practical Truth', p. 153.
[54] 'Practical Inference', p. 145.
[55] 'Practical Truth', p. 154. And she adds: 'We ask: "With *what* rightness?" It must be rightness of the "right desire" in the decision of the agent when that is sound' (p. 154).

For its part, if the desire is wrong, then the conclusion will be an instance of practical falsehood.[56]

At this point we might ask: Is the mere validity not enough to account for the practical syllogism as the kind of reasoning involved in human action? No, because we engage in practical syllogistic reasoning as an *exercise* of our capacity to achieve a desired end and, thus, as a means to do what we regard as truly good. In the absence of the actual desire of an end (as something truly good), there would not be any exercise of practical reasoning and, thus, there will not be any instance of a practical syllogism. Validity is a necessary but not sufficient condition for the exercise of the human capacity of reasoning practically. It is not enough, because the agent aims at drawing a true conclusion. In this sense, truth-value is essential to the conclusion. A conclusion that is neither true nor false is not the conclusion of a practical syllogism, properly speaking.

Just as the distinction apparent/real good presupposes that we take the chosen action to be (really) good, we necessarily consider the conclusion to be true, and this truth depends on the truth of both premises. If we were unable to characterize the action as good (in opposition to bad), there would not be any action at all, since the object of our desire will not be characterized as good (and thus as desirable). For the same reason, the conclusion must be either true or false, if there is to be practical reasoning at all.

This seems to be the ultimate reason for Anscombe's criticism of von Wright.[57] His position amounted to the claim that the 'business of practical thinking is simply *truth in agreement with desire*' and Anscombe considers that insufficient.[58] She admits that such criticism is a bit unfair to von Wright, because in his paper he is not addressing the question about the nature of the business of practical thinking, at least not in comparison with Aristotle. For Aristotle—Anscombe claims—practical thinking is not just about

---

[56] I think that the distinction introduced by Anscombe is somehow parallel to the one between the practico-technical and the practico-ethical syllogism, because the validity of a practical syllogism depends on technical knowledge, whereas the rectitude of the desire is an ethical question. Both syllogisms are practical proper, but any technical syllogism is part of a broader ethical syllogism. See 'Thought and Action in Aristotle', pp. 68–70.

[57] Anscombe's 'Practical Inference' is a response to Georg Henrik von Wright, 'On So-Called Practical Inference', *Acta Sociologica* 15 (1972):39–53.

[58] 'Practical Inference', p. 144.

'getting things the way one wants them to be' but also about 'getting things a way it's all right to want them to be'.[59] Anscombe criticizes von Wright precisely for not posing that question, since the truth about it is 'a necessary component of the essential characterization of practical inference',[60] which was the topic of his paper. The nature of practical inference and reasoning remains unexplained until that question has been addressed.

We already know Anscombe's position in this regard and her reasons. For our topic, it is relevant to note that 'truth in agreement with *right* desire' is precisely the definition of practical truth and, thus, it can be said that practical truth is an essential part of the characterization of practical inference and reasoning. Anscombe clearly argues that goodness of the end — on which the soundness of the syllogism depends — is not (completely) external to the validity of the reasoning, because good is the object of action and preserving such goodness is 'an essential associate of the validity' of practical reasoning.[61]

In the next section I explore how to determine the truth of the major premise, that is, the rightness of the desire.

2.5. On the rightness of ends and 'doing well' as the description of any action

In section 2.2 I explained that three steps can be distinguished in the characterization of an action as good. The *first* step consists in considering the action to be good because it is a suitable means towards the end the agent is pursuing. The *second* step relates a particular means to other ends that the agent *also* pursues, because actions are not compartmentalized or isolated. From this perspective, a certain action can be rejected (instead of chosen) because it is incompatible with another end that we also desire to obtain (or to preserve). Anscombe gives an example of this kind of situation: burning the house down to roast a pig.[62] Let us assume that burning the house down is a way of properly roasting the pig. It could, nevertheless, be considered to be a bad choice because it makes impossible the end of resting that night (the house is

---

[59] See 'Practical Inference', p. 144.
[60] See 'Practical Inference', p. 144.
[61] See 'Practical Inference', p. 146. I am here paraphrasing Anscombe.
[62] 'Practical Inference', p. 145.

needed for that). In this situation, burning the house to roast the pig can no longer be performed 'under the guise of the good'.

In terms of the distinction between action theory and ethics, the first two steps belong to the understanding of action. In the *third* step, however, the question arises about the hierarchy of ends, that is, which are *preferable*: for instance, why preserving the house (not only to rest tonight) is more important (or desirable) than doing a good job of roasting the pig. The comparison or ordering of ends can only be done if there is an ultimate, architectonic end.[63] Such is happiness, or the good life.

I do not think it is necessary to elaborate on this here. I just want to make clear that there are two different issues involved in the necessity of having an ultimate end: (1) that the agent *must have* such an end (if she is to be an agent), and (2) the *specific content* of the ultimate end, that is, what the agents considers to be the good life.[64] I argue that the analysis of the practical syllogism leads us to accept (1), but leaves (2) as an open question. For instance, even though Aristotle and Kant (or an Aristotelian and a Kantian agent) disagree about what the good life consists in and, thus, have a different answer for (2), they both would accept (1). Accepting (1) is the mark of strong or substantive (opposed to merely technical/instrumental) models of practical rationality, because they claim that any human action is moral. The answer to (2) is an ethical business, in which other philosophical (anthropological, metaphysical) considerations about 'human life' are usually taken into account (such as life according to reason in Aristotle or autonomy in Kant).[65]

---

[63] 'Practical Inference', p. 147. And she adds: 'Only on this condition can that illusory "moral ought" be exorcised, while leaving open the possibility of criticizing a piece of practical reasoning, valid in the strict and narrow sense in which in theoretical contexts validity contrasts with truth. The criticism will be of the practical reasoning as not leading to the doing of good action. An action of course is good if it is not bad, but being inimical to the last architectonic end would prove that it was not good' ('Practical Inference', p. 147).

[64] Even though the truth of the conclusion of practical reasoning depends on what is in fact the good life, there is also practical falsehood, which appears in the conclusion when the agent is wrong about the content of the good life. In either case the necessary components of practical reasoning are present.

[65] See 'Thought and Action in Aristotle', p. 75. This position is at odds with the one exemplified by Hare, because he rules out the possibility of determining (2): 'If pressed to justify a decision completely, we have to give a complete specification of the way of life of which it is a part [...] If the inquirer still

The distinction between (1) and (2) is another way of putting Anscombe's thesis that, on the one hand, the practical syllogism does not have moral content (i.e. is independent of (2)) but, on the other hand, its proper conclusion is the good action, because practical reasoning is not independent of the ultimate end or the agent's conception of the good life (because of (1)). Practical reasoning does not have moral content, because morality is not a 'content' in the sense of something added or different from the action itself.[66] Practical rationality is structurally moral: it is moral insofar as it is practical. Acting, practical reasoning, is about doing good and, in the end, leading a good life.

If I am right, this is the sense in which Anscombe claims that 'doing well' is a 'final description of what every praxis—every "action" in this limited sense—aims at being'.[67] What we do has different names or descriptions: healing the sick person, doing my job, improving my family life, etc. But the description 'doing well' is also included, precisely because we act 'under the guise of the good' and the particular end one pursues at a particular time is connected to her other ends and her life as whole.[68] Practical truth is the truth of that action description. Such truth (or falsehood) belongs to the action (or is predicated of the action), because 'doing well' is something that, properly speaking, can only be *done* (not just wished, thought, etc.). Practical truth is not (just) about being right on the meaning of the good life, but about *leading* a good life. Whether it is true that what we do can be described as 'living well' is something only ethics (both as a discipline and as the moral knowledge of the agent) can determine.

---

goes on asking "But why *should* I live like that?" then there is no further answer to give him.' Richard M. Hare, *The Language of Morals* (Oxford: Oxford University Press, 1952), p. 69. For Hare 'there is no further answer' because it is impossible to establish a hierarchy among the ends. I think this is what Anscombe was referring to when she talked about 'corruption of the mind' in 'Modern Moral Philosophy': not that someone holds an outrageous ethical opinion, but that her way of *reasoning* does not allow her to see that it is outrageous or, even worse, it makes it impossible to consider anything to be morally outrageous. See 'Modern Moral Philosophy', p. 191.

[66] 'Action, Intention and "Double Effect"', in *HLAE*, pp. 209–210.
[67] See 'Practical Truth', p. 157; see 'Thought and Action in Aristotle', p. 75.
[68] Practical truth/falsehood does not consist *merely* in 'making true' a description of the action, as other natural causes make true certain proposition. See 'Practical Truth', p. 157.

If the preceding analysis of the notion of practical truth is right, we might conclude that acting rationally is acting morally, but not necessarily acting morally well. Our actions have both truth-value and goodness-value: they necessarily are good or bad.[69]

---

[69] Previous versions of this chapter were presented at Università Gregoriana (Rome), Universidad Carlos III (Madrid) and Università di Genova (Italy). I would like to thank the audiences for their comments and suggestions. I am also thankful to Jennifer Frey for reading and discussing the first draft, to David Zapero Maier for his insightful comments and, particularly, to Roger Teichmann and David Albert Jones for their thorough comments and criticism. Research for this chapter was conducted as part of Research Project FFI2012-38737-C03-01, Ministry of Science and Innovation, Government of Spain.

Matthew B. O'Brien

On Obligation and the Virtues of Law

Today students of Anglophone philosophy are taught that virtue ethics is one of three main alternative moral theories on offer, with the other two being utilitarianism and deontology. These three rival theories are distinguished by which ethical notion they prioritize: virtue ethics is supposed to prioritize the good *habits* or *dispositions* that issue in actions, utilitarianism to prioritize good *consequences* of actions, and deontology to prioritize (the rules of) *right actions* themselves.

Elizabeth Anscombe is widely regarded as a founder of modern virtue ethics, on account of her essay 'Modern Moral Philosophy', in which she argues that much of modern moral theory is incoherent due to its neglect of the virtues and reliance upon a confused conception of the 'moral ought'. Anscombe's critique of modern moral theory in this essay and her subsequent works does not amount to a brief on behalf of the contemporary understanding of virtue ethics, however.[1] For Anscombe's critique rejects the whole tendency of modern moral theorists to prioritize a single ethical category against all others. On the contrary, Anscombe's critique suggests a picture of ethics in which neither virtues, consequences nor rules serve a more basic explanatory role than the others. She is a pluralist about ethical categories,

---

[1] See Philippa Foot, 'Rationality and Goodness', in Anthony O'Hear (ed.), *Modern Moral Philosophy*, Royal Institute of Philosophy Supplement: 54 (Cambridge: Cambridge University Press, 2004), pp. 1–13, and Christopher Miles Coope, 'Modern Virtue Ethics', in T.D.J. Chappel (ed.), *Values and Virtues: Aristotelianism in Contemporary Ethics* (Oxford: Oxford University Press, 2006).

which implies that virtues, consequences and rules answer to complementary and mutually implicating explanatory needs. A human action may be bad either if it springs from a vicious disposition, produces certain bad consequences or violates a rule; it can be good only by avoiding all of these pitfalls.

Perhaps the most well-known of Anscombe's contentions in 'Modern Moral Philosophy' is her rejection of 'obligation, and duty—*moral* obligation and *moral* duty, that is to say—and of what is *morally* right and wrong, and of the *moral* sense of "ought" […]'.[2] The brusqueness of Anscombe's rhetoric in the essay, along with her recommendation of the virtues, can distract from the fact that her rejection of obligation, duty, right, wrong and ought is quite focused: it extends only to a specifically *moral* sense of these terms. The argument of 'Modern Moral Philosophy', especially when read in light of Anscombe's later work, can be interpreted as a defence of obligation rightly understood, as much as an attack on certain characteristic distortions of it.[3] Anscombe herself never gave a systematic, positive account of obligation. My aim in this chapter is to flesh out the lines that such an account might take by elaborating upon some of what she did say. In particular, I wish to show how Anscombe's rather grand claims about the genealogy of obligation are connected to a closely-argued account of necessity and practical inference.

Anscombe's various discussions of obligation are broadly Thomistic in spirit, and they suggest an account in which obligation is understood as a normative force of practical reason that is essentially linked with law and authority.[4] One attractive feature of this picture is that it shows how law and virtue need not be

---

[2] 'Modern Moral Philosophy', in *CPP3*, p. 27. Thus she goes on to say, 'It would be a great improvement if, instead of "morally wrong", one always named a genus such as "untruthful", "unchaste", "unjust". We should no longer ask whether doing something was "wrong", passing directly from some description of an action to this notion; we should ask whether, e.g., it was unjust; and the answer would sometimes be clear at once' (p. 33).

[3] Julia Driver points out that 'Modern Moral Philosophy' can be read as a *modus tollens* demonstrating the necessity of theological ethics. See 'Gertrude Elizabeth Margaret Anscombe', *The Stanford Encyclopedia of Philosophy* (Fall 2009 Edition), edited by Edward N. Zalta, [Online] http://plato.stanford.edu/archives/fall2009/entries/anscombe/.

[4] Portions of this chapter appeared in an earlier form in Matthew B. O'Brien, *Practical Necessity: A Study in Ethics, Law, and Human Action*, PhD Thesis (Austin, Texas: University of Texas, 2011).

considered alternative ethical frameworks, but might cohere within a single framework. Thus law is the kind of norm that binds those who are subject to it with the force of obligation, and authority and obedience are the co-relative virtues that persons must possess if the directives they make and follow are to count as genuine laws.[5] The existence of genuine law, therefore, presupposes an authoritative lawgiver at its source. When the law in question is the moral law, as opposed to the civil or criminal law of some positive legal system, then the only viable candidate for lawgiver is God.[6] The alternative to the specifically *moral* sense of obligation that Anscombe rejects is a generic sense of obligation. I shall begin by elaborating this generic conception of obligation, understood as the practical mode of necessity. In the second and third parts I shall discuss some of the logical, legal and theological aspects of Anscombe's account of obligation, and compare her account with an argument of Peter Geach about the necessity of acting virtuously.

1. Obligation as practical necessity

In her book *Intention,* Anscombe insists that moral reasoning does not have its own special form, but rather is just ordinary reasoning, whose topic happens to be moral: *viz.,* what somebody ought and ought not to do.

> Contemplating the accounts [of the practical syllogism] given by modern commentators, one might easily wonder why no one has ever pointed out the mince pie syllogism: the peculiarity of this would be that it was about mince pies, and an example would be 'All mince pies have suet in them—this is a mince pie—therefore

---

[5] Calling 'authority' a virtue may initially sound odd, but I think this characterization is justified, because authority is a personal attribute that is correlative with obedience, which manifestly *is* a virtue, and, like virtues generally, the legitimate and just exercise of authority is an excellence that lies in a mean between excess and deficiency. A person with authority has the right to be obeyed partly because of his *ability* to perform some task, and partly because of the need for this task to be performed.

[6] It is beyond the scope of this chapter to consider how Anscombe's remarks about law related to contemporary legal theory. Suffice it to say that her analysis of obligation is unrelated to the crude form of 'orders backed by threats' positivism upended by the work of H.L.A. Hart. In fact, 'Modern Moral Philosophy' is surprisingly complementary with Hart's early essay 'Legal and Moral Obligation', in A.I. Melden (ed.), *Essays in Moral Philosophy* (Seattle: University of Washington Press, 1958).

etc.' Certainly ethics is of importance to human beings in a way that mince pies are not; but such importance cannot justify us speaking of a special sort of reasoning.[7]

Similarly, we are not justified in speaking of a special sense of *moral* obligation, any more than we are justified in speaking about a special sense of *mince pie* reasoning, say, that involves *sui generis* categories of reasons and inferences for cooking and eating mince pies. A good person has the aim of acting well, just as a good cook, let us say, has the aim of baking tasty mince pies. Given these aims, rational necessities arise for the good person and the good cook which demand what must be done and what must be avoided by each of them. Although the most philosophically interesting and pressing instances of obligation arise in morality, rather than in less fraught practices such as cooking, the concept of obligation figures generally in social practices. We speak of the *duties* of a shortstop on a baseball team or a paediatrician in a hospital, for example, at least as sensibly as the *duties* of conscience or morality.[8]

The obligations of morality are central and distinctive features of human life when compared to instances of obligation in other social practices like etiquette, medicine, baseball or cooking. The centrality and distinctiveness of moral obligation is a function of the subject matter of morality, however, and not of the structure or form that the concept of obligation has within morality. Because morality touches every deliberate thought and action, philosophers are often misled into treating the obligations of morality as if they were *sui generis* and unlike anything else in practical life. On the contrary, being under a moral obligation is structurally quite like a doctor being under an obligation of good medical practice or the member of a political community being under an obligation of his legal system.[9]

---

[7] *I*, p. 58.

[8] Note Anscombe's remark in *Intention*, 'In thinking of the word for "should", "ought" etc. (*dei*) as it occurs in Aristotle, we should think of it as it occurs in ordinary language [...] and not just as it occurs in the examples of "moral discourse" given by most moral philosophers [...], [because] "should" is a rather light word with unlimited contexts of application [...]' (p. 64).

[9] An obligation of medicine or of law may ultimately be coextensive with genuine moral obligations, but these are not just *examples* of moral obligation because there may be cases in which morality requires violating the obligations of medicine or law.

When we speak of obligation we express the idea of practical necessity. Obligation expresses a specific mode of practical reason's normative force: the rational force of demand.[10] This means that when an agent is obligated to perform or forbear from some action, it is a force of reason that binds him. Practical necessity is an instance of hypothetical or suppositional necessity: 'that without which some good will not be obtained or some evil averted.'[11] To be obligated to φ, on this account, is to be under a rational necessity to φ as means that is either instrumental to or constitutive of some good that is willed as an end. The willing of the good as an end generates the rational force of the demand on the agent to choose what contributes to the end. This initially simple idea of suppositional necessity is the root of the complex structure of obligation in human agency. It is important to clarify from the outset that this Aristotelian-Thomistic idea of hypothetical necessity is in some respects similar, but not equivalent, to the Kantian idea of the hypothetical imperative, because it belongs to a picture of normativity and practical reasoning that avoids the Kantian package of categorical *versus* hypothetical imperatives. I shall return to this point later on.

Consider authority. Authority is the virtue that consists in possessing the power to command subjects who have the duty to obey.[12] For someone with authority, to command is for him to impose a binding, rationally necessary requirement upon his subject's action. An authoritative requirement provides practical reasons to its subjects that exclude considerations that might otherwise be relevant to the subjects' decision to act in the absence of the authoritative requirement, and pre-empt further deliberation. Although requests, pleas, petitions, advice, suggestions, counsels and recommendations all express normative claims upon an agent's practical reasoning, they do not generate requirements that have the rationally binding force of necessity in the way that authoritative commands do. Whoever petitions, counsels or admonishes another person does not do so *qua* authority.

---

[10] Here and elsewhere I am indebted to the schema developed by Thomas Pink in 'Moral Obligation', in Anthony O'Hear (ed.), *Modern Moral Philosophy* (Cambridge: Cambridge University Press, 2004) and his other works, in spite of our differing conclusions.

[11] 'On the Source of the Authority of the State', in *CPP3*, p. 139.

[12] Throughout I take 'authority' to mean 'legitimate authority'.

Authority, therefore, entails command and command gives rise to obligation.

Given that we speak about the obligations of doctors, the demands of etiquette, and the duties of a baseball team's shortstop, obligation and its associated concepts are not unique to morality. If we examine both philosophical and everyday uses of the concept of obligation, it appears that obligation plays two structural roles within social practices, which need to be distinguished, at least at the outset. Any general theory of obligation will have to be capable of explaining both of these roles.

Anscombe is very clear that one sense of obligation rightly understood is the necessity of avoiding certain intrinsically bad actions:

> [I]f someone really thinks, *in advance*, that it is open to question whether such an action as procuring the judicial execution of the innocent should be quite excluded from consideration—I do not want to argue with him; he shows a corrupt mind.[13]

Anscombe's assertion of absolutism is of a piece with her proposal to return to Aristotelian ethics. For Aristotle also identifies certain actions as intrinsically bad, which 'imply by their names that they are themselves bad', so that '[i]t is not possible, then, ever to be right with regard to them; one must always be wrong'.[14] Furthermore, like Anscombe, Aristotle argues that perceiving the baseness or nobility of certain actions and emotions is prerequisite to engaging in philosophical ethics, so theoretical debate with 'a corrupt mind' who failed to possess the starting points of moral theory would be pointless.[15]

One need not already agree with Anscombe's assertions in order to see that intrinsically bad actions are one sense of what people mean when they speak of obligations; this is the first of the two forms of obligation that I wish to isolate. Therefore, when

---

[13] 'Modern Moral Philosophy', p. 40.
[14] *Nicomachean Ethics* (*NE*) 1107a12–14, trans. Ross in J. Barnes, *The Complete Works of Aristotle: The Revised Oxford Translation* (Princeton: Princeton University Press, 1984). Aristotle mentions spite, shamelessness, grudgingness, adultery, theft and murder as actions or emotions that it is intrinsically wrong to choose to do or to feel.
[15] *NE*, 1.4 and 10.9. Cf. Myles Burnyeat, 'Aristotle on Learning to be Good', in A.O. Rorty (ed.), *Essays on Aristotle's Ethics* (Berkeley: University of California Press, 1981).

someone asks, 'what is moral obligation?' or 'are there any moral obligations?' one question he might be asking is:

(1) Is there anything that's *always* wrong?

This question may be put more precisely: are there exceptionless moral norms that pick out intrinsically bad types of action? If there are, then what such norms imply is that for an agent to act virtuously he must strategically avoid doing certain things, whatever else he does. An agent does not guarantee for himself that he will act virtuously by avoiding intrinsically bad actions, but by choosing them he does guarantee that he will act viciously, and so he *must* avoid them if he is to act well. In spite of all the attention they receive from moral theorists, such exceptionless norms only pick out a very small part of the moral landscape—the cliffs and precipices. It would be impossible to act well merely by respecting those negative moral norms that are exceptionless. Attempting this would be like trying to eat healthfully merely by avoiding lethal poisons; it would be quite easy to avoid lethal poisons entirely and still die from malnutrition or indeed from the cumulative effects of excess or deficiency of elements that are healthy in moderation. But if a prospective action satisfies certain prohibited act descriptions, then this fact automatically rules out that action as a moral possibility, regardless of whatever further goods it respects or promotes.

We can construe proposals about exceptionless moral norms as claims about 'normative modality', as it were. To say that there are intrinsically bad actions is to say that there are actions that are morally impossible. This point is not distinctive of the practice of morality, however, because it could equally be made about language, law or baseball, for example. Some actions, like a batter running to second base without touching first base, are strictly impossible for someone who is playing baseball. To attempt such an action is not to play baseball badly, as it would be for a runner not to tag-up on a caught fly ball with no outs, but it is to fail to play baseball at all. Certain strategic and exceptionless norms partially constitute baseball as a game and following them is a necessary condition on playing the game at all. Similarly, a language user cannot speak meaningfully if he violates certain basic grammatical rules, although there is certainly more flexibility in grammar than baseball.

The second structural role that obligation appears to play in a practice is not limited and strategic, but comprehensive and architectonic. People implicate this role, for example, when in the course of deliberating they feel the pangs of conscience 'to do the right thing', or 'to be moral', whatever that may amount to, and even though they are at the moment unsure of what this is. When, say, someone finally sees what the generous gesture to his friend would consist in, his conscience tells him that he *must* do this generous thing. In seeing the prospective action as generous, the agent sees the goodness in it and recognizes that reason recommends choosing it, and perhaps recommends it on balance more strongly than any other course of action. His voice of conscience amplifies the force of reason's recommendation with the force of demand. Such pangs of conscience are of course not universal to human experience, but they are familiar enough. In any case, the idea of a general conscientious requirement to do the right thing or to be moral implies an affirmative answer to the question:

(2) Is it obligatory to be good; is it rationally necessary to act virtuously?

This question picks out the second role that obligation can take: given that moral agents *do well* to act virtuously, are they also obliged and bound—necessitated—to act virtuously? To answer affirmatively is to say that morality also necessitates the actions that it recommends.[16] Whereas the limited and strategic practical necessities pick out act descriptions that cannot be chosen by a moral agent *within* morality, this second form of necessity compels the practice of morality as a whole. Engaging in the morality practice is not optional. Even if an agent doesn't see the good in or feel the pull of acting virtuously, he is nevertheless subject to an inescapable norm that rationally compels virtuous action.[17] If obligation plays this architectonic role in morality, then all-things-considered moral reasons for action or forbearance don't merely recommend virtuous actions in comparison to vicious ones, but such reasons pre-empt further deliberation about alternative courses of action and exclude considerations about other reasons

---

[16] Depending on the moral theory, what's purportedly necessitated might be a single determinate action or a range of equally eligible actions.
[17] Cf. 'On Promising and its Justice, and Whether it Need be Respected *in foro interno*', in *CPP3*, pp. 18–19.

from arising.[18] In this case, moral reasons authoritatively demand compliance. For example, consider a case where in given circumstances an agent's φ-ing would be just and his not φ-ing would be unjust. The virtuous feature of φ-ing, which is its justice, gives the agent a good reason to φ. Now if we add to this situation the further claim that an agent *must* act morally, then the merely good reason to φ becomes an obliging reason to φ, and, as such, the obliging reason both pre-empts further deliberating and excludes other considerations that may have been relevant otherwise.

It is common to think that it is not possible rationally to opt out from an interest in the practice of morality, as one might opt out, say, from an interest in baseball.[19] Indeed, the person who does try to opt out of morality is considered shameless and subject to blame, while the person who opts out of baseball is not. Moral obligation and the 'moral ought' have been thought to express comprehensive and architectonic practical necessity and thereby to bind all rational agents. Christine Korsgaard is an influential proponent of this view. Morality, she thinks, is capable of answering 'the normative question', which is the question 'why should I be moral?' as asked by someone who has lost confidence or interest in the reasonableness of morality's claims.[20] Although Korsgaard herself does not call attention to the two different roles that obligation plays—strategic versus architectonic—and that I have tried to distinguish, she clearly thinks that any respectable moral theory should be able to justify the rational necessity of acting virtuously for any moral agent. On this view, the amoralist who spurns ethics is not merely blind to or neglectful of a form of

---

[18] This language of exclusionary and pre-emptive reasons implies the idea of authority. Cf. Joseph Raz, *The Morality of Freedom* (New York: Oxford University Press, 1988). We could put the same question thus: *does morality have authority?*

[19] It is important to see what's packed into this sense of non-optional. If it is necessary to act well, then morality is non-optional in that failing to act morally would amount to logical contradiction.

[20] Christine M. Korsgaard, 'The Normative Question', in her *The Sources of Normativity* (Cambridge: Harvard University Press, 1996). Korsgaard's normative question is equivalent to what Prichard thinks is the mistaken question which moral philosophy rests upon: should '[…] we really ought to do what in our non-reflective consciousness we have hitherto believed we ought to do, or if not, […] what, if any, are the other things which we really ought to do?' (H.A. Prichard, 'Does Moral Philosophy Rest on a Mistake?', *Mind* 21(81) 1912:37).

value, and he is not merely senseless, unjust or shameless, but he is rationally incoherent and logically self-contradictory.[21] As Korsgaard puts it, the amoralist destroys his identity as an agent by failing to follow the norms that are constitutive of agency.[22]

Thus far I have avoided using the Kantian distinction between hypothetical and categorical imperatives. I have avoided this common way of characterizing these issues because it confusingly elides two separate matters that need to be kept apart. First, there is the *scope of application* that a normative consideration has, which may be universal or restricted. Second, there is the *force* with which a normative consideration is justified, which may be imperatival or recommendatory. By assuming that hypothetical and categorical norms *both* have imperatival force, Kantians neglect the normative force of recommendation entirely. Consider an example of how the scope of application and force of reason come apart. If I am a physician and you are my patient, then my reason to give you the medicine you need applies to me specially, given my role as your physician. Someone else who doesn't have this role may have no reason to spend his time administering you the treatment. Depending upon the facts about our situation, the reason to give you the medicine that applies to me might *demand* that I give you the medicine or alternatively, it might *recommend* my medicating you as one among other eligible actions that would also discharge my responsibilities as a doctor. If the hospital is overwhelmed with patients after some catastrophe, for instance, then reason might recommend my medicating you and perhaps recommend equally well my assisting other patients instead of you. As Anscombe observes in her little essay, 'Who is Wronged?', I might do one or the other and still act well.[23] If the hospital is empty and your condition is grave, then all other things being equal, reason might demand that I medicate you, and my

---

[21] As Philippa Foot says, 'Irrational actions are those in which a man in some way defeats his own purposes, doing what is calculated to be disadvantageous or to frustrate his ends.' Philippa Foot, 'Morality as a System of Hypothetical Imperatives', *The Philosophical Review* 81(3) 1972:310. The question is whether or not immorality necessarily involves such irrational action.
[22] For a persuasive criticism of this view, see David Enoch, 'Agency, Schmagency: Why Normativity Won't Come from What is Constitutive of Action', *Philosophical Review* 115(2) 2006:169–198.
[23] 'Who is Wronged? Philippa Foot on Double-Effect: One Point', in *HLAE*, pp. 249–251.

choosing not to would amount to harming you by negligence. Whatever strength the rational force turns out to be, it will be a function of how medicating you in such and such circumstances fits into the good practice of medicine, given that I am a medical practitioner with you under my care.[24] Quite generally, therefore, if I have a reason to φ, then we can always ask two questions about this reason's status. First, we can ask what the *scope* of the reason's application is: whose reason is it, does it apply to someone categorically and irrespective of his contingent interests, or only in a restricted fashion, given that (perhaps as a consequence of a certain role of his) he intends to ψ? Second, given that the reason does apply to someone, we can ask what the *force* of the reason is: does it demand his φ-ing or does it merely recommend it? The Kantian package of hypothetical and categorical imperatives primes us to miss the distinctiveness of these two questions by eliding reason's scope and force. Moral reasons may apply with universal scope and bind with recommendatory force, and they may apply with restricted scope and bind with demanding force.

In this section I have distinguished two ways in which the concept of obligation is used. The contrast I have sketched is between practical necessity as (a) expressed in limited and strategic norms *within* a practice, which are necessary conditions on acting well according to that practice, and as (b) expressed in the comprehensive and architectonic demandingness *of* a practice as a whole. It is consistent to acknowledge the existence of (a) strategic necessities, while denying that morality as a whole speaks with (b) the authoritative voice of obligation. Indeed, subject to some qualifications, this seems to be the position of Aristotle.

It isn't possible to formulate a claim expressing architectonic obligation in terms that are faithful to Aristotle's ethics. We might formulate a recognizably Aristotelian ethical master principle — e.g. you do best in acting, and (consenting to) feeling, so as to promote excellent activity of your soul over the course of a complete life — but the normative force of such a principle is indicative rather than imperative, so it expresses the force of recommendation, not demand. What it is best for you to do is not what you must do, unless there is an argument that explains why 'best' and 'must' should be identified. Consequentialists have often made

---

[24] In order to simplify the case, I am assuming that there is no further overriding reason why I should cease to consider my role as a physician.

this identification, but they have merely asserted it. Strategic obligations have purchase with agents who see the reasonableness of acting well, and who wish to know more clearly what commitment to acting well consists in and consists in avoiding. Architectonic obligation applies to all moral agents as such and purports to bind them to participate in morality whatever their commitments or interests.

2. Obligation and practical inference

Anscombe is well-known for her historical claim that the concept of moral obligation in modern moral theory is an instance of 'the survival of a concept outside the framework of thought that made it a really intelligible one […]'. This framework, she argues, is the framework of divine law, more or less shared by Jews, Stoics and Christians.[25] Less well-known, however, is Anscombe's account of how obligation, rightly understood, figures in the logic of practical inference.[26] In 'On Promising and its Justice' Anscombe gives a long and difficult argument to show 'that a man will not act well —do what is good', if he fails to act justly in keeping his contracts.[27] She is adamant that, even if her argument is successful, someone still may concede that unjust action is bad action, 'but refuse to infer from this that it is necessary not to act unjustly'.[28] As we have seen, this further inference fails because of the difference between *what* there is reason to do, and the normative force *with which* reason favours what there is reason to do. It makes perfect sense to recognize that something is bad and yet to ask why one *must* avoid doing this bad thing. This question is not the same as the ultimately nonsensical question, 'what reason do I have to do what is good?' For this question is equivalent to asking, 'what reason do I have to do what is reasonable?' To recognize an action as good just is to see that reason favours doing it.[29] The legitimate question is about the *necessity* of doing good and avoiding bad, not the reasonableness of doing good and avoiding

---

[25] 'Modern Moral Philosophy', p. 31.
[26] There doesn't appear to be a straightforward connection here to deontic symbolic logic.
[27] The argument runs from page 10 to 19 and is, she suggests, 'one of the several roots of the idea of *justice*'. 'On Promising and its Justice', p. 19.
[28] 'On Promising and its Justice', p. 19.
[29] For Anscombe's definition of a reason for action, see her 'Practical Inference', in *HLAE*, p. 147.

bad. The fact that people talk about 'necessary evils' shows that the meanings of evaluative and deontic appraisals come apart in the way that Anscombe observes. It is common to think that a necessary evil is a bad act that someone is permitted and maybe even required to do. Even if in fact there are no necessary or permissible evils, it is an intelligible notion.

The particular example of acting justly in the matter of contracts that Anscombe discusses is a placeholder and her observations seem meant to apply equally to any particular genus of virtue or acting well. Making and keeping contracts 'is an instrument whose use is part and parcel of an enormous amount of human activity and hence of human good [...]'.[30] This enormous amount of human activity and human good can and does persist even though people routinely fail to keep their contracts. No doubt eventually a tipping point is reached and the failure of enough people to keep their contracts undermines the ability of contract making to contribute to human good. But in the very wide interim, which is certainly our present condition,

> [if] you think that you can attain your own good without acting well, and even if this is not true, it is not shown to be untrue by the considerations which show that acting unjustly is not acting well. For this reason it is intelligible for a man to say that he sees no necessity to act well in that matter, that is, no necessity for himself to take contracts seriously except as it serves his purposes. But if someone does genuinely *take* a proof that without doing X he cannot act well as a proof that he must do X, then this shows, not that he has an extra premise [*viz.*, the premise, 'it is necessary to do what is good and avoid what is bad'], but that he *has a purpose* that can be served only by acting well, as such.[31]

The confusions surrounding the 'moral ought' arise when philosophers fail to grasp the difference between a *premise* of practical inference and a *principle* of practical inference. The goodness or badness that someone sees in a prospective action will figure in his reasoning as a premise in his practical inference that concludes in the performance or avoidance of the action, as the case may be. The premise includes a 'desirability characterization', and when this mentions something that is genuinely good, it gives the agent's reason for the action that applies with the force of

---

[30] 'On Promising and its Justice', p. 18.
[31] 'On Promising and its Justice', p. 19.

recommendation.[32] It is rationally necessary, or obligatory, for someone to do good and avoid evil only if two further criteria are fulfilled: (a) the agent aims at a substantive purpose that governs his practical reasoning, and (b) he knows it to be true that doing evil is strictly incompatible with pursuing this governing purpose. In such a case, the agent's ultimate goal functions for him as a principle of practical inference, which generates the obliging force that compels the avoidance of bad actions. Since he reasons about what to do under this principle, such a moral agent 'would need no step from the proof that doing X is acting ill to the conclusion that he must not do X. For here there is no room for the question "Granted this is acting ill, still may not it be necessary for me — i.e. be that without which I cannot attain my end?"'.[33] He thus not only has reason to avoid X, but he is rationally compelled to avoid X, on his supposition of a governing purpose.

Anscombe's claim about the source of practical necessity is related to a logical point about theoretical reasoning made by Lewis Carroll in his famous mock dialogue 'What the Tortoise Said to Achilles'.[34] Carroll's discussion between Achilles and the tortoise is meant to show, among other things, how the logical rule of *modus ponens* properly functions as a principle, and not as a premise, of theoretical inference. Confusions about the 'logical ought' arise when the difference between a principle or rule of inference and a premise is confounded, as Carroll has Achilles confound it in his responses to the sceptical questioning of the tortoise. Someone who merely asserts *modus ponens* as a premise in an argument is not thereby logically compelled to draw a conclusion that would follow by the supposition of *modus ponens* as a principle or rule.[35] For example, if you assert P and $P \rightarrow Q$, then Q follows validly from these asserted premises; but the logical necessity of actually inferring Q only arises on the active supposition of *modus ponens* as a principle of inference, operating

---

[32] *I*, pp. 71–72.
[33] 'On Promising and its Justice', p. 20.
[34] *Mind* 4(14) April 1895:278–280.
[35] Cf. Anscombe's quotation of Wittgenstein in the prescript to her essay 'Practical Inference': 'Logic is interested in the UNASSERTED propositions' (p. 109). See also Gilbert Ryle, '"If", "So", and "Because"', in his *Collected Papers, Volume II, 1929–1968* (New York: Barnes & Noble, 1971), pp. 239ff.; Anselm Winifred Mueller, 'Acting Well', in Anthony O'Hear (ed.), *Modern Moral Philosophy*, pp. 32–35.

in tandem with the assertion of the premises. There is a broad parallel between the logical structure of reasoning towards belief and the conceptual connection between 'judgment' and 'truth', on the one hand, and reasoning towards action and the conceptual connection between 'wanting' and 'good' on the other.[36] In the case of practical reasoning, the necessity of doing good and avoiding evil arises only from the agent reasoning about what to do under the supposition of a certain principle. Anscombe rejects 'the conception of the practical syllogism as of its nature ethical, and thus as a proof about what one ought to do, which somehow culminates in action'.[37] For her the 'ought' of practical inference is a function of the end that the deliberating agent has in view. The premises of a practical inference include the characterization of some action as good or desirable, but '[...] the fact that *some* desirability characterisation is required [among the premises] does not have the least tendency to shew that *any* is endowed with some kind of necessity [...]'.[38] The conclusion of practical inference 'is an action whose point is shewn by the premises', but not necessitated by the premises.[39]

Although people may *treat* the necessity of doing good and avoiding evil as an axiom of their moral reasoning, the difficulty is that as an axiom it 'is not capable of demonstration except as generally holding'.[40] Even if it may be evident that people generally need to do good and avoid evil in order to be happy, it isn't evident that they always must. Therefore, someone who was already questioning the need to follow reason's recommendation against an action he knew to be bad would not be reinforced by supplying him with an axiom that itself is contestable. This person might even recognize the goodness of a life free from any deliberate evildoing, but if he thinks some other good is achievable for him by deliberately acting badly, then he need not see any necessity in avoiding bad acts.[41] He need not, that is, unless he has some higher purpose that is incompatible with acting badly.

---

[36] *I*, §40.
[37] *I*, p. 78.
[38] *I*, p. 76.
[39] *I*, p. 60.
[40] 'On Promising and its Justice', p. 20.
[41] See Anscombe's discussion of *bonum est multiplex* in *I*, pp. 74–77.

What candidates are there for such a higher purpose? Anscombe seems to think that there are two possibilities: first, there is the higher purpose whose incompatibility with acting badly is merely formal, because it excludes bad action by definition. This is the aim 'to *be moral*'.[42] If someone makes his main aim in life to 'be moral', or to act virtuously, then he will be rationally necessitated to avoid choosing badly. (Of course hard questions still arise about just which actions really are bad, immoral or vicious.) To use the schema from the first section of this paper, it is rationally necessary for such a person to act virtuously because he makes the practice of morality his highest aim. Aristotle seems to hold something like this view, because his conception of the highest good, or *eudaimonia*, is a 'moralized' conception of happiness. The problem with this sort of view is that it invites the question, which on its own terms is unanswerable: why *must* I be moral?

God, understood as legislator, is the second candidate for a highest good that cannot rationally be pursued while choosing badly. Here we can see the connection between Anscombe's historical thesis about the origins of the concept of moral obligation and her discussions about how necessity figures in practical inference. The Jews, Stoics and Christians have an intelligible conception of moral obligation because they conceive of moral agency as essentially structured by a final end, *viz.* God. But not every conception of God has like implications for practical reasoning. By conceiving of man's final end as knowing, obeying and loving a *personal* God who *legislates*, the Jews, Stoics and Christians define practical reasoning in terms of a '[...] substantive aim the attainment of which is conceived to be, and really is, happiness', and which 'obviously could not be attained but only hindered by acting ill [...]'.[43] Whatever else their differences, the Hebrew, Christian and Stoic conceptions of God each satisfy these criteria. When this conception of God operates as the governing principle of someone's practical reasoning, it really is clear why he rationally must do good and avoid evil. Without a higher purpose of this sort, the rational force of obligation fades, although its

---

[42] 'On Promising and its Justice', pp. 20–21.
[43] 'On Promising and its Justice', p. 20.

'mesmeric' and 'psychological' force may remain as a piece of inherited cultural baggage.[44]

It's worth contrasting the structure of the Hebrew, Christian and Stoic conception of happiness with Aristotelian *eudaimonia*. Aristotle includes in his account of the final end an essential role for divinity, but not in a way that involves divine legislation or moral obligation. Aristotle fails to have a law conception of ethics in the sense relevant to moral obligation, because his conception of God—*nous kai theos*, as Anscombe reminds us—does not include personal legislating or giving orders.[45] Aristotle's God is the supremely attractive object of contemplation, which is the highest humanly possible activity, but his God did not create the world and does not providentially superintend it. Aristotle's God may be contemplated, but not obeyed.

Hasty readers of 'Modern Moral Philosophy' have seen in Anscombe's remarks about moral obligation a kind of crude voluntarism, in which law's obliging force amounts to a mere order backed by a threat, after the fashion of Austinite legal positivism.[46] This reading is mistaken. For Anscombe the force of obligation is a force of reason, as the above discussion of practical inference shows.[47] Indeed, the substance of her discussions of law and obligation closely track the natural law theism of Aquinas. '[I]t really does add something to the description "unjust"', Anscombe claims, 'to say that there is an obligation not to do it; for what obliges is the divine law—as rules oblige in a game [...].'[48] Just as *modus ponens* obliges as a rule in the 'game' of

---

[44] 'Modern Moral Philosophy', p. 32.
[45] Anscombe points to *Metaphysics*, Book VII, and *Eudemian Ethics*, Book VIII, 1249b15-17. '[...] I cite [Aristotle] to show that one may hold that reason demands the worship and contemplation of God without holding that sins are behaviours contrary to divine law.' 'Sin: The McGivney Lectures', in *FHG*, pp. 120-121.
[46] Cf. John Austin, *The Province of Jurisprudence Determined*, edited by W. Rumble (Cambridge: Cambridge University Press, 1995).
[47] Although she calls obligation 'a taboo or sacredness which is annexed' by convention to practices such as contract-making, Anscombe goes on to give an account of obligation's rational force that explicitly contrasts with obligation construed as the mere 'terror of the law'. 'On Promising and its Justice', p. 19.
[48] She continues: 'And it is because "morally wrong" is heir of this concept, and an heir that is cut off from the family of concepts from which it sprang, that "morally wrong" *both* goes beyond the merely factual description "unjust"

theoretical inference, so 'Love the Lord your God and love your neighbour as yourself' obliges as a rule in the 'game' of the moral life.

3. Obligation, authority and law

Moral norms count as laws if they oblige and not merely recommend. Obligation and recommendation are two degrees of normative force, which the Scholastics called *vis directiva*, and normative force expresses the strength with which practical reason favours or disfavours the performance of actions. A rational norm may favour some action without demanding it, but for Anscombe, as for Aquinas, 'law' just is the sort of rational norm that applies with the demanding force of obligation, and in turn the force of obligation implies a law that generates it. *Consilia* favour actions and *praecepta* demand them.[49] Aquinas states, 'law [*lex*] is a certain rule and measure of actions, according to which someone is induced to act or restrained from acting; for "law" [*lex*] derives from "binding" [*ligando*], because it obliges to action.' Even rational norms that favour doing what conforms to virtue and contributes to the common good do not count as laws unless they bind with obligation. Aquinas also thinks that legal norms must have a specific source in directives issued by an authority: 'all law arises from the reason and will of the legislator.' To the extent that the acts of specific virtues have a 'preceptive', obliging character, they are an aspect of obedience.[50] The natural law is legal because a divine legislator commands it and it is natural because the content of the divine commands reproduce the immanent requirements of natural human fulfilment. Or as Anscombe puts it, 'To have a *law* conception of ethics is to hold that what is needed for conformity with the virtues failure in which is the mark of being bad *qua* man (and not merely, say *qua* craftsman or logician) — that

---

and seems to have no discernible content except a certain compelling force, which I should call purely psychological.' 'Modern Moral Philosophy', p. 42.
[49] Cf. Francisco Suarez, *De Legibus*, Book 2, Chapter 6, 'Is the natural law truly a preceptive divine law?'.
[50] Furthermore, it is possible to perform acts of specific virtues without adverting to their preceptive, obliging character: '*ad obedientiam pertinent omnes actus virtutum prout sunt in praecepto [...] licet actus virtutis cadat sub praecepto, tamen potest aliquis implere actum virtutis non attendens ad rationem praecepti*', *Summa theologiae* II–II, q. 104, a. 3 ad 2.

what is needed for *this*, is required by divine law.'[51] It is possible to know one and the same thing under different descriptions; as Aquinas remarks in connection with natural knowledge about God, 'to know that someone is approaching is not the same as to know that Peter is approaching, even though it is Peter who is approaching.'[52] In reflecting upon my own happiness and the virtues, therefore, I might come to know what is in fact the natural law, without knowing it under the description 'law'. In this case I would 'have' the requirements of the natural law within me as requirements of human nature, but I would know them *qua* requirements of natural goodness, without additionally knowing their ultimate legal character, which is the character that confers on requirements the normative force of obligation.

Anscombe insists, '[i]f our nature is a divine creation, the divine law would be different if the nature created was different, and it would command and forbid the things that would then be good and bad according to that nature's need. These things reason could work out without belief in divine commandments.'[53] Acting badly is correctly defined as acting contrary to right reason, and this definition is coextensive with a definition of acting badly as acting contrary to divine law. Anscombe observes that this latter definition, unlike the first, introduces 'a concept of obedience and disobedience' into the meaning of bad action.[54] Following or flouting someone's demands only counts as obedience or disobedience, respectively, if the demands are made by someone who has authority, so it also follows that the concepts of obedience and disobedience imply the concept of authority. Just as following a rational norm as such doesn't amount to *obeying*, neither does the normativity of reason amount to *authoritative* demand. For this reason, the normativity of Philippa Foot's 'natural goodness', for example, which finds moral norms in human virtues and is explicitly non-theological, does not generate a moral law, even if it includes an account of intrinsically bad actions. According to Anscombe, 'In *this* sense the notion of a "norm" brings us nearer to an Aristotelian than a law conception of ethics.' The philosopher who proposes such an account 'ought to recognize

---

[51] 'Modern Moral Philosophy', p. 30.
[52] Aquinas, *Summa theologiae* I, q. 2, a. 1 ad 1.
[53] 'Sin: The McGivney Lectures', in *FHG*, p. 123.
[54] 'Sin', p. 123.

what has happened to the term "norm," which he wanted to mean "law—without bringing God in": it has ceased to mean "law" at all'.[55]

Anscombe seems to be genuinely ambivalent about the crucial, further question of whether the conception of God as providential legislator that is prerequisite to justifying moral obligation is itself discoverable through unaided human reason, or whether this conception depends upon divine revelation.[56] She does not seem to dissent from the solidly Thomistic view that reverence for God is knowable as a 'dictate of natural reason' unaided by revelation, and that the corresponding virtue of religion is an ordinary moral, and not a properly theological virtue such as the supernatural virtues of faith, hope or charity.[57] Yet there is a gap between owing reverence to someone and owing full-bore obedience to him. Aristotle, as we have seen, has a place for reverence to divinity without any role for obedience.[58] Plato's Socrates, by contrast, has an acute sense of owing God a debt of obedience, which he believes places him 'under orders', as it were, to avoid wrongdoing at any cost.[59] Anscombe might have illustrated her conception of obligation by emphasizing the contrast between Socrates and Aristotle, but for whatever reason she did not. She remarks, 'the motives, spirit, meaning, and purpose of the moral life of Christians depend on revelation', even though 'the content of the moral law, i.e., the actions which are good and just, is not essentially a matter of revelation'.[60] These motives, spirit, meaning and purpose of moral agency involve rendering obedience, for obedience is correlative with authority, and *caritas* cannot exist without it.[61]

Bracketing the question of whether divine legislation belongs to natural or revealed theology, we can nevertheless see that Anscombe's claims about the dependence of moral obligation upon a divine lawgiver are at once ontological *and* epistemic.

---

[55] 'Modern Moral Philosophy', p. 38.
[56] See 'Sin', p. 123.
[57] *Summa theologiae* II–II, q. 2 ad 3; q. 5.
[58] See, e.g., *NE*, 1179a22–32.
[59] C. Steven Evans, *God and Moral Obligation* (Oxford: Oxford University Press, 2013), pp. 16–19.
[60] 'Authority in Morals', in *CPP3*, p. 50.
[61] Charity 'cannot exist apart from obedience [*caritate, quae sine obedientia esse non potest*]', *Summa theologiae* II–II, q. 104, a. 3 co.

Moral obligation exists because God truly is man's ultimate end, who creates mankind with a nature ordered toward communion with him, and who commands obedience with his creative plan. Someone's belief in this conception of God is what makes that person's belief in the reality of moral obligation justified. Someone who recognizes the reality of moral obligation, but lacks this conception of God, is in an epistemically unstable position. He should either reconsider belief in moral obligation, which is Anscombe's suggestion in 'Modern Moral Philosophy' to her secularist colleagues, or reconsider the rational grounds for theistic natural law.[62]

In order to see just how divine law adds obliging force to the recommendatory force of the virtues, and how this makes a difference to concrete instances of practical reasoning, consider an argument proposed by Peter Geach in 'The Moral Law and the Law of God' about the difference that divine law makes to a moral code.[63] Geach's argument is on to something, but I want to suggest that it can be improved by re-stating it in Anscombe's terms. In a discussion of intrinsically bad acts, Geach contends, 'somebody might very well admit that not only is there something bad about certain acts, but also that it is desirable to become the sort of person who needs to act in the contrary way; and yet *not* admit that such acts are to be avoided in all circumstances and at any price.'[64] Like Anscombe, Geach rejects the view that all ethical appraisals of actions as good or bad are logically dependent upon knowledge of God's existence.[65] Although knowledge of God isn't required in order to have any moral knowledge at all, he argues that knowledge of God—indeed, of God as a providential creator—is required to know that it is rationally necessary to do good and

---

[62] 'Modern Moral Philosophy', p. 32.
[63] Peter Geach, 'The Moral Law and the Law of God', in his *God and the Soul* (London: Routledge & Keegan Paul, 1969).
[64] 'The Moral Law and the Law of God', p. 123.
[65] 'The Moral Law and the Law of God', p. 119; Anscombe, 'Contraception and Chastity', in *HLAE*, p. 179: '"Natural law" is simply a way of speaking about the whole of morality, used by Catholic thinkers because they believe the general precepts of morality are *laws* promulgated by God our Creator in the enlightened human understanding when it is thinking in general terms about what are good and what are bad actions. That is to say, the discoveries of reflection and reasoning when we think straight about these things *are* God's legislation to us (whether we realise this or not).'

avoid evil.[66] Geach asserts that this knowledge is available to natural reasoning, independent of any revelation.[67]

The course of Geach's argument is rather roundabout. His aim is to prove a conditional: *if* someone accepts that God exists and governs men by command and counsel (i.e. providentially), *then* he will be justified in having a different moral code from an atheist or agnostic. Geach is interested in establishing this conditional in order to refute a very common claim, which Anscombe similarly scorns in 'Modern Moral Philosophy'. This is the claim that theological and non-theological ethics are not significantly different, because, as Anscombe summarizes the view, '[i]f someone does have a divine law conception of ethics, all the same, he has to agree that he has to have a judgment that he *ought* (morally ought) to obey the divine law; so his ethic is in exactly the same position as any other [...].'[68] The different moral code that Geach thinks follows from knowledge of a providential God is one in which it is necessary to act virtuously. Geach's argument makes two assumptions: first, that we can know that God exists and governs men providentially, and second, that we can know that certain practices, such as lying, adultery and murder, are generally bad and we ought not even to think in advance of resorting to them. But are such practices nevertheless completely forbidden? Geach supposes, for *reductio ad absurdum*, that they are not. If such practices aren't forbidden, then there will be situations in which we should consider engaging in such practices, even though making this decision, *viz.* to do what we ought routinely to avoid thinking of doing, would be systematically clouded by our tendency to permissive self-indulgence, and would require relying upon our grossly fallible knowledge of present circumstances and still more unreliable conjectures about the future. If such situations naturally arose in the course of human life, then their occurrence would entail that our moral reasoning is inherently unreliable as a guide for living a good human life. But moral reasoning just is our capacity to respond to commands and counsels, which (as was assumed) is the means by which God governs men, so it must be reliable. Therefore, the supposition that generically bad acts are not completely forbidden must be rejected, Geach says, since it

---

[66] 'The Moral Law and the Law of God', p. 120.
[67] 'The Moral Law and the Law of God', p. 123.
[68] 'Modern Moral Philosophy', p. 32.

contradicts the initial stipulated premise that God exists and governs men by command and counsel. He concludes,

> The rational recognition that a practice is generally undesirable and that it is best for people on the whole not even to think of resorting to it is thus *in fact* a promulgation to a man of the Divine law forbidding the practice, even if he does not realize that this is a promulgation of the Divine law, even if he does not believe there is a God.[69]

Geach's argument is not persuasive. The difficulty of deciding for grave reasons whether or not to do some intrinsically bad act may be harrowing and fraught with pitfalls, but it doesn't seem any more difficult in principle than many other real life dilemmas, which arise regularly enough and don't seem to impugn God's endowment of mankind with rational powers of self-direction.[70]

But consider the rub of Geach's argument re-stated in terms of Anscombe's discussion of practical inference: '[…] may not someone be criticizable for pursuing a certain end, thus characterizable as a sort of good of his, where and when it is quite inappropriate for him to do so, or by means inimical to other ends which he ought to have?' Indeed, someone such as this is criticizable, and criticizable for having violated the obliging force of reason, '[…] only if man has a last end which governs all'.[71] Geach fails to make clear that the agent must not only idly *believe* in a providential lawgiver, but he must make that belief active by taking communion with and obedience to that lawgiver the final end of his practical reasoning. For it is having and pursuing a last end that quite literally 'governs all', as a providential creator governs his finite creatures, which makes it strictly irrational for someone to choose a lesser good by means of some acknowledged evil and thereby spurn the highest good, by whose pleasure 'his wits hold together' to entertain choosing the lesser.[72] 'Now, that practical reasoning so understood should be of use to understanding action, including the action of a society', is something that no doubt Geach, like Anscombe, could accept.[73]

---

[69] 'The Moral Law and the Law of God', pp. 124–125.
[70] I'm grateful to David Albert Jones for pressing this point.
[71] 'Practical Inference,' p. 146.
[72] 'The Moral Law and the Law of God', p. 127.
[73] 'Practical Inference', p. 147.

Thomas Pink

Anscombe, Williams and the Positivization of Moral Obligation

1. Obligation and its place in morality

Moral obligation or duty is a part of morality that is directive. We communicate obligations to direct people into doing what is right — what is morally obligatory or required as a matter of duty — and away from what is morally wrong. The direction given is demanding. And this demandingness seems linked to a criticism that is distinctively condemnatory. People who breach moral obligations and who do so without excuse are subject to blame. And the content of blame is that they are morally responsible for having done wrong.

This moral responsibility seems importantly different from anything invoked in ordinary rational criticism. We can be subject to rational criticism for our general attitudes as well as for our actions. Fears, wants and other passions and emotions can be foolish or sensible. But moral responsibility is commonly understood to be specifically for agency — for action and omission. We can only be morally responsible for our actions and omissions and their consequences, and not — unless indirectly, as consequences of our own prior agency — for the feelings and emotions that come over us. And just as moral responsibility is for agency, so too are the moral obligations that we are responsible for keeping. We can only be under a moral obligation to act or to refrain from action — not to experience desires or to have feelings.

Morality shares the language of obligation, responsibility and blame with positive law — the law contingently legislated by political authorities for the specific human communities subject to their jurisdiction. 'You have an obligation to pay the money' could be said by a moralist asserting a moral obligation—or by a judge or state official asserting a legal obligation, that is an obligation under some system of positive law. And just as one can be under obligations that are legal as well as moral, so one can be held legally as well as morally responsible, and legally as well as morally to blame.

Besides this shared language of obligation and responsibility linking morality with positive law, there seems to be a shared directive function. It is very natural to think that in imposing legal obligations positive law likewise serves to direct human action and thereby the various outcomes that can be produced or prevented through human action. And there is a historically influential view of how, at least in the case of positive legal obligation, this action-directive function operates.

According to this view, positive legal direction, at least when effective, is of the voluntary—those outcomes that are subject to our will or decision, and that we produce or prevent by our own agency, through deciding so to do. The law makes a certain outcome—that our car not be parked on a double yellow line—legally obligatory, and threatens sanctions should this outcome not arise. We are motivated, either by a concern to be law-abiding, or, as often, by a further dislike of the sanctions, to decide to do what is required to ensure the obligatory outcome. And so we act on the basis of that decision to produce the outcome and avoid the sanctions.

That morality shares a language of obligation and responsibility with the positive law, and that both moral and legal obligations seem alike directive of action, has long suggested the idea that in obligation morality too contains a form of law—a specifically moral law. Behind this conception of a specifically moral law stands an idea of law in general. Law, according to this conception, is any system of obligations as demanding directives on action, addressing a distinctive responsibility for meeting those obligations, a responsibility that we are supposed to possess for action and omission and its outcomes. Law addresses us as peculiarly responsible for what we do, and demands that we exercise that responsibility to do what is right and to avoid doing what is wrong. Direction by law so understood is distinct from the application of more general normative principles. Law is to be distinguished from more general principles of reason—principles that are merely advisory, and that presuppose no special responsibility for how we act, but serve to appraise attitudes and emotions generally simply as reasonable or unreasonable.

How might morality, in particular, take the form of action-directive law? One approach is to apply an understanding of positive legal obligation to the moral case as well. For if moral obligation might seem puzzling and in need of explanation, we are all too familiar with legal obligations and systems of humanly created positive law. Why not use the familiar positive case to model the moral case? A moral obligation is a moral directive that functions as a moral version of a legal obligation. The account would then proceed by selecting those salient aspects of legal direction that seem most plausibly to admit of some form of moral equivalent, and use them to identify what is constitutive of moral obligation. To characterize moral obligation in this way is to propose what I shall term a *positivizing* model of moral obligation.

Positivizing models of moral obligation can take a variety of forms. We might, for example, characterize moral obligations as moral directives that, like legal obligations, are the decrees of some appropriate law-giving authority—in the case of moral obligation, a specifically moral authority above any human legal authority, and that governs humanity generally, such as God. Just as to deny the very existence of a legislative authority is also to deny the existence of the legal obligations dependent on its authority, so denying the existence of such a moral legislator is to deny the very existence of moral obligations. For Elizabeth Anscombe, absent continued belief in God as divine lawgiver, all we are left with in morality is a metaphorical use of the term 'obligation'; we must give up belief in the literal reality of moral obligatoriness. The term 'moral obligation', she claimed, will now be empty, without any further literal application. Moral obligatoriness can no more exist without the divine decrees that constitute it than can criminality without the institution of criminal law:

> But if a divine command conception is dominant for many centuries, and then is given up, it is a natural result that the concepts of 'obligation', of being bound or required as by a law, should remain though they had lost their root [...] it is as if the notion 'criminal' were to remain when criminal courts had been abolished and forgotten [...][1]

---

1 'Modern Moral Philosophy', in *HLAE*, p. 176.

But positivizing models can take secular form as well. The existence of moral obligations need not be tied to some form of theism. We might instead take moral obligations to be directives backed by some form of sanction, imposed if not by a moral legislator, at least by members of any community where the moral obligation applies.

Thus Bernard Williams characterizes moral obligations as, properly understood, directing us to meet standards of voluntary behaviour that matter socially. Moral obligation

> is grounded in the basic issue of what people should be able to rely on. People must rely as far as possible on not being killed or used as a resource, and on having some space and objects and relations with other people that they can count as their own. It also serves their interests if, to some extent at least, they can count on not being lied to.[2]

So the standards on voluntary action which protect these vital interests are properly classed as morally obligatory, and are reinforced by social pressure—the appropriateness of some kind of reinforcing pressure being, on this view, of the essence of obligation in all its forms. Our ethical training is designed to leave us strongly motivated towards performing those actions which count as morally obligatory, and away from those which count as wrong and forbidden. We are left concerned to do what is obligatory and to avoid doing what is wrong, and then through this concern thoughts about moral obligation motivate us voluntarily to do what is obligatory as a means to complying with our moral obligations. So the pressure that comes with moral obligatoriness enforces and encourages a certain practical conclusion—a concern to do what is morally obligatory:

> [...] moral obligation is expressed in one especially important kind of deliberative conclusion—a conclusion that is directed toward what to do [...] The fact that moral obligation is a kind of practical conclusion explains several of its features. An obligation applies to someone with respect to an action—it is an obligation to do something [...][3]

---

[2] Bernard Williams, *Ethics and the Limits of Philosophy* (London: Fontana, 1985), p. 185.
[3] Williams, *Ethics and the Limits of Philosophy*, pp. 174–175.

The central form of social pressure is blame, whether communicated from without, by others, or once one is trained socially, communicated from within, by oneself to oneself in self-blame and remorse. Blame, like obligation-enforcing pressure generally, is likewise directed at the voluntary:

> [...] blame always tends to share the particularized, practical character of moral obligation in the technical sense. Its negative reaction is focused closely on an action or omission, and this is what is blamed. Moreover—although there are many inevitable anomalies in its actual working—the aspiration of blame is that it should apply only to the extent that the undesired outcome is the product of voluntary action on the particular occasion.[4]

Positivizing models of moral obligation have important implications for the place of moral obligation within wider morality. For besides moral obligation there are other aspects to morality. There is, for example, the appraisal as morally admirable or contemptible in various ways, not only of people's actions, but of their characters, inclinations and dispositions too. This is the part of morality that is concerned with virtues and vices. And a positivizing view of moral obligation tends to distance moral obligation from the morality of virtue and vice. For standards of virtue and vice seem not to depend on any legislation, or on the availability of sanctions to enforce them. And virtues or vices, such as courageousness or temperance, do not seem voluntary or subject to the will as are the actions and outcomes that, on the positivizing model, are subject to legal direction. We do not acquire courage, say, just by deciding to, on receipt of some directive to be courageous. If moral obligation is understood to involve a form of action-directive law, and then the morally legal direction it involves is understood on the basis of natural models of positive law, it will seem that moral obligation is very different from the general morality of virtue and vice. Moral obligation will seem to form a distinctive part of morality with a special concern of its own—the direction of the voluntary—and to depend on special elements, such as sanctions and legislation, that are not generally essential to virtue and vice.

Hume assumed that the idea of moral obligation as a form of action-directive law was a deep mistake just because, in his view,

---

[4] Williams, *Ethics and the Limits of Philosophy*, p. 193.

morality, the morality of obligation and blame properly understood being included by him in this, did not generally involve any kind of sanction-backed direction of the voluntary. The supposition otherwise was the invention of theologians, who had tried to remodel moral obligation and blame on the basis of some sort of fictitious cosmic version of positive law:

> Philosophers, or rather divines under that disguise, treating all morals as on a like footing with civil laws, guarded by sanctions of reward and punishment, were necessarily led to render this circumstance, of voluntary or involuntary, the foundation of their whole theory [...] but this, in mean time, must be allowed, that *sentiments* are every day experienced of blame and praise, which have objects beyond the dominion of the will or choice, and of which it behoves us, if not as moralists, as speculative philosophers at least, to give some satisfactory theory and explication.[5]

In Hume's view, wrongful breach of moral obligation or duty — moral 'crime' — is not anything like positive legal crime. Moral 'crime' is not the violation of some sanction-backed directive on the voluntary, but is simply a failure to meet a standard of admirability, a standard moreover that immediately applies not to voluntary actions, but to non-voluntary states of motivation and character.

> A blemish, a fault, a vice, a crime; these expressions seem to denote different degrees of censure and disapprobation; which are, however, all of them, at the bottom, pretty nearly of the same kind or species.[6]

One violates natural duty in morality as a parent, not just through failing to look after one's children, but by lacking a natural affection or care for them. This, in Hume's view, is the fundamental moral wrong, a failure of non-voluntary motivation, of which the neglect of children at the point of the voluntary is but a symptom or effect.

> We blame a father for neglecting his child. Why? Because it shows a want of natural affection, which is the duty of every parent. Were not natural affection a duty, care of children cou'd not be a duty;

---

[5] David Hume, *An Enquiry Concerning the Principles of Morals*, ed. P.H. Nidditch (Oxford: Clarendon Press, 1975), Appendix IV, 'Of some verbal disputes', p. 322.
[6] Hume, *An Enquiry Concerning the Principles of Morals*, Appendix IV, p. 322.

and 'twere impossible we cou'd have the duty in our eye in the attention we give to our offspring.[7]

So a positivizing understanding of what moral law would involve can, as with Hume, lead to a rejection of the very idea of moral obligation or duty as action-directive law. Or else, as with Anscombe and Williams, who, despite his admiration for Hume, reasoned here as one of Hume's 'divines' in philosophical disguise, that positivizing understanding can still leave moral obligation as something action-directive. But then, since it is taken to resemble positive law in its directive function, the morality of obligation is viewed as detached from and importantly different from the morality of virtue and vice.

But this view of how moral obligation might take the form of action-directive law is very debatable, and alien to an important part of the Catholic intellectual tradition. In late medieval and early modern Catholicism, moral obligation was certainly conceived as action-directive law. But it was not conceived as different in its basis from the morality of virtue and vice. Rather the morality of obligation was part of the morality of virtue and vice. Moral law was, in effect, the morality of virtue and vice as concerned not with morally admirable or disadmirable characteristics in general, but those parts of the morally admirable and disadmirable that fell within our control. Moral obligation was the morality of virtue and vice as it applied to our exercise of freedom —a power to determine what we do that applies in particular to how we exercise the will itself as well as to what is subject to the will and voluntary.

This very different view of moral obligation as a form of law should not be a surprise. For besides positivizing theories of moral obligation, there is also the natural law tradition. And the natural law tradition takes a very different view of moral law. Far from moral law being understood on the model of positive law, for the natural law tradition moral law is a form of law that is importantly prior to law in positive form. Moral law is a demanding form of moral direction that comes with our human nature. Whereas positive law is a secondary form of law that when it does its proper job, serves to extend the force of moral law, and to render its requirements more specific, in ways that serve ends

---

[7] David Hume, *A Treatise of Human Nature*, ed. P.H. Nidditch (Oxford: Clarendon Press, 1978), p. 478.

of personal and communal happiness and justice that the moral law requires us to pursue.

Because positive law is a secondary and special form of law, many features of it may go beyond what is required for the legal direction of action in itself, and may not apply to moral law. So legislative origin, the involvement of sanctions, a special concern with direction of the specifically voluntary—these features of positive law may not apply to the moral law at all; and yet moral obligation may still be demandingly directive of a distinctive responsibility for action, just as any genuine law must be.

In the moral theory of late scholasticism, we find a systematic defence of moral obligation as embodying natural law that radically distances moral obligation from positive legal obligation, and that does so by assimilating moral obligation to a special case of a wider morality of virtue and vice. Central to this approach is a distinctive approach to a fundamental problem within the theory of normativity—the problem of the relation of normative direction to normative appraisal.

2. Normativity—direction and appraisal

We can distinguish two aspects to normativity. First, there is a directive function, a function that, unless taking the form of a specifically legal direction, is not restricted to action and omission, but which can apply to attitudes generally. Normative standards may not only direct us to do things or refrain from them, but may also direct us to want or to believe things. So standards that are normative for us may possess a directive role. They may point us in a given direction or support us taking it; and are *strongly* directive when they point us in that direction and away from any other—when they not only support A, but oppose any contrary B. And as directive, normative standards address a capacity to respond to that direction—to register or cognize the direction being given, and to respond to and follow that direction.

But secondly there is an appraisive aspect to normativity. People who meet or exceed standards that are normative may be praised or judged favourably for having done so; while those who breach or fail to meet the standards may be criticized or judged unfavourably for this failure. So besides any capacity we might have to register direction and respond to it, there are the capacities and activities that normative standards serve to appraise. Besides providing various kinds of direction, normative standards support various forms of appraisal; and there may be a variety in the kinds of normativity corresponding to the different sorts of capacity and activity appraised.

These two aspects to normativity, the directive and the appraisive, are importantly distinct. Obviously, there can be standards of appraisal that apply to objects that cannot be directed. A vase's goodness has to do with its form and utility, not with its responsiveness to any form of direction. And even as humans the capacities for which we are appraised need not have much to with our responsiveness to direction either. People are praised for being amusing or for being inventive. But neither talent need be easily subject to direction or much dependent on receptiveness to direction. At the same time standards may serve to give direction without supporting much by way of appraisal of those being directed: consider an instruction manual. Obviously one could use the manual as a basis for appraising people in terms of whether they followed it correctly or not. But this would be vastly peripheral to the main point of the manual—which is simply to provide a set of directions.

Ethical standards give direction. They guide us to do what is right and good, and to avoid what is wrong and bad. But they also serve as a very important basis of appraisal both of actions and of the agents who perform them, and in a way that seems profoundly connected to direction. The term 'a good thing to do' may communicate a directive in support of performing the action in question. But the term 'good' also serves favourably to appraise the action, as well as to appraise the agent who performs it. If the action is a good thing to do, it may have been good of the agent to perform it. The combination of the directive and the appraisive is central to ethical standards as we ordinarily understand them. But how to relate the appraisive and directive in morality?

Is direction primary? In which case understanding ethical standards begins with the basic notion of a directive, say to want or to do something; and appraisal is then explained in terms of the theory of direction: the capacity addressed by ethical standards is simply the capacity to receive and respond to ethical direction, and ethical appraisal of agents is then for whether they follow ethical directives or not. Or perhaps direction is not primary. Perhaps the appraisive side of ethical standards should be viewed as in certain respects importantly independent of and even explanatory of the directive. It may be that ethical appraisal is of capacities that go significantly beyond the capacity to respond to ethical direction. And these further capacities and their ethical significance may then inform and shape not only ethical appraisal but even the use of ethical terms to give direction.

In recent philosophy the prevalent assumption has been that quite generally, or at least in the moral sphere, normativity is identical with reason. Standards that are normative for us, it is assumed, are just standards that it is reasonable for us to meet. Indeed, the identity of normativity with reason is typically presented as if it were trivial or obvious. Thus Joseph Raz:

> Aspects of the world are normative in as much as they or their existence constitute reasons for persons, that is, grounds which make certain beliefs, moods, emotions, intentions, or actions appropriate or inappropriate.[8]

If as philosophers we identify normativity with reason, then we will tend to concentrate our attention on the directive side of normative standards, as opposed to their agent-appraisive function. And indeed, it is direction and our capacity to respond to it that has dominated much recent philosophical discussion of normativity. This is because in relation to reason it seems to be agent-direction rather than agent-appraisal that takes centre stage. Standards of reason are indeed used to appraise agents; but they are used to appraise agents just in terms of their responsiveness to rational direction. So in relation to reason, it seems to be the directive side of normativity that is primary, the appraisive side to be explained in terms of the directive.

Reason provides directions in the form of justifications. And rational justifications, it seems, are immediately justifications for or against forming and holding psychological attitudes, whether beliefs, or emotions, desires, intentions and various kinds of content-bearing motivations for action generally.[9] The justifications derive from possible objects of thought at which content-bearing attitudes might be directed, and from the various justification-providing properties those objects of thought might have—such as likelihood of truth in the case of belief, of goodness

---

[8] 'Explaining normativity: On rationality and the justification of reason', in Joseph Raz, *Engaging Reason* (Oxford: Oxford University Press, 1999), p. 66.

[9] As T.M. Scanlon puts it: judgment-sensitive attitudes constitute the class of things for which reasons in the standard normative sense can sensibly be asked for or offered. T.M. Scanlon, *What We Owe to Each Other* (Cambridge: Harvard University Press, 1998), p. 21.

or desirability in the case of desires and other motivations. These justifications direct us towards the attitudes that they support, and away from the attitudes they oppose.

Favourable rational appraisal makes use of terms such as 'reasonable', 'sensible', 'rational' and so forth; and unfavourable rational appraisal correspondingly uses terms such as 'foolish', 'less than sensible', 'unreasonable', 'irrational' and the like. It is very plausible that to be subject to appraisal in such terms at all—to count at all either as reasonable or as unreasonable—is always to have some capacity to cognize and respond to justifications and the direction that they provide, whether that capacity be exercised competently or incompetently. Lower animals, such as sharks and mice, which are clearly quite incapable of recognizing or responding to justifications, equally clearly fall outside the sphere of reason. In other words, they are a-rational, and no more capable of being genuinely foolish or unreasonable than they are capable of being sensible or reasonable. Lacking any capacity to respond to rational direction, such lower animals are beyond rational criticism or appraisal.

Not only does rational appraisal presuppose some capacity in the agent appraised to respond to rational direction. Rational appraisal is also precisely for our responsiveness to such direction. The sensible or reasonable agent is just one who is responsive to rational direction—who is moved by justifications to form the attitudes justified; and an unreasonable agent is one who fails to respond properly to justifications—who, despite having the general capacity to respond to reason, is unmoved by justifications, and who is moved to form those attitudes that the justifications oppose. The capacity addressed by standards of rational appraisal—the capacity for rationality or reasonableness—just is the capacity to respond to rational direction.

If we identify all normativity purely and simply with reason, then we may be tempted to adopt the position that I shall call 'ethical rationalism'. This view does not simply regard ethical standards as reasons—a claim I should myself wish to support—but claims that the capacity addressed and governed by ethical standards is simply the general capacity to respond to rational direction.[10] According to the ethical rationalist, there is nothing

---

[10] Consider Scanlon's view of moral responsibility or our responsibility to ethical standards. The capacity addressed seems to be not much more than the

more to ethical direction than general rational direction as applied to moral questions; and ethical appraisal is entirely of our responsiveness to such rational direction. Hence for the ethical rationalist it is the directive aspect of normativity that is fundamental to ethical theory.

But the identity of ethical normativity with reason is hardly trivial, for otherwise the ethical project of David Hume would be unintelligible — which it seems not to be. Hume certainly allows that ethical standards are normative for us; he supposes that ethical standards make a call on us to meet them, and support appraisal of us in terms of whether or not we meet the standards. But he denies that the call is that of reason, and that ethical appraisal is of us as reasonable or unreasonable.

> Actions may be laudable or blameable; but they cannot be reasonable or unreasonable: Laudable or blameable, therefore, are not the same with reasonable or unreasonable.[11]

Hume replaces the notion of reason in the theory of ethical normativity with that of *merit*. Merit is a particular form of personal goodness or admirability. It is admirability that takes the form of talent. In other words merit is admirability or excellence in relation to arts or skills. And for Hume moral admirability or virtue is just another form of talent. The supposed distinction between moral virtue and talent is, in Hume's view, wholly verbal.[12] The moral person is good at morals and as admirable or estimable in moral terms as, say, the able singer is good at singing and so estimable in terms of standards supplied by the art of singing.

The assimilation of virtue to talent, of moral admirability to a form of merit, tends to broaden the focus of a theory of ethical normativity from being narrowly on reason — which is what Hume intended. It also prevents the theory of ethical normativity from assuming a primacy of the directive over the appraisive. For to possess talent is obviously not in general a mode of being reasonable, just as to lack talent is not in general to be

---

general capacity for reason: '[...] "being responsible" is mainly a matter of the appropriateness of demanding reasons [...].' Scanlon, *What We Owe to Each Other*, p. 22.

[11] Hume, *A Treatise of Human Nature*, p. 458.

[12] See again Hume's *An Enquiry Concerning the Principles of Morals*, Appendix IV, 'Of some verbal disputes'.

unreasonable. There are plenty of arts and skills that are not greatly dependent on, still less a function of our reason; consider, for example, a talent for song or ballet. And to be appraisable as good or bad in terms of an art or skill may or may not be to possess a capacity to respond to any particular form of direction, let alone to that provided by reason. Some talents may consist in a largely undirectable knack; and their exercise be largely an expression of that knack. Consider again wit, or the talent to amuse.

How far merit appraisal is of our capacity to respond to any form of direction depends on the nature of the art or skill in question, and of the kinds of capacity which practice of the art or skill involves. The immediate question raised by the appeal to merit is the question that ethical rationalism assumes from the very start to have been answered—what kinds of capacity are involved in morality, and what kind of practice is it that involves their exercise? Is more involved than just some general capacity to respond to rational direction? What is it that we are appraising when we appraise people ethically?

Hume needed the appeal to merit because he had already denied himself any recourse to reason. And that is because Hume's psychological theory committed him to a complete denial of the very possibility of any form of practical reason—of reason, that is, in a form governing what ethical standards centrally apply to, namely motivations and the actions which those motivations guide and explain. According to Hume, motivations are contentless feelings, akin to sensations of pain and pleasure.

> When I am angry, I am actually possest with the passion, and in that emotion have no more a reference to any other object, than when I am thirsty, or sick, or more than five foot high.[13]

Motivations, as contentless feelings, are not attitudes towards some object of thought in terms of which they might be justified. So motivations and the actions they explain are, in Hume's view, subject neither to rational direction nor to rational appraisal. Reason, to the extent that Hume admits the notion, is simply directive of belief.

Even if we do not find this wholesale denial of practical reason credible, there is still a question how far ethical normativity in

---

[13] Hume, *A Treatise of Human Nature*, p. 415.

particular is a normativity of reason. For the view that laudable and blameable are not the same as reasonable or unreasonable is clearly right in the general case. As we have noted there can be merit and demerit in relation to arts and skills that does not consist in reason or unreason. We certainly can praise and criticize people other than as reasonable or unreasonable—for forms of excellence or its lack that are not a matter of rationality or reasonableness or its lack. And even in the ethical case it is not obvious that praise and criticism are as reasonable or unreasonable. For the most immediate terms of ethical appraisal are surely not 'reasonable' and 'unreasonable', still less 'sensible' and 'foolish', but, exactly as Hume supposed, 'good' and 'bad'. Immoral people are bad people—that seems obvious. It is not quite so obvious that they are unreasonable, still less that they are foolish; which is why establishing that immorality is contrary to reason has in the past seemed to many a substantial philosophical problem.

At the same time, Hume's scepticism about practical reason is based on a psychology that renders very problematic any satisfactory theory of ethical direction. Hume certainly did not deny that ethical standards serve to direct us. Such a denial would have been quite incredible. But the form this direction took is left rather mysterious. For Hume, as we have noted, motivations are not content-bearing attitudes formed in response to some object of thought—an object that might serve as justification for the attitudes. Motivations, for Hume, are just contentless feelings, that are no more attitudes towards an object than is (say) a stab of pain; and, as we have seen, that is fundamental to his general scepticism about practical reason. But how is someone to be directed into or out of feeling a contentless sensation, such as a pain or pleasure? There is no satisfactory account of how mere feelings might be sensitive to normative direction.

But it is very important to our conception of ethical appraisal, whether as good or as bad, that it really is of agents who are capable of ethical direction. Just as to be unreasonable, as opposed to falling a-rationally outside the sphere of reason as might a shark or a mouse, an agent must have at least some capacity to respond to rational direction; so, too, to be genuinely immoral, it might be thought, an agent must have at least some capacity to understand and respond to ethical direction.

Badness in terms of many arts or skills—being bad at them—may, when sufficiently pronounced, detach the talentless from any capacity even to be directed towards excellence. But immorality seems different. To be morally very bad arguably always presupposes some capacity for being directed ethically—and at the very least therefore some cognitive grasp at least of the kinds of ethical standard being disregarded. If that capacity is absent then one is not immoral or bad in moral terms. One falls outside the class of those who are morally appraisable. A shark is not morally bad any more than a shark is foolish. Quite incapable of being directed ethically, sharks fall outside morality just as they fall outside reason.

We now have the basis of two contrary positions, occupying opposing extremes. The first is what I have called 'ethical rationalism'. This certainly provides a theory of ethical direction—one taken from a general theory of rational direction. Yet nothing more is said about moral practice and about moral appraisal in relation to that practice than that the capacity involved and appraised is the capacity to receive and respond to rational direction. But if nothing more than that were involved, why would ethical appraisal be immediately intelligible in terms that are not obviously and immediately those of rational appraisal? Why does ethical appraisal immediately involve terms familiar from general merit appraisal, which takes the form of appraisal of agents as good or bad—terms which leave it to some degree a question whether immorality is *ipso facto* a form of folly or unreason? For Hume was perfectly right to note that where a person or action is concerned, being laudable or good is not the same as being reasonable.

On the other extreme we have the reason-scepticism of Hume, which treats the appraisive function of ethical standards as primary. Ethical standards are introduced just as standards of merit or personal admirability. But the disavowal of any appeal to reason leaves a void as far as explaining ethical direction is concerned. Hume thought that he could accommodate the directiveness of ethical standards; and, in particular, that he could accommodate even the directiveness of obligation. But it is not clear that his appraisive model supplies, on its own, the required basis for explaining ethical direction.

3. Obligation and appraisal

Positivizing theories of moral obligation as directive law appeal to some distinctive form of direction associated with positive law—

such as direction through legislative decree, or direction backed by threat of sanction. But it may be that to understand moral obligation as action-directive law we should appeal instead to a distinctive form of appraisal—and characterize the distinctively demanding direction provided by moral obligation in terms of that.

Late scholasticism provides a theory of moral law as a wholly natural form of action-directive law—a theory that is not positivizing. The theory constitutes a *via media* between ethical rationalism with its prioritization of normative direction, and reason-scepticism with its exclusive attention to normative appraisal. As natural law, moral obligation provides a form of rational direction, and so addresses motivation as a capacity to respond to that direction. But the peculiarly demanding and action-specific direction that comes with obligation is explained in terms of a theory of ethical appraisal, and by reference to capacities subject to that appraisal that go beyond a simple capacity to respond to rational direction. The theory of normative direction is a theory of practical reason. But this theory is informed by a theory of normative appraisal that goes beyond a simple theory of rationality and reason—a theory of appraisal elements of which survived, detached from the general theory of rational direction, to form Hume's theory of merit.

Aquinas thought, just as did Hume, that moral obligation is linked to a negative form of moral appraisal. As for Hume, moral obligation is a standard to breach which is to be disadmirable or bad. Wrongdoing involves demerit. But, by contrast to Hume, the negative appraisal that relates to breach of moral obligation is not just ordinary negative evaluation, but takes a distinctive form—as moral blame.

Blame for doing wrong is distinctively condemnatory as a criticism because it does not just detect a fault in the agent's action, but condemns that fault as bad, and then attributes that fault so understood to the agent as their fault, condemning the agent himself. Not only was what they did bad, but it was bad of them to do it. And as Aquinas argued, this condemnation of the agent as bad to have done what he did involves a central and distinguishing human capacity—the capacity for freedom:

> Hence a human action is worthy of praise or blame in so far as it is good or bad. For praise and blame is nothing other than for the goodness or badness of his action to be imputed to someone. Now

> an action is imputed to an agent when it is within his power, so that he has dominion over the act. But this is the case with all actions involving the will: for it is through the will that man has dominion over his action [...] Hence it follows that good or bad in actions of the will alone justifies praise and blame; for in such actions badness, fault and blame come to one and the same.[14]

Hume did not recognize this capacity for freedom as of moral significance—which is why he reduced moral blame to nothing more than a mere negative evaluation. But there is another difference between Aquinas and Hume. For Aquinas, moral blame is a form of rational criticism, and addresses a failure to follow a form of rational direction. This direction comes not as rational advice, but as rational demand. This is a distinctive form of direction that is identified by the special form of negative appraisal, moral blame, that is made of those who disregard the direction—who breach moral obligation.

The directive aspect of normativity, just considered in itself, does not easily distinguish between obligation and advice. We can be strongly directed to do what is advisable just as we can be directed to do what is obligatory. In each case, direction can be conveyed in terms that imply marked criticism of those that disregard it. 'It would be foolish or deeply inadvisable not to do that', and 'Not to do that would be very bad and quite wrong'. What distinguishes obligation and advice lies at the level of appraisal— the way in which failure to follow the rational direction is negatively appraised. In the case of duty or obligation, the negative appraisal does not allege folly or lack of sense. That is the criticism that meets disregard of advice. Rather the criticism takes the form of moral blame. And the message of moral blame is that the agent is a wrongdoer, and that in the absence of excuse the agent was therefore bad to have done what they did.

So the direction given by moral obligation is located by the scholastic tradition within a general framework of rational direction. But the peculiar kind of rational direction involved is then explained in terms of a theory of appraisal—appraisal that is not simply of the agent's capacity to respond to reason, but of how the agent exercises freedom.

---

[14] Thomas Aquinas, *Summa theologiae* I–II, q. 21, a. 2 resp. (Turin: Marietti, 1950), p. 122.

The general theory of rational direction takes motivations, the agent's decisions and intentions, to be directed at objects of thought—objects that specify various voluntary actions between which the agent must decide, and which he will perform on the basis of deciding to perform them. Thus I might have to decide between keeping a sum of money and giving it to someone else. Each voluntary action may have various reason-giving features that rationally support its performance. Thus keeping the money allows me to spend it on myself. Giving it to another might repay a debt.

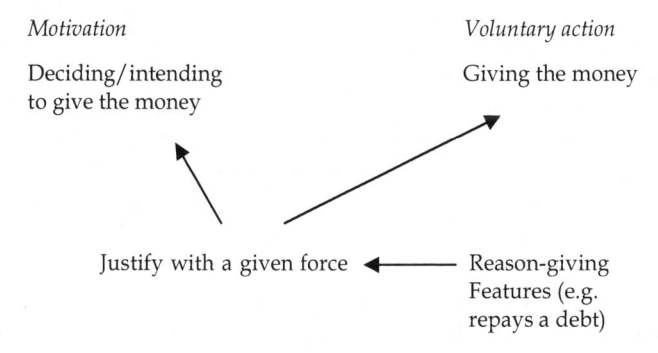

Motivation   *Voluntary action*

Deciding/intending   Giving the money
to give the money

Justify with a given force ◄──────── Reason-giving
                                       Features (e.g.
                                       repays a debt)

Besides these reason-giving features and the justification they provide, we need the idea of various kinds of directive force with which these features might support or justify both the voluntary actions that possess them and the motivations for performing these voluntary actions. The difference between advisability and obligatoriness is then explained as a difference in respect of justificatory force—a difference between recommendation and demand—that is unpacked, in turn, in terms of a theory of appraisal. To disregard the force of advice is to be criticized as foolish or less than sensible. To disregard the force of obligation is to act badly so that, where there is no excuse such as from ignorance or lack of control, it was bad of one so to act.

In the practical sphere the pair 'sensible' and 'foolish' shares with 'good' and 'bad' a set of common properties. Each pair similarly applies both to voluntary actions and to prior motivations to act, and in a way that both conveys direction, and that serves to appraise people for their response to such direction.

The terms 'sensible' or 'foolish' can be used of voluntary actions to pick them out as possessing features that support or oppose their performance and leave that performance advisable or inadvisable. But they also apply to the motivations to perform those voluntary actions; and then they track the application to those motivations of the justificatory force generated by their voluntary objects. If it is sensible to give the money, then to intend or to be motivated to give the money is sensible too. And correspondingly if it is foolish to hand the money over, then it is foolish to be motivated to hand over the money. Finally those terms 'sensible' and 'foolish' serve to appraise agents for their responsiveness to the force of the justification provided, both for voluntary actions and the prior motivations to perform them. Agents who are sensible act and are motivated to act in ways that are sensible.

But the same pattern applies to 'morally good' and 'morally bad'. The terms can similarly be used to pick out voluntary actions as possessing features that support or oppose their performance. And just as with 'sensible' and 'foolish' this support applies also to the motivations to perform those actions. Giving the money might be morally good because it helps another or fulfils a promise. And if it is good to give the money, it is correspondingly good to intend or be motivated to give the money; if morally bad or wrong to give the money, then it is equally bad or wrong to intend to give the money. And finally 'good' and 'bad' similarly serve to appraise agents for their responsiveness to the normative support or lack of it for various voluntary actions and the motivations to perform them.

So 'morally good' and 'morally bad' are used in the same way as 'sensible' and 'foolish' in relation to objects of thought, to communicate the support given by them to psychological attitudes. And they are used in the same way in arguments to support the formation of motivations directed at those objects of thought. Both 'bad/wrong' and 'foolish' are used to convey strong direction in a way that we immediately treat and understand as equally argumentatively conclusive in each case. To point out that doing A would be foolish is plainly not a merely preliminary step in a rational argument against doing A that would need to be completed by somehow showing that (therefore) it would be wrong or bad of one to do A. But nor is pointing out that it would be bad or wrong of one to do A merely the first step in a rational argument against doing A that would need to be completed by somehow showing that (therefore) it would be foolish of one to do A. Once either the folly or the wrongness and badness of an action has been established, each is on its own enough to convey an argumentative and rational rejection of the action as an option. Advisability and obligatoriness is each a genuine force of reason, and neither needs to be buttressed by the other.

There is in late scholasticism a systematic project of using this appraisal-based account of moral obligation and the rational direction it provides to detach moral obligation from divine commands, and so from the tie to legislation and sanction so characteristic of positive law:

> Since even if God never gave any command about the matter, it would still be bad to kill a human being without reason, to show contempt for one's superiors, or to expose oneself to clear danger of death, therefore even if natural law did not do so by way of any particular commandment given by God, natural law would still forbid such actions. [...] [F]or by the natural law we understand that on account of which some action is good or bad independently of any positive law, and so insofar as there would still be very many good and bad actions even if there were no divine commands, there would still be a natural law even in the absence of such commands.[15]

Even Suarez, trying to defend a dependence of moral obligation on divine legislation, remains within the same framework of appraisal-centred natural law — a framework he shares with the many early modern Catholic disbelievers in such dependence. Unlike Anscombe, Suarez does not appeal to divine commands to explain what moral obligations are. He and his opponents already share the same conception of what moral obligations are. They involve a justificatory force identified by a distinctive kind of negative appraisal. So Suarez is quite happy to assume the very notion of obligation to characterize the content of the decree of the divine will necessary, in his view, to the generation of moral obligations. The content of the divine decision that generates moral obligation, and that in Suarez's view is necessary to its very existence, is that a given action be *morally obligatory*. And, again, when Suarez attempts to argue for the dependence of moral obligation on divine legislation, he does so within the terms of an appraisal-centred theory, by alleging that without that legislation

---

[15] John Punch, commentary on Scotus on the Decalogue, *distinction* 37, in Duns Scotus, *Opera Omnia*, vol. 7, ed. Luke Wadding (Lyons, 1639), pp. 855-877.

there would not exist a peculiar form of badness—that which he terms *praevaricatio* or transgression, and which in his view is necessary to genuine wrong-doing.

> I therefore reply that in a human action there is indeed some goodness or badness by virtue of the object positively aimed at, in as much as that object is compatible or incompatible with right reason, so that by right reason the action can be counted as bad, and a fault and blameworthy in that regard, apart from any relation to law proper. But beyond this a human action has a *particular character of being good or bad* in relation to God, when we add divine law forbidding or decreeing, and in respect of that the human action counts in a particular way as a fault or blameworthy in relation to God by virtue of its breaching of the genuine law of God himself, which *particular badness Paul seems to have referred to by the name of transgression* when he said, 'Where there is not law, neither is there any transgression'.[16]

Whether or not Suarez's position is convincing, it is clear that moral obligation and its directiveness is still being characterized, even by him, in terms of a 'particular badness'. The peculiarly demanding direction that constitutes moral obligation is being characterized in terms of a distinctive form of moral appraisal.

The natural law tradition views moral law as prior to positive law, and moral obligation or duty as prior to positive legal obligation or duty. But there is more to the tradition than just that priority. In characterizing moral obligation, rather than appeal immediately to some distinctively legal form of direction, such as might be involved in positive law, the Catholic natural law tradition came to view legal direction as indeed distinctive—but in ways that had to be understood in terms of a theory of ethical appraisal, and as involving a special form of the general morality of virtue and vice. Anscombe and Williams, by contrast, agree on a very different and positivizing view of moral obligation. Despite the many other differences between them, together these two philosophers exemplify, in a strikingly similar manner, the great distance between modern ethical theory and that earlier natural law tradition.

---

[16] Francisco Suarez, *De legibus ac legislatore deo*, in *Opera Omnia*, vol. 5, ed. Charles Berton (Paris: Louis Vives, 1856), p. 110 (my emphases).

Candace Vogler

Anscombe on Promising

Elizabeth Anscombe thought that David Hume correctly identified two problems about understanding promises: first the problem of understanding what a promise is, and second the problem of understanding how, given that there are promises, these can generate obligations. She takes up both explicitly in two essays — 'On Promising and its Justice, and Whether it Need be Respected *in Foro Interno*' (1969) and 'Rules, Rights and Promises' (1978).[1] As is often the case in reading Anscombe, lining up her work on promises with recent Anglophone philosophical forays into the topic is not perfectly straightforward. The problems that capture her interest are more basic than those that haunt the pages of recent books and journal articles, and surface similarities can be misleading.

For example, philosophers have recently devoted significant attention to the centrality of practices or institutions to promises — a topic crucial to Anscombe. But Anscombe approaches this question in a way that has become unusual. Given that no one can make a promise inadvertently — in order to make a promise, I have to think that I am doing so — she asks after the content of this thought. The thought is only possible, she argues, if both the person making the promise and the person receiving the promise are operating from a single convention — for Anscombe, following Wittgenstein, a language game, a common source that allows both parties to be of one mind with respect to what's happening when a

---

[1] Both essays are reprinted in *CPP3*. Page number references to these essays will be taken from the *CPP3*: 'On Promising and its Justice and Whether it Need be Respected *in Foro Interno*' (pp. 10–21); 'Rules, Rights and Promises' (pp. 97–103). Anscombe agrees with Hume that promises are unintelligible apart from our conventions (although, unlike Hume, she does not think that this fact makes promises different from other uses of natural language).

promise is made. More often drawing from John Rawls' work than Anscombe's, recent work uses the idiom of *practices* or *institutions* to point to this feature of promising.[2]

A large literature concerned with the philosophical psychology of assurance and trust (as supported by the institution) attends much contemporary philosophical work on promises. Concern with interlocking beliefs and expectations, and how these might be brought to bear on questions about the character of the obligation to do one's word, is at the centre of much recent work on promising, often eclipsing interest in newer versions of the problems that attracted Anscombe's attention. For example, in his highly influential treatment of the topic, Tim Scanlon urges that, although promising as we know it involves convention, the practice-involving or institutional character of promising is irrelevant to understanding the kind of obligation generated by promises. He reaches this conclusion in part because of an intuition:

> Suppose I am stranded in a strange land. In an attempt to get myself something to eat, I make a spear. I am not very good at using it, however, and when I hurl it at a deer it goes wide of the mark and sails across a […] river. As I stand there gazing forlornly at my spear […] a boomerang comes sailing across and lands near me. Soon a strange person appears on the opposite bank, picks up my spear, and looks around in a puzzled way, evidently searching for the boomerang. It now occurs to me that I might regain my spear without getting wet by getting this person to believe that if he throws my spear across the river I will return his boomerang. Suppose that I am successful in this: I get him to form this belief; he returns my spear; and I walk off into the woods with it, leaving the boomerang where it fell.
>
> Now it seems to me that, intuitively, what I have done in this example is no less wrong than it would have been if I had

---

[2] See Tim Scanlon, 'Promises and Practices', *Philosophy & Public Affairs* 19, 1990:199–226; and *What We Owe to Each Other* (Cambridge: Harvard University Press, 1998), ch.7. The most thorough treatment of this topic is to be found in Michael Thompson's recent work. See Thompson, 'What is it to Wrong Someone? A Puzzle about Justice', in R. Jay Wallace, Philip Pettit, Samuel Scheffler, and Michael Smith (eds.), *Reason and Value: Themes from the Moral Philosophy of Joseph Raz* (Oxford: Clarendon Press, 2004), pp. 333–384. See also Michael Thompson, *Life and Action: Elementary Structures of Practice and Practical Thought* (Cambridge: Harvard University Press, 2008), Pt. III, pp. 149–212. Thompson draws from Anscombe in much of his work.

promised the stranger that I would return his boomerang if he threw back my spear. Yet nothing like a social practice of agreement-making is presupposed in the example.[3]

Scanlon thinks that the obligation to do one's word is a special case of a more general obligation not to foster false expectations on the part of our fellows. He takes it that this is a crucial aspect of promising because, he thinks, the view that sees fidelity as grounded in a beneficial practice cannot, all by itself, account for the sense in which breaking my promise to you wrongs, specifically, *you*, and not the practice or our fellow practitioners. In an effort to capture the sense in which the wrong I do in breaking a promise is personal, he focuses instead on the many ways in which we lead others to expect that we will do one thing rather than another. Scanlon's view has been the focus of a lot of recent work, and I will put Scanlon into conversation with Anscombe as a way into her view.

1. Scanlon's concern

Scanlon takes, as his starting point, John Rawls' account of promising as a mutually beneficial social practice, and of the obligation to do one's word as an obligation to do one's part if one enjoys the benefits of the practice. Now, it is very hard to come up with examples of people who do not enjoy any of the benefits of cooperation made possible by the institutions that rest on our capacity to give and do our word — people who use *none* of the goods made possible by a structured economy, for instance, and whose material lives are in no way dependent upon those of us who *are* participants in a structured economy. For this reason, Rawls' account has the kind of majestic sweep one nowadays seeks in work on considerations of morality. But the very breadth of the kinds of things that might be brought forward as instances of enjoying the benefits of those institutions that rely upon promising, contract and the like is related to the structural point that leads Scanlon to reject Rawls' account of fidelity. In effect, if I break a Rawlsian promise to you, then I am a free rider. You primarily are an *occasion* for my bad behaviour rather than, primarily, my victim. Scanlon points out that this can't be right. When I fail to keep my side of our bargain I wrong *you*.

---

[3] Scanlon, *What We Owe to Each Other*, p. 297.

He sets out to capture the nature of the personal wrong at issue by means of a series of increasingly demanding principles governing our interactions. Unless I am playing poker with you or engaged in espionage activities, or some such, I must not manipulate you into having a false expectation about my own future actions; and next, more than this, I must exercise due care not to lead you to form reasonable, but false, expectations about what I will do, when you stand to lose a lot by relying on such expectations; next, I must take reasonable steps to prevent you from suffering this loss (ordinarily, by warning you). But even the combination of avoiding intentional manipulation, exercising due care and giving you fair warning if I no longer intend to do what you expect of me does not, Scanlon argues, take us all the way to fidelity. Each offers some sort of assurance about my future conduct, but not enough of the right sort of assurance. To give you the right sort of assurance, we need a proper principle of fidelity. Here is Scanlon's formulation of the principle:

> *Principle F*: If (1) A voluntarily and intentionally leads B to expect that A will do X (unless B consents to A's not doing so); (2) A knows that B wants to be assured of this; (3) A acts with the aim of providing this assurance, and has good reason to believe that he or she has done so; (4) B knows that A has the beliefs and intentions just described; (5) A intends for B to know this, and knows that B does know it; and (6) B knows that A has just this knowledge and intent; then, in the absence of some special justification, A must do X unless B consents to X's not being done.[4]

From Scanlon's perspective, it is a great strength of the account that, although applicable to promising, the fidelity principle does not require that A and B be participants in a shared social practice or institution. A and B can be strangers on the road who have nothing much in common beyond some interest in cooperation. It matters, Scanlon thinks, that A indicates to B that A abides by this principle *because* failing to do so will wrong B: 'I indicate to you that I believe and take seriously the fact that, once I have declared this intention under the circumstances, and have reason to believe that you are convinced by it, it would be wrong of me not to [do what I have indicated I will do] (in the absence of some good justification [...]).'[5]

---

[4] Scanlon, *What We Owe to Each Other*, p. 304.
[5] Scanlon, *What We Owe to Each Other*, p. 307.

He takes it that such a thing could be possible in the boomerang and spear case—and he *has* to think so, as near as I can tell. In Scanlon's state of nature, the two strangers have no common language, have no common culture, are not bound by the same legal institutions and so on. Scanlon uses the slightly slippery formulation 'no less wrong' to describe how he thinks about the failure to throw the boomerang across the stream—it is no less wrong than breaking a promise. He seems to want something stronger—not merely no *less* wrong, but in no way *differently* wrong—because he thinks that the obligation to keep promises is of a piece with the sense that he ought not to have wandered off with the spear without throwing the boomerang across the river.

Notice, for a moment, that Scanlon's account could be made to fit situations in which I seek sustained interaction with a feral cat (if you like, the stranger across the river might be a non-human primate that wants my banana, while I want its coconut—but I'll stick with cats, because I know more about them). I want the cat to let down its guard because I love cats and want this one to trust me. The cat is cautiously willing to let down its guard, bit-by-bit, for whatever reason feral cats occasionally are willing to do such a thing. Each of us has begun moving toward some sort of rapprochement with the other. The kind of communication involved is complex, and declarations and assurances take complicated behavioural forms, but Scanlon's picture *may* be broad enough to cover many, many kinds of situations involving cultivation of trust between sentient creatures of different species. Here is how I build trust with an alley cat:

I voluntarily and deliberately place a small bowl on my porch while the cat watches from the alley, and, looking the cat in the eye, fill the dish with cat food (if the cat flees, I remove the bowl and go back inside).

I step back from the bowl of food, still looking the cat in the eye, then lower my gaze and stand still.

I lower my gaze, step back, and stand still in order to assure the cat that I mean it no harm and mean for it to have the food.

Breaking off eye contact by lowering one's gaze and ceding territory by stepping back are feline behavioural techniques indicating that one will not challenge a cat's access to some important resource.

The cat is equipped to recognize such signals as such and my behaviour is meant to communicate my interest in giving the cat food.

The cat comes onto the porch and eats the food; I repeat the actions, supplementing them with soothing vocalizations, until the cat becomes accustomed to routine, scent-marks the porch, and will signal its hunger to me when it wants more food, at which point the cat will complain if I stop feeding it.

Scanlon could object to the suggestion that non-human animals can know and intend, declare things behaviourally or be the addressees of behavioural declarations and the like from humans, but it is hard to see how to make sense of the complexity of human interaction with dogs, cats, horses and the like if something like this isn't possible. Of course none of the non-humans that live and work with people seems equipped to attribute moral seriousness to any of us (Scanlon wants faithful people to exhibit moral seriousness). But it is equally hard to write an attribution of specifically moral seriousness into a one-off encounter with a creature at the far side of a river that has somehow got the impression that one of us is trustworthy. Plain trust normally requires repeated encounters.

What is lacking in the case of interspecies communication that may be driving Scanlon's intuition is the hidden force of a thought about property. David Jones suggested that part of what makes Scanlon's intuition plausible is the idea that the boomerang *belongs* to the stranger, and the spear *belongs* to Scanlon.[6] Scanlon has worked up a spear out of whatever was on hand. The stranger has worked up a boomerang out of whatever was on hand. If we thought that manipulating materials produced not merely boomerangs and spears but also property rights in manufactured objects, then we might think that Scanlon *owns* the spear and the stranger *owns* the boomerang. But thought about property normally brings with it precisely the sort of institutional framework that Scanlon means to exclude. Recall this crucial moment in Jean-Jacques Rousseau's state of nature thought experiment:

> The first person who, having fenced off a plot of ground, took it into his head to say *this is mine* and found people simple enough to believe him, was the true founder of civil society. What crimes, wars, murders, what miseries and horrors would the human race have been spared by someone who, uprooting the stakes or filling in the ditch, had shouted to his fellow-men: Beware of listening to

---

[6] In discussion, September 2013.

this imposter; you are lost if you forget that the fruits belong to all and the earth to no one![7]

Rousseau goes on to give a complex just-so story about the development of social relations adequate to supporting institutions of property. Scanlon's state of nature has more in common with Hobbes' household than Rousseau's vanishing wilderness. Hobbes invites the reader inclined to doubt that the state of nature is a state of violent conflict to reflect on this point:

> Let him therefore consider with him-selfe [...] what opinion he has of his [...] fellow Citizens, when he locks his dores; and of his children, and servants, when he locks his chests. Does he not there as much accuse mankind by his actions, as I do by my words?[8]

In the Hobbesean household, concern over property is the air one breathes. But the Hobbesean householder lives in a world shaped by promise-involving institutions of property and a judiciary prepared to defend property rights: 'he knows there bee Lawes, and publike Officers, armed, to revenge all injuries shall bee done to him.'[9] Scanlon's account depends upon excluding such a context from the banks of the river.

2. Scanlon's encounter with Anscombe

Whatever we make of *my* spear and *his* boomerang, Scanlon puts himself in conversation with Anscombe almost immediately after attaching his motivational caveat to the principle of fidelity. His concern is with her circularity objection to attempts to account for promising in terms of interlocking intentions, utterances and expectations outside the context provided by a social practice or other institution. In short, Anscombe anticipates precisely the sort of account that Scanlon gives. Here is Scanlon's reading of Anscombe's objection:

> According to accounts [like Scanlon's] saying "I promise to..." creates an obligation only if it convinces the recipient of the

---

[7] Jean-Jacques Rousseau, *Discourse on the Origin and Foundation of Inequality Among Men*, in *The First and Second Discourses*, edited by Roger D. Masters, translated by Roger D. and Judith R. Masters (New York: St. Martin's Press, 1964), pp. 141–142.
[8] Thomas Hobbes, *Leviathan*, edited by C.B. Macpherson (Harmondsworth: Penguin Books, 1985), pp. 186–187.
[9] Hobbes, *Leviathan*, p. 187.

speaker's intention to do the thing in question. But it can do this only insofar as it gives the recipient reason to believe that the speaker has reason to do that thing. What is this reason? On the analysis proposed, it is the speaker's awareness of the fact that it would be wrong, having said "I promise," to fail to follow through. But it would be wrong to do this only if saying "I promise" created an obligation, and creates an obligation only if it gives the recipient reason to believe that the speaker has a reason to do the thing promised. So there appears to be a circle here.[10]

Anscombe's objection is not exactly this, if I understand her, although it is close. She notices, for example, that there are special content restrictions on promising that are no part of Scanlon's story—for example if the thing that you want me to do, and that I say that I mean to do, is wicked, fidelity drops out of the picture—assurances that I will assist you in your foul scheme, in exchange for your assurances that you will help me with mine, do not generate moral obligations, even though they might trigger the kinds of interlocking intentions and well-grounded expectations that are the stuff of Scanlon's account.[11] Anscombe recognizes that the temptation will be to treat this as a strange point, or to chalk it up to some sort of defeasibility. So she goes at the matter more directly.

The way in which she goes at it is through a discussion of language, rules and pairs of modals—the 'must' in Scanlon's fidelity principle falls within the range of the things that Anscombe discusses. If I *must* do what I have said that I will do (in the sense at issue in promising rather than through coercion, compulsion, physical necessity, etc.), then the recipient of my word has a right against me that I perform, and I will have wronged precisely that person if, barring misfortune, I fail to perform. Such a linguistic instrument is thoroughly conventional and, Anscombe thinks, captures the personal dimension at issue in noticing that breaking my promise to you wrongs *you*.

Now, Scanlon is not much concerned with thinking how natural language users busily using declarations and the like to strike the bargains might manage to do such a thing at all, or even to take it into their heads that such a thing might be done. Part of the reason that I mentioned the feral cat was because Scanlon's

---

[10] Scanlon, *What We Owe to Each Other*, p. 307.
[11] 'Rules, Rights and Promises', p. 98.

account presupposes a great deal of what Anscombe thinks needs to be discussed in order to understand promises, and the best way I could see to strip away that presupposition was by imagining interspecies interaction, where there really *isn't* human convention. Anscombe argues that having the linguistic apparatus in the context of its conventional use is required in order to make sense of promising. This is why she offers funny examples of idiosyncratic procedures to bind my own future conduct—I have to do it because I green-inked it! I must do it because I blipped it! But virtually everyone working in the way that Scanlon is working presupposes that the conventions required if promising is to be so much as possible already are in place. There is, as Anscombe put it, a language game.

In assuming the existence of the language game which already must be in place in order to explain how I could so much as imagine getting others to do my will by getting them to say that they will, Scanlon already is riding piggyback on a social practice that he wants to treat as optional. What sort of beast is a promise? A conventional linguistic instrument deployed in an established institution or social practice in order to bind others' future conduct in circumstances where others have no independent reason to do our will. It is the institution or practice—not the word *promise*—that is at issue in Anscombe's account. She writes:

> 'I'll help you today; will you help me tomorrow?'—'Yes!' Here are promises given and received. The question is what it is for them to be *promises*. They are or contain descriptions of possible future states of affairs. They are made true by performance. But they are not merely predictions, not even merely the sort of pre-diction which is an expression of intention.[12]

Leave that concern to the side. Imagine Scanlon working to see how we might understand promises through the formation of interlocking intentions and expectations. In effect, under certain conditions, A uses some form of communication to trigger B's expectations about A's future conduct. When all goes well, B can rest assured that A will do what A has indicated that she will do. Why will B believe and place her faith in A?

Scanlon's account of the grounds for B's assurance involves deploying the principles of due care and manipulation-avoidance.

---

[12] 'Rules, Rights and Promises', p. 99.

B will understand that A abides by these principles, that A is trying to persuade B about what A will do, and that A will work to avoid misleading or disappointing B. Perhaps because Scanlon thinks that the obligation to keep my promises is just a special instance of a more general obligation not to let others down, he thinks that this will be enough to move us from interlocking systems of intention and expectation to promises. He thinks that my working to get you to expect me to do various things (outside special situations like gaming tables, competitive sport, theatre and my work for the French Resistance) is enough to oblige me to do them when what you expect of me matters a lot to you. Like Hobbes and Hume, Anscombe did not share this intuition. She writes:

> Hume's own conclusion was 'that promises have no force antecedent to human conventions.' If this is found offensive, that will be by a misunderstanding. God himself can make no promises to man except in a human language. The regularity of the seasons, and the applicability of the rational probability calculus in matters of chance, are not divine *promises*. A spouse who has always come home at a certain hour has not *eo ipso* broken any promise (only perhaps acted inconsiderately) by suddenly and willfully failing to do so. There is indeed such a thing as implicit contract, and there might be one in this case. But that is two-sided. Mere fostering of expectations can't be making an implicit contract.[13]

Like Hobbes and Hume, Anscombe was struck by our need for some way of binding each other's future conduct. The social practice comes into play when you have no independent reason to want to do my will, and, when the time comes for you to do your side of our bargain, there will always be something else you would rather do. This point is at the heart of Niko Kolodny and R. Jay Wallace's recent work on Scanlon's account. In effect, they argue that either Scanlon's picture of my trust in your word is based in my understanding that you have a moral-practice-based reason to do what you say you will do, or it is based on your belief that I have a non-moral reason to do my word independently of our joint participation in the practice of promising. Kolodny and Wallace write:

> [T]he distinctive utility of promising is not simply that it allows A to assure B that A will do X when A has prior or [non-moral-

---

[13] 'Rules, Rights and Promises', p. 99.

practice] reasons to do X that he prefers not to communicate to B, but also that it allows A to assure B when A does not have *any* prior or [non-moral-practice] reasons to do X at all. This is precisely what makes promising so beneficial in cases such as that of Hume's farmers, in which the parties have no prior or [non-moral-practice] reason to do what they have promised, and in which the lack of such independent reasons is common knowledge. On Scanlon's view, promises can no longer perform this vital service. If A can promise to do X only by leading B to believe that A has some prior or [non-moral-practice] reason to do X, then in a situation in which A has no [such reason], A cannot promise at all.[14]

Scanlon tries to build fidelity out of interlocking systems of intention and expectation fuelled by a motivational engine that is a bit perplexing. If I understand him, he wants the engine to be an engine of moral motivation, and hopes to escape Anscombe's circularity objection by treating the wrong involved in breaking my promise as something other than the distinctive failure to give you your due at issue when my undertaking has made some bit of my future conduct something that *is* your due. Instead, my fidelity is supposed to be rooted in the many ways that I want to avoid disappointing others. I confess that I hate being a disappointment to others. But that is not a good way of describing my relationship with my mortgage lender.

3. Anscombe's account

I have mentioned that Anscombe does not think that mere fostering of interlocking intentions and expectations is enough to get us all the way to promising. For all that, it is worth noticing that fostering of expectations may give you *better* grounds for predicting what I will do than extracting a promise from me does. Consider: you and I spend weeks discussing an upcoming rock concert — we each love the band. Although we have merely fostered the expectation that each of us will be there, you have good grounds to expect me to go. If, on the other hand, I am made nervous by crowds and find loud music daunting, and so you get me to *promise* to go, it's not a big surprise when I ring you up the day before to tell you that I'm not feeling well and will not be going. In general, if you rely upon extracting promises in order to

---

[14] Niko Kolodny and R. Jay Wallace, 'Promises and Practices Revisited', *Philosophy and Public Affairs*, 31(2) Spring 2003:143.

bind my future doings, it is *because* there is no reason to think that I otherwise will be inclined to do your will when the time comes. (Incidentally, this *does* characterize my relationship with my mortgage lender.)

I have suggested that Scanlon can be read as describing how things are for people once the institution of promising already is in place. This is the force of noticing that he assumes what one might call the *grammar* of the language game, and proceeds to give one sort of account of *a* moral psychology made possible by that game. Although careful discussion of a practice or a language-game might explain how many different people can be of one mind on the occasion of an undertaking, it cannot explain why any of them *should* do her word. The mere exploration of the facts that people enter into such arrangements, and of the stunning coincidence in their thoughts and actions when they do, is not enough to baptize such doings with justice. Scanlon thinks that he can supply the additional element—the account of the good or the point of promising—by focusing on the way it fosters the formation of interlocking intentions and expectations. If I understand her, Anscombe will think that this is not quite enough.

It is helpful, at this point, to re-describe the twofold task Anscombe sets herself. The first part, saying what a promise *is*, involves showing how an undertaking can restrict one's possibilities of acting without incurring reproach. People will complain about broken promises. Scanlon can be read as discussing protection against incurring reproach—if I never disappoint you, then you are unlikely to complain about what I do or fail to do. But Scanlon hopes to give the same account of why I *ought to* incur reproach if I fail to do my word. And here, I think, Anscombe will urge that he locates the utility of promising in the wrong place. She writes:

> What ways are there of getting human beings to do things? You can make a man fall over by pushing him; you cannot usefully make his hand write a letter or mix concrete by pushing; for in general if you have to push his hand in the right way, you might as well not use him at all. You can order him to do what you want, and if you have authority he will perhaps obey you. Again if you have power to hurt him or help him according as he disregards or obeys your orders, or if he loves you so as to accord with your requests, you have a way of getting him to do things. However, few people have authority over everyone they need to get to do things, and few people either have power to hurt or help others

without damage to themselves or command affection from others to such an extent as to be able to get them to do the things they need others to do. Those who have extensive authority and power cannot exercise it to get all the other people to do the things that meet their mutual requirements. So, though physical force seems a more certain way of producing the desired physical results than any other, and authority and power to hurt or help and sometimes affection too, more potent than the feeble procedure of such a language-game [as promising], yet in default of the possibility or utility of exerting physical force, and of the possibility of exercising authority or power to hurt and help, or of commanding affection, this feeble means is at least a means of getting people to do things. Now getting one another to do things without the application of physical force is a necessity for human life, and that far beyond what could be secured by those other means.[15]

The utility of promising — the point or good of it — lies in this perfectly general human need rather than in the aggregate misfortune of defeated expectations. In a Hobbesean vein, Anscombe thinks that what made those expectations reasonable *in the first place* was not the sympathetic tendencies we may or may not detect in each other. It was the institution of promising — a human invention that can restrict our possibilities not merely of acting in such a way as to avoid reproach and avoid disappointing each other (the stuff of *faring* well, as one used to say), but also our possibilities of acting well. She gives a task-based account of the justice of doing one's word and the principal beneficiaries are the indefinitely many people who are drawn into pairwise relations with each other insofar as they are, as Michael Thompson will put it, bearers of a unified and singular practice of promising. Thompson argues, in an Anscombean vein, that there *is* nothing to the disposition to do one's word but the social practice internalized.[16]

4. A glance at Michael Thompson in conclusion

Thompson does not give an account of the good of the practice of promising. His efforts are directed at giving a fuller account than anyone else working from Rawls or Anscombe has managed of the sense in which any individual disposition to fidelity derives its

---

[15] 'On Promising and its Justice', p. 18.
[16] Michael Thompson, 'Two Forms of Practical Generality', in Christopher W. Morris and Arthur Ripstein (eds.), *Practical Rationality and Preference: Essays for David Gauthier* (Cambridge: Cambridge University Press, 2001), pp. 121–152.

intelligibility from the practice. Of course the practice can't exist without individual practitioners. But this ought not to lead us to suppose that we can build up the practice out of interlocking individual psychologies or, worse, reduce it to these.

By way of analogy, Thompson points out that there is no such thing as a species unless there are individual members of that species. Nevertheless, we presuppose an understanding of the human species in confidently making judgments about individual human beings.[17] Thompson writes:

> We can say, in light of *my* form, which is the specifically human form, that these are arms—a bit weak, maybe, but fairly together [rather than] *legs* [...] — only horribly deformed and not much good for crawling with [...] Or mutilated wings.[18]

Implicitly following Anscombe's lead, Thompson argues that an understanding of the social practice of promising likewise allows us to apprehend some instances of speaking, writing, clasping hands and the like as undertakings.

I expect that Thompson will handle cases in which you and I collude in a scheme to rob others this way:

> [I]f the practice [of promising] makes some action good, then any action the practice cannot make good does not express the practice. This is evidently consistent with the view that such acts of promise-keeping as *are* good are only made good by the practice.[19]

Promising cannot make the acts involved in implementing our scheme good. It is true that even robbers need to rely on each other, but their handshake will be parasitic on the practice, in Thompson's view, rather than an expression or instance of it.

Anscombe could explain this by pointing to the general point of the practice—that human good of the sort at stake in a structured economy, marriage, lunch dates, office hours, scheduled professional meetings and other promise-involving modes of sociality is the point of the practice. Promises, covenants, contracts and the like are the feeble instruments we have to make such things possible.

---

[17] Thompson, *Life and Action*, pp. 199–207.
[18] Thompson, *Life and Action*, p. 61.
[19] Thompson, *Life and Action*, p. 188.

Luke Gormally

On Killing Human Beings

This chapter falls into three parts. In the first, I offer an overview of Elizabeth Anscombe's thinking on the topic; in the second and third I explore further two of the key themes in that thinking.

In the Michaelmas term of the first full academic year (1970-71) after she moved from Oxford to the Chair of Philosophy at Cambridge, Elizabeth Anscombe offered a seminar for the Faculties of Divinity, Law and Medicine under the title 'On killing human beings'. She pursued this topic in seminars and lectures in the Michaelmas terms of the following three academic years. In writing this chapter I've drawn on unpublished writings of hers from this period[1] as well as on the two principal published papers which embody some of the fruits of her thinking from this period: 'On the Source of the Authority of the State'[2] and 'Murder and the Morality of Euthanasia'.[3]

1. Exposition of Anscombe on killing human beings

Killings of one human being by another attract a variety of descriptions: 'He slipped on the branch, fell out of the tree and broke his companion's neck' (they were picking apples together); 'He shot him in self-defence'; 'He executed him after the judge had

---

[1] These are referred to in the footnotes by the File number in the Interim Archive of Professor Anscombe's papers (e.g. AIA 39). The archive is referred to as 'interim' because the ordering of papers simply follows the chronological order in which they were found. A considerable further reorganization of the papers is needed.

[2] *CPP3*, pp. 30-55 (the paper was originally published in 1978). As she remarks in the Introduction to that volume: 'I would have said I got interested in political philosophy in the 1970s simply out of an interest in the concept of murder' (p. vii).

[3] *HLAE*, pp. 261-277 (the paper was originally published in 1982).

imposed the death penalty'; 'He shot the enemy soldier on the battlefield'; 'He terminated the pregnancy (euphemism) in the second trimester'; 'He cut the baby's spinal cord after delivering her' (Kermit Gosnell's *modus operandi*); 'He gave a lethal overdose of morphine to the pain-wracked patient at the patient's request'; 'He killed the patient who was sure to die in order to obtain his organs for another patient'; 'He withheld nutrition and hydration from the patient so that he starved to death'; 'He shot the tyrant'; 'He burned the house down to obtain insurance and three of his children died as a result.'

Killings of one human being by another raise questions of responsibility. Responsibility is a three-level concept. It may be used in reference, firstly, to being a cause or contributory condition of x happening; secondly, to being callable to account for x happening; and, thirdly, to being guilty for the occurrence of x, i.e. when one lacks an exonerating answer when called to account for causing or contributing to x happening.

Murder is the killing of one human being by another which involves the degree of responsibility for death which is guilt. If a killing is not to be counted as murderous there must be an exonerating answer for why it occurred or was carried out.

Anscombe is insistent that murder is not to be defined as 'impermissible intentional killing'.[4] To do so would be to rule out

---

[4] See unpublished lecture, 'Killing and Murder: Introductory' (AIA 511, p. 2): 'Nowadays if this question is asked ['Is that sign, the strict commandment {i.e. the prohibition of murder}, a *false* sign?'], someone will say that the word "murder" simply means impermissible killing. If that should be true, "Thou shalt do no murder" only means "Thou shalt not kill human beings in cases where thou shalt not". Then the commandment, however venerable, will be *no* sort of contribution to an argument that something is damnable because it is murder. For it will always *first* have to be determined that the killing of someone is wrong before it can be determined whether it is murder, and so it cannot effectively be argued that it should not be done because it is murder. It will also cease to be a substantial question whether it can be justifiable to murder.' See further AIA 298, pp. 4–5: 'There is an inclination to imagine a strong case for justifying a particular killing, from the point of view only of the urgently felt desirability of the consequences in the particular situation. If we let the existence of an *at least discussable case for* killing someone on such grounds imply that perhaps the act is *not* to be called "murder", then we are surreptitiously undermining a certain pattern of reasoning about conduct. The pattern goes like this, where some here-and-now proceeding or plan is in question:
1. To do *that* would be to do such and such.

the question 'Is it ever right to commit murder?', a question which Anscombe thought G.E. Moore was correct in raising.[5] Moore in fact thought that there could be affirmative answers to the question. But the justification of murder would be similar, Anscombe observes, to the justification of treachery. If one betrayed someone to an enemy after promising them protection and one justified one's betrayal on the grounds that it was 'for the best' in the circumstances, it would be treachery that would be being justified. Likewise:

> there is one 'justification' which, even if it is admitted as a justification as it is by Moore, does not take away the character of 'murder'. That is where the justification of a piece of deliberate killing is on the sole ground of advantageous consequences to be gained, or disadvantageous consequences to be avoided, in the particular situation.[6]

The type of action which gives us the central case of what counts as murder is intentional killing of the innocent.[7] Responsibility for that is unambiguous precisely because it is intentional. And there is no exonerating justification because the human being killed is innocent—a paradigm case of injustice. Justice in this domain rests on the valuation of human life. In murderous killing an individual human being is done away with not because he

---

2. Such an action is, or of this kind is, or in these circumstances is: dishonest/cruel/cowardly/an act of treachery/adultery/theft/murder/etc.
3. Therefore to do *that* in this case would be to commit an act of dishonesty or cruelty or ... etc. ...
This is a powerful piece of practical reasoning. I mean a *will* not to be dishonest, cruel, cowardly, a thief, adulterous, treacherous or murderous may very well exist, and where there is such a will, the possessor of it will tend to be moved by this reasoning. It undoubtedly can have a strong effect on the mind to be forced to contemplate one's proposed actions under descriptions of this sort, the applicability of which may be arguable or evident from the undeniable circumstances of the case.'

[5] See G.E. Moore, *Principia Ethica* (London: Cambridge University Press, [1903] 1971), pp. 148ff. The openness of the question is compatible with an answer to it that argues to the conclusion that murder is necessarily wrong.

[6] AIA 298, p. 9.

[7] The innocent are all those who are *not* engaged in unauthorized actions which have as their object the death of others or foreseeably threaten their lives. Those who do so act—the 'nocents'—do not because of that lose their intrinsic dignity as human beings. This places constraints on what can count as an acceptable justification for killing 'nocents'.

deserves to die but for the sake of others or because his continued existence is judged not worthwhile or an evil, or because of hatred. 'So *his* existence is counted as worth nothing in comparison with the ends of others.'[8] But a human life is not to be so devalued. Human worth or dignity goes with being a person of human kind, characterized as it is by rational nature.

> [...] [M]an is spirit. [Anscombe wrote] He moves in the categories of innocence and answerability and desert—one of the many signs of a leap to another kind of existence from the life of the other animals. The very question 'Why may we not kill innocent people' asks whether it may not be *justified* to do so, and this is itself a manifestation of this different life.[9]

Not all murders involve intending to bring about the death of the victim, or even intending harm or danger to the victim. A killer may be simply aiming to badly hurt a victim, or, as in the case of the father burning down his house to claim insurance, may have no victim in mind but be indifferent to whether there is one. Such killings may exhibit contempt for human life more extreme than is exhibited by many intentional killings.[10]

The intrinsic wrongfulness of murder and therefore its prohibition, Anscombe observes, is very basic. One can point to the character of rational argument for moral norms to see why murder is prohibited:

> The arguments are of the form 'Obedience to this law is needed for human good'. The unit whose good the argument seeks is the human individual, considered generally. To kill him, then, is to destroy that being which is the point of those considerations.[11]

Because the prohibition of murder is in this way fundamental it is prior to and grounds the right not to be murdered.[12]

Intentional killing of the innocent remains the core of the concept of murder and under that description is unjust. This position can be maintained only if a proposed action can be identified as unjust regardless of its further consequences. If it were not possible to do this in regard to killing human beings then they are

---

[8] AIA 289, p. 4.
[9] 'Murder and the Morality of Euthanasia', in *HLAE*, p. 267.
[10] See 'Murder and the Morality of Euthanasia', p. 263.
[11] 'Murder and the Morality of Euthanasia', p. 266.
[12] 'Murder and the Morality of Euthanasia', p. 266.

already devalued. 'Terrible consequences to others of *not* killing this innocent person will be enough to prove it just to kill him, so he is devalued.'[13] Insofar as an action is identifiably an intentional killing of the innocent it is identifiable as unjust regardless of further consequences. Recognition of the injustice rests ultimately, of course, on the proper valuation of human life.

Clarity about the injustice of the intentional killing of the innocent is possible, however, only if we distinguish between the intended and the foreseen consequences of an action.

> For what is an action? Usually the totality consisting of some movement in a certain context in which that movement has certain consequences. For example, I pull a trigger; the movement of my finger in this context is shooting a man. So consequences make up what an action is. We cannot then speak as if 'being a consequence' were a classification of events distinct from actions. But if pulling the trigger in these circumstances is shooting a man dead and that is my intention, then in pulling the trigger I am intentionally killing the man. If the action under that description is already unjust, it is possible to say 'don't think about further consequences'. For I certainly will be doing that intentional action if I pull the trigger with that intention. But if any foreseen or foreseeable consequences are to be included in any intentional action, then I will *also* be intentionally killing men if, for example, I build a fleet of fishing vessels; for some innocent men will get drowned. It will not be reasonable to say: never do any action from which foreseeably some death will follow. So if what is foreseen and what is intended are the same, it will not be reasonable to say: never commit the intentional action of killing an innocent man.[14]

The norm also requires us to make a particular distinction between acts and omissions. If I omit to do x there are consequences different from the consequences of my doing x. But an agent can be called to account for his omitting to do x only if it was both possible and necessary for him to do x. One may, however, intentionally omit to act precisely to bring about a particular outcome. If a clinician withholds nutrition and fluids from a dependent patient with the intention of ending the patient's life and the patient dies as a result the clinician has murdered the patient. It cannot, however, 'be "necessary" to kill an innocent person except in the sense that you won't secure a given end

---

[13] AIA 289, p. 4.
[14] AIA 289, p. 5.

unless you do; on the contrary, it is *out of the question* to do so with justice'.[15] The omission of this act has the consequence perhaps of many others being killed. But abstention from a wicked act is not the murder of those persons.

Anscombe considers a number of types of killings of human beings which are not murderous because there is an exonerating answer for carrying them out. The killing of violent offenders by the forces established by civil authority to protect innocent citizens; killing in war by soldiers; and the assassination of tyrants. I omit consideration of killing in warfare because it is the subject of Fr Goodill's contribution to this volume.

What distinguishes civil authority, for Anscombe, is precisely the actual or threatened exercise of violent coercive power. And it is distinguished from the Mafia's exercise of violent coercive power precisely by the authority to command such violence. Authority in general she defines as 'a regular right to be obeyed in a domain of decision'. 'Authority arises from the necessity of a task whose performance requires a certain sort and extent of obedience on the part of those for whom the task is supposed to be done.'[16] What grounds civil authority's exercise of coercive power is the need to protect innocent and peaceable citizens from those of their fellow citizens disposed to attack them and violently impede their activities and enterprises. It is this evil reality which provides the human need for government and laws backed by force. Except in emergency situations in which the forces of law and order are obliged to kill to prevent the murder of an innocent citizen, what justifies the exercise of coercive power is the existence of laws and a legal system designed to establish guilt. Within such a framework the infliction of punishment (including capital punishment) requires both that the offender be found guilty and that the person inflicting the punishment has the authority to do so. A guilty offender may be wronged by getting his deserts at the hands of private parties.

What gets justified in invoking the need for civil authority to inflict punishment are primarily the particular laws in the light of which punishment is inflicted and the institutions of law enforcement. For it is these that are meant to ensure justice in

---

[15] AIA 289, p. 5.
[16] AIA 513, p. 4.

punishment, for without just laws and the establishing of desert punishment cannot normally be justified.

If one lacks the authority of civil government to kill, it is readily assumed that assassination must always be murder. But a legitimate government may be violently usurped, or, on the other hand, there may be gross failures to perform the tasks of government such that civil authority lapses, since such authority derives from the need for those tasks to be performed. '[I]t would be absurd', Anscombe wrote, 'to say that because he has no official commission to do so, a man who can may never strike down the usurpers of power as they are first seating themselves.'[17] The assassin, however, has to get things right in two respects if his killing is to be justifiable. First it must be clear that the usurper deserves to be killed. The legitimate target of assassination must be a usurper of political authority who is acting with gross injustice. But secondly, it must be reasonable to think that removal of the abnormality of tyranny will be succeeded by the normality of civil government. Otherwise the assassin will be responsible for ensuing evils.

This rapid account of the main lines of Anscombe's thought on killing human beings might prompt reflection on a number of topics; I will confine discussion to two of them: human dignity, and the distinction between what is intended and side effects.

2. Killing and human dignity

In what follows I give a fuller account of the concept of human dignity than can be found in Anscombe, but it is an account that I believe is called for by what she in fact says about dignity.

As I've noted, Anscombe regarded unjust killing as that in which a person's 'existence is counted as worth nothing in comparison with the ends of others'. Human worth or dignity stands in the way of unjust killing. Anscombe spoke of dignity as made evident in a human being's life moving 'in the categories of innocence and answerability and desert — one of the many signs of a leap to another kind of existence from the life of the other animals'. One might be tempted to interpret this along the lines of contemporary voluntaristic interpretations of Kant's understanding of human dignity, according to which its only possessors are

---

[17] AIA 515, p. 5.

those who are actively capable of exercising rational agency — such a presently exercisable capacity would then be what counted as the 'leap to another kind of existence'. The interpretation (unfaithful to Kant)[18] is a consequence of the modern tendency to locate the origin of value in human willing.[19] This goes with the 'personism' which is the plague of bioethics, according to which only a restricted class of human beings, those in possession of a range of presently exercisable psychological abilities, count as persons and enjoy basic human rights.

This is manifestly not Anscombe's position, for whom

> A human being is a person because the kind to which he belongs is characterised by rational nature. Thus we have the same individual, and have the same person when we have the same human being. One is a person just by being of this kind, and that does indeed import a tremendous dignity.[20]

So procured abortion, as intentional killing of an innocent human being, is murder, whatever its legal classification.

Anscombe's locating dignity in human nature rather than human willing assumes a particular anthropology. It rests on a teleological understanding of human nature which finds its clearest exposition in Aquinas.

Exercisable psychological abilities presuppose second-order capacities to develop those abilities. These are referred to by Aquinas as 'powers of the soul'. The rational soul is the 'form and life-long actuality' which gives dynamic unity to the complex material organisms we are and to the expression of our various powers in multifarious activities. In his Commentary on Lombard's *Sentences* Aquinas wrote: 'from the essence of the soul flow powers which are essentially different […] but which are all united in the soul's essence as in a root.'[21] The powers of the soul,

---

[18] Dignity for Kant belongs to the moral law present in human beings and to human beings as capable of independently subjecting themselves to the moral law. '[…] [M]orality, and humanity in so far as it is capable of morality, is that which alone has dignity.' *Groundwork of the Metaphysics of Morals*, A435, in Immanuel Kant, *Practical Philosophy*, edited and translated by Mary J. Gregor (Cambridge: Cambridge University Press, 1996), p. 84.

[19] On this see Michael Rosen, *Dignity:. Its History and Meaning* (Cambridge, MA, and London: Harvard University Press, 2012), p. 93.

[20] 'Murder and the Morality of Euthanasia', p. 268.

[21] *II Sent.* d. 26, q. 1, a. 4c.

as mostly[22] undeveloped, radical capacities, are given to each individual at the beginning of his or her existence. Anscombe, following Aquinas, was reluctant to say precisely that about the early embryo, a point David Jones discusses in his contribution to this volume. But, like him, I think it is what should be said.

It is because human beings are endowed with capacities through which they can realize a distinctive kind of goodness that they possess the dignity they do. So dignity attaches to our natural constitution understood as having an immanent *telos*. Aquinas's general definition of dignity is 'something's goodness on account of itself (*propter seipsum*)'.[23] The distinctive goodness which belongs to us in virtue of being human consists in the fact that we are equipped by nature for a transcendent fulfilment, we are born with a dynamic orientation to such a fulfilment. It is intellect and will which equip us for this fulfilment as capacities to know the truth and to choose to do what is good. We enjoy the freedom of self-determination to succeed or fail in these respects. So the radical capacity[24] for self-determination is an intrinsic feature of what makes for our dignity. But in its exercise it does so not by some autonomous determination of what is to count as valuable but rather by choosing to act in the knowledge of what are the true goods of the human form of life. And it is the necessities of preserving or realizing these goods that is at the root of obligations.

Since we are social animals, among these goods is the fundamental good of justice, of right relationships between human beings. And fundamental to the good of justice is the prohibition of murder which grounds the right not to be murdered.

One can find three concepts of human dignity in Aquinas's thought:[25] (1) the dignity which belongs to our constitution and

---

[22] Some are manifested *ab initio*, otherwise development could not get underway.

[23] *III Sent.* d. 35, q. 1, a. 4, sol. 1c.

[24] 'Radical' as possessed prior to its development as an exercisable capacity.

[25] Bearing in mind Aquinas's definition of dignity as 'something's goodness on account of itself', what is said here about 'levels' of human dignity follows from Aquinas's distinctions about the 'imago Dei' in man in *Summa theologiae* 1, q. 93, a. 4: '[...] we see that the image of God is in man in three ways. First, inasmuch as man possesses a natural aptitude for understanding and loving God; and this aptitude consists in the very nature of the mind, which is common to all men. Secondly, inasmuch as man actually or habitually knows and loves God, though imperfectly; and this image consists in the conformity of grace. Thirdly, inasmuch as man knows and loves God perfectly; and this

the immanent *telos* of our nature, the one I've been discussing, which one might call 'intrinsic dignity', a dignity which one cannot lose;[26] (2) the dignity of those who live a virtuous life, which one might call 'acquired dignity',[27] and which one might fail to acquire and, if acquired, lose; and (3) the definitive dignity of those who have achieved our human destiny, the dignity of 'beatitude'.

It is important to be clear that it is intrinsic not acquired dignity which enters into Anscombe's explanation of why capital punishment (at least in principle if not in practice) and tyrannicide can be consistent with respect for human dignity if those killed get what they deserved. For to hold someone deserving of death is to see them as 'moving in the categories of answerability and desert'. But the dignity that is being implicitly affirmed in judgments of desert is not the acquired dignity of the criminal or the tyrant, which one assumes they inadequately exhibit, but the dignity that attaches to the capacities which make possible movement in the categories of 'answerability and desert'. This is respected precisely in holding someone to account and deserving of death.

I earlier quoted Anscombe as saying that the 'existence' of the person murdered 'is counted as worth nothing in comparison with the ends of others'. But, on the face of it, it is the person to be killed who makes the judgment about the worth of his life in the case of voluntary euthanasia, and the ends of others don't seem to enter into consideration. Do considerations of human dignity stand in the way of voluntary euthanasia? If one locates value in the will, i.e. if one holds that what is to count as valuable in a life is determined by the choice of an individual, then one may well have a conception of human dignity which commends voluntary euthanasia as a reasonable choice. For a decision for euthanasiast killing seems clearly based, when voluntary, on the would-be decedent's judgment that his life is no longer worth living.

---

image consists in the likeness of glory.' For commentary see Jaroslav Pelikan, 'Imago Dei: An Explication of *Summa theologiae*, Part 1, Question 93' in A. Parel (ed.), *Calgary Aquinas Studies* (Toronto: Pontifical Institute of Medieval Studies, 1978), pp. 27–48.

[26] See *Summa theologiae*, I–II, q. 85, a. 1c.

[27] In a number of previous publications I've referred to 'intrinsic dignity' as 'connatural dignity', and 'acquired dignity' as 'existential dignity', but readers have found these terms ambiguous.

For anyone who thinks, as Anscombe clearly did, that human beings possess intrinsic human dignity,[28] the question arises whether a person's judgment that his life is no longer worth living is compatible with respecting the dignity of that person. When we are discussing euthanasia we are discussing one human being killing another. Advocates of legalization would have doctors do the killing. Since doctors are themselves responsible agents and not automata, their justification for killing must be that they concur in their patient's judgment that his life is no longer worth living. In agreeing with the patient who says 'It's simply not worth continuing to live in the wretched condition I'm in' are they thereby committed to saying that the patient lacks fundamental worth or dignity? Surely the judgments are distinguishable in what they refer to; in the one case, the worthwhileness of living in a certain condition, in the other, the value of a person. But if you talk about the value (or dignity) of a person you are talking about something which holds good of the *actuality* of that person. To say that something has value though its *actual existence* lacks value is surely nonsense. There may be a notional distinction between the thought that a person's life is not worth going on with and the thought that the person, whose life it is, lacks value. But the former thought surely commits one to the latter thought. To think otherwise seems to rest on the assumption that the *being* of a human person is distinct from his or her ongoing life. But a human person just is a living human body, and the life of that person (i.e. the *being* of that person—*esse viventibus est vivere*) is the life of that body. Hence to say that the ongoing life of a particular living human being is not worthwhile is to deny value to the person whose life it is.[29]

This matters because, as Anscombe makes clear, justice in the matter of killing rests on the valuation one recognizes in being a human being. Those who deny the existence of intrinsic human

---

[28] See, e.g., her statement: 'There is just one impregnable equality of all human beings. It lies in the value and dignity of being a human being.' 'The Dignity of the Human Being', in *HLAE*, p. 67.

[29] I here largely repeat what I said in response to an objection from The Rev Dr Gerald Gleeson at a seminar I gave at the John Plunkett Centre for Ethics in Health Care in Sydney on 10 November 1995. The Proceedings of the Seminar were published by the Centre in 1996: Luke Gormally, *Why the Select Committee on Medical Ethics of the House of Lords Unanimously Rejected the Legalization of Euthanasia*. See pp. 21–22.

dignity and see dignity in voluntaristic terms, i.e. as determined by a person's own choices, face a quite fundamental difficulty over what is to count as justice in the matter of killing. It is common in the contemporary literature of bioethics to associate the notion of dignity with self-determination to the point that what is to count as the value of a life is determined by the person whose life it is. But self-conferral of value assumes a developed capacity to do so, and there are developmental stages in the life of a human being during which no such exercisable capacity exists, and there can be periods of decline and debility during which any such capacity may be lost. At what point in development the capacity for self-valuation emerges and at what point it is lost are things unavoidably determined in a more or less arbitrary fashion. But if justice in the matter of killing rests on the valuation of a human life there can't be justice where who counts as possessing value or dignity is determined in an arbitrary fashion.[30]

It would be a pragmatic solution to this difficulty, arising for those who deny the existence of intrinsic dignity but instead distinguish between mere biological life and 'personal life' as a phase in the existence of a human being, if they were to grant that a non-arbitrary determination of who are the subjects of justice requires the assumption that all living human beings have some title to be treated justly. But as the candidate title to the right not to be murdered is indeed intrinsic human dignity the assumption is not readily entertained. It is not entertained for two reasons: the continuing influence of post-Cartesian mechanism in the understanding of human life, and rejection of the doctrine of creation which provides the ultimate explanation for the anthropology which underpins the notion of intrinsic human dignity. For the explanation for the existence of natures immanently ordered to specific ends is the Divine Creative Intelligence.[31] So what underpins the immanent ordering of human nature to a distinctive kind of goodness, an ordering in which the dignity of being human

---

[30] The arbitrariness in question here—over who is to count as entitled to just treatment—is of an altogether different order from the kind of arbitrariness which is often unavoidable in defining many social rules (e.g. in respect of membership of clubs). The latter does not affect one's most basic claims to just treatment.

[31] The reference here is to Aquinas's 'Fifth Way'; see *Summa theologiae* I, q. 2, a. 3. For a brief and lucid exposition see Edward Feser, *Aquinas* (Oxford: One World, 2009), pp. 110–120.

consists, is divine creation. This means that the notion of intrinsic human dignity is at root a religious concept.

Anscombe speaks of it as such most clearly when she considers propaganda in favour of death as a remedy for suffering. Such propaganda, she says, is 'irreligious'. A religious attitude to the mystery of human life may be incipient or developed. In its incipient form it refuses 'to make a "quality of life" judgment to terminate a human being'. In its developed form it is responsive to the *telos* of every human being—as made by God, to know and love him.

> The love of God is the direction of the will to its true end. The human heart and will are set on amenity; they may also be set on what is just[32]; that is (when it comes to dying) set in acceptance of life—which is God's gift—and of death, as it comes from him. [...] [W]here there is intellectual consciousness [...] the human being operates under one or the other of these conceptions of what counts ultimately for him: either amenity only, or acceptance, which is obedience in spirit, which is justice. Acceptance of life and death is what justice is in circumstances of unavoidable dying: it is accord with God's will. Such perception of what a human being is makes one perceive human death as awesome, human life as always to be treated with a respect which is a sign and acknowledgement of what it is for.[33]

That last phrase confirms, I think, the specific teleological understanding of human life which grounds Anscombe's understanding of human dignity and therefore of the valuation of human life which lies behind her understanding of the ethics of killing.

3. Distinguishing what is intended from side effects

What in particular cases is to count as intentional killing of the innocent depends on clearly distinguishing between the intended consequences of an action from what are identifiable as side effects. There is controversy about whether Anscombe was consistent in drawing the distinction. John Finnis, for example, thinks Anscombe's 1982 paper 'Action, Intention and "Double Effect"'[34] deploys an 'ethics-oriented analysis' that overlooks 'the act-analysis (intention-analysis) employed in her non-ethical

---

[32] See St Anselm, *De Casu Diaboli*, c. 12. [Anscombe's reference.]
[33] 'Murder and the Morality of Euthanasia', pp. 269–270.
[34] Reprinted in *HLAE*, pp. 207–226.

writings'.[35] Specifically, he objected to the following observations in Anscombe's discussion of the case of the stuck pot-holer blocking escape for his companions from rising waters; they can escape if they move a rock which, however, will involve crushing the head of the man who is stuck.

> All this is relevant to our pot-holer only where the crushing of his head is an immediate effect of moving the rock. Here a ground for saying you can intend to move the rock and not intend to crush the head is that you might not know that in moving the rock you would crush the head. [...] But if you *do* know, then where the crushing is immediate you cannot pretend not to intend it if you are willing to move the rock.[36]

Two paragraphs before this Anscombe made the general observation: 'Circumstances and the immediate facts about the means you are choosing to your ends, dictate what descriptions of your intention you must admit.'

Finnis comments as follows:

> I think this attempt to distinguish the intended from the unintended by reference to sheer physical 'immediacy' of cause and effect is unsound, a confusion of categories, an elision of human behaviour with human action. I know of no *argument* that Anscombe has brought against her own analysis, twenty five years earlier in her book *Intention*, of the intentions of the man who pumps poisoned water into a house. In one variant of the situation, 'the man's intention might not be to poison [the inhabitants] but only to earn his pay' by doing his usual job:
>
>> In that case although he knows concerning an intentional action of his—for it, namely replenishing the house water-supply, is intentional by our criteria—that it is *also* an act of replenishing the house-water-supply with *poisoned* water, it would be incorrect by our criteria, to say that his act of replenishing the house supply with poisoned water was intentional. And I do not doubt the correctness of the conclusion; it seems to shew that our criteria are rather good.[37]

Notice how fine-grained is the analysis which Anscombe accepted as correct: not merely that the poisoning of the inhabitants—which

---

[35] See John Finnis, 'Anscombe on Spirit and Intention', in his *Intention & Identity. Collected Essays: Volume II* [hereafter: Finnis, *Intention & Identity*] (Oxford: Oxford University Press, 2011), p. 77.

[36] 'Action, Intention and "Double Effect"', p. 224.

[37] *I*, p. 42 (para. 25).

is not physically 'immediate'—is not intentional, but that the *replenishing of the house water supply with poisoned water* is not intentional [because that the water be poisoned is not part of the pumper's proposal, *viz.* to do his usual job of replenishing the water supply]. Nothing could be more 'immediate' than the known presence of the poison in the water supply: as *behaviour*, replenishing the supply with water *just is*, in this case replenishing it with poisoned water. Yet the criteria for a sound analysis of intention(ality) and that of *action* require that we distinguish knowingly pumping in poisoned water from intentionally pumping in poisoned water (or: pumping water with intent to contaminate the water supply). That the water supply be poisoned was, for this man on this occasion, a side effect.[38]

Finnis is of the view that the head-crushing should be seen as a side effect because 'that the head be crushed' is no necessary part of a *proposal* adopted on the basis of deliberation to seek egress from the cave by moving the stone. Like considerations are supposed to allow a doctor who has performed a craniotomy (by emptying a baby's skull and then crushing it in a case of obstructed labour) to say:

> 'No way do I intend to kill the baby' and 'It is no part of my purpose to kill the baby'.[39]

The death of the baby is to be classified as a side effect rather than part of what is intended by the doctor. The object of the act—what is intended—'is to reduce the size of the baby's head so that the baby or its corpse can be removed from the birth canal'.[40]

The general thesis lying behind these delimitations of what is intended is that

> [...] one's intention is defined by one's practical reason in terms of the desirability characterization under which one wills the end and the description under which one judges one's chosen means appropriate to that end.[41]

In other words, the desirability characterization of one's end/purpose controls the specification of what one is prepared to count as means to achieving it. The thesis abstracts practical reasoning about means from consideration of their intrinsic efficacy as

---

[38] 'Intention and Side Effects' in Finnis, *Intention & Identity*, pp. 192–193.
[39] 'Direct and Indirect in Action', in Finnis, *Intention & Identity*, p. 251.
[40] 'Direct and Indirect in Action', in Finnis, *Intention & Identity*, p. 252.
[41] 'Intention and Side Effects', in Finnis, *Intention & Identity*, p. 189.

characterizing those means. But it is surely only insofar as they have a certain *kind* of efficacy that an agent chooses the means he does. He therefore cannot fail to enjoy practical certainty that what he concretely aims to do has an intrinsic kind of causal efficacy.

Anscombe's *Intention* was based on the lectures she gave in Oxford in the Hilary Term of the academic year 1956–57 following the debate about what precisely President Truman intended in signing the order to drop the atomic bombs on Hiroshima and Nagasaki. There were those who were saying that all the man did was sign a piece of paper, so why was Anscombe objecting [in 1956] to Oxford University conferring an honorary degree on him? What Anscombe was interested in exploring for her audience was how to determine what an agent intended in doing whatever he did. And to that end what he had to *say* in response to the question 'Why are you doing X?' would have particular relevance if it identified the agent's reasons for doing what he did.[42] The 'Why?' question is not seeking an answer based on observation or inferences from observation but looks for a spontaneous answer that reveals the agent's end and chosen means. 'Spontaneous', because answers to 'Why?' questions exhibit the non-observational practical knowledge which is 'the cause of what it understands'[43] 'It is the agent's knowledge of what he is doing that gives the descriptions under which what is going on is the execution of intention.'[44] Those descriptions exhibit a teleological pattern of means to end identified by a succession of 'Why?' questions prompted by interest in establishing the precise

---

[42] One should note that Anscombe was of the view that much of what an agent intended would be evident prior to asking him or her 'Why are you doing X?': 'Well, if you want to say at least some true things about a man's intentions, you will have a strong chance of success if you mention what he actually did or is doing. For whatever else he may intend, or whatever may be his intentions in doing what he does, the greater number of things you would say straight off a man did or was doing, will be things he intends.' *I*, p. 8. Contrast with this Finnis, 'Introduction', *Intention & Identity*, p. 13: 'But the actions and reasoning towards the choice(s) whose carrying out is what human action centrally is, are complex and often subtle. Transparent to a really clear-headed chooser, they are for observers always more or less a matter of inference or of belief in testimony [...]'

[43] *I*, p. 87. See also p. 47: 'It is in fact only if the thought "I'm only doing my usual job" is spontaneous rather than deliberate that its occurrence has some face-value relevance to the question what the man's intentions really are.'

[44] *I*, p. 87.

relevance of what he is doing to the *intention with which he is acting* (his end/purpose). The description of the means identifies 'How' the agent's purpose is achieved.

'It is a person's knowledge of what he is doing that gives the descriptions under which what is going on is the execution of intention.' What are the implications of this for the subject of craniotomy? Anscombe published nothing on this topic in her life but there are two short manuscripts about it among her papers. The relevant part of the text of the first one[45] is as follows:

> 'Certainty' comes into the question whether doing this is *eo ipso* doing that.
>
> E.g. shooting an arrow is not *eo ipso* transfixing a man, so you might shoot an arrow in a certain direction for a certain purpose without having to be *eo ipso* intentionally transfixing a man. But there might be *danger* that you would transfix a man; and then the question of your accusability in that matter, if a man got transfixed, would be determined by the gravity of the *need* to shoot the arrow in that direction, weighed against the greatness of the risk and the gravity of what it is a risk of.
>
> But if your purpose in shooting the arrow is one that can only be attained *by transfixing* a man, so that transfixing a man is your

---

[45] In AIA 240. The full text is published in Luke Gormally, 'Intention and Side Effects: John Finnis and Elizabeth Anscombe', in John Keown and Robert P. George (eds.), *Reason, Morality and Law: The Philosophy of John Finnis* [hereafter: Keown & George, *Reason, Morality and Law*] (Oxford: Oxford University Press, 2013), pp. 96–97. The relevant part of the second text, AIA 312, reads as follows: 'The strict doctrine says: Don't kill intentionally, don't kill as a means or as an end. Now when it's an end (as in most modern abortion) that's unambiguous: *this life is wanted out of the way*, we don't want to be lumbered with it. When the killing is a means, as in more old fashioned medical abortion, the life isn't wanted done away with, it's just that the killing was done because without it it was thought the end (saving the mother) couldn't be achieved. Now that being so, someone could say the death, if you like, can be called unintended, it's just that you have to cut the head off, *that's* intentional, but the death can be called a side effect. The answer of course was: don't be absurd, as things are you can't intend to cut someone's head off without intending to kill him: it's not a question of what *you feel a desire for*. To this is objected: if *as things are* in any particular case you can't do A without B being involved, how can you, in any particular case, say that A can be intended, B not? It is a question of (a) whether this head being cut off is a way of effecting your aim, and (b) whether the head off is death. In another case, even though you *can't* do A without B being involved, the occurrence of A isn't the occurrence of B, so the fact that bringing A about is a way of effecting your aim doesn't mean the bringing B about is.'

means to the accomplishment of the purpose, *then* you could not argue that you were only *transfixing* him with the arrow, not damaging him with the arrow, on the ground that your purpose would be attained by transfixing without damage, were that possible. For *if* transfixing a man with an arrow is certainly damaging him, and *if* you may absolutely not try to damage him, you may not try to transfix him.

Thus the question is not: 'may I do so-and-so with my hands?' but 'may I cut off the child's head?' Thus in one way certainty of upshot is not what is in question. For the question is: what is the agent trying to do? In the case of the shooting the answer is: to transfix the man (let us suppose). And this may not be a *certain* result of 'the way he moves his hands'. Similarly, then, for the surgeon: the relevant immediacy is not that between how he moves his hands and the child's death, but between what he is trying to do *in* moving his hands and the child's death.

Why should we think that a doctor, in carrying out a craniotomy, enjoys a certainty about what he is aiming to do which does not allow him to refuse application of the question 'Why are you killing the baby?'? It is because to evacuate the contents of the skull of an unborn baby and then crush it is *eo ipso* to kill the baby. In the case of *eo ipso* act identities, the applicability of an act description (in this case 'killing the baby') to what the agent is doing does not derive from the articulation of the practical reasoning of the agent (as 'replenishing the water supply' applies to 'pumping the water') but rather from the character of the intrinsic efficacy required by the practical reasoning which informs one's chosen action together with what anyone can know who knows enough about the world. *Eo ipso* act identities reflect this. And it would be normal that one enjoyed certainty that they characterized what one intended to do; in that way they would become a part of practical knowledge. In the case of craniotomy, 'killing the baby' is applicable in virtue of the intrinsic efficacy of what the surgeon chooses to do and of the role of skull and brains in the life of a human being. Since, then, the question 'Why are you killing the baby?' has legitimate application one can call killing the baby intentional under that description.[46]

In reply to this claim Finnis observes:

---

[46] Part of what I say in this paragraph is indebted to observations made by Roger Teichmann on my paper published in Keown & George, *Reason, Morality and Law*.

For so too, no more and no less, B's pumping of poisoned water into the house 'just was', 'also', '*eo ipso*', poisoning the water supply, yet equally (as Anscombe in *Intention* holds) it simply *was not* the intentional [...] act of poisoning the water supply.[47]

The water pumper, however, acts under the description 'replenishing the water supply' (with a view to doing his usual job) not under the description 'poisoning the water supply'. So the poisoned character of the water has no role to play in his chosen mode of causal activity. What he is up to in what he chooses to do is not *of its nature* 'poisoning activity'.

By contrast, a surgeon who says that all he is interested in is reducing 'the size of the baby's head so that the baby or its corpse can be removed from the birth canal' may reasonably be asked the question 'How do you propose to do that?'. And the answer, 'by evacuating the contents of the baby's skull and then crushing it', identifies an intentional act which *under that description* is intrinsically lethal.

Finnis says that my analysis 'obliterates [a host of] act-analytical and humanly real distinctions' such as between 'jumping from the top of the World Trade Centre on 9/11 to escape the oily fireball and jumping to commit suicide; [...] between giving a life-shortening dose of analgesics as the only dose that will suppress a terminally ill patient's pain and giving the same dose to shorten her life and "unblock" her bed'.[48]

I can best explain the basis of my response to this criticism by quoting what I wrote some years ago:

> Just as there are *per se* effects of natural causes so there are *per se* effects of intentional acts, effects that a particular kind of intentional act tends to produce. And such effects are part of the significance of what one chooses to do in choosing to do that type of act. It may be that what is of particular significance for an agent in what he chooses to do does not make explicit all that belongs to the meaning of his chosen action, but *if the description of the act under which he chooses to perform it identifies an aspect of its efficacy which tends of its nature to produce another effect then that other effect belongs to the meaning of what he does.* That this other effect belongs to the proper characterization of what a person intentionally does follows from the nature of the type of causal efficacy chosen to achieve the precise effect the acting person seeks to achieve. It is

---

[47] Keown & George, *Reason, Morality and Law*, p. 481.
[48] Keown & George, *Reason, Morality and Law*, p. 481.

because it is in the nature of a particular kind of causal efficacy to tend to produce a particular kind of effect, that one can speak of entailment between cause and effect, such that if it is intrinsic to the meaning of a doing of X that it tends to be a doing of Y one cannot say that one is not choosing to do Y in choosing to do X, or that Y is simply a side effect of doing X. It is important to recognise that the entailment is such as to characterise one's *intention*.[49]

And that is because the chosen mode of causal efficacy is identifiable *by the description under which one chooses to act.*

What does this mean for 'the humanly real distinctions' that Finnis says I have obliterated? In the case of the World Trade Centre escapee, one can be fairly certain that his jump was chosen *qua* avoidance of being burnt alive. Its efficacy in that respect did not entail his death. By contrast, the suicide jumper chooses to jump precisely with a view to the jump's efficacy in causing his own death.

A doctor who administers very high doses of analgesics *qua* apt to control otherwise uncontrollable pain chooses to do so with a view to their efficacy *in that respect*, and their efficacy in that respect is not as such lethal.[50] By contrast, a doctor who administers the same dose to kill his patient chooses to do so with a view to its being lethally efficacious. And a doctor who chooses to control painful breathing by giving drugs in quantities aimed precisely at totally suppressing respiration intends to kill his patient.

In the final section of this chapter I have sought to show reason for Anscombe's position on craniotomy[51] by arguing that there is a

---

[49] Luke Gormally, 'Personal and Social Responsibility in the Context of the Defence of Human Life: The Question of Cooperation in Evil', in Elio Sgreccia and Jean Laffitte (eds.), *Christian Conscience in Support of the Right to Life* (Vatican City: Libreria Editrice Vaticana, 2008), pp. 92–111, at 99–100. Text also available online at www.academiavita.org/_pdf/assemblies/13/Christian_conscience_in_support_of_the_right_to_life.pdf, at pp. 58–70.

[50] Contemporary palliative care physicians are understandably irritated by moralists using the administration of analgesics with lethal effect as a standard example in discussions of double effect. As they point out, carefully titrated administration of analgesia will more often delay rather than hasten dying in those who are terminally ill.

[51] In this chapter I leave aside discussion of whether in the case of the potholers their prior certainty that what they intended to do would immediately cause the crushing of the head of the man stuck in the entrance to the cave amounted to the intention to crush his head.

kind of 'immediacy' to what a person does which arises from the intrinsic causal character[52] of his chosen course of action and which implies that the character of one's means in acting cannot be delimited 'by what one chose, under the description which made it attractive to choice'.[53] The *per se* effects of intentional acts means that the killing which is involved in craniotomy cannot be described as a state of affairs 'which one foresees will result from carrying out one's plan or proposal, but *which one does not need or want* as part of one's way of bringing about what one plans or proposes to bring about'.[54] One surely does not want it, but there is reason to think that what one aims to do in craniotomy is unavoidably intentional killing of the innocent.[55,56]

---

[52] It will be evident that my argument rests on the Aristotelian claim that efficient causality is not adequately intelligible without the notion of final causality and so rejects Humean notions of causation which seem to be assumed by those who divorce their understanding of intention from notions of causal efficacy. I comment further on this in the paper referred to in footnote 49.

[53] 'Intention and Side Effects', in Finnis, *Intention & Identity*, p. 191.

[54] 'Human Acts', in Finnis, *Intention & Identity*, p. 143, emphasis added.

[55] One should not think of craniotomy in obstetric emergencies as wholly a thing of the past. It is a procedure which is not infrequently employed in countries where health services are seriously under-resourced. See, for example, Shane Duffy, 'Obstetric Haemorrhage in Gimbie, Ethiopia', *The Obstetrician and Gynaecologist* 9, 2007:121–126, recording eight cases of 'destructive craniotomy-aided vaginal delivery' in an audit of 595 consecutive deliveries in Gimbie Hospital in 2005.

[56] I am indebted to Fr Kevin Flannery SJ, David Albert Jones, and Roger Teichmann for their critical observations on previous drafts of this chapter.

David Goodill OP

Elizabeth Anscombe on Just War

1. Anscombe's three papers on war

Elizabeth Anscombe wrote three papers on the subject of justice and war.[1] The first paper, 'The Justice of the Present War Examined',[2] was the first part of a pamphlet co-authored with Norman Daniel in 1939 in response to the British entry into war with Germany. The second, 'Mr Truman's Degree',[3] put forward the case against President Truman receiving an honorary degree from Oxford in 1956, and the third[4] was published as part of the collection *Nuclear Weapons: A Catholic Response*, edited by Walter Stein in 1961.[5] The earliest paper is concerned with both the just conditions for entering into war (*Jus ad bellum*) and with the proposed means of fighting the war (*Jus in bello*), whereas the latter two focus largely on the conditions for justice within war (*Jus in bello*), particularly in relation to the use of nuclear weapons.

In each of these papers Anscombe sought to apply principles of justice derived from natural moral law to the conditions of contemporary warfare. In this sense they can be seen as contributions to the tradition of Just War Theory.[6] Thus in the paper written in 1939 she was to write:

---

[1] I would like to thank Dr Michael Black, Professor David Jones and Rev Dr Robert Ombres OP for their discussion of and comments on this chapter.
[2] Reprinted in *CPP3*, pp. 72–81.
[3] Reprinted in *CPP3*, pp. 62–71.
[4] Reprinted in *CPP3*, pp. 51–61.
[5] Walter Stein, *Nuclear Weapons: A Catholic Response* (London: The Merlin Press Ltd, 1961).
[6] Talk of a just war tradition can give the impression of a unified theory, however, the application of principles of justice to war has developed through

> It is our duty to resist passion and to consider carefully whether all the conditions of a just war are satisfied in this present war, lest we sin against the natural law by participating in it.[7]

She further underlines the central importance of natural moral law by arguing that: 'The idea of natural moral law is one which modern men have lost; but without it they cannot live in peace within themselves, or socially, or internationally.'[8] Here a number of things are held to be true. Firstly, that natural moral law does exist. Secondly, that modern people have lost an idea of this law, and thirdly that without an idea of this law modern people cannot live in peace. The implication of this analysis is that the state of conflict in Europe on the eve of the Second World War resulted from the loss of this idea. Furthermore, Anscombe argued throughout the three papers on war that entering into and conducting a war outside the natural moral law will not lead to a state of peace, in fact quite the opposite. Thus towards the end of the paper a lengthy quotation from Pope Pius XII's first encyclical, *Summi pontificatus*, is given in which the Pontiff warns that a victory not founded upon justice will breed further violence.

Anscombe's case against the justice of the war being entered into by the United Kingdom in 1939 is thus built upon the application of principles taken from the just war tradition to contemporary events. There are seven conditions for just war listed in 'The Justice of the Present War Examined',[9] which cover both conditions for entering into war and those for just conduct within war.[10]

---

a varied and complex historical process which makes talk of *a* tradition somewhat misleading. I use the term 'just war tradition' with this in mind, in a similar way to that in which the term 'natural law tradition' is used as a useful term for referring to a complex and varied group of theories, principles, laws and practices. For an account of the complex history of just war tradition see James Turner Johnson, *Just War Tradition and the Restraint of War: A Moral and Historical Inquiry* (Princeton: Princeton University Press, 1981).

[7] CPP3, p. 72.
[8] CPP3, p. 72.
[9] CPP3, p. 73.
[10] In listing these seven conditions Anscombe follows the standard list given in manuals of moral theology current at the time. Oliver O'Donovan notes in his book on just war that the distinction between conditions *ad bellum* and conditions *in bello* is a later modern division, and James Turner Johnson traces the expansion of these conditions to seven to the modern period. See Oliver

In regard to the application of principles of justice to modern warfare there are two principal challenges. The first challenge accepts the legitimacy of just war tradition, but argues that it is impossible to conduct modern wars justly. Thus, it may be argued[11] that the power and mobility of modern weapons makes discrimination in their usage virtually impossible, and inevitably leads to a greater balance of evil over good as the result of war. Such arguments depend upon analysis of modern weaponry and particular conflicts, and thus cannot make a case which would rule out the just use of force in every case of modern war. In 'War and Murder' Anscombe rejects the argument that: 'The old "conditions for a just war" are irrelevant to the conditions of modern warfare, so that must be condemned out of hand.'[12] She argues that those who use this argument have in mind 'only major wars between the Great Powers',[13] but these are not the only kinds of modern wars.

The second challenge to the application of just conditions to modern warfare argues that the conditions for just war developed within the just war tradition are contradictory.[14] Thus it is not directed specifically to contemporary conditions, but seeks to show that any attempt in any historical period to justify war on the basis of principles of justice fails. Such arguments can be made by those who are advocating pacifism, but, as Anscombe notes in 'War and Murder', the pacifist argument that war is of its nature contrary to justice can convince those who are not pacifist that war is an area where principles of ruthless effectiveness should prevail:

> Now pacifism teaches people to make no distinction between the shedding of innocent blood and the shedding of any human blood.

O'Donovan, *The Just War Revisited, Current Issues in Theology* (Cambridge & New York: Cambridge University Press, 2003).

[11] For an examination of the justice of modern warfare see James Turner Johnson, *Can Modern War Be Just?* (New Haven: Yale University Press, 1984).

[12] *CPP3*, pp. 59–60.

[13] *CPP3*, p. 60.

[14] For an example of such an attack on the coherence of Just War Theory see David Rodin, *War and Self Defence* (Oxford & New York: Clarendon Press, 2002). The argument which we will examine by Nicholas Denyer is also of this kind, see his 'Just War', in Roger Teichmann (ed.) *Logic, Cause & Action: Essays in Honour of Elizabeth Anscombe, Royal Institute of Philosophy Supplement* (Cambridge & New York: Cambridge University Press, 2000), pp. 137–151.

And in this way pacifism corrupted enormous numbers of people who will not act according to its tenets. They become convinced that a number of things are wicked which are not; hence seeing no way of avoiding wickedness, they set no limits to it.[15]

Given the attacks on Just War Theory, is there an alternative means of limiting the violence of war, one which does not require agreement on a controversial moral theory? We may be given encouragement in such a venture by observing that the setting of limitations on war is not exclusively the concern of the just war tradition, and international law has played a primary role in drawing limits to the violence of war since the Second World War. Should we, with the hindsight of the last sixty years, conclude that Anscombe's argument here is somewhat overstated? Could it be argued that in the light of challenges to Just War Theory we no longer require a shared moral framework for drawing the limits of war, but that international law provides an effective set of limits without the need for moral justification? In this chapter I will examine a challenge put forward by Nicholas Denyer[16] to the notion of just war in general and in particular against Anscombe's use of just war principles. In defence of Anscombe's position I will use a key principle she draws upon in her understanding of the legitimacy of killing, and in so doing seek to show that not only are her own writings on just war coherent, but they contain an essential principle in understanding how principles of justice are to be applied to war. Moreover, I will argue that Anscombe's analysis of the legitimacy of killing in war can be extended to cases of killing within the state to provide a rationale, but also a limit, for the killing of enemies within the state for the sake of the common good.

2. Denyer's criticism of Anscombe and the just war tradition

Nicholas Denyer, in his essay 'Just War',[17] argues that the limitation of violence in war makes no sense according to principles of justice, but should be seen as the task of international law. In particular Denyer argues that the medieval moral distinction between innocence and non-innocence is incapable of providing

---

[15] *CPP3*, p. 59.
[16] Denyer, 'Just War'.
[17] Denyer, 'Just War'.

the basis upon which war can be conducted. In contrast he argues that international law has developed a distinction between combatants and non-combatants which does not use 'moral-cum-causal criteria: nothing about wrong enters in the law's definitions of these notions'.[18] Denyer asserts that the distinction between non-combatants and combatants is not a moral one, but offers no rationale for this assertion beyond the observation that it is used in international law. I will follow Anscombe in arguing that this distinction does have a moral basis, but one which is of a different nature to that between innocent and guilty (see section 3 below). In the meantime I will refer to it as a legal distinction, but this does not entail it is not also a moral distinction.

Denyer's purpose in criticizing Just War Theory is not to undermine objective morality, nor is it to elevate positive law, rather his intentions are moral and pacifist. If we accept that there is no just basis on which to conduct war, and if we accept that war is an evil, then:

> The best course of all may be to abolish war itself, and therefore abolish with it those institutions whose violence creates the need for a law of war. That would require one world state, or else no states whatsoever.[19]

I do not have the scope in this chapter to comment on Denyer's pacifist solution to war. He is not proposing a naïve solution to war: 'it achieves nothing simply to forbid violence between states. Better then that their violence be channelled and limited by the law of war.'[20] Nor is he saying that such limitations are purely legal with no moral basis. The use of 'better' here indicates that the legal limitation of violence has a moral purpose. What he is objecting to is the notion that war itself can be morally justified. To this end he compares warfare with the practice of duelling between aristocrats:

> So long as there was an aristocracy, whose members had the power to conduct disputes between themselves by force, it was as well for there to be the institution of duelling, to channel and limit the damage done.[21]

---

[18] Denyer, 'Just War', p. 144.
[19] Denyer, 'Just War', p. 151.
[20] Denyer, 'Just War', p. 151.
[21] Denyer, 'Just War', p. 150.

Denyer's point here is that, in the same way that we would not think of duelling aristocrats as conducting their fight on the basis of justice, so we should not think of warring states as fighting according to just principles. The analogy here developed would seem to be persuasive so long as we accept Denyer's premise that the distinction between non-combatant and combatant is a non-moral distinction based upon law and lacking a moral basis. He criticizes Anscombe for her attempt to derive this legal distinction from the moral distinction between innocence and non-innocence.[22]

Denyer provides three arguments to show how the distinction between innocent and non-innocent differs from the distinction between non-combatant and combatant. I will focus here on his third argument, which I believe is his most compelling. Denyer's third argument is that: 'there are of necessity combatants on both sides, whereas according to our twin principles there need be nocents[23] only on one, the side without a just cause.'[24] This lack of parallel is for Denyer the essential factor in determining that not only must we distinguish non-combatant and combatant from innocence and non-innocence, but that the former distinction is in no way derivable from the latter. Here Denyer puts forward a series of arguments to establish the conclusion that the legal distinction is not compatible with the moral one. For example, he argues that law allows that: 'Combatants have a liberty right to use force';[25] in contrast, if we use the moral criterion, only those who are not guilty can legitimately use force. Similarly, he notes that in law combatants are not tried according to the standards of civilian guilt, and civilians are not entitled to conduct war against the guilty,[26] whereas a moral criterion would entail both of these.

It is outside the scope of this chapter to explore how international law is framed in these matters, but it is sufficient for my argument to make the general observation that the lack of coincidence between law and morality does not entail that law is not framed on the basis of morality. Although law may give a

---

[22] Denyer, 'Just War', p. 138.
[23] Denyer uses the word nocent rather than guilty, I will use the term non-innocent in place of Denyer's nocent.
[24] *Op. cit.*, p. 145.
[25] Denyer, 'Just War', p. 148.
[26] Denyer, 'Just War', p. 147; here Denyer notes that Anscombe argues 'that prisoners may not be tried and punished by the captor'.

party the legal right to do that which is morally wrong this does not entail that the party is not morally wrong in exercising that legal right. In the absence of effective international adjudication and enforcement the best option may be to allow this liberty right together with the risk of its abuse. It is the task of experts in international law and conflict to judge these matters. What is clear, however, is that the existence of such a legal right does not morally justify its exercise. Those who within the state do immoral things are not justified in doing so by the fact they are permitted to do so, nor are those who suffer the effects of these immoral actions wrong in using just means to combat them. Denyer's argument that international law provides a non-moral set of criteria for the conduct of war is only valid if it is assumed that the existence of a liberty right justifies its exercise. This in turn only makes sense if we have already accepted that what is permissible is defined by law alone with no reference to the natural moral law. But why accept this? In her writings on war Anscombe does not offer a defence of natural law, she does, however, issue a challenge to those who reject the idea of a natural moral law. The challenge is to show how without the idea of a natural moral law we can distinguish just from unjust killing. It is the application of natural moral law principles to contemporary conflicts which guided Anscombe in distinguishing between legitimate killing and murder. Here she argues that the general principle that rulers have the right to fight enemies of the common good applies not only within the state, but also to external struggle:

> [...] [T]here are occasions when the authority has to fight its internal enemy to the point of killing, as happens in the struggle with external belligerent forces in international warfare; and then the characterization of its enemy as non-innocent has not been ratified by legal process.[27]

We are left, nevertheless, with the task of showing *how* the legal distinction between non-combatants and combatants is justified according to the moral distinction between innocence and non-innocence. In other words we need to show how the legal distinction enables the rights of the innocent to be protected against the non-innocent.

---

[27] *CPP3*, p. 53.

3. A moral distinction?

It is necessary first to understand the nature of the distinction between non-combatant and combatant, before determining whether it can be derived from the distinction between innocent and non-innocent. In the previous section we noted how Denyer asserts that this distinction is a non-moral one,[28] but offers no argument for this assertion. Perhaps Denyer is taking it as self-evident that this is not a moral distinction on the grounds that external status in itself does not involve a judgment of innocence or guilt. Thus, the fact that an individual has the status of combatant does not in itself entail a judgment of innocence or guilt, because considered in itself taking on this status does not involve a moral judgment on the individual concerned, unless the status is one which of its nature is morally wrong. In concrete particular circumstances an individual will need to judge whether it is just to enter into this army under these circumstances,[29] but in itself becoming a soldier is not morally good or evil. What Denyer fails to see is that once an individual has taken on a particular role his or her moral status may change in certain respects. Thus teachers have certain rights and responsibilities in regard to their students which a non-teacher does not (for example expecting students to complete homework or helping students to pass exams).

It is the moral consequences of changing status from non-combatant to combatant that Anscombe draws attention to in her explanation of the justification for attacking combatants in war. Here she argues that force used against combatants is not dependent upon the moral guilt of the particular combatant, nor is the immunity of non-combatants dependent upon their lack of guilt. In Anscombe's paper 'Mr Truman's Degree' she argues that innocence in war is not a term referring to personal responsibility:

> Now who are 'the innocent' in war? They are all those who are not fighting and not engaged in supplying those who are with the means of fighting [...] 'Innocent' here is not a term referring to

---

[28] I thank Mary Geach for her comments in helping me to see that this is not a purely positive distinction.
[29] Such judgments are not unique to the military, since any individual considering whether or not to take on a special status (e.g. whether to become a teacher or an accountant) has to assess the particular circumstances in order to make the right decision.

personal responsibility at all. It means rather 'not harming'. But the people fighting are 'harming', so they can be attacked.[30]

She adds to this principle that, just as the police are only justified in using force proportionate to the immediate threat posed, so in warfare the force used against an enemy should be proportionate to the threat posed and have the objective of removing the threat, not of inflicting personal punishment: 'it is true that the enemy should not be attacked more ferociously than is necessary to put them *hors de combat*.'[31] Such measures are punitive insofar as they inflict harm upon an enemy as a response to the unjust use of force, but they are to be distinguished from the punishment that is imposed as a result of a judicial process establishing personal innocence and guilt.

It is important to be clear here what Anscombe is not saying. She is not saying that subjective guilt cannot be attributed to soldiers in war. Rather she is determining the principles for carrying out military action. In the case that a soldier knows that the cause he or she is fighting for is unjust, or is indifferent to the justice of the conflict, any injustice caused to the innocent is to some degree culpable. When a solider believes he or she is fighting for a just cause, but it turns out to be unjust, the personal responsibility of the soldier depends (among other factors, such as the degree of duress they are under in fighting) upon the degree to which he or she can be considered culpable for their wrong judgment. The category of combatant has developed to take this into account, by placing limits on the presumed responsibility of combatants. By limiting what may be done to combatants and how they are to be judged for their role in a given conflict,[32] it is accepted that combatants are often not in a position to determine the justice of the cause they are fighting for, and furthermore may be fighting under duress.

But can we say that their culpability could be completely removed? There may be cases in which a soldier is not subjectively guilty. Yet in such cases it cannot be said that the soldier is 'innocent' in the sense of not harming. An analogy with the appropriate

---

[30] *CPP3*, p. 67.
[31] *CPP3*, p. 67.
[32] Which is not to say that combatants cannot be held personally responsible for their actions, but allowance is made for the role they hold as combatant in making such judgments.

police response to criminal activity is instructive. Society has the right to protect itself against criminal activity even when those engaging in such activity are non-culpably ignorant of the fact they are committing crime. If we accept, as Anscombe does in 'War and Murder', that authority in society sometimes 'has to fight its internal enemy to the point of killing',[33] then there could be cases in which society is right in intentionally killing a person who is non-culpably ignorant of killing the innocent. Take for example the case in which a person presents a serious threat to others, and we can impute responsibility to that person for this threat.[34] There may be cases in which we cannot prevent this person from inflicting this harm other than by killing. Even if this person is not subjectively guilty of the crime they are committing they lose their status of innocent by their intention to inflict harm on others. This is a risk that anyone who seeks to seriously harm others runs, that in those cases in which a person's decision to use force turns out to be wrong, even when no culpability can be imputed to that person for this wrong decision, force can be used to prevent serious harm to the innocent; up to the point of killing.

4. Deriving non-combatant and combatant from innocent and non-innocent

So far we have established that the distinction between non-combatant and combatant involves a moral distinction, but we have yet to demonstrate how it is founded upon the moral distinction between innocence and non-innocence. The kind of demonstration I think is required here is one which draws upon the historical experience[35] of how the non-combatant/combatant distinction has served to limit violence against the innocent, whilst allowing for due punishment for those who act unjustly in war.

---

[33] CPP3, p. 53.
[34] Here I would argue that it is not only those who intend harm, but also those who without intending harm can be deemed responsible for bringing about harm to others, that Anscombe has in mind. For a person may inflict harm without intending to do so, but could nevertheless be regarded as responsible for causing that harm.
[35] This does not entail that the argument is relative to historical circumstances, but rather that it is only in concrete historical circumstances that the implications of a distinction such as this can be fully determined.

In his classic work *Just War Tradition and Restraint of War: A Moral and Historical Inquiry*[36] James Turner Johnson traces how the notion of non-combatant immunity developed in medieval theory and practice. Johnson's explanation begins with the interchangeability of the two principal terms used for war and armed conflict during the middle ages, *bellum* and *duellum*. Although they were clearly distinguished, *bellum* and *duellum* were often used interchangeably in the middle ages, thus Johnson notes:

> A *duellum* is essentially a private combat, even if it takes place within a *bellum*; the latter is essentially public combat. Yet at the same time every war, *bellum*, is in a secondary sense a duel, *duellum*, and under certain social conditions this secondary overlap in meaning can be of the greatest importance.[37]

This secondary overlapping of meaning enabled knightly codes of chivalry to be extended from individual combat to groups of knights, which was particularly important in developing the notion of non-combatant immunity, and hence in defining the conditions of what would later be termed *jus in bello*.[38] Here history would seem to support Denyer's picture according to which we see the notion of non-combatant immunity in war as the extension of aristocratic attempts to limit violence, rather than as the application of principles of justice. Yet Johnson argues that although our later notion of non-combatant immunity has an origin in knightly codes of chivalry, and retains to some degree features of this origin, it was also shaped by medieval canon law. Whereas knightly chivalry protected those non-combatants under the patronage of the knight so long as he was able to defend them: 'In the canon law, those persons named as non-combatants are spared the ravages of war by simple justice.'[39] The opposition Denyer draws between a medieval moral distinction and a modern legal distinction does not stand up to historical scrutiny. The history is far more complex than that of the replacement of a moral criterion with a non-moral legal distinction, and shows that the distinction was developed in the middle ages precisely in order to protect the innocent.

---

[36] See Johnson, *Just War Tradition and the Restraint of War: A Moral and Historical Inquiry*.
[37] Johnson, *Just War Tradition and the Restraint of War*, pp. 44–45.
[38] Johnson, *Just War Tradition and the Restraint of War*, p. 48.
[39] Johnson, *Just War Tradition and the Restraint of War*, p. 138.

By drawing upon this historical account we can see how the non-combatant/combatant distinction can be derived from that between innocent and non-innocent. Firstly, by limiting what can be done in war against combatants to what is required to remove the threat they pose it accepts that any punitive measures taken against enemy troops within the immediate action of a war is not based on what is proportionate to their subjective degree of guilt. This protects those who are subjectively innocent,[40] whilst allowing that justice can be served later. Secondly, non-combatants are protected from military attack, and hence justice is served in the case of the innocent, and in the case of the guilty justice is not denied, but can again be served at a later time. These arguments do not rely on the degree of overlap between non-combatant and combatant and innocent and non-innocent. In the case where every combatant is subjectively innocent of carrying out an unjust attack, by limiting our action against them to removing the harm they pose, we serve the cause of right, whilst limiting as much as possible the harm done to the subjectively innocent. Similarly, if most non-combatants happen to be subjectively guilty this does not prevent justice being carried out when military action is concluded. Anscombe does argue that combatants should not be tried on criminal charges, but qualifies this to say that this is not because they have no personal responsibility for their actions:

> [T]he people fighting are 'harming', so they can be attacked; but if they surrender they become in this sense innocent and so may not be maltreated or killed. Nor is there ground for trying them on a criminal charge; not, indeed, because a man has no personal responsibility for fighting, but because they are not the subjects of the state whose prisoners they are.[41]

Here I do not believe that Anscombe is denying in all circumstances that states can try those who are not its citizens: it is a clear principle of justice that those living in a foreign state or visiting are bound by the laws of that state (with the normal qualifications that we are not bound to obey unjust laws). I believe that what she is getting at is that in the case of war enemies have in no sense consented to obey the laws of the state they are fighting. This does

---

[40] I thank David Jones for pointing this out to me. Of course this does not just protect the just innocent, but also the guilty. In the case of the guilty proportionate punishment may be carried out after the end of the conflict.
[41] *CCP3*, p. 67.

not, however, absolve them from obeying the natural moral law, nor does it imply that international courts cannot establish penalties for those found guilty of infringing international law (where this embodies natural justice).

5. Intentionally killing the enemy

In chapter five of his book *In Defence of War*[42] Nigel Biggar defends the just war tradition against an attack made upon it by David Rodin.[43] Rodin's arguments in many respects run parallel to those put forward by Denyer, and Biggar responds through a restatement and defence of the just war tradition, in which he argues that war can legitimately be conducted for the sake of overcoming injustice, with the proviso that: 'it aims to defend genuine and important human goods against grave and unjust threat.'[44] Whilst I am in agreement with a great deal that Biggar has to say in his criticism of Rodin there is one central issue upon which I believe his approach to be confused, an issue which Anscombe more than any philosopher in recent history has helped us to see more clearly: intention. Biggar, like Anscombe, argues that it is legitimate to kill enemy combatants on the grounds that they are objectively doing harm, as opposed to judgments of subjective guilt:

> In rare cases unjust agents might not be at all guilty in fact, because although responsible for judging the moral quality of their own cause their ignorance of its injustice might be excusable; and in rarer cases this might be known to their just opponents. Nevertheless, their possession of a right not to be harmed does not lie entirely in the control of their own moral choices. Its loss can be caused by factors other than their incurring guilt. Their threatening or causing objective injustice is one factor, necessary but not sufficient.[45]

So far Biggar and Anscombe are in agreement, the point of difference emerges with the other factor which Biggar argues is necessary for an attack on the subjectively non-culpable. Biggar

---

[42] Nigel Biggar, *In Defence of War* (Oxford & New York: Oxford University Press, 2013).
[43] Rodin, *War and Self Defense*.
[44] Biggar, *In Defence of War*, p. 212.
[45] Biggar, *In Defence of War*, pp. 212–213.

argues that in attacking the subjectively non-culpable we should not intend to kill them:

> What is also necessary is that those who kill them do not intend (that is, maliciously want) their deaths, that they kill only as a last resort, and that they do so with proportionate reason.[46]

Biggar's account of intention is laid out in chapter three of *In Defence of War* in which he offers the following analysis of intention: 'to intend something is not just to *choose* it, but also to *want* it.'[47] Here Biggar fails to distinguish between motive, objective and intention in a context in which these distinctions are significant. In regard to the distinction between motive and intention Anscombe observes in *Intention* that although:

> Popularly motive and intention are not treated as so distinct in meaning [...] Nevertheless there is a popular distinction between the meaning of 'motive' and the meaning of 'intention.' E.g. if a man kills someone, he may be said to have done it out of love and pity, or to have done it out of hatred; [...] 'motive for an action' has a rather wider and more diverse application than 'intention with which the action was done.'[48]

In seeking to clarify this popular distinction Anscombe is not setting out a hard and fast rule, but rather reflecting on the ordinary distinctions we make in our everyday language. The distinction between intention and objective is also one which is not always distinct in ordinary language, but we do distinguish between proximate intentions and more remote objectives. We often do choose to do things which we do not want to do, for the sake of our objectives. This is not, however, to say we do not intend those things. To deny that a soldier is intending to kill an enemy when the soldier purposely acts so as to bring about the enemy's death is to re-describe the soldier's act in a manner which Anscombe argues against in *Intention*. Thus, in the following passage she writes in opposition to the notion that intention can be determined by re-describing a person's actions based upon what his or her objective is:

> 'Roughly speaking, a man intends to do what he does'. But of course that is *very* roughly speaking. It is right to formulate it,

---

[46] Biggar, *In Defence of War*, p. 213.
[47] Biggar, *In Defence of War*, p. 104.
[48] *I*, pp. 18–19.

> however, as an antidote against the absurd thesis which is sometimes maintained: that a man's intended action is only described by describing his *objective*.[49]

Thus, if the solider aiming at an enemy were to reply to the question 'what are you doing?' by saying that there is no intention to kill the enemy, but to remove the enemy from the battle with no malice intended, we may be somewhat perplexed. Our confusion is not due to the lack of malice, nor to the soldier articulating his or her objective, but to the soldier's denial of what they are actually doing. We may conclude the soldier has psychological reasons for responding in this manner or is using a kind of special military language, but the answer we would accept to the question 'what are you doing?' is that the soldier is aiming to kill the enemy. This is clearly what is intended, albeit with the motivation of seeking to wrong an injustice by removing an enemy from the conflict. There is a moral distinction between the act of a soldier who aims to kill the enemy and maliciously wants to kill, and the soldier who aims to kill not maliciously wanting to kill, but reluctantly to prevent the enemy from carrying out a great injustice. In both cases, however, there is an intention to kill.[50]

Intentional killing is problematic for Biggar in all cases. This is because he argues that although it is possible that some people may be subjectively so evil that to kill them is to 'intend harm to nothing of value [...] the history of a person's spiritual and moral corruption is largely opaque to human view; and his fellows would be wise to refrain from claiming the competence to judge it irreversible'.[51] Here Biggar's argument seems to be that in intending to kill we are judging the person to lack value, a judgment we are not in a position to make. Yet Biggar holds the traditional doctrine (which we saw Anscombe follow) that those with the authority to act on behalf of the common good of society can legitimately act to remove a serious threat to society, but adds that in this case: 'the public officer does not intend (in the broader sense) the wrongdoer's death, but only accepts it.'[52] It is difficult to

---

[49] *I*, p. 45.
[50] This is not to say that in most cases there is an intention to kill, but that there will be cases in which the soldier's actions show a clear intention to kill.
[51] Biggar, *In Defence of War*, pp. 107–108.
[52] Biggar, *In Defence of War*, p. 109.

make sense of the idea that a public officer who orders the death of a criminal does not intend that death.

Rather than perform gymnastics with the notion of intention, the solution to the problem of how someone intending to kill another human being can do so without thereby denying the dignity of that person's life can be found by extending Anscombe's argument regarding the grounds for attacking combatants in war. Here in intending to kill enemy combatants we are not judging that they have forfeited their human dignity as a result of carrying out objectively unjust acts, but that they are seriously harming others (or we have sufficient evidence that they will seriously harm) in a manner that only killing them will prevent. Here the intention to kill should be both proportionate to the harm inflicted or threatened, and have the objective of removing the criminal from causing harm; for which killing is a last resort: two conditions which Biggar attaches to legitimate killing. Thus we are not intending to kill the person as that individual with their intrinsic worth, but as a person who is harming. The intention is to kill that person, but this does not mean we kill them on the basis of a judgment of personal worth.

We can extend this analysis to other cases of intending to kill for the common good. Thus, in the case of seeking to kill a criminal, we can argue that the reason for intending the death of the criminal in defence of the common good does not derive from a judgment of the criminal's lack of human dignity, but an assessment of the objective harm they perpetrate or threaten.[53] This solution saves a great deal of what Biggar seeks to achieve with his theory of legitimate killing, but not at the cost of denying that those who are involved in such killing are intending to kill.

6. Conclusion

In this exposition of Anscombe's writings on just war I have attempted to show that although her three articles were written in particular historical contexts they continue to cast light on

---

[53] This analysis of the justification for intentionally killing criminals is not intended to provide a theory of punishment; any such theory should take into account a criminal's subjective guilt, even if this cannot be the only measure for punishment. It is rather concerned with police actions against criminals who can only be resisted effectively by use of potentially lethal force (for example in a shoot-out when the criminals start firing first).

important moral questions. In particular the question of legitimate killing; both in terms of the grounds for, and the limitations which should be placed upon, any such killings. I focused upon a particular challenge to Anscombe's theory of just war, but this is a general and fundamental challenge to which any just war theory must respond. Denyer argues that within the context of war the ordinary categories of moral responsibility are not applicable, so any use of such categories in connection with war is mistaken. For Denyer the mistake is a dangerous one, for it can be used to justify the continuation of warfare. In response to this challenge I have argued that Anscombe's notion that combatants are 'non-innocent' insofar as they harm provides the rationale for using violence against them, up to the point of killing. It also explains why the force used against combatants should be proportionate to the threat they pose, as opposed to their subjective guilt, thus placing limitations on the use of force against them during a conflict. Anscombe's notion of combatants as 'non-innocent' also explains why force is not used against non-combatants. It is because they are not harming that non-combatants should not be targeted in a conflict, not because they are subjectively innocent. Thus the distinction between combatant and non-combatant provides a means of limiting the use of force against both combatants and non-combatants, whilst allowing protection for those who are innocent (here in the ordinary sense of innocence) from serious violations of their basic rights.

In the latter part of the chapter I have examined Biggar's defence of legitimate killing in the light of Anscombe's writings. Again it is important to stress that there is a great deal of agreement between Biggar and Anscombe: both set out to show how the just war tradition is still relevant to contemporary conflicts. The point of disagreement is on the nature of intention and in particular the intention to kill. Here I have argued that Biggar's notion of intention is confused, but that his overall purpose, to provide a rationale for legitimate killing and to place definite limits to such killings (they are proportionate and a last resort), is saved by Anscombe's notion: that it is legitimate for those in authority to use force against persons who voluntarily harm, to the point of killing. Furthermore, I have argued that this notion also provides a rationale for killings which are within the state, but also places clear limitation to such killings. As with many of Anscombe's writings the solution she here offers to a complex and contested moral question is simple, yet this simplicity should not be mistaken for a lack of subtlety, for it is only when we come to appreciate the subtlety of her writings that we come to grasp something of the immense contribution she has made to moral thought.

David Albert Jones

Anscombe on the Human Embryo

1. Anscombe on personhood

To understand the thought of Elizabeth Anscombe on the human embryo it is useful to place her in the context of what she called 'modern moral philosophy'[1] (roughly, the predominant form of moral philosophy practised in the English speaking world in the nineteenth and twentieth centuries), a context whence there emerged, in the late twentieth century, certain philosophical arguments developed to excuse the killing of unborn infants.

If we take a further step back, to put those arguments in a longer historical context, it is well known that Jews and Christians were distinctive in the ancient world for their opposition to the common practices of abortion and infanticide.[2] The Christian objection to such practices is well summarized in an early second-century work known as the *Didache*, 'You shall not kill a child by abortion nor kill it after it is born.'[3] Infanticide and abortion are forms of homicide and they are abominable acts because it is an archetypal injustice to kill an innocent human being.

Over the centuries it was the civilizing effect of Christianity that gradually shifted social attitudes towards the protection of infants born and unborn. How that protection was enacted in law varied from place to place and from time to time but it was only in the twentieth century that countries began to abandon this protection altogether and deliberately to liberalize their abortion laws.

---

[1] 'Modern Moral Philosophy' in *CPP3*, pp. 26–42.
[2] D.A. Jones, *The Soul of the Embryo: An enquiry into the status of the human embryo in the Christian tradition* (London: Continuum, 2004), pp. 33–74.
[3] *Didache* 2:2.

It was also from this time that philosophers in these societies began to construct arguments in defence of abortion and sometimes also in defence of infanticide. Perhaps the most prominent such argument is based on the claim that what makes human beings valuable or worthy of protection is some extra quality in virtue of which a human being qualifies as a 'human person'.

A usefully clear example is provided by John Harris: 'most current accounts of the criteria for personhood follow John Locke in identifying self-consciousness coupled with fairly rudimentary intelligence as the most important features [... the human individual] will gradually move from being a potential or a pre-person into an actual person when she becomes capable of valuing her own existence. And if, eventually, she permanently loses this capacity, she will have ceased to be a person.'[4] Harris goes on to say 'This account, very starkly presented, yields a difference in the morality of ending the lives of persons and that of ending the lives of all other creatures including human non-persons.'[5] Harris may be exaggerating slightly when he says 'most' current accounts of personhood are of this kind, but certainly there are many contemporary philosophers and bioethicists who give similar such accounts.

Such a view of acquired personhood is also accepted by some theologians. For example, Gerard Hughes, in a recent discussion on the status of the human embryo, argued that 'From the very beginning, therefore, it seems to me we are human beings and potentially human persons. We are human beings because our DNA is human. But a human person is defined in terms of being able to perform the activities which are characteristic of a person rather than a tomato. So I think that we become persons gradually over time.'[6]

Anscombe regarded this argument as 'a mere trick' by which 'thinkers trade on the weight of the word "person", although they define it wrongly in terms of characteristics which may come and go and which are a matter of degree'.[7]

---

[4] J. Harris, 'Euthanasia and the Value of Life', in J. Keown (ed.), *Euthanasia Examined* (Cambridge: Cambridge University Press, 1995) [hereafter: Harris, 'Euthanasia'], pp. 8–9.
[5] Harris, 'Euthanasia', pp. 9–10.
[6] G. Hughes, 'Personhood as a Process', in L. Woodhead *et al.*, 'What People Really Believe About Abortion', *Modern Believing* 55(1) 2014:7–14, at pp. 10–11.
[7] 'Murder and the Morality of Euthanasia' in *HLAE*, p. 267.

In exposing this sophistry, Anscombe was aware that she was rejecting an opinion that had become prevalent among analytic philosophers. In a short paper briefly setting out twenty erroneous opinions common among modern Anglo-American philosophers, the second listed opinion is that 'A human being comes to be a person through the development of the characteristics which make something a person. A human being in decay may also cease to be a person without ceasing to be a human being. In short: being a person is something that gets added to a human being who develops properly, and that may disappear in old age or imbecility.'[8]

In contrast Anscombe herself held that, 'A human being is a person because the kind to which he belongs is characterised by a rational nature. Thus we have the same individual, and hence the same person, when we have the same human being.'[9] Whereas the account of personhood provided by John Harris and others traces its roots back to John Locke, Anscombe's account is rooted in an older tradition, in the philosophy of Thomas Aquinas, Boethius and Aristotle. A human being is a particular kind of animal, a living being with a specific nature, and a human being possesses this nature for as long as he or she exists. If a person is understood to be 'an individual substance of a rational nature',[10] then a human being is always a human person in virtue of his or her very nature, notwithstanding that immaturity, injury or senescence might impede the use of his or her rational powers.

As well as the clear Aristotelian influence here one may also detect a *genealogical* argument, similar to that she develops in 'On Modern Moral Philosophy'.[11] There Anscombe asserts that those philosophers who argue that it can be 'morally right' to kill an innocent man are invoking concepts of 'morally right' and 'morally wrong' to which they are not entitled. According to Anscombe, the concept of 'morally wrong' is the heir of the notion of 'illicit' and belongs to a divine law theory of ethics. Once the divine law context has been lost, the idea that an act might be

---

[8] 'Twenty Opinions Common among Modern Anglo-American Philosophers' in *FHG*, pp. 66–67.
[9] 'Murder and the Morality of Euthanasia', p. 268.
[10] Boethius, *On the Two Natures of Christ*; see Thomas Aquinas, *Summa theologiae* I, q. 29, a. 1.
[11] *CPP3*, pp. 26–42.

'morally wrong' is then 'cut off from the family of concepts from which it sprang'.[12] In just the same way, Anscombe argues that the modern analytic concept of 'personhood' trades on the moral weight of an earlier concept of 'person' but no longer has the context to justify the moral significance it is given.

In Anscombe's act of exposing the misuse by philosophers of a word that has been taken from its original context we can also discern the influence of Wittgenstein: '[...] one must always ask oneself: is the word ever actually used in this way in the language-game which is its original home? What *we* do is to bring words back from their metaphysical to their everyday use.'[13] Wittgenstein characteristically regarded with suspicion terms used by philosophers in a special sense distinct from their everyday use, and typically regarded such ways of talking as obscuring rather than as better disclosing the world. Thus, our recognition of the humanity of another person is not based on arguments framed by such 'metaphysical' words but is a kind of predisposition, 'My attitude towards him is an attitude towards a soul. I am not of the *opinion* that he has a soul.'[14] The claim that such an attitude towards a living human being might be set aside, on the basis of a nice philosophical argument, because the human being in question did not conform to the *a priori* concept of 'personhood' is precisely the kind of malign effect of 'metaphysical' terms which Wittgenstein repeatedly sought to undermine: 'What we are destroying is nothing but houses of cards and we are clearing up the ground of language on which they stand.'[15]

What Anscombe adds to Wittgenstein is a greater historical sense of the use of terms in ancient and medieval philosophy. Thus when Anscombe uncovers 'one or another piece of plain nonsense'[16] what remains is not 'only bits of stone and rubble' but is a route to the renewed appreciation of the richer and more robust concepts of philosophers of an earlier age, concepts developed by thinkers such as Thomas Aquinas and Aristotle. In this way Anscombe both draws on and improves on Wittgenstein.

---

[12] *CPP3*, p. 41. This is a move that was generalized into a broader argument about tradition and virtue by Alasdair MacIntyre.
[13] L. Wittgenstein, *Philosophical Investigations* (Oxford: Basil Blackwell, 1958), §116.
[14] Wittgenstein, *Philosophical Investigations*, p. 178.
[15] Wittgenstein, *Philosophical Investigations*, §119.
[16] Wittgenstein, *Philosophical Investigations*, §119.

2. Anscombe on delayed hominization

For Anscombe, then, 'you cannot be killing a human being and not be killing a person.'[17] From this it might be thought that Anscombe believed the human embryo to be a human being from the moment of fertilization such that all abortion is homicide *sensu stricto*. However, Anscombe was unwilling to commit herself to this thesis. 'I have long myself had doubts about what is called "immediate animation" and might more aptly be called "immediate hominisation".'[18]

To be sure, Anscombe regarded *some* abortion as homicide: 'the killing that is done at a stage where the baby is, if only seen, visibly a human being.'[19] However, she was doubtful that the early embryo was 'a human being' in the sense of 'a *Mensch* if we are talking German, an *anthropos* in Greek, a *homo* in Latin', hence she regarded Catholics who oppose abortion as misguided if they base their opposition to abortion solely on the thesis that 'the zygote is a human being'.[20]

In this Anscombe is, again, very close to the thought of Aristotle[21] and of Thomas Aquinas,[22] both of whom regarded

---

[17] 'Murder and the Morality of Euthanasia', p. 268.
[18] 'Embryos and Final Causes' in *HLAE*, p. 46.
[19] 'The Early Embryo: Theoretical Doubts and Practical Certainties' in *FHG*, p. 218.
[20] 'Embryos and Final Causes', p. 45.
[21] The primary text of Aristotle on the development of the embryo is his *De generatione animalium* but there are other important references in the *History of animals*, *De anima*, *Physics* and *Metaphysics* and in a number of other works. For secondary discussion of Aristotle's embryology, see C.A. Freeland, 'Aristotle on Bodies, Matter and Potentiality', in Gotthelf and Lennox (eds.), *Philosophical Issues in Aristotle's Biology* (Cambridge: Cambridge University Press, 1987); D. Balme, 'Human is Generated by Human', in G. Dunstan (ed.), *The Human Embryo: Aristotle and the Arabic and European Traditions* (Exeter: University of Exeter Press, 1990); K. Flannery, 'Applying Aristotle in Contemporary Embryology', *Thomist* 67(2) 2003:249–278; Jones, *The Soul of the Embryo*, chapter 2; and D.A. Jones, 'Thomas Aquinas, Augustine and Aristotle on "Delayed Animation"', *Thomist* 76(1) 2012:1–36.
[22] The two key passages for Aquinas on the embryo are *Summa theologiae* I, q. 118, and *De potentia* III, a. 9–a. 12. In general Thomas follows Aristotle's account very closely, indeed citing him 29 times in the four articles of the *De potentia* on human generation. In the late twentieth century the political debates over abortion and over the use of human embryos in research have added currency and contention to the interpretation of Aquinas on the embryo. See, for example, J. Donceel, 'Immediate Animation and Delayed

embryonic development as a gradual process such that the embryo receives its final specifically human form at the end of generation, which for male foetuses Aristotle places at around six weeks and for females around thirteen weeks.[23] Regarding this account, Anscombe states that 'I do not find St Thomas's ideas absurd, though we must think his physiology rather quaint.'[24] As for those who assert that embryonic development manifests 'government by [...] the soul of the embryo',[25] and hence the presence of the specifically human soul from the beginning, Anscombe thinks they confuse formal and final causality. The process of development is teleological and is to be understood in relation to the form of the human body which is being generated. However, this does not mean that the form of the human being is *already present*.

> 'No'. What is governing here is the principle of unity of a new and coming life, the animal life of movement and sensation which is not there yet. But one cannot doubt that what is done—the action of the living embryo in its early stages—is done for the development of that animal life—the production of the beating heart, of inchoate sense organs, of the limbs and of the brain; the existence of almost all of which is necessary if there is to be the life of an animal.[26]

Hominisation', *Theological Studies* 31(1) 1970:75–105; B. Ashley, 'A Critique of the Theory of Delayed Animation', in D. McCarthy and A. Moraczewski, *An Ethical Evaluation of Fetal Experimentation: An Interdisciplinary Study* (St Louis, MO: Pope John XXIII Centre, 1976); S. Heaney 'Aquinas on the Presence of the Human Rational Soul in the Early Embryo', *Thomist* 56(1) 1991:19–48; J. Haldane and P. Lee, 'Aquinas on Human Ensoulment, Abortion, and the Value of Life', *Philosophy* 78(2) 2003:253–276; R. Pasnau, 'Souls and the Beginning of Life: A Reply to Haldane and Lee', *Philosophy* 78(4) 2003:521–531; J.T. Eberl, 'Aquinas's Account of Human Embryogenesis and Recent Interpretations', *Journal of Medicine and Philosophy* 30(4) 2005:379–394; D.A. Jones, 'Aquinas as an Advocate of Abortion? The Appeal to "Delayed Animation" in Contemporary Christian Ethical Debates on the Human Embryo', *Studies in Christian Ethics* 26(1) 2013:97–124. Anscombe did not engage directly with such secondary literature but she was aware of at least some of it, as is evident by her use of the terms 'immediate animation' and 'immediate hominization'.

[23] Thomas Aquinas, *Commentary on the sentences* III, d. 3, q. 5, a. 2, citing Aristotle, *History of Animals* 7.3, 583b 3–5; see Jones 'Thomas Aquinas, Augustine and Aristotle'.
[24] 'The Early Embryo', p. 217.
[25] 'Embryos and Final Causes', p. 57.
[26] 'Embryos and Final Causes', p. 57.

Thus according to Anscombe, and indeed to Aquinas, while the successful development of the embryo is only understandable in relation to the specifically human form, this specific form is the *final* cause of development not the *formal* cause of the actual life of the embryo as it is now. Anscombe would not then have agreed with Tertullian that, 'He who will one day be a man is a man already.'[27]

It is noticeable that Anscombe is confident that the embryo is a human being from the time that 'the baby is, if only seen, visibly a human being'[28] which she also seems to place at around six weeks. In another place she is even more explicit about the significance she gives to outward appearance, 'I assume that [Aquinas] would rely on the human appearance of the baby for saying that it was now a human being. In a rather similar way, I incline to rely on its outward form and its having human organs.'[29] This reliance on the presence of visible bodily form to disclose the presence of the human soul is a point of contact between Aristotle, for whom the soul is 'the form of a natural body which has life in potentiality',[30] and Wittgenstein, for whom 'the human body is the best picture of the human soul'.[31] The soul is not some hidden inner substance but is the form of a living being and is evident in the visible activities of its body. This is seen not only in physical shape but also, and more so, by behaviour. It is significant that Anscombe gives the example of an ectopic human embryo who was 'observed to swim vigorously with a breast stroke'.[32] It is such outward behaviour rather than speculation about the inner development of certain kinds of neurones which is the basis for her view that this is already a living animal, and thus possessed of a sensitive soul. This seems to be exactly parallel to Wittgenstein's example of the 'wriggling fly' whose behaviour allows psychological terms 'to get a foothold'.[33] It is not necessary to ask about what is happening in the head of the fly (as it were) to see that it is in distress.

---

[27] *Apology* 9.6, see Pope John Paul II, *Evangelium Vitae*, §61, though note that this is my example, not Anscombe's.
[28] 'The Early Embryo', p. 218.
[29] 'The Early Embryo', p. 217.
[30] Aristotle, *De Anima* ii 1, 412a20–1.
[31] Wittgenstein, *Philosophical Investigations*, p. 178.
[32] 'The Early Embryo', p. 217.
[33] Wittgenstein, *Philosophical Investigations*, §284.

There are of course important differences between the thought of Aristotle and Wittgenstein, in method, interests, interlocutors and influence. Nevertheless, there are some family resemblances that it would be perverse to ignore, in that both thinkers emphasize the significance of the form of this visible world, and hence the form of the living human body. Thus in giving the significance she does to visible bodily structures and activities, Anscombe is also drawing on both Aristotle and Wittgenstein, as well as Aquinas, whom she cites in a number of places.

3. Deductions from embryology and the significance of twinning

One response to the view of Anscombe is to say that, while it is true that Thomas Aquinas and Aristotle accepted a form of delayed hominization, modern biology has now demonstrated that the embryo is a human being. According to this response, the fact that Aquinas's account of physiology is 'rather quaint'[34] cannot be dismissed in the way that Anscombe seems to do. Biology does not directly address questions of philosophy, but philosophical reflection on human nature must take account of biology. A number of philosophers and theologians have argued that, if Thomist principles are applied to modern biology, they demonstrate beyond reasonable doubt that a human being, with a rational soul, is present from fertilization.

This position is relatively common among contemporary Thomist philosophers, but for Anscombe, her primary interlocutor was 'the famous geneticist Jerome Lejeune [who was] confident that the zygote is not merely human but is a human being'.[35] Lejeune gave evidence in a number of court cases appealing to advances in biology, especially to knowledge of genetics and embryology, as providing proof that the embryo was a human being: 'Science has a very simple conception of man; as soon as he has been conceived, a man is a man.'[36] He bases this conclusion on the fact that from the very beginning in the 'genetic information and the molecular structure of the egg'[37] you have everything

---

[34] 'The Early Embryo', p. 217.
[35] 'Embryos and Final Causes', p. 45.
[36] 'Embryos and Final Causes', pp. 45–46.
[37] 'Embryos and Final Causes', p. 46.

inherent needed for the later development of the human individual.

Anscombe met Lejeune and had a great respect for him, but she was not convinced by his arguments. She agreed that the basis for human development was present in the zygote (the embryo at the single cell stage) and that this development was only comprehensible in relation to the form of a human being. However, as already mentioned, she did not think that this power of development (this final causality) demonstrated the presence of the actual form of human being in the embryo (formal causality). Anscombe thought that the identification of the human embryo (even as a single cell) as a human being was made plausible by the fact that most adults could trace their life continuously back to a single cell, a zygote, whereas this cell, quite uniquely, was formed not by division but by the union of two cells, the sperm and the egg. If I am the same individual living being as the zygote, then it seems that each of us was once a zygote, and hence that a zygote is a human being.

Anscombe's response to this argument was to say, 'What this indicates is that they suddenly forget about identical twins.'[38] Identical twins originate from a single zygote which splits sometime in the first few days of existence. Therefore the twins do not have their unique origin until sometime after fertilization (though within the first 13 days). Lejeune did not think that this negated the significance of fertilization as he argued that, in the case of identical twins, the early embryo was programmed to twin and so fertilization was the beginning of two individuals both of whom were present within one body. Anscombe considers his argument but notes that he himself admits that he does not have proof for this. He thinks that somehow it must be so, but this is not sufficient for Anscombe who questions whether it must be so. From a philosophical perspective, there is no clear reason why twinning must be construed in this way, as one embryo that somehow was or contained two human beings. Twinning might be understood in various ways: as a process by which a second human being buds off from an original; or as a human being splitting to become two; or as a human entity which is alive and human but is not yet one or two human beings but which after a certain point becomes two human beings.

---

[38] 'Were You a Zygote?', in *HLAE*, p. 39.

The phenomenon of twinning was significant for Anscombe because it was a lens through which she questioned deductions from biology, and in particular questioned the arguments of Lejeune that biology provides demonstrative proof that human beings begin at fertilization. The possibility of other interpretations, and especially the interpretation whereby the embryo is regarded as a human entity but not yet a human being (nor two human beings), functions as it were as a *sed contra*, a contrary indication sufficient to make one reserve judgment prior to further consideration of the question.

Anscombe did not think that the phenomenon of twinning and the various ways in which it might be construed provided a *proof* that the zygote was not a human being. In this way her view should be distinguished from that of Richard McCormick or Norman Ford who thought that the early embryo (which McCormick called the 'pre-embryo') became a human individual, and hence a human being, only from the point where twinning was no longer possible, at 14 days or so.[39] In contrast Anscombe did not think that arguments from biology demonstrated when the human being was present (from fertilization, from 14 days or from any other particular time). Indeed she is clear that twinning is logically compatible with immediate animation and defends those who hold this view.[40] Nevertheless, she regarded the ambiguity of twinning as sufficient to undermine the simple genetic argument for equating fertilization with the beginning of a human individual. In the absence of any other such demonstration, general philosophical considerations inclined Anscombe 'to rely on its outward form […] where the baby is, if only seen, visibly a human being',[41] a stage which she placed at around six weeks.

---

[39] R. McCormick, 'Who or What is the Pre-Embryo?', *Kennedy Institute of Ethics Journal* 1(1) 1991:1–15; N. Ford, *When Did I begin? Conception of the Human Individual in History, Philosophy and Science* (Cambridge: Cambridge University Press, 1988). Ford provides what is arguably the most robust, and certainly is the most extended, defence of delayed hominization on the basis of delayed individuation. Note, however, that Ford subsequently revised his opinion and from 2008 has held that the zygote is indeed a human being, see N. Ford 'A Catholic Ethical Approach to Human Reproductive Technology', *Ethics, Bioscience and Life* 17 (Supp. 3) 2008:39–48.
[40] 'Embryos and Final Causes', p. 53.
[41] 'The Early Embryo', pp. 217–218.

4. Anscombe 'not that sort of "good Aristotelian"'

In many respects Anscombe's views on the early embryo were typical of Thomists of an earlier generation (such as Hering[42] or Maritain[43]) and close to the views of some of her contemporaries, especially those of Norman Ford.[44] However, in certain other respects her approach was distinctive to the point of being idiosyncratic.

One way to illustrate this is to consider the answer she gives to the question 'Were you a zygote?' and compare it to the answer Ford gave to the question 'When did I begin?'. For Ford, the fact of twinning meant that an individual did not come to be until twinning was impossible, at around 14 days; this is when he thought he began. He quotes Ann McLaren with approval as saying, 'This was when I began being me.'[45] Anscombe also thinks twinning important and remarks that, 'if I ask you "Were you a zygote?" you might intelligently reply, "No I was an identical twin".'[46] Anscombe reminds us that for identical twins there is no zygote with which one or the other could singly and uniquely identify him- or herself. Nevertheless, Anscombe argues that it could be truly said of identical twins, 'you and your twin jointly were once a zygote.'[47] This might be taken to mean that two human beings could be present in the same body (as Lejeune believed) but Anscombe does not think any human being yet existed when the zygote existed. She states that the identical twins *were* that zygote because that zygote was the beginning of those human beings, though at that stage it was not yet a human being (nor two human beings). It is in this sense that she thinks that twins could say that they, jointly, were once a zygote. To the objection that the twins cannot jointly be identical with the zygote because they are not identical with one another, Anscombe states

---

[42] H.M. Hering, 'De tempore animationis foetus humani', *Angelicum* 28, 1951:18–29.
[43] J. Maritain, *Untrammeled Approaches*, trans. B. Doering (Notre Dame: University of Notre Dame Press, 1997).
[44] Ford, *When Did I Begin?*
[45] Ford, *When Did I Begin?*, p. 174.
[46] 'Were You a Zygote?', p. 39.
[47] 'Were You a Zygote?', p. 39.

that, 'present non-identity of B and C does not prove that B and C *were* not identical with A and so with one another.'[48]

For the majority of people, who are not twins, Anscombe argues that each can truthfully say 'I (singly) was that zygote'[49] because that zygote was the beginning of the same life that the person has now, even if it was not yet the life of a human being. 'So I wasn't yet *a* human? That seems correct'[50] or again 'for some "what" I am the same somewhat as that zygote that I once was, even if when I was a zygote I wasn't yet a human.'[51]

Anscombe is aware that in speaking in this way she is departing from Aquinas. Thomas Aquinas regarded generation as 'a series of generations and corruptions',[52] and thus as a series of substantial changes. He did not regard the early embryo as that same substance (the same being, the same life, the same living thing) as the foetus. In contrast, Anscombe claims that while the specific human form is not present from the beginning, its gradual emergence is not through a series of generations and corruptions but by a gradual acquisition of form. Hence, she says, Aquinas 'need not think that the changes from vegetative to animal to rational life have to be seen as substantial changes'.[53] Furthermore, whereas Aquinas follows Aristotle very closely in his account of embryonic development, Anscombe points out that Aristotle nowhere characterizes embryonic development as a series of generations *and corruptions*. This is an addition by Aquinas. It could be argued that Aquinas is doing no more than applying to embryology the account of substantial change that Aristotle

---

[48] 'Were You a Zygote?', p. 41, emphasis in the original. Such problems of apparent intransitivity, which might seem *prima facie* incompatible with the logic of identity, have led philosophers such as Derek Parfit to reject diachronic personal identity in favour of 'continuity' of some sort. Anscombe does not take this route. She does not treat the case of embryonic development as analogous to the identity of a human person over time but neither does she consider it an example of substantial change. It may be that in the case of the gradual acquisition of form some idea of 'relative identity' is in play. It may also be that there may be scope for exploring whether the apparent contradiction in this case may be resolved by appeal to Arthur Prior's 'tensed logic'. Such explorations are, however, outside the scope of this chapter.
[49] 'Were You a Zygote?', p. 43.
[50] 'Were You a Zygote?', p. 43.
[51] 'The Early Embryo', p. 217.
[52] *Summa theologiae* I, q. 118, a. 2, ad 2.
[53] 'The Early Embryo', p. 217.

develops in his other writings. That the acquisition of a new form implies corruption of the previous form is simply what a 'good Aristotelian' would say. In answer to this objection, Anscombe points out that, in relation to embryonic development, Aristotle himself was 'not that sort of "good Aristotelian"'[54] for Aristotle claims that when the embryo first becomes an animal it is not an animal of any particular species! The passage that Anscombe refers to is from Aristotle's work on the generation of animals:

> As they develop they also acquire the sensitive soul in virtue of which an animal is an animal. For e.g. an animal does not become at the same time an animal and a man or a horse or any other particular animal. For the end is developed last, and the peculiar character of the species is the end of the generation in each individual.[55]

This is a passage with which Aquinas was familiar and he uses it to defend his own account against the objection that it seems to make the embryo 'pass from one species to another'.[56] The embryo does not change from one species to another because an embryo is not a perfect being but a being 'on the way to perfection',[57] it therefore does not belong to any species accept 'by reduction':[58] it may not yet have the specific form of a human being, but it is already an embryo of a human being (not of any other animal).

The claim that the embryo is an animal but is not 'a man or a horse or any other particular animal'[59] is implicit in Aristotle's view that the specific form, which is the perfection of generation, is acquired only at the end of a process of development. However, if Aristotle can maintain this seemingly un-Aristotelian idea — of an animal without a specific form — then there is no reason to deny that he could also maintain the seemingly un-Aristotelian idea that the embryo could gradually acquire form without the corruption of the previous form. Here Anscombe arguably provides a

---

[54] 'The Early Embryo', p. 217.
[55] Aristotle, *De gener. animal.* 2.3.736b2–5.
[56] Aquinas, *De potentia* III, a. 9, obj. 10.
[57] Aquinas, *De potentia* III, a. 9, ad 10.
[58] Aquinas, *De potentia* III, a. 9, ad 10.
[59] Aristotle, *De gener. animal.* 2.3.736b2–5.

more convincing interpretation of Aristotle than that provided by Aquinas.[60]

5. When does the embryo become 'visibly a human being'?

According to Anscombe, the life of 'that zygote' was *my* life, and I am the same living being and the same substance and the same individual as that zygote; why then deny that the zygote was the same human being as I am now? She says that the fact of twinning counts against it, but acknowledges that there are many ways to understand twinning without denying immediate hominization. Similarly, Anscombe claims that formal and final causality are distinct but, again, she does not say that 'formal and final causes are never the same: on the contrary [...]'.[61] However, Anscombe fails to acknowledge that, where final and formal causes are distinct, the final cause must inhere in *some other formal cause*. According to Aquinas this other form is the form of the male parent, thus development occurs *in* the embryo but is not a power *of* the embryo. It is shaped from outside by the parent. This premise (which he takes from Aristotle) is important for him. Without it there would be no link between final and formal causality in embryonic development.

Anscombe shows little interest in the biological writings of Aristotle[62] or in this question. She describes the biology as 'rather quaint'[63] but does not acknowledge that Aristotle's biology plays a crucial role in Thomas's account. If the development of the embryo is due to a power of that embryo, as seems undeniable in

---

[60] On the distinction between Aristotle's account of the human embryo and that of Thomas, and the ambiguity of the former, see Jones, 'Thomas Aquinas, Augustine and Aristotle'.

[61] 'The Early Embryo', p. 220.

[62] On Aristotle as a biologist and the importance of biology for Aristotle's philosophy see, amongst others, W.D. Thompson, *On Aristotle as a Biologist* (Oxford: Clarendon Press, 1913); M. Grene, *A Portrait of Aristotle* (Chicago: University of Chicago Press, 1963); M. Nussbaum, *Aristotle's De motu animalium: Text with translation, commentary, and interpretive essays* (Princeton: Princeton University Press, 1978); A. Gotthelf (ed.), *Aristotle on Nature and Living Things* (Pittsburg and Bristol: Mathesis Publications and Bristol Classical Press, 1985); A. Gotthelf and J. Lennox (eds.), *Philosophical Issues in Aristotle's Biology* (Cambridge: Cambridge University Press, 1987); and J. Lennox, *Aristotle's Philosophy of Biology* (Cambridge: Cambridge University Press, 2001).

[63] 'The Early Embryo', p. 217.

relation to modern biology, then the final cause inheres in an already present formal cause in the embryo. Every embryo is already an embryo of a distinct species (*pace* Aristotle) and develops according to its specific kind.

Anscombe's reluctance to regard the embryo as a human being seems to be based on its appearance: that it does not appear to be 'if only seen, visibly a human being'.[64] It may reasonably be asked, however, why a human being is thought always to have the same shape. Does not an embryo possess the shape that a human being (or any other organism) has at that stage of development? There is perhaps in Anscombe's rejection of immediate animation a suspicion of the Cartesian hidden ego, in contrast to the belief, shared in different ways by Aristotle and Wittgenstein, that the soul is something visible in the life of the body. However, someone who holds that the embryo is a human being need not believe that the soul is hidden. Embryonic development is a *visible* process and the developmental power of the human embryo is something specifically human.

In relation to the great majority of embryos which are not produced by twinning, and which do not go on to form twins, Anscombe is surely correct to say that the life of the zygote is the same life as the life of the adult; these are different moments of the biological life story of a single organism. However, having accepted the unity and identity of this biological life, Anscombe has no grounds to deny that the zygote is the same human being as the adult. Nor is the language of 'two materially distinct carriers of the life'[65] helpful, and still less the claim that the chromosomes and genes of the embryo 'provide a marvellous example of the *proximate matter* of a human being'.[66] The principle of life, as Aristotle understood so clearly, is a kind of form: if the embryo has the same life, this cannot be because it has the same matter, but only because it has the same form, the same *psuche*.

From a Thomist perspective, faced with the claim that 'when I was a zygote I wasn't yet a human',[67] one would naturally ask — what then am 'I'? If the correct answer is that I am a human

---

[64] 'The Early Embryo', p. 218.
[65] 'Were You a Zygote?', p. 44.
[66] 'Embryos and Final Causes', p. 58.
[67] 'The Early Embryo', p. 217.

being,[68] then we face a choice: either the zygote was not a human being and not me, or if the zygote was me, then it was a human being. Anscombe states that the same substance, the same individual, the same life is present in zygote, infant, and adult human, and that there is no substantial change through development. She therefore had no good reason to resist acknowledging that the human embryo is 'a human'.

6. Anscombe on the moral status of the embryo

In summary, Anscombe held that every human being was a human person but doubted that every human embryo was a human being and hence doubted that deliberate destruction of an early human embryo (in vivo or in vitro) was homicide *sensu stricto*. Someone unfamiliar with Anscombe's thought might therefore imagine that she was liberal on abortion or that she was motivated to deny that embryo destruction was homicide precisely to exonerate the practice of abortion. Certainly, from the 1960s onwards, both within the Church and outside it, a prevalent desire to promote acceptance of abortion seems to have been an important reason for the revival of interest in the concept of 'delayed animation'.[69] The idea seemed to offer a medieval precedent for modern proposals to promote access to abortion.

In the case of Anscombe, however, it is clear that she regarded abortion as a gravely wrong and indeed as an abominable act. The inference that if Anscombe did not think early abortion to be homicide then she must think it permissible would only be valid if all acts were morally permissible other than homicide, narrowly

---

[68] The legitimacy of this question and the relevance of the answer do not depend on taking the proposition 'I am a human being' to be a proposition of identity, as though the 'I' were the name of an object. Anscombe famously argued that a sentence such as 'I am this thing here' is *not* a proposition of identity ('The First Person', in *CPP2*, pp. 21–36). Nevertheless, she regarded this sentence as 'a real proposition' of a kind which could be true or false. Her account therefore still allows one to ask, 'what am I?' If this question can be answered by reference to an individual substance (in an Aristotelian sense), which it can in the case of adult human beings, and if there is a true answer to the question 'when did I begin?', then this answer will be the same as the answer to the question 'when did this individual substance begin to be?' The latter question will not have the same meaning as the first question but its answer will have the same truth conditions.

[69] Jones, 'Aquinas as an Advocate of Abortion?'.

defined. This is of course a false premise. The logical independence of these propositions can be illustrated by a simple diagram.

	Abortion gravely wrong	Abortion not gravely wrong
Abortion homicide	X	
Abortion not homicide		X

It might be assumed that if abortion is homicide then abortion is gravely wrong whereas if abortion is not homicide then abortion is not gravely wrong. In which case only the diagonal boxes would be filled (e.g. by Pope John Paul II top left and John Harris bottom right). However, while homicide is one reason that an act may be wrong, it is clearly not the only reason, hence abortion might be morally wrong even if it were not homicide. Similarly, while homicide is a reason that an act may be wrong, in certain exceptional cases homicide might be excusable or even justifiable, as in the case of reasonable self-defence.

There are thus philosophers who represent each combination of positions. Some modern apologists for elective abortion defend the practice even on the premise that it involves homicide, most notably Judith Jarvis Thomson (putting her in the top right box). Such arguments are outside the scope of this chapter and they were not addressed by Anscombe, except when they involved appeal to the principle of double effect. Anscombe regarded 'the principle of side effects', as she called it, as valid and important but also as being open to abuse. Her analysis of killing as an unintended side effect of action is explored by Gormally in another chapter of this volume.

With regard to early abortion (i.e. before six weeks) Anscombe represents the bottom left position, that it is gravely wrong even though it is not homicide. Why does Anscombe regard early abortion as gravely wrong? Anscombe stands in the intellectual tradition of Thomas Aquinas, and with much of the Western Christian tradition, which has held that 'after the sin of murder, whereby a human nature already in actual existence is destroyed, this sort of sin seems to hold the second place, whereby the generation of human nature is precluded.'[70] Aquinas thus condemned both contraceptive intercourse and destruction of the embryo prior to ensoulment. Anscombe also argues that contraceptive intercourse is contrary to the virtue of chastity. Nevertheless, while Anscombe rejects both contraception and early abortion, she seems to regard these as different kinds of acts, wrong for different reasons.[71] The moral evaluation of contraception primarily concerns the virtue of chastity and the relationship between sexual acts and the goods of marriage. The moral evaluation of abortion, on the other hand, primarily concerns the virtue of justice and the act of killing a human embryo or foetus.

Anscombe understands the deliberate destruction of the human embryo as something very close to homicide, even if not homicide in the strict sense. She says that destruction of an embryo should fall under the term murder even though it would not if one had a 'rigid' definition of murder and were to be 'pedantic' and 'stick to this [definition] in an obstinate fashion'.[72]

How are we to make sense of this claim? If homicide is killing a human being, how can killing what, *ex hypothesi*, is not a human being be morally equivalent to homicide? The defence that Anscombe provides for this moral position[73] is frustratingly brief. In one place she states that embryo destruction, even if not homicide, 'has evidently the same sort of malice as killing it later on when it is unquestionably a human, or more than one'.[74] This might suggest an analogy with attempted murder, which may share the malice of murder, and may be subject to severe legal sanction, even if no human being is killed. However, with attempted murder there is an actual human being who is the

---

[70] *Summa contra gentiles* III, q. 122, see also *Commentary on the sentences* IV, d. 31, q. 4; note that it is not clear whether Thomas is referring to contraception or to early abortion or if indeed he made a distinction between them.
[71] In contrast to the interpretation of the tradition given by D.A. Dombrowski and R. Deltete, *A Brief Liberal Catholic Defense of Abortion* (Urbana: University of Illinois Press, 2000); Jones, 'Thomas Aquinas, Augustine and Aristotle', p. 12.
[72] 'The Early Embryo', p. 221.
[73] Anscombe writes more frequently and at greater length on the theoretical question of whether the embryo is a human being than on the moral implications of the answer to that question. The most extended discussion of the moral implications of her theoretical account is in 'The Early Embryo'.
[74] 'The Early Embryo', p. 221, though, *pace* Anscombe, it is not 'evident' to everyone that the same malice is involved in this case.

object of the malice. Who is the object of homicidal malice in the case of embryo destruction?

One possible answer would be that it is the future human being who is the object of the malice. The problem with this response is that there will be no future human being from this embryo if the embryo is destroyed. There is not and will not be any human being who is harmed. At this point some philosophers might seek to identify a harm suffered by the future human being that *would have existed* had this embryo not been destroyed. However, it is clear that Anscombe is not such a philosopher. She is highly critical of the attempt to identify states of affairs or individuals that would have been had the world been different, 'there [is] not, quite generally, any such thing as what would have happened if what did happen had not happened, and that in particular there [is] no such thing as what someone would have done if… and certainly that there [is] no such thing as how someone would have spent his life if he had not died as a child.'[75] On the premise that an embryo is not yet a human being there is no particular human-being-who-would-have-been-born had this embryo not been destroyed.

It is not in relation to future 'possible persons' that the harm of embryo destruction is to be understood but in relation to the actual status of the embryo that is destroyed. Anscombe's account of the moral status of the human embryo reflects her theoretical account of embryonic development. In a letter signed by a number of philosophers, Anscombe affirms that 'at fertilisation we have for the first time an entity which we can identify with the later foetus, newborn, teenager, etc.'[76] Destroying an embryo is thus categorically different from destroying gametes that can be combined variously and which cannot be identified with the future organism.[77] While Anscombe does not accept that the human embryo is a human being, she thinks that every human being (either singly or together with his or her twin) was once a zygote. A human being can therefore say to him- or herself, 'when I was a zygote I wasn't yet a human.'[78] From this it follows that someone

---

[75] 'Introduction', in *CPP2*, p. vii.
[76] G.E.M. Anscombe *et al.*, 'Destructive Research Upon Human Embryos', March 1990.
[77] 'Destructive Research', see also 'The Early Embryo', p. 218.
[78] 'The Early Embryo', p. 217.

could truthfully say 'had you killed that zygote you would have been ending my life.' The life of *that* zygote was *my* life and thus killing that embryo is not merely preventing me from coming into existence (as preventing my parents meeting would have prevented my coming into existence), rather it would be the ending of a life that had already begun, my life.

Each of us was once a zygote and killing a zygote is killing 'that very same living thing'[79] that we once were. In the words of a recent EU citizens' initiative, the human embryo is 'one of us'.[80] It has been argued in this chapter that, given philosophical and biological premises which she accepted, Anscombe did not have good grounds to resist the claim that a human embryo is a human being. Nevertheless, notwithstanding her scepticism on this point, on her account of the embryo, I was once an embryo and destroying that embryo would have ended my life. Killing a human embryo is, on this account, something very like homicide and is unjust for the same kinds of reasons that homicide is unjust.

---

[79] 'The Early Embryo', p. 218.
[80] Commission registration number: ECI(2012)000005, subject matter: 'Juridical protection of the dignity, the right to life and of the integrity of every human being from conception in the areas of EU competence in which such protection is of particular importance.'

Kevin L. Flannery SJ[1]

Anscombe on Two Jesuits and Lying

In a number of places, Elizabeth Anscombe speaks about lying, invariably at least suggesting that it is always wrong. In the essay 'Does Oxford Moral Philosophy Corrupt the Youth?', for instance, she criticizes the way that moral philosophy today bases itself upon intuitions about '"our" standards'. The image 'conjured up', she says ironically, is of 'people free of crime, behaving nicely (they will always tell lies to avoid betraying friends), and also looking for improvement [...]'.[2] And in the essay 'Action, Intention and "Double Effect"', she acknowledges that the 'application' of the term 'lying' is 'somewhat obscure or disputable'. She immediately rejects, however, the notion that this 'creates a conceptual difficulty about the notion of absolute wrongness—whether great wrongness, or small as in many instances of lying'.[3]

But, in the one place where Anscombe discusses lying most extensively, the essay entitled 'Two Moral Theologians', she suggests that some lies might be permissible.[4] We shall get to these remarks later in this essay. But before that I would like to consider in some detail what she says about a couple of Jesuits, and especially about the Belgian Jesuit, Arthur Vermeersch. My interest in Vermeersch is due not just to the fact that he taught at

---

[1] I am grateful to a number of people who made comments regarding earlier versions of this essay. They include Nicanor Austriaco, Charles Fried, Kevin Fitzpatrick, Mary Geach, Luke Gormally, Daniel Hill, David Albert Jones, Hugh MacKenzie, Anselm Müller, Matthew O'Brien, Roger Teichmann, Candace Vogler, and Helen Watt.
[2] 'Does Oxford Moral Philosophy Corrupt the Youth?', in *HLAE*, p. 166.
[3] 'Action, Intention and "Double Effect"', in *HLAE*, p. 219.
[4] 'Two Moral Theologians', *FHG*, pp. 157–169.

the Gregorian University, where I presently teach.[5] Vermeersch was, as Anscombe acknowledges, a gifted moral theologian. She also calls the essay she criticizes 'interesting and learned'; and it certainly is that.[6] I shall argue that some of the ideas he puts forward help one to solve difficulties connected with Anscombe's own position in 'Two Moral Theologians'.

Anscombe contrasts Vermeersch with Bruno Schüller, the other Jesuit (but not of the Gregorian University), whose work she calls '*quite* interesting'[7] but also wonders 'how people could be snowed by such writing'.[8] She maintains that there is a 'curious resemblance' between Vermeersch and Schüller:

> Our two moral theologians both play Humpty Dumpty with words and both use well known facts, which do make their topic more difficult than a naïf person would think, to justify themselves. There the similarity ends: Vermeersch *thinks* he is strictly maintaining a strict doctrine; Schüller's bent is to make hay of any strict doctrine.[9]

Schüller, as we are told in a note to this essay, 'advanced a "proportionalist" (consequentialist) understanding of Christian ethics'.[10] Anscombe calls his thesis that traditional Catholic morality is consequentialist 'a startling impudence'.[11]

---

[5] He taught at the Gregorian from 1918 to 1934.
[6] Arthur Vermeersch, 'De mendacio et necessitatibus commercii humani', *Gregorianum* 1 (1920):11–40, 425–474. In what follows, the abbreviation 'De mendacio' stands for this essay.
[7] 'Two Moral Theologians', p. 162, emphasis added.
[8] 'Two Moral Theologians', p. 161. The work she criticizes is Bruno Schüller, *Die Begründung sittlicher Urteile: Typen ethischer Argumentation in der Moraltheologie* (Düsseldorf: Patmos, 1980).
[9] 'Two Moral Theologians', p. 162. The emphasis is in the original. In subsequent quotations, unless otherwise noted, emphasis is in the original.
[10] 'Two Moral Theologians', p. 160.
[11] 'Two Moral Theologians', p. 166. Although Anscombe considers Schüller a consequentialist pretty much throughout this essay, at one point she does say: 'Now I am not quite clear to what extent Schüller is a consequentialist. He sometimes I think forgets the totality of opinion involved in defining the "teleologist"—a "teleologist" thinks *all* acts are determined in their moral character by their consequences or tendency to produce certain consequences' ('Two Moral Theologians', p. 164). (She understands here Schüller's term 'teleologist' as equivalent to 'consequentialist'.)

1. Defending Vermeersch

Vermeersch's essay, 'De mendacio et necessitatibus commercii humani' (or 'On Lying and the Necessities of Human Life in Common') is long—nearly 80 pages—and is divided into three parts: the first considering the 'idea or description of lying'; the second considering the 'wrongness [malitia]' of lying; and the third (by far the longest) considering the issue, 'In what way provision is to be made for the necessities of human life in common.' Vermeersch's methodology is largely historical, although in the third part he waxes more speculative—which gets him into trouble, as we shall see. The historical spadework that Vermeersch has done itself makes his essay extremely valuable: he gives quotations from, summaries of, and precise references to, a huge array of writings by authors from Augustine to his fellow Belgian and ally Gustavus Waffelaert (1847–1931).[12] The list includes Thomas Aquinas (of course), Cajetan (1469–1534), Medina (1527–1581), de Valentia (1551–1603), Sanchez (1550–1610), Suárez (1548–1617), Lessius (1554–1623), Laymann (1574–1635), Alphonsus (1696–1787) and many others.

In the first part of his essay, Vermeersch discusses the standard definition of lying: 'a false signification contrary to the mind with the intention of deceiving.' Surprisingly (given what he says later), he emphasizes the first words of the definition ('falsa significatio contra mentem'), rather than the rest ('cum intentione fallendi'). And so he writes:

> Because today there is no obvious reason why we should insert into the definition words that are not necessary, if we wish to speak in unison with Catholic scholars who have lived since the time of St. Augustine, we must choose the following brief definition, by means of which lying is described: *A locution contrary to the mind*.[13]

In maintaining that the words 'cum intentione fallendi' are not necessary, Vermeersch is following Thomas, who maintains that the intention to deceive does not belong to the formal species of lying but amounts to a certain 'perfection' of it. A locution contrary to the mind but lacking the intention to deceive is prevented

---

[12] Beyond these parameters, Vermeersch makes mention of Xenophon, Plato and Aristotle and (at the other extreme) Antonin-Gilbert Sertillanges, O.P. (1863–1948).
[13] 'De mendacio', p. 19.

by that lack from effecting what its nature (such as it is) 'wants' to effect. Thomas uses the example of a heavy object, which, by its nature, falls but, contrary to that nature, can be held aloft. Thus, Thomas and Vermeersch both allow that there could be a genuine lie that does not involve the intention to deceive.[14] In Thomas (and presumably in Vermeersch) that means that one lies even if one's intention is, say, simply to get a laugh out of someone.

The second part of the essay, on the wrongness of lying, begins with a section demonstrating that the tradition of that Church is decidedly against lying: 'Therefore', this section concludes, 'we deplore any retreat from the traditional severity with which the learned [summi Doctores] maintained that not even to save a life —either one's own or that of another—is it permitted to lie.'[15] In the second 'article' of the same second part, Vermeersch considers various explanations for the wrongness of lying and rejects one which is of particular interest. A number of authors argue that lying is wrong because it *'corrupts the only instrument of intercourse among men'*.[16] He mentions a number of authors who maintain this position, including St. Ephrem and an unnamed commentator on Scotus who, he says, greatly exaggerates the evil of lying, writing that, if lying were not wrong, 'Society and human conversation would be totally destroyed'.[17] This argument, says Vermeersch, proves too much since some lies are 'socially useful'.[18] Nonetheless, he clearly holds that there is some truth in the argument, for he states later on that lying is immoral because 'consideration of the individual man, no less than consideration of the social man, requires communication among men.'[19]

Vermeersch's objection to the argument about the corruption of society is that sometimes a lie is simply not that important. In

---

[14] *Summa theologiae* II–II, q. 110, a. 1c. In this same article, Thomas also explains how the word 'falsa' in 'falsa significatio contra mentem' is to be understood. One can utter a truth and still lie, if one *thinks* that the locution is false. In this case, the utterance is formally false, materially true. Vermeersch cites Thomas in these regards ('De mendacio', pp. 16–17).

[15] 'De mendacio', p. 28.

[16] 'De mendacio', p. 29.

[17] 'De mendacio', p. 30. Vermeersch also cites Cardinal Juan de Lugo (1583–1660) ('De mendacio', p. 30), who says, more moderately, that lying impedes human intercourse and renders a man unreliable. It is this position that, according to Vermeersch, the Scotist unduly exaggerates ('valde exaggerat').

[18] 'Two Moral Theologians', p. 157.

[19] 'De mendacio', p. 33.

this regard, he cites Thomas, who says, in answer to the question 'Whether every lie is a mortal sin', that, 'properly speaking, a mortal sin is that which is repugnant [repugnat] to charity, by which the soul lives conjoined to God.'[20] There are, however, he says, various ways in which an act can be contrary to charity. These include being contrary 'in itself [secundum se]' and being contrary with respect to the end intended. The first of these has to do with the 'false signification' itself. If this pertains somehow to the good of man, the lie is a mortal sin; if, however, it makes no difference to one's neighbour whether the opinion generated by the signification is false or not, so that no injury is done by the lie, the sin is venial. As for the end intended in telling a lie, this might not be contrary to charity at all, as happens with the jocose or officious lie, which are intended respectively to delight or to help one's neighbour; neither is, therefore, a mortal sin.

Explicitly adhering to these ideas of Thomas's, Vermeersch acknowledges that a lie, even *qua* false locution, does go against charity. On the other hand:

> [...] since a man is himself a contingent being and the truth of which he deprives other men through a lie is per se merely a truth of *his* mind, to know which is minimally essential for others, a lie leaves the order of charity towards others substantially intact.[21]

He also acknowledges that, when someone lies out of hatred or by lying does injury to another or has a special obligation to tell the truth, the act is a mortal sin.[22] A couple of paragraphs later he remarks that, although the order pertaining to a locution itself has a connection with charity and although a lie does upset that order, 'nonetheless, it is only beside [praeter] the order of charity'; it 'leaves the order of charity towards others substantially intact'.[23] In other words, it does not attack charity directly—it is not 'repugnant' to it—but neither *is* it a charitable act, as such an act should be.

Anscombe recounts all of this, but, having done so, remarks:

> His [Vermeersch's] conclusion seems admirable but his thinking here is a bit odd. If the order of speech is inviolable because and

---

[20] *Summa theologiae* II–II, q. 110, a. 4c.
[21] 'De mendacio', p. 36, emphasis added.
[22] 'De mendacio', p. 36.
[23] 'De mendacio', p. 37.

only because speech relates to the 'order of charity,' how is it that that doesn't show, not merely that lying is always wrong, but that it is always a violation of the 'order of charity'? Or if it is not always a violation of the 'order of charity,' how does its relation to the order of charity manage to show that it is always wrong? To repeat, I am not disputing his conclusion that lying is always wrong but not always mortally sinful. I am only criticising the reasons he offers for his conclusion.[24]

Here I must come to the defence of my fellow Jesuit. Since in the argument just expounded, but also earlier when discussing the proper definition of charity, Vermeersch not only cites but is clearly following Thomas, his reasons for saying both that lying is *per se* wrong but, at the same time, not necessarily gravely wrong can be judged no more 'odd' — or inadequate — than Thomas's own. And in this regard we have already encountered the Dominican's idea that a lie might remain short of its 'perfection' — which it does 'achieve' when its speaker's intention is precisely to deceive — as when a stone remains short of its proper perfection when held aloft by some other force. It is for this reason that Vermeersch says that we can dispense with the words 'with the intention of deceiving' and define lying simply as 'a false signification contrary to the mind'. It is also on this basis that he maintains that all lying is disordered, that is, since there is a break of intelligibility between the mind and what is signified. And yet only some lies are gravely disordered, since what a lie *could* be, by its very nature, it is not always.

A mother might be weary after a stressful day and quite deliberately snap at her child, not because she does not love the child or intends its harm but because she is tired and gives in momentarily to her emotions. Her act is very different from that of a mother who snaps at a child in order to harm the child psychologically. Both acts are wrong because they go against charity, but only the latter is seriously wrong, because the intention is to harm. Similarly, as Thomas says in *Summa theologiae* II–II, q. 110, a. 4c, with some lies the other person might be led astray 'in some contingent particulars that do not pertain to him': it may make little real difference whether he knows the truth or not. An untruth with respect to such contingent particulars does not pertain 'to the good of man — to, for example, the perfection of knowledge or the

---

[24] 'Two Moral Theologians', pp. 158–159.

understanding of morals'. But a lie that *does* pertain to an individual's good (in this sense) is a mortal sin. These distinctions in Thomas seem to me not at all odd but perfectly reasonable.

2. Agreeing with Anscombe, against Vermeersch

The third part of Vermeersch's essay—entitled, as mentioned earlier, 'In what way provision is to be made for the necessities of human life in common'—begins with this paragraph:

> Lying is never permissible. Living, however, is. As is living humanly. It is necessary that secrets be capable of remaining inviolate. Nor are men to be undone on account of words. How these things can be reconciled among themselves and such necessities be combined with the absolute exclusion of lying is what we now propose to investigate.[25]

Vermeersch then describes briefly the larger historical context within which he confronts these issues.[26] He mentions thinkers who, in order to reconcile the absolute prohibition of lying with the necessities of life, proposed the use of ambiguities, equivocation, 'mental restrictions' and the like in answering questions, the straightforward answers to which would violate trust or betray persons.[27] He mentions also Kant and Fichte, who, having rejected all such artifices of speech, pushed the 'austere conclusions of Augustine' even further than the latter does himself. This is followed by a rich and detailed presentation and critique of the various ways in which thinkers—almost all Catholic thinkers—have attempted to deal with the 'hard cases', in which straightforward answers would violate trust or betray the innocent.[28]

---

[25] 'De mendacio', p. 425.
[26] 'De mendacio', pp. 425–427.
[27] Anscombe makes some useful remarks about why we ought not to translate 'restrictio mentalis' as 'mental reservation' ('Two Moral Theologians', p. 159). Also useful is chapter 10 of Albert R. Jonsen and Stephen Toulmin, *The Abuse of Casuistry: A history of moral reasoning* (Berkeley: University of California Press, 1988). The chapter finishes with a consideration of the Holy Office's condemnation of certain theses regarding equivocation put forward by the Jesuits Thomas Sanchez and Leonardus Lessius. See *Enchiridion symbolorum definitionum et declarationum de rebus fidei et morum / Compendium of Creeds, Definitions, and Declarations on Matters of Faith and Morals*, edited by Heinrich Denzinger and Peter Hünermann (San Francisco: Ignatius Press, 2012), §§2126–2128.
[28] 'De mendacio', pp. 428–460.

Finally, having rejected the majority of the theories regarding how to deal with such hard cases, Vermeersch offers his own 'Solution of the problem'.[29]

I do not wish to spend too much time discussing Vermeersch's own solution, which is disappointingly contrived and unconvincing. But something must be said about it, if only to finish off the story of Vermeersch on lying. As a preface to his solution, Vermeersch invokes a principle he takes from Suárez.[30] To speak — in the sense relevant to the definition of lying: 'locutio contra mentem' — is not just to utter words and to direct them at another: this happens also in the theatre. Required also is that the speaker make it apparent in executing that act — 'as if through the intrinsic reflection of the act itself upon itself' — that he is revealing what he thinks about the way things stand in reality.[31] A 'locution against

---

[29] 'De mendacio', pp. 460–471.

[30] 'De mendacio', p. 462. He also cites in this regard the lesser known Gilles [Aegidius] de Coninck, *De moralitate: natura et effectibus actuum supernaturalium in genere et fide, spe, ac caritate speciatim* (Antwerp: Martinus Nutius, 1623), disp. 9, dub. 5, n. 57 (p. 173). Says de Coninck: 'Note that, when Peter, for example, says to me "John is dead," he not only signifies to me that John is dead but also that he judges this to be the case and that he wishes to indicate this to me — and, indeed, that he in fact does this.' The principle that Vermeersch invokes is similar to the idea that Anscombe analyses in 'What is it to Believe Someone?', in *FHG*, pp. 1–10.

[31] 'Loqui itaque non est tantum verba exterius proferre eaque ad alium dirigere; sed essentiale locutioni quoque est ut qui, *in actu signato* verba profert, *in actu exercito* "quasi per intrinsecam reflexionem eiusdem actus in se ipsum", dicat se dicere, seu mentem suam a se communicari' ('To speak, therefore, is not just to utter words exteriorly and to direct them at another, but it is essential to a locution also that the person who *in the act signified* utters words, *in the act exercised*, "as if through an intrinsic reflection of the very act upon itself", says that he speaks or that his mind is by him communicated') ('De mendacio', p. 462). In a note Vermeersch refers to Francisco Suárez, *Opera Omnia*, vol. 12: *De Fide Theologica*, edited by M. André and Carolus Berton (Paris: L. Vivès, 1858), d. 3, sect. 12 n. 12 (pp. 105–106). In this passage Suárez draws a distinction between two ways in which God can say that he is revealing something. He can actually *say* this, as when Christ says, 'My Father has revealed' (such and such). Here, in fact, we have 'the revelation of a revelation'. The other way that God can say that he is revealing something is when, 'in the act exercised', God speaks 'as if through the intrinsic reflection of the act itself upon itself'. Here God does not *say* that he is revealing; he simply reveals. The locution has within itself an implicit reference to itself implying that it is a revelation of the speaker's (here, God's) mind regarding the way

the mind' obviously goes against such a dynamic. Vermeersch interprets this principle in such a way that, just as the circumstances (for instance) of a play make it apparent that the actors are not speaking their own minds, so also whenever there is a doubt about whether any speaker is communicating his mind, 'there would be present a true and proper ambiguity, which itself [...] excludes lying'.[32]

On this basis, then, Vermeersch maintains the following:

> A wife who is questioned and denies having committed adultery and a culprit who denies having committed a crime are not exonerated of lying on the grounds that the word 'adultery' [adulterium] can also mean 'idolatry' or because the culprit tacitly adds 'I did not do it today, this hour' but rather because these responses objectively signify one of the following: either 'I did not do it' or 'I do not wish to admit it.' These are not 'contrary to the mind' [contra mentem]. Also the loveable St. Francis, when he wished to save the life of a man whom [others] pursued, in order that without lying he might respond 'He has not passed this way,' did not need with his hand to indicate his sleeve or with his foot to designate the place where he stood. His response itself bore this ambiguity: either 'He has not passed this way' or 'I am not betraying the man.' ('De mendacio', pp. 462–463)

Anscombe is certainly right to call this nonsense.[33] Not only are the contexts supposed here—questioning whether someone has done something or whether someone has passed by—not at all like the context of a stage, but also a doubt present in the mind of one who hears a speaker does not make what that speaker says ambiguous.

---

things stand—or should stand—in reality. (Of course, in speaking about God any reference to his 'mind' must be understood analogically.)

[32] 'Si ita res se habent, quotiescumque ex adiunctis rationabiliter colligitur, exteriora verba non dici ab aliquo qui mentem sitam communicat, aberit, cum ipsa locutione, copia mendacii; et quotiescumque idem dubitabitur, aderit vera et propria ambiguitas sermonis, quae ipsa, ea quam supra diximus ratione, mendacium excludit' ('De mendacio', p. 462). The back reference ('ea quam supra diximus') is to his earlier comments on ambiguity in which he acknowledges that the utterance of some ambiguities is not lying ('De mendacio', p. 444–446).

[33] Anscombe says of Vermeersch's solution that it 'is much more nonsense than some of the contentions of the mental restrictioners were' ('Two Moral Theologians', p. 160).

Vermeersch maintains that his own 'solution to the problem' is more straightforward than the various equivocations (and the like) he discusses—which, in comparison with some of them, it certainly is—but this limited advantage costs him dearly: the result is that certain locutions would, according to him, no longer mean what they clearly *mean*.[34] The Vermeersch who proposes this solution is, as Anscombe puts it, 'Vermeersch in his world-pleasing role'.[35] He is concerned *at all costs* to deflect the criticism directed at Catholic authors that, on this topic, they inevitably resort to 'subtle tricks' ('calliditates') such as pointing to one's sleeve, equivocation, mental restriction, etc. It is almost as if Vermeersch's overall strategy was to set out, in the earlier parts of the essay, 'with absolute rigor'[36] the position that lying is always wrong, so that, in the final part, his own novel attempt to satisfy the critics might be received as traditional. If this was his strategy, it was not successful.

3. Anscombe's solution

But what is Anscombe's solution to the problem? It comes during a biting criticism of the other Jesuit, Bruno Schüller, who sets up a dilemma for the non-consequentialist which he believes demonstrates that consequentialism is the only reasonable solution to the lying-related hard cases.[37] She notes, first of all, that Schüller tends to simplify matters: to write, that is, '*as if* there were only two possibilities when there are evidently, or likely to be, more'.[38] For example:

---

[34] This makes the position incompatible with the Suárezian principle invoked by Vermeersch himself. Suárez's position—like that of Thomas Aquinas in *Summa theologiae* II-II, q. 110, a. 1c—looks primarily to the locution itself: it is (as he says) as if the locution *itself* says, 'This is being said as something to be believed.' See above, note 31. Decisive for Vermeersch is rather the context within which the locution is uttered.

[35] 'Two Moral Theologians', p. 166.

[36] 'De mendacio', p. 40.

[37] In this section, Anscombe speaks about Schüller's concept of the 'teleologist': 'a "teleologist" thinks that actions are to be judged only by their consequences, or their tendency to produce good or bad consequences.' So, the terms 'teleologist' and 'consequentialist' are equivalent. Anscombe adds: 'Schüller maintains that "teleological" ethics is the right Catholic sort' ('Two Moral Theologians', p. 163).

[38] 'Two Moral Theologians', pp. 162-163.

> If you must preserve a secret, are asked a question about it and 'silence will betray'; well then—to betray the secret is excluded; so you must *either* lie *or* if you think you must not lie you must *give an answer* which *is* an answer but which doesn't betray; in giving it you use a restrictive concept of lying so that what you say, by that concept, doesn't count as a lie.[39]

Anscombe's setting out here of the possibilities offered by Schüller is not particularly clear. She actually speaks of three possibilities, one of which, silence, is eliminated at the outset, leaving the two: either lie or 'use a restrictive concept of lying so that what you say, by that concept, doesn't count as a lie'. It is also true, however, that for the non-consequentialist only one of these two is a real option, since he refuses to lie. In effect, Schüller forces the non-consequentialist down the only path he (the non-consequentialist) believes he can follow morally—the one that does not involve lying but only the use of equivocation or some other 'restrictive concept of lying'—in order to demonstrate that one should just become a consequentialist and take the alternative path of lying since the other path involves mere ruses intended to mask the fact that a decision has been made on consequentialist grounds that the innocent person must be saved.

In any case, as we have seen, Anscombe protests that Schüller does not consider other possibilities. Among the possibilities not mentioned by Schüller, says Anscombe, would be 'feigning a faint' and 'making a distracting joke'. She then adds to this list of possibilities the following:

> That if you can see no possibility except to give some information you must not give, or to lie, you will do better to lie than, say, to betray the unjustly persecuted fugitive—this is sufficiently obvious but does not get mentioned. The most that is mentioned is that you may not be clever enough, which is unfair. For the discussions are all about how to *avoid any sin* at all. But the truth is: you might not be good enough to do that.[40]

Schüller's suggestion that 'you may not be clever enough' to come up with a dodge of some sort is unfair, according to Anscombe, not because you might *indeed* be clever enough but because he never *really* offers to the non-consequentialist the possibility of simply lying (that is, sinning by lying). This is apparent from what

---

[39] 'Two Moral Theologians', p. 163.
[40] 'Two Moral Theologians', p. 163.

Anscombe says immediately after the words 'which is unfair': 'For the discussions are all about how to *avoid any sin* at all. But the truth is: you might not be good enough to do that.' In fact, although she introduces the other possibilities (of 'feigning a faint' and 'making a distracting joke'), Anscombe ultimately, in at least some cases, excludes them for the same reason that Schüller cites: in some cases, certain people will not be clever enough to come up with such an honest dodge.

Anscombe goes on to acknowledge that the difference between a consequentialist such as Schüller and one who rejects that approach is that, for the latter, there are 'some kinds of actions one should not do—not for any advantage to be gained or evil to be avoided'.[41] She then begins an ostensibly anti-consequentialist argument, the conclusion of which is that, in certain circumstances, one should lie. It must be quoted at its full length.[42]

[1] Lying is one of the candidates [that is, for status as actions 'one should not do']. This makes the discussion of it rather interesting.

[2] I said one should lie about the thing *rather* than give the fugitive away. How come? Isn't that doing something bad for the sake of avoiding an evil?—namely the evil of the fugitive being caught? This must be what incites Schüller to say that the devices invented to show what would *not* be a lie come as near as anything to teleology. Aren't we going by consequences?

[3] People may easily be incited to say that the devices invented to show that something would not be a lie come as near as you like to saying 'Lie for the good purpose, or to avoid the evil, and I'll tell you a way of muddling your mind into thinking it isn't a lie.' Now *aren't* we just going by consequences here?

[4] No, and the point is important. If it is absolutely clear that someone can't be persuaded to avoid wrongdoing altogether in some matter, it is good to persuade him to commit some lesser sin than what he is minded to do. If you *cannot* see any alternative to committing one sin or another, you act better if you choose[43] the lesser sin. And you may not have time or cleverness to find out a better possibility. To betray the fugitive, we will suppose, is a

---

[41] 'Two Moral Theologians', p. 164.

[42] For the sake of clarity, I have numbered the argument's paragraphs and also interjected a few words in square brackets. The argument appears at 'Two Moral Theologians', p. 164.

[43] The published version actually reads 'you act better if you chose the lesser sin' ('Two Moral Theologians', p. 164]. I take it that this is a typographical error.

> gravely wicked thing to do. Telling the pursuers he is there *is* betraying him. So in this case telling that truth is a wicked act—more than telling the lie that he is not there. But suppose that somebody else threatened that *he* would give the fugitive away unless you told some lie? That case would be different. If you are a consequentialist, you are likely to say you should tell that lie just as much as the other one. But I didn't say you *should* tell the other one, only that you should do it *rather* than commit an act of betrayal by what you tell the pursuers. If you are a consequentialist you will hold that you are responsible for all the consequences of your acts and omissions and therefore that you are responsible for the capture of the fugitive if he was caught because you refused to tell the lie demanded by the person who betrayed him—just as much as if you betrayed him.

Anscombe's choice of words in the first sentence here is indicative of what is to come. She has just said (as we have seen) that for the non-consequentialists, among whom she certainly places herself, there are 'some kinds of actions one should not do—not for any advantage to be gained or evil to be avoided'. But now she says that lying is one such *candidate*. In fact, she goes on immediately to assert that 'one should lie about the thing *rather* than give the fugitive away.' The emphasis here ('*rather*') is important and is explained later in the quotation, in paragraph [4].

Paragraphs [2] and [3] have primarily to do with Schüller's position (already alluded to) that crass equivocation and other such devices are just consequentialism in disguise. But, over the course of this brief discussion, Anscombe asks rhetorically a number of times whether her own position is not consequentialist. 'Isn't [lying to the pursuers] doing something bad for the sake of avoiding an evil?—namely the evil of the fugitive being caught?' 'No,' she says very decisively at the beginning of the fourth paragraph, 'and the point is important.'

And then (in paragraph [4]) come two sentences that, placed together as they are, constitute a first argument in support of her solution. The two sentences are as follows:

> If it is absolutely clear that someone can't be persuaded to avoid wrongdoing altogether in some matter, it is good to persuade him to commit some lesser sin than what he is minded to do. If you *cannot* see any alternative to committing one sin or another, you act better if you choose the lesser sin.

The first sentence articulates a thesis with solid support in classical moral theology, that is, the thesis that, when nothing can be done to impede a person from committing at least one of a number of evil deeds, it is permissible to counsel that person to commit a lesser of the same evils: the 'minus malum'.[44] The second sentence articulates quite a different thesis: that if *you* can see no other way —as in the hidden fugitive case—then *you* should commit (as Anscombe puts it) 'the lesser sin'. Anscombe apparently believes that the thesis regarding counselling the lesser evil gives support to her own position that the lesser sin (the lie) should be chosen rather than give the fugitive away. We shall come back to these two sentences—and the relationship between them—below.

In the rest of paragraph [4], Anscombe offers a second argument to the effect that her position—that, in the circumstances presupposed so far, one should tell the lie—does not amount to consequentialism. She asks us to 'suppose that somebody else threatened that *he* would give the fugitive away unless you told some lie?' The difference between this scenario and the one discussed previously is that here you would not be choosing between your lying rather than *your* betraying but between your lying and *someone else's* betraying. The latter choice, she maintains, could only be justified on consequentialist grounds. As she says at the end of the quotation: 'If you are a consequentialist you will hold that you are responsible for all the consequences of your acts and omissions and therefore that you are responsible for the capture of the fugitive if he was caught because you refused to tell the lie demanded by the person who betrayed him—just as much as if you betrayed him.'[45]

---

[44] On this moral issue, see Kevin L. Flannery, 'On Counseling the Lesser Evil', *The Thomist* 75 (2011):245–289.

[45] See 'War and Murder', in *CPP3*, p. 58: 'But if I am answerable for the foreseen consequences of an action or refusal, as much as for the action itself, then these prohibitions will break down. If someone innocent will die unless I do a wicked thing, then on this view I am his murderer in refusing: so all that is left to me is to weigh up evils.' See also Anscombe's remark on a case considered in connection with the principle of double effect: whether to save one person stranded on a rock (this is the example she uses) or many stranded on another. She suggests that a man would not necessarily act immorally if he saves the one. 'I do not mean that "because they are more" isn't a good reason for helping these and not that one, or these rather than those. It is a perfectly intelligible reason. But it doesn't follow from that that a man acts badly if he doesn't make it his reason. He acts badly if human need for what is in his power to give doesn't work in him as a reason' ('Who is Wronged? Philippa Foot on Double Effect: One Point', in *HLAE*, p. 251).

4. A criticism of Anscombe's theory

What are we to make of these various arguments? Well, there is certainly something right about the idea that the transition into consequentialist thinking can be almost indiscernible even to the person who makes the transition and even though the shift to consequentialism is philosophically a radical move. In my own teaching, I have found that students very often resist the idea that a lie is always wrong and (like Anscombe) say that one should tell the lie in order to save the innocent fugitive. But they are also stopped short by the question: 'Let us say that someone says to himself, "No, I refuse to lie" and the fugitive is discovered. Has he committed a sin?' Of course, some will proceed to argue that, yes, he has sinned; but it is clear at that point that a line has been crossed. Once it is crossed, if one is to be consistent, one will have to make the basis of one's moral theory 'all the consequences of your acts and omissions' (such consequences including also the acts done by others) and to do away with absolute prohibitions, such as the prohibition against lying. Anscombe traces this idea back to Henry Sidgwick and argues that it has infected 'modern moral philosophy' ever since.[46]

Granted then that Anscombe's position is not a consequentialist position, problems remain, however, in other parts of her argumentation. One of them occurs at the very beginning of her account of the choices that Schüller's places before the non-consequentialist. There, as we saw, even before speaking of the two possibilities—to lie or to 'use a restrictive concept of lying'—another option is excluded: silence. But ought it to have been? Let us say that the situation is this: you know that there is a hostage named Stein hiding in the attic and his pursuers come to the door and say: 'We are looking for Stein. Do you know where he is?' Anscombe excludes remaining silent ('silence will betray'[47]). It is hard to know—or rather to imagine—just what is being excluded here. Is it saying nothing at all? We can grant that this would amount to betraying, although it might happen in a number of ways. If, upon the enquiry, you remain resolutely stone-faced, looking off into the distance, it is likely you mean to betray Stein. You might as well say 'He's in the attic.' In any case, we can also grant that this would be to act immorally. On the other hand, you

---

[46] 'Modern Moral Philosophy', in *CPP3*, pp. 33–34.
[47] 'Two Moral Theologians', p. 163.

might just freeze up and for that reason say nothing, in which case Stein will also have been 'betrayed', that is, discovered. You will not, however, have done anything immoral. We will come back to this possibility shortly.

There is also a problem with the first argument in paragraph [4] of the longer, numbered passage above. That argument, as we have seen, consists of a parallel between the classical position that it is sometimes licit to counsel the lesser evil and the thesis that, if a person cannot see any alternative to committing 'one sin or another', he acts better if he chooses 'the lesser sin'.[48] On the face of it, this is a false parallel. When you successfully counsel the lesser evil, *you* do not commit that evil: the act is performed by the other person, who otherwise would have committed a greater evil. Your own act consists simply in reducing the amount of damage (evil) done. But, when you choose to lie rather than to betray the fugitive, the lying is your act.

It might be argued that there is a way of exonerating Anscombe here. The traditional teaching on counselling the lesser evil always sets things up in such a way that, when such counsel is permissible, there is absolutely nothing that the counsellor can do in order to convince the other person to commit no sin at all. So, he counsels the lesser evil. But we can imagine that, when the pursuers come to the door, in that half second before answering (or not answering), the person who knows that Stein is in the attic truly *cannot* think of an alternative to lying. Perhaps, then, we can extend the traditional teaching to cover such momentary 'traps': in effect, one would be counselling oneself to perform 'the lesser sin'.

The problem with this approach, however, is that, as we have seen, Anscombe herself has, on doubtful grounds, limited the possibilities on offer. In fact, the "counsellor" (who counsels himself) is not forced to give that counsel. We can concede that stone-faced silence is excluded, as are likely-to-be-successful honest dodges — supposing that the person answering the door is not clever or quick enough to come up with one. But it is always possible at least to *attempt* some dodge, even while knowing that it

---

[48] Regarding the classical position, it is important to bear in mind that not *any* instance of counselling the lesser evil is permissible. The situation must be one in which the person doing the counselling is morally certain that the other will perform at least the lesser evil, no matter what. Again, see the article referred to above in note 44.

is quite likely to fail. The attempt might manifest itself in nothing other than the person's simply stuttering and then freezing up—or freezing up without stuttering—so that the fugitive is discovered. In any such scenario, the person answering the door can be said to have betrayed the fugitive, in the sense that the pursuers do discover the fugitive (presuming that they do). The person, however, is certainly not guilty of *betrayal*. But if this is the case, there is an option never really considered by Anscombe and which is a better option than choosing the 'lesser sin'. The person who tries to come up with something but fails does nothing wrong; but the person who tells the lie—as Anscombe acknowledges—commits a sin. Since the former possibility is morally better than the latter, in the circumstances described, the person answering the door should not tell the lie but should attempt somehow to protect the fugitive without lying.

What then about the second argument of that fourth paragraph: that there is a difference—significant with respect to involvement in consequentialist thinking—between (on the one hand) your lying rather than your betraying the fugitive and (on the other hand) your lying and someone else's betraying the fugitive? As already indicated, I am quite willing to accept that this distinction does point to a difference—or a possible difference—between two mentalities, one consequentialist and the other non-consequentialist. But I fail to see how this has a bearing upon the basic question: whether it is permissible to lie, even (for instance) in order to save a fugitive. After all, even a non-consequentialist can do something that is not permitted.[49]

---

[49] In the discussion after a version of this paper was presented in Oxford and also in conversations (some by email) in the hours and days that followed that initial discussion, the suggestion was made to me that Anscombe does not say in a straightforward way that one should lie but only that, given certain *conditions*, one should lie. In other words, she does not detach the proposition 'one should lie' from the conditional 'if the situation is such, one should lie'. But Anscombe often says that one ought never to lie, no matter what the circumstances, i.e., no matter what the conditional. See, for instance, the remark (mentioned near the beginning of the present essay) in 'Action, Intention and "Double Effect"' where she speaks of the 'absolute wrongness' even of small lies (*HLAE*, p. 219). See also 'The Justice of the Present War Considered', in *CPP3*, p. 79, where she says: '[...] we may not commit any sin, however small, for the sake of any good, however great, and if the choice lies between our total destruction and the commission of sin, then we must choose to be destroyed.' If one holds that one ought never to lie, whatever the circumstances, even if

The strongest argument for the sort of position that Anscombe wants to defend would be based, in my opinion, upon an understanding of sin such as gives her pause when discussing Vermeersch. In studying what this Jesuit, following Thomas, says about the difference between venial and mortal sin, we saw above that it consists in the fact that the venial sin 'leaves the order of charity towards others substantially intact'.[50] Following Thomas, we might specify that, for a Christian, a venial sin leaves intact one's relationship, within the theological virtue of charity, not only with one's neighbour, but also with God.[51]

If this is true, it is not *wholly* unreasonable to lie to the pursuers of an innocent fugitive in order thereby to avoid the great evil that the fugitive be discovered and killed. The fugitive would be saved and one's relationship with God would not be harmed irreparably. It is true: charity towards one's neighbour would, for the moment, have been set aside; but there would not be much 'love lost' between you and the pursuers. Just as, according to Thomas, even a person who unjustly attacks an innocent person still enjoys certain rights—the person attacked cannot, for instance, use disproportionate means to repel the attacker[52]—so also the pursuers at the door ought not to be lied to. But, if they are lied to, no one is going to suffer irreparable moral harm as a consequence of the lie.

Thomas in effect explains why this is so in his discussion (in *Summa theologiae* II–II, q. 47, a. 8) of prudence and its characterizing function as 'ordering' (*praecipere*). Prudence is an intellectual virtue and it is the basis of all of ethics in the natural realm. The fact that it is the *basis* is what distinguishes a genuinely Thomistic theory of ethics from a consequentialist theory. Within a Thomistic theory, one certainly can—and often must—make choices with a view to consequences; consequences, however, never become the basis of the theory: if there is a possible conflict, reason always trumps consequences. But the intellectual character of prudence is also inherently orientated toward action; and so one can be

---

one's saying that one should (sometimes) lie remains within a conditional (as in, 'if the situation is such, one should lie'), one's position is untenable since the two propositions are contradictory: 'one ought not to lie whatever the conditions' and 'in some conditions, one ought to lie'.

[50] 'De mendacio', p. 37.
[51] See *Summa theologiae* I–II, q. 72, a. 5c. See also *De malo* 7.2c, which concludes: 'Et ideo peccatum veniale nullo modo caritatem habitam diminuit.'
[52] *Summa theologiae* II–II, q. 64, a. 7.

accused of 'inconstancy' (as Thomas calls it at *Summa theologiae* II–II, q. 53, a. 5) if one knows what is the most reasonable thing to do and does not do it: if one does not, that is, 'give the order' to oneself to act in accordance with what prudence dictates. This makes prudence different from a craft (or *ars*). A master craftsman might actually demonstrate his mastery of a craft by making a mistake: doing so deliberately, for instance, in order to teach apprentices how not to proceed. 'And so', says Thomas:

> that craftsman is considered better who errs willingly in an art, as having right judgment, rather than the one who errs unwillingly, which appears to issue from a defect of judgment. But with prudence the converse is the case, as is said in the sixth book of the *Nicomachean Ethics*, for more imprudent is the one who errs willingly, as being defective in the principal act of prudence, which is to order, than the one who errs unwillingly.[53]

Applying these ideas to the case at hand, for a person to use prudence in order to do what prudence says is not the most reasonable thing to do — that is, to lie to the pursuers rather than to do whatever else one can — is an abuse of prudence since it amounts to understanding what is the most reasonable thing to do but not giving oneself the order to act in accordance with what that understanding dictates. This does not mean that lying in such circumstances is utterly unreasonable. On the other hand, to argue that lying is *the* reasonable thing to do — which is, in effect, to assert that refusing absolutely to lie is to do wrong to the person who is thereby discovered — is to fall into consequentialism.

These ideas apply also in the realm of the theological — or infused — virtues, such as depend ultimately upon charity, for charity is not present in a person's soul without the infused virtue of prudence, not to mention its natural counterpart, 'acquired' prudence.[54] As we have seen, the continued presence of charity in the soul is what differentiates venial from mortal sin. One cannot choose in perfect charity to lie, although in certain circumstances a lie does not utterly destroy one's communion with God. Which is not to say that, even in such circumstances, choosing to lie is the

---

[53] *Summa theologiae* II–II, q. 47, a. 8. The idea comes from Aristotle's *Nicomachean Ethics*, 6.5.1140b22–24; see also *Eudemian Ethics*, 7.13.1246a31–35. (In some editions, chapter 7.13 of the latter work is designated as chapter 8.1.)
[54] See *Summa theologiae* II–II, q. 47, a. 14.

most charitable thing to do, since all charity is in the first instance about one's relationship with God.

5. Conclusion

To conclude then very briefly, the person who tells the lie will have done something that lacks inherent intelligibility: he will have uttered a 'locution contrary to the mind' within a context in which, 'as if through the intrinsic reflection of the act itself upon itself', his locution says that it is *not* contrary to his mind. Invoking this Suárezian principle does not allow anyone to 'play Humpty Dumpty with words' and to argue, as Vermeersch might do, that the person answering the door and saying that the fugitive is not there actually *means* that he does not wish to reveal the correct information.[55] His words mean what they clearly mean: he tells a lie, and lies are always disordered and therefore bad.

When the pursuers came to the door, the person answering the door would have done better had he been able to come up with an efficacious and honest dodge or even tried to do so and failed in such a way that the pursuers suspected that he was hiding someone. In either of these cases he would have done nothing even minimally wrong. But he might also have decided to lie, in effect entrusting himself to the mercy of God. If he knows his Thomas Aquinas, he will have done so with some confidence, knowing that such a sin is 'beside [*praeter*] the order of charity' but not repugnant to it. But that same knowledge will not tell him that refusing to lie would have been immoral. It would rather have been the reasonable thing to do.

---

[55] See 'De mendacio', pp. 462–463.

Roger Teichmann

Sincerity in Thought

A person can be responsible for an outcome, can be held to account for it, despite not having intended it or even foreseen it. The babysitter who brings her Rottweiler along with her and leaves it with the baby while she nips out to buy some cigarettes will be responsible for the baby's injuries. She didn't, let us assume, intend the dog to attack the baby. And she may well not have foreseen this outcome either, if that means foreseeing it as likely, since it might not have been a likely thing to happen, merely something made more likely by her absence. Let us imagine that she is asked, 'Why did you leave the dog with the baby?', and replies: 'I assumed the dog would stay still for the short time I was at the shop.' A question that arises about statements like this is whether they are fully sincere, or *bona fide*, or genuine.

In her article, 'On Being in Good Faith',[1] Elizabeth Anscombe discusses the phenomenon of insincerity in connection with issues of responsibility, voluntariness and so on. It might be thought that insincerity must attach to statements made to, or behaviour directed towards, other people; but as Anscombe argues, sincerity and insincerity can be features of thoughts themselves. Indeed, a statement can be insincere on account of its expressing an insincere thought of the speaker's—rather than on account of its not expressing the thought the speaker really has. One consequence of this for ethics is that when someone's responsibility for an action or omission depends on the sort of account the person could truthfully give, e.g. in answer to such questions as 'Why didn't you do X?', it is not enough that such possible answers not be *lies*—for the person may not know that her response is false or dubious, and so

---

[1] In *FHG*, pp. 101–112.

may not be lying. But in the case of insincerity, 'not knowing' doesn't supply an excuse, as it might in other cases, but is itself a source of culpability.

1

It is natural to suppose that the sincerity of an assertion is a matter of the utterance's being an expression of what the person thinks; in some sense, the public and conventional meaning of the utterance, together with the point or purpose of the language-game within which it is made, determine that you should say such-and-such only if you think that p. (Reference to the point of the language-game is needed so as to allow for jokes, play-acting and the like—contexts where you needn't think what you say.) Such a model seems to be inapplicable to thoughts: if a thought can be called insincere, surely this won't mean that it's at odds with some other thought standing behind it? At any rate, if the second thought is meant to be the same sort of thing as the first, it would apparently have to be sincere in its turn, i.e. in line with some thought standing behind it, and so on *ad infinitum*. So what can the insincerity of a thought consist in?

As Anscombe remarks, 'It need not mean that some feeling of hesitancy or difficulty accompanied the thought. For it depends on the context of the thought whether a feeling of difficulty would be counted as showing that the man did not sincerely think it.'[2] She mentions a man who 'believes in the assurance of a friend that there are no steps to fall down in a dark passage, but who has uneasy feelings as he walks the passage';[3] such a man still quite sincerely thinks that there are no steps to fall down. Of course, the uneasiness that might accompany the babysitter's thought, 'The dog is sure to stay put on the sofa' will very likely be a symptom of insincerity, or not full sincerity, and this seems to be because a rational person knowing the facts is unlikely to arrive at such a thought without 'suppressing the knowledge that makes the thought doubtful'. (The phrase is Anscombe's, and we shall be taking a closer look at it later on.[4]) In other words, it is the doubtfulness of the thought, given the known facts, that lends a certain character to any feelings of uneasiness or difficulty; and this fact is

---

[2] 'On Being in Good Faith', p. 102.
[3] 'On Being in Good Faith', p. 103.
[4] See 'On Being in Good Faith', p. 103.

an indication that it is the doubtfulness of the thought which is the key issue when it comes to the thought's insincerity, in ways we shall see.

We need at this point to make a distinction, between thoughts as occurrences and thoughts as more settled states of a person.[5] Anscombe appears to be talking about the first; and someone might object that to the extent that occurrent thoughts are statements made to oneself or occurring inwardly, e.g. as heard with one's 'inner ear', the sincerity or insincerity of *these* will be very like that of external statements. I can, after all, say something to myself I don't believe at all, such as 'The Wykeham Professor has three heads.' What I *believe*, the objector goes on, is in fact something lying behind my occurrent thoughts and with which those thoughts may or may not be in harmony.

But what is the nature of this background belief? If it is said to be a certain disposition of the person, we must ask what manifestations this disposition is supposed to have. A disposition to have occurrent thoughts with a certain content will bring us back to the question whether these occurrent thoughts are sincere or not. For surely I can be disposed to say jokingly to myself, 'The Wykeham Professor has three heads', perhaps even several times a day? And yet I do not believe this, and these inner assertions are not meant sincerely. It is natural at this point to look to the person's non-linguistic behaviour, and to attempt to cast a standing belief as a behavioural disposition, possibly a multi-track one *à la* Gilbert Ryle. But restricting ourselves to non-linguistic manifestations of a belief, as it seems we must, puts many beliefs out of the range of our analysis; what non-linguistic behaviour could manifest my belief that Hannibal ate meat, for instance? Moreover, non-linguistic behaviour shares with linguistic behaviour the problematic feature that it can be sincere or insincere, genuine or fake.

It is worth pausing to consider this last point. What does the insincerity of a bit of behaviour consist in—a smile, say, or some attentive nodding? It cannot consist simply in a disharmony

---

[5] This distinction is not intended to be either exhaustive or precise, nor do I mean by employing it to be addressing the question 'What sort of *mental state* is thinking/thought?' As Wittgenstein said, 'thinking' is 'a widely ramified concept. A concept that comprises many manifestations of life' (*Zettel*, p. 110); and he advised that we 'look at the word "to think" as a tool' (*Philosophical Investigations*, p. 360). The distinction between 'occurrent' and 'settled' thoughts is itself merely a tool, whose usefulness is relative to the enquiry.

between the behaviour and an accompanying thought or feeling, if that thought or feeling is an 'inner statement', since that inner statement might itself not be sincere, as we have seen. Perhaps the accompanying thought or feeling is a standing disposition of some sort, such as an attitude of unfriendliness. The insincere smile then counts as insincere because smiling (of that sort) is a sign of friendliness, the contrary of unfriendliness. The smile, in other words, is misleading. Not all misleading signs are insincere, to be sure; the listener who closes his eyes during a lecture may appear to be dozing, and may know that he appears so, and may even relish the thought that he appears so — when in fact he is simply avoiding the strong glare of a lamp on the stage. He is not pretending to doze, for to do that he would have to *mean* to mislead people. And, as Anscombe showed us, meaning or intending something can't be equated with inwardly saying something: once again, any such inner sayings would themselves have to be 'meant'.

Is a positive intention to mislead a necessary condition of some behaviour's being insincere? No; for not all insincere behaviour is pretence. An insincere smile can be part of the repertoire of behaviour of someone who is phony, or sycophantic, a repertoire even including behaviours that are involuntary or not fully voluntary, such as laughing or crying. Nevertheless, phony behaviour is insincere — a phony smile is misleading, and not accidentally so. (To say it is misleading is not to say that it does or will mislead, of course; the phoniness might be ineffectual phoniness.)

It should be clear now that to call a smile insincere because it is in conflict with a background behavioural disposition, e.g. unfriendliness, assumes that *this* disposition is a more genuine aspect of the person's character than the disposition embodied in what I called the repertoire of phony behaviour. For evidently insincerity is itself very often a disposition of a person. Smith says and does all these things, indicating friendliness to his boss — and he also says and does these various other things (we may include inward thoughts here) indicating unfriendliness to his boss. Which words, deeds and thoughts are genuine? The question does not seem to have to do with any statistical preponderance of friendly or unfriendly behaviour. Throwing up our hands, we may decide that there is just a mess of behaviour, in which two opposing dispositions or tendencies may be discerned, or perhaps as many dispositions or tendencies as we care to pick out, as one picks out shapes and patterns in the bark of a tree.

In fact, of course, we will probably regard the friendliness towards the boss as insincere, given the signs elsewhere of unfriendliness; and this is because there is reason to suck up to your boss. That might suggest that we are simply casting our holistic net wider, so as to include more facts about the person's psychology—as, that he wants to get on in his career. But our thoughts are guided not just by what we 'discover' about the person before us, which is often not very much, but by what is normal and natural for human beings. After all, if we do end up saying that the man wants to get on in his career, it may well be on account of behaviour we have *already* classified as sycophantic, just through observing it. A smile and a bow in a particular social context—e.g. in the presence of the boss—can simply strike us as obviously phony, and our being struck that way is an unmediated reaction, not the forming of a hypothesis. Our propensity to react in that way arises from and develops through experience of life, though it must start off from quite instinctive modes of interpersonal reaction. And although I said that a reaction to some phoniness would not typically have the character of a hypothesis, such a reaction and what one says in expressing it are not free-floating things, but point in some directions and not others, can be confirmed or disconfirmed, and so on.[6]

I said above that in some cases of insincere behaviour, namely certain kinds of pretending, a person will intend to mislead—but that such an intention isn't a necessary condition of insincerity. Now remember that Anscombe's central criterion of intention is what somebody says, or would say, in answer to the question 'Why?' (as in 'Why did you do that?'). If we follow Anscombe on this, as I think we should, we shall conclude that someone who intends to mislead by his behaviour would answer the question 'Why?' by saying, 'So as to mislead'; that is, if he answers sincerely, something he is unlikely to do. Evidently we have to assume that an answer to the criterial question 'Why?' is a sincere

---

[6] Cf. Wittgenstein, *Philosophical Investigations*, trans. G.E.M. Anscombe (Oxford: Basil Blackwell, 2nd ed., 1958), ii, p. 228: 'Imponderable evidence includes subtleties of glance, of gesture, of tone. I may recognize a genuine loving look, distinguish it from a pretended one (and here there can, of course, be a "ponderable" confirmation of my judgment).'

one. Is this working assumption itself tantamount to the supposition that an answer to 'Why did you give that answer to "Why?"?' would be along the lines of, 'So as to answer truthfully'? We could perhaps say such a thing; though the rule 'Answer truthfully' is as it were built into the language-game, so there is a sense in which 'So as to answer truthfully' could hardly be an informative response.[7] Certainly, the further question 'But why answer my questions truthfully?' would in normal circumstances be crazy or silly, not to mention self-undermining.

2

Why did I claim that an intention to mislead isn't a necessary condition of insincerity? After all, even if the sycophant wouldn't answer 'Why did you smile like that?' by saying 'So as to butter up the boss', isn't that just because he's insincere? If he were being sincere about it, he surely would give some such reply? – It is worth drawing a distinction here, between the cunning hypocrite and what we may call the natural sycophant, or complete sycophant, as in 'compleat angler'. The statement, 'If he were being sincere, he'd admit he was aiming to mislead' applies straightforwardly to the cunning hypocrite; but in the case of the natural sycophant, he is insincere all the way down, and there is a sense in which he *can't* tell us what he's really up to. Some will suggest he has a subconscious intention to mislead, and so is self-deceived. But I think it might be more accurate to say that he lacks self-knowledge: the concept of self-deception typically brings with it some notion of struggle or tension within the person's overall character, and there might not be any of that in the natural sycophant. Perhaps he answers our question, 'Why did you smile like that?' by saying, 'Because I think him a truly wonderful man!' This answer itself would be insincere, but not because of clashing with any belief or attitude of the sycophant himself. What it clashes with is *our* assessment of the situation, as one in which he's merely buttering up the boss. But what has our assessment got going for it that his assessment does not?

---

[7] This fact helps us to see why no vicious regress is involved in its being necessary that the answer 'So as to answer truthfully' would itself have to be sincere. Sincerity is the default position, and is conceptually prior to insincerity in the way in which a pound coin is conceptually prior to a fake pound coin.

It is here that we can turn back to Anscombe's discussion, and also to the question of the sincerity of thoughts. The sycophant, I imagined, tells us that he smiled at the boss like that because he thinks him a truly wonderful man. It is the doubtfulness of this thought that is the issue, as it was the doubtfulness of the babysitter's thought that her dog was sure to stay put. Anscombe puts the matter thus:

> It [the sincerity of one's thoughts] is the purity of one's intentions in thinking these thoughts. By the purity of intention I mean not the ultimate purpose but the immediate purpose in thinking. The thought is thought, or there is an inclination to think it, because it appears to be the relevant truth on the matter in hand; as opposed to its appearing to be the relevant truth on the matter in hand because it is a convenient or otherwise tempting thought, i.e. because there is an inclination to think it.[8]

Despite her reference to someone's intentions in thinking something, Anscombe's use of the word 'because' in this passage does not seem to point towards any possible giving of reasons by the subject herself. After all, the sincere person will not say, 'My reason for thinking that p is this: that it seems to me to be true that p.' That is hardly a *reason*.[9] Still less will the insincere person say, 'The reason it seems to me to be true that p is this: that I'm inclined to think that p.' Nevertheless, the sincere person will typically *be in a position* to give reasons for her belief that p; and this is what is usually conveyed by saying 'It seems to her to be true that p.' By contrast, the explanation by appeal to what it's convenient or otherwise tempting to think is of the nature of a causal explanation, in a broad sense of 'causal'. That we reach for such an explanation shows our assessment of 'p' as being a doubtful or dubious thing to think in those circumstances and given what the person can be expected to have known.[10]

---

[8] 'On Being in Good Faith', p. 103.
[9] Might she instead say, 'I have arrived at the thought that p in order to think the truth about such-and-such'? If 'in order to' points to means–end *reasoning*, this answer would be incoherent, as we shall see later on (pp. 222–3); but it nevertheless makes sense to impute to the person a purpose, *thinking the truth about such-and-such*, such that thinking that p achieves that purpose.
[10] This last phrase covers a tangle of issues. A person may end up embracing a thought that happens to be true and reasonable in those circumstances, though doubtful relative to what he believes, and this doubtfulness could render his thought insincere (or rather: warrant the thought's being counted a

It might seem that we get an idea of what *sort* of causal explanation is at issue from Anscombe's description of the insincere person as 'suppressing the knowledge that makes the thought doubtful'. But in fact what Anscombe's surrounding discussion brings out is not the occurrence of any hypothetical acts of suppressing, so much as certain failures on the part of the person — in particular, the failure to reflect or think properly. The babysitter who thinks to herself 'The dog is sure to stay put' fails to reflect properly on the facts, something which those around her may explain by reference to her desire to go to the shops. And the phrase 'suppression of knowledge' is apt only because we are liable to protest, 'But you *knew* the dog might move!' But as Anscombe says, 'in other cases we say rather "You would have known if you had thought"'[11] — and it seems clear that the condition of responsibility is in general not knowledge that one's action or the circumstances are of a certain kind, so much as the capacity to think, consider or reflect. Of course this capacity itself presupposes that one have *some* knowledge of relevant facts, if only of a general kind (e.g. concerning dogs).

At the start of this chapter, I imagined the negligent babysitter telling us, 'I assumed the dog would stay put.' This statement could of course be mere pretence, if the babysitter had fully realized the dangers of what she was doing, and is now trying to cover things up. But we have been considering the sort of case where what she *thinks*, not just what she *says*, is insincere or not fully sincere; and we seem to have arrived at a point where we can characterize this insincerity. It is not that her thought is in conflict with an occurrent thought standing behind it — nor is it even that her thought directly conflicts with (i.e. contradicts) certain settled

---

manifestation of insincerity). But this raises the further question whether his 'beliefs' are themselves sincere — not that this raises any spectre of a vicious regress. Further, someone's falsely believing X to be right or wrong, good or bad, etc. will not count as innocent error, in the way in which e.g. falsely believing that the transparent liquid in a bottle is water might be innocent; cf. Anscombe: 'ignorance of principle is not a cause of involuntariness, but of scoundrelism, according to Aristotle and those who have followed him' ('On Being in Good Faith', p. 104). The distinction between matters of principle and matters of fact sounds like, though for various reasons it cannot be equated with, the Humean distinction between values and facts. Anscombe discusses it at length in 'Two Kinds of Error in Action', in *CPP3*, pp. 3–9.
[11] 'On Being in Good Faith', p. 106.

beliefs or items of knowledge had by her. It is that she failed to think or reflect properly on the matter when she ought to have done, this failure being naturally explicable as arising from the standing temptation to go and buy some cigarettes, and being such as to enable her to embrace a doubtful thought, namely 'The dog is sure to stay put.'

Insincerity of thought is thus above all a sort of failure, the failure to think properly. And of course that means that many insincere utterances, namely the ones not involving actual pretence, are likewise cases of such failure, being expressions of insincere thoughts. It will now be apparent why it is significant for our discussion that there are forms of outward insincerity not involving actual pretence, such as sycophancy; since if insincerity were tied to pretending, in the sense of having an intention to mislead, then it would be obvious that thoughts could not be insincere. But it is not so tied.

3

Now it is natural to say that the reason the failure to think properly is culpable is that, if the person had thought properly, she would have realized that such-and-such, and would therefore not have embraced the doubtful thought. And in fact I think this is probably Anscombe's view. But this sort of counterfactual does not seem to be true of my natural sycophant and people like him. It might not be possible to say to the natural sycophant: 'You know the boss is awful, really, don't you?' — nor yet, 'If you'd just think about it a bit, you'd see that he's awful.' The sycophant is insincere all the way down, as I put it. Does he or doesn't he 'really mean' his protestations of adulation? One can reply to this in the manner of Aristotle, saying, 'In one way, yes — in another way, no.' But if one does choose to say 'No, he doesn't really mean them', this is on account of the inappropriateness of those protestations in the face of the observable character of the boss, and on our consequent interpretation of the sycophant's behaviour as *buttering up*. The psychology of buttering up can be quite complex, and may or may not have to do with possible kick-back benefits to the sycophant; people often adopt a servile stance in the presence of mere worldly success. And even where it is a matter of possible kick-back benefits, we need not posit an *aim*, e.g. subconscious, of getting those benefits. It may be that, like the character Berg in Tolstoy's *War and Peace*, the person just instinctively does and says those things, mixes with those people, etc., which in the long run stand to benefit him—as a bee is attracted to certain flowers. Thus if the boss is unremittingly rude back to him, the sycophant may just take that as part of the natural order of things, and still continue with his habits of sycophancy. He's unlucky in his boss, as a bee can be unlucky in its flower.

Remarks along these lines apply also, it seems to me, to cases of insincere thought. It may on a natural interpretation be false that, had Smith thought about it, he would have realized the doubtfulness of what he was thinking, and thus quite probably of what he was doing. I say 'on a natural interpretation'; but there is another, perhaps equally natural, interpretation of the relevant counterfactuals which in effect takes them as saying 'It was objectively possible to think properly about this matter, and someone thinking properly about it would not, etc. etc.' We are interested in Smith's character, after all, and it may be *part* of his character that he often fails to think properly about certain matters, whether or not there is even a remote chance that he could be brought to see his failures as failures and do something about them.

Relevant here is what Anscombe has to say about invincible ignorance:

> 'Invincible ignorance' is sometimes spoken of as if it were a psychological condition—not necessarily of mental defect or insanity. I am suggesting that it means 'ignorance that the man himself could not overcome'; as appears from the standard example, that the man who has never heard of Christ is invincibly ignorant of Christianity. Here the impossibility is not an impossibility because of the bent of his mind; he simply has not the information available to attend to.[12]

'Invincible ignorance' is supposed to serve as an excuse. But an impossibility that is due to the bent of your mind will not excuse you, since it is in a sense the bent of your mind that stands accused. And the bent of your mind, e.g. if you are prone to insincere thoughts, may make it hard or impossible for you to think properly about certain matters.

In the end, the fault in thinking insincerely lies in the doubtfulness of the thought. For what counts as 'not thinking properly about a matter'? Surely any thinking which, in those

---

[12] 'On Being in Good Faith', p. 111.

circumstances, leads to the babysitter's concluding that the dog is sure to stay put will *prima facie* count as not thinking properly. It is a different matter, to be sure, if the babysitter is for some reason ignorant of the habits and capacities of dogs or babies; but if she is an adult of normal experience, then her thinking will be improper *in virtue of* its yielding such conclusions. The case is rather like that of necessary truth in geometry: some measurements that appear to show that the angles of a certain triangle on a flat surface add up to 200° will *thereby* count as flawed, even if we have no inkling which part of the actual measuring procedure was to blame, and indeed even if the whole procedure were captured on film and no flaw could be detected. (The measurements will not throw even a scintilla of doubt on the truths of trigonometry, though if such measurements kept on and on occurring, trigonometry as a practice would eventually become undermined.) Likewise, in Descartes' *Meditations* it looks as if the clarity and distinctness of your ideas must in the end *consist in* their not producing falsehood — unluckily for Descartes.

If this is right, then the failure of which the insincere person stands accused is what it is only because of the positive fact, if you like, of that person's embracing a dubious thought. This sort of failure is unlike the failure that consists in not doing some necessary thing. In the latter case, the relation between what you fail to do and the outcome of that failure is typically external rather than internal. Externality of relation is relative to description-under-which, to be sure; but even where the only description we can come up with of some failure is 'failure to prevent X's happening' — which is indeed internally related to 'X happened' — still, where the person is deemed *responsible* for the failure, he is *ipso facto* deemed to have been *able* to prevent X's happening, something which really does depend on there being some independent description of what he could have done to prevent X's happening. Thus, even if we don't know why the soup tastes nasty, it is still the fault of the cook if, and only if, there is some independently specifiable means of preventing this, such as putting salt in, which could be invoked when framing a charge of negligence. By contrast, there often isn't such an independent description of what someone didn't do when he didn't think properly.

Moreover, the sort of 'thinking properly' a person can be blamed for not doing cannot itself be regarded as the adoption of certain mental means towards some goal, e.g. that of arriving at an answer to a practical question. This has been demonstrated by Anselm Müller in the course of his arguing that many forms of thinking exhibit what he calls 'unreasoned teleology'. The babysitter who, when considering whether to go to the shops, reflects properly, does so for a purpose, namely — given the circumstances — the purpose of forming any available true judgment of the form *the dog could do such-and-such undesirable thing if I leave it here for 10 minutes*. She succeeds in her purpose if she arrives at the thought *the dog could molest the baby if I leave it here for 10 minutes*. Having this thought is in this sense a means to the end she has set herself in reflecting; if she arrives at the thought she will have achieved her end. But clearly if the babysitter were to *adopt*, as a means, *having the thought that the dog could molest the baby if I leave it here for 10 minutes*, she would already have achieved her end: in just conceiving of her means as a suitable means she would have succeeded in her purpose, for she would be thinking, 'The dog could molest the baby if I leave it here for 10 minutes.' But this is absurd. The purposiveness of her thinking, in other words, cannot be understood in terms of a practical syllogism. As Müller puts it, 'You may decide that *this* is the right way to behave and yet not behave this way. But you cannot decide that *this* is the right way to judge concerning a given topic without thereby judging this way.'[13]

4

The habit of not thinking properly and the habit of thinking dubious thoughts[14] both sound as if they must be intellectual vices, and we might therefore wonder how they can be objects of ethical blame. The idea that there is a hard-and-fast line between the intellectual and the ethical has in modern times often gone with the idea of a corresponding distinction between the factual and the evaluative, the cognitive and the conative, and so on. One of Anscombe's enduring contributions has been to undermine thoroughly the so-called 'fact/value distinction' and the Humean psychology which is at the root of it. But I'm sure Anscombe

---

[13] A. Müller, 'Mental Teleology', *Proceedings of the Aristotelian Society* XCII, part 2, (1992):161–183, at p. 178.

[14] As has been indicated, this phrase means something like 'thoughts it is dubious to have given what the person can be expected to have known and relative to his actual beliefs.' See the tangle mentioned in n. 10, above.

would in the main go along with the Aristotelian distinction between intellectual and ethical vices; and we might ask of not thinking properly, and of insincerity in thought, 'Are these vices intellectual or ethical?'

Perhaps the main difference between the two species of vice or defect, for Aristotle, lies in the way the will is involved with each. If you misspell a word by accident, that shows that you're a bad or imperfect speller in a way that your misspelling it on purpose won't; whereas going off with someone else's wallet by accident does not show you to be ethically imperfect (i.e. dishonest) — going off with it on purpose does. To have an ethical virtue means more than being *able* to do a certain good sort of act, it means being inclined to, wanting to; if you accidentally remove someone's wallet, that probably means you didn't want to remove it. To have an intellectual virtue it is typically enough to be able to do whatever it is well; something similar goes for skills.

The intellectually sincere person seems to be someone who wants to say and think the truth, something that shows itself in various ways, including in how the person thinks and in what he ends up thinking. There is also, as we've seen, sincerity in behaviour — in expressions of friendliness, interest, love, indignation and so on. Anscombe might say that such sincerity involves wanting to 'do the truth' (a favourite phrase of hers); and certainly, as we have seen, even the smile of the natural sycophant who harbours no secret intention to mislead is a misleading smile, a smile which 'means something' that is the opposite of the truth.[15] Now it is not that the intellectually insincere person *wants* to embrace falsehoods, and nor need the behaviourally insincere person *want* to embody falsehood in his behaviour. And this is the sort of fact which can lead people to infer that, since the will is not involved, any defect here cannot be an ethical one — for ethical virtues and vices involve the will. But the inference is unsound. This can be shown in two steps: first, by showing that when someone's intentions or wants are relevant to their culpability, this is not typically on account of their wanting to act badly, but rather on account of their wanting to do X, where doing X is acting

---

[15] What does the smile mean? One could say it means, 'This is a smile' — i.e. 'This is a real/true/genuine/authentic smile.'

badly;[16] and second, by showing that in any case, as Anscombe says, 'sin essentially requires, not intention but voluntariness.'[17]

It is the second of these points that is most germane to our discussion. The babysitter in our example doesn't intend the baby to get bitten; and if she thinks to herself, 'The dog is sure to stay put', she doesn't intend to think a false or dubious thought. We do not blame her for her intentional action, i.e. going out to the shops, but for her not securing the dog somehow (given that she was going to the shops); and this failure of hers was not intentional, but voluntary. Likewise, in calling her thought an insincere one, we imply blame for a failure of hers, the failure to think properly, behind which there is likely to be a more general failure, the failure to want to think the truth. Perhaps we should say: the failure to want it enough, for of course in many matters the babysitter will want very much to think what's true. But if how much someone wants to think the truth depends on the subject matter, we may well have the sort of situation described by Anscombe as one in which something 'appears to be the relevant truth on the matter in hand because it is a convenient or otherwise tempting thought'. The phrase 'otherwise tempting' covers a wide range of cases, and the temptation in question may not be self-interested, in the way in which the temptation to say or think what will excuse your behaviour is self-interested. Thus laziness is in general tempting, and laziness of *thought* often involves the sort of sloppiness or falling into cliché which renders what is thought dubious and also insincere.

It is also tempting to cut a certain sort of figure, in the eyes of others but also in your own eyes, and it is perhaps a bit unclear whether this is a matter of self-interest or not. This temptation can lead to one important species of insincerity, namely hypocrisy. Anscombe discusses the hypocrisy that is outward pretence, taking pretence to be a sort of wanting-to-seem, and writes: 'It is characteristic of this sort of wanting-to-seem that it carries with it

---

[16] The way in which what you want or intend is relevant to blame is parallel to the way in which what you knowingly do is relevant to blame; in both cases, the notion of a 'description under which' is crucial. See Anscombe's discussion of the doctrine that mortal sin requires 'full knowledge': 'This, then, will be the meaning of the condition "full knowledge": given that to do X is gravely wrong, then a man is guilty of wrongdoing in doing what is in fact doing X, only if he knows that he is doing X' ('On Being in Good Faith', p. 104).

[17] 'On Being in Good Faith', p. 105.

an implicit demand for respect for an atmosphere evoked by the pretender, which surrounds not the reality, but the *idea* of such things as being principled, or cultured, or saintly, or rich, or important.'[18] I have argued that intention to mislead is not a necessary condition of insincerity, and Anscombe's 'wanting to seem' is different from 'intending to seem' — so it is possible to extend her account of outward hypocrisy to inward hypocrisy of thought: e.g. a person can be in the habit of thinking deep-seeming thoughts because he in some sense *wants* to seem deep to himself. His thoughts will manifest inward hypocrisy, and will be insincere (or not fully sincere).

Insincerity of thought is evidently a vice that is both intellectual and ethical. On the one hand it concerns thinking and judging, and on the other it concerns a failure of the will in connection with an important human good or goods, namely having and sharing the truth; the virtue of sincerity in thought involves wanting to think the truth. There is a failure of will because of the voluntariness (not intentionalness) that can be ascribed to thoughts. To show more fully than I have here that voluntariness *can* properly be ascribed to thoughts, and also to the *not having* of thoughts, would require further argument.[19] But that is a topic for another occasion.

---

[18] 'Pretending', in *CPP2*, pp: 83–93, at p. 93.
[19] The topic is discussed in R. Teichmann, 'The Voluntary and the Involuntary: Themes from Anscombe', *The American Catholic Philosophical Quarterly* 88(3) (2014):465–486.

Mary Geach
Anscombe on Sexual Ethics

Anscombe did not believe that ethical considerations were the same for every rational being.[1] She thought that the study of virtues and vices was part of ethics,[2] and that ethics was not formally independent of the facts of human life.[3] She thought that to call some quality a virtue or a vice was not merely to express feelings of approval or disapproval of it[4] but to state a truth or, alternatively, a falsehood: in the case of human virtues, a truth or falsehood about human nature. The behaviour of the virtuous, we might add, is important to the understanding of human life in the way that the conduct of a healthy digestive system is important to an understanding of human physiology. Just as passage through the gut is not merely one of the things which can happen to food when we eat it, so payment of a debt is not merely one of the things that can happen when we incur debt. If we vomit, or if we default, some departure from the norm[5] has occurred, a departure which stands in need of explanation. In the case of failing to pay the debt, the explanation may be that the debtor is a bilker, one who has a bad habit in regard to debt. Such a bad habit is a vice, and its contrary is a part of the virtue of justice.

---

[1] See number 5 of her 'Twenty Opinions Common Among Modern Anglo-American Philosophers', *FHG*, p. 67. (Hereafter 'Twenty Opinions'.) Peter Geach called this index of objectionable opinions her 'Twenty distinct damnations'.
[2] 'Twenty Opinions', opinion 9, p. 67.
[3] 'Twenty Opinions', opinion 8, p. 67.
[4] 'Twenty Opinions', opinion 10, p. 67.
[5] Both these norms are usually conformed to, but I here use the term 'norm' in the non-statistical sense which Anscombe uses in 'Modern Moral Philosophy', where she gives the example of a man with a complete set of teeth as a norm. *HLAE*, p. 188.

Thus Anscombe rejected the doctrine 'There ain't no sin and there ain't no virtue. There's just things folks do.' The ex-preacher who says this in *The Grapes of Wrath* has been led to this opinion by his own habit of fornicating after revival meetings, and many people would share this view precisely with regard to such matters, though they might think that habitual failure to pay debts — to pay just wages, for example — was indeed contrary to virtue. Anscombe on the other hand thought that there was a virtue which had to do with sexual matters: the virtue of chastity. It was, she said, a solid useful sort of virtue, but thought that its value went beyond the utilitarian and had also a mystical part.[6] The traditional way of classifying the virtue, deriving from the Greeks who saw it as a part of temperance, was, she said, inadequate because it did not allow for this mystical aspect, shown in the reverence which the Greeks themselves had for virginity. She thought that the Christian standard of chastity had never been generally lived by, but that if it were, it would be colossally productive of earthly happiness.[7]

Anscombe's distinction between the utilitarian and the mystical suggests two ways of investigating a virtue: one is to show that it is needed if society is to run well; another is to consider the aims of the person who has it. These aims might be such that the pursuit of them will produce good order in society without this good order being what the virtuous person is primarily and ultimately aiming at when he makes his virtuous choices. A philosopher who can see this may realize that the sort of person who has a useful virtue may usually have goals other than what has been called 'utility'. The utilitarian might think these goals chimerical, but because what he cares for is utility, he prefers to leave people in a state which results in more good than would result from their disillusionment. Thus in matters of sexual morality, the aims of a person having the virtue called chastity might have been scorned by utilitarians, but so much good results if people avoid non-marital intercourse that the desire and respect for purity, especially in women, has been something which utilitarians in power might wish to leave intact. Many rulers regard increase of population as a vast and urgently threatening evil, and for this reason systematically assault the sexual virtue of the

---

[6] 'Contraception, Chastity, and the Vocation of Marriage', *FHG*, p. 212.
[7] 'Contraception and Chastity', *FHG*, p. 188.

people. However, where civilization lasts it is through at least the old heathen morality mentioned by Anscombe.[8] According to this morality, honest women behave in such a way that fathers are confident in owning their children,[9] and good men respect the chastity of such women. From this knowledge of paternity results the stable family, which is the building-brick of civilized society, being the place where children learn respect for authority and for law.

If there is a virtue of chastity, it is a disposition of our sexuality itself. If we say that chastity is a disposition of our sexuality which always disinclines us from incest, promiscuity, adultery and rape, the usefulness to society of this disposition indicates in an external way that chastity is a virtue, since the behaviour of the virtuous members of a social species will be consistent with the good of society. Unless our sexuality itself is disposed against these things, the strength of our passion is apt to cause us to act in ways which are contrary to justice, kindness and prudence. For this reason, chastity has to be a disposition of the male as well as the female psyche with regard to sexual matters. Also, since sexuality is so universal and profound a part of the human make-up, affecting and affected by many parts of our mind and our emotions, a good sexual disposition is a part of what it takes to be a good and

---

[8] 'Contraception and Chastity', p. 171.
[9] As an alternative to this, Andrew Koppelman (A. Koppelman, 'Judging the Case Against Same-Sex Marriage', Northwestern University School of Law, Public Law and Legal Theory Series No. 13-08, http://papers.ssrn.com/sol3/papers.cfm?abstract_id=2257557, subsequently published in 2014(2) *U. of Illinois Law Review*: 431–466) recommends what he calls the 'new middle class ethic'. He says that he himself has children whom he treats as a father should. However, he does not explain how, where women are promiscuous, fathers in general can still be confident about paternity, or how uncertainty about paternity is not to have those effects on society which for its more prosperous members can be to some extent mollified by the security which wealth provides, and by the common interest which may prevent people from dividing their property. He blames the remnants of an ideal of chastity in the lower classes of his society for the failure of these people to conform perfectly to his new morality, which involves delaying childbearing by means of abortion and contraception, so that one can go to university and attain to a comfortable box on the middle class hillside. But we should consider the effects of this morality upon society as a whole, especially where the middle class, through the media, through organizations like Planned Parenthood, through an effectively compulsory system of state education, and through the welfare system, plays so large a part in forming the minds and habits of the poor.

fulfilled human being. It can in this be contrasted with good habits with regard to the handling of guns or motor cars, in that while a virtuous man will have these habits if he is a user of these implements, it is not a part of being human, or a defining part of being a happy and fulfilled human being, that one should be a user of them. We cannot shed our sexuality by being celibate, and so there remains for celibates as for sexually active people a question of how they are to behave in connection with this part of their nature, whereas for those who have not driven there is no driving part of their nature for good driving habits to be a part of.

Now, I wish to make an internal examination of this virtue: to investigate the reason, the principle, which informs the sexuality of those who have the virtue, and to find the way (or ways) that these people pursue.

Some people think that virtue in these matters consists in being a considerate lover, good in bed. However, to think this is to ignore the fact that a good man must be one who so orders his sexuality that he will avoid the bad effects which can arise from distorted and uncontrolled passion. It might be said that the disposition to want mutual provision of sexual satisfaction is inconsistent with the sort of sexuality which makes one person maltreat another, but to say this is to ignore the human tendency to sexual possessiveness and jealousy, which, if it is ever justified, means that there is a relational dimension to sexuality, which has to do with more than the single encounter. Thus, if there is such a thing as justified sexual jealousy and possessiveness, the desire and ability to be what is called 'good in bed' is not inconsistent with sexual wrong to the other party, or to a third party. One important part of human sexuality is that it gives rise to possessiveness and jealousy, so if these are always unjustified, it remains the case that the sexuality of virtuous people has to be formed and controlled by habit, in that they will have done away entirely with the desire to possess, and the desire to be possessed exclusively. Thus there cannot be in the virtuous a free human sexuality uninhibited by a self-discipline which suppresses common human inclinations: either the inclination to be jealous is always contrary to virtue (since it is never reasonable to treat as ours by right a thing which is not ours by right) or the inclination to fancy other people than the one who does possess us by right is an inclination to wrongdoing. To do away with either of these inclinations would require a self-discipline which for many would be quite severe.

There are also the various evils which result from uncontrolled behaviour. But what habit is likely to result in behaviour which avoids the evils which uncontrolled sexuality can produce, even by the agency of those who are what is called 'good in bed'? Anscombe rejects the idea that people who are bent upon and obtain a lot of sexual enjoyment are more gentle, merciful and kind than those who live in voluntary continence.[10] She also sees as unrealistic the picture that some social evils which result from uncontrolled sexual behaviour can now be prevented by careful contraception: people just won't be so careful, and this results in a supposed need for abortion. Anscombe held that people at large would not avoid this bad consequence of disordered sexuality unless inspired by a positive ideal of chastity.[11]. Nor, we may add, can they avoid all the other bad consequences unless they have this virtue.

Anscombe's distinction between the mystical and the utilitarian aspects of the virtue does not mean that the good consequences, the good order in society, which result from chastity are themselves without what she would regard as a mystical significance. Though wealth and health, and the pleasures which go with these, result from chaste behaviour, this is because of the maintenance of stable families. Chastity on the part of women makes for such families because of the desire of men to know which children in the world are really their children, which desire surely derives from what Anscombe would count as a mystical perception of human relationships. Also, the misery of not knowing who one's father is derives from perceptions which are 'mystical' in the very general sense in which Anscombe uses that term.[12] Whatever one may think of this undefined concept of the mystical, it remains the case that the utility of chastity derives not only from the convenience of the family as an arrangement for looking after children, but from the satisfaction of desires which

---

[10] 'Contraception and Chastity', p. 188.
[11] 'Contraception and Chastity', p. 172.
[12] Instances of the very general way in which Anscombe uses the term can be seen in the essay 'Frustration of the Majority by the Fulfilment of the Majority's Will', CPP3, pp. 124–125. She supposes people might think, for instance, that participation in political decision-making is itself valuable, 'or perhaps one should say, is itself a value. Such a value is mystical, of course. I don't mean a criticism in saying so'. She also calls 'mystical' the sentiment a voter on the losing side might nevertheless have that 'we' have made a democratic decision.

are for things naturally valued for themselves and not only for their effects.

Anscombe held that this virtue itself was not of the highest, could perhaps hardly be said to exist, unless it was one aspect of the quality called purity of heart,[13] as in the Beatitude 'Blessed are the pure in heart, for they shall see God.'[14] This saying of Christ reminds us of what Aristotle had already said at the end of the *Eudemian Ethics*, that any choice of living which either through excess or defect impeded the service and contemplation of God was bad. Aristotle held in this passage that the superior part of ourselves should be in command, and that the highest way to follow was one in which the irrational part of the soul, *qua* irrational, was least attended to.[15] What this ancient ideal means in practice is worked out in the writings of Anscombe on the topic of chastity.

So let us approach the virtue from this end, as one aspect of the purity of heart which, as Anscombe says, we acquire in ways which involve persistently declining to act from contemptible motives.[16] (Anscombe points out that we can choose whether to act from a particular motive, instancing the choice made by Plato when he said to his slave 'I would beat you were I not angry.'[17]) However, sexual desire seems itself to be a motive belonging to the baser part of ourselves: to act upon it seems to be to attend to the irrational part of the human psyche. Reason, it seems, can hardly be said to be in control when we engage in such activity. Sophocles, in a story told of him in the *Republic*, says in his old age about the natural force which enables a man to serve Aphrodite (i.e. to enjoy venereal pleasures) that he feels that he has escaped from a savage beast of a master.[18] So some people have concluded

---

[13] 'Contraception, Chastity, and the Vocation of Marriage', p. 212.
[14] *Matt*.5:8.
[15] Aristotle, *Eudemian Ethics*, 1249b. Anscombe told me with satisfaction about the work of Anthony Kenny on this subject, which casts doubt on the common view that this work is a product of an early Platonist phase in Aristotle's philosophy. For a brief statement of his argument, with references to his previous publications, that the *Eudemian Ethics* is a mature work of Aristotle's see the Introduction to his translation of Aristotle, *The Eudemian Ethics* (Oxford: Oxford University Press, 2011), p. xi.
[16] 'Contraception, Chastity, and the Vocation of Marriage', p. 212.
[17] *I*, p. 22.
[18] Plato, *Republic*, Book 1 329.

that sexual activity is bad in itself. Such was the view of the Manicheans, who also thought generation itself an evil, since it trapped soul in body.

Aristotle, however, and Anscombe herself, did not think of a human soul as being trapped in the body. She knew that a human person is essentially an animal, and the human soul is the life of a rational animal. Generation of persons is good and the life conceived is always to be honoured.[19] Generation being good, the kind of action by which human beings generate is a good kind of action. It is by living a life with another, a life of which this action forms a small but important part, that human beings reproduce and secure the right environment for their children. Just as there is an animal way in which the vegetative function of sexual reproduction is carried out, so there is a rational way in which this animal act is performed: the normative human copulation is the marriage act, which is the expression of a freely chosen lifelong relationship, and is good in kind. The irrational part of the soul, I would add, does not have to be attended to *qua* irrational when one performs a marriage act, since the action can be a manifestation of an appetite which is conforming to the *ratio* of its nature. Aristotle's qualification '*qua* irrational' is important, as it makes the sentence about not attending to the irrational part of the soul consistent with the view that the virtues can inform the lower powers. Thus, as I have been arguing, the virtue of chastity must inform our sexuality itself, in all its aspects.

These aspects are all manifested in the marriage act, which is the kind of action which reproduces, and occurs in the context of marriage, which is the human state suitable for reproduction. It is thus an act of a good kind. However, an action might be of a good kind and yet in the individual case be a bad human action, for instance when it is performed from base motives. Thus it has been taught that the sexual union of husband and wife is bad if engaged in 'purely for pleasure'. Anscombe accepts this teaching, interpreting it to mean that such union is bad if sensuality is in command: if it is, then the couple is acting intemperately. We are back with Aristotle, and his conclusion that the superior part of

---

[19] Even if (as she thought possible) there is a stage in that life which precedes the conceptus's becoming a human individual. See 'Were You a Zygote?', *HLAE*, p. 39; 'The Early Embryo: Theoretical Doubts and Practical Certainties', *FHG*, p. 214.

ourselves should be in command. Anscombe also recalls that G.E. Moore counted lasciviousness as a great intrinsic evil. One test of whether sensuality is in command is whether the couple can go without for a while, which is necessary sometimes anyway, e.g. for medical reasons. Clearly, we can add, if sensuality is in command, then only circumstance will prevent the bad effects of uncontrolled passion.[20]

Some people have thought of sexual activity as requiring excuse, so that unless we are specifically aiming at reproduction, we are acting purely for pleasure and are letting the irrational part of ourselves rule our actions. Anscombe regarded this kind of attitude as coming from a faulty moral psychology. The activity being good, the desire for it is good, and the desire is for the activity as pleasurable. If the context is marriage, the way in which the marriage bond is expressed is in this activity, and the way it works is that desire tends to arise without our calculation. But if our marriage act is not very imprudent or lascivious, it is just part of married life, significant of the bond and strengthening of it, a rational activity in which sensuality is not in command.[21] That it should be a habitual part of married life goes with the fact that on the whole generation occurs without our knowing which act did the generating: children arise out of the married relation, which is a generative sort of relation, enacted and expressed by copulations which, as copulations, are generative in kind.

When we speak of sensuality not being in command, we are in disagreement with Hume,[22] who thinks that reason has no power to move us, but only to discover facts in the light of which we can pursue the objects of our passions. Anscombe in face of this points out that only rational beings can have generic ends,[23] ones which they formulate as to be pursued through life, and that when we have such ends, they are such as can be rationally criticized. Thus we can make sense of the idea of an activity being in accordance with reason, since it may or may not be in accordance with generic ends, and these may or may not be ones to which reason presents

---

[20] For example, a man in whom sensuality is habitually allowed to be in command is likely under certain circumstances to commit rape or incest, while women who are like this render the paternity of their children uncertain.
[21] 'Contraception and Chastity', p. 189.
[22] David Hume, *A Treatise of Human Nature*, Book II, Part III, Section I.
[23] 'Sin', *FHG*, p. 119. This does not mean that all generic ends are good ones for a human being to have.

no objection, and which reason presents to us as fine, noble or worthwhile.[24]

Now, what is the generic end pursued by a person having the virtue of chastity? What, that is, beside the end of living a life in which there is much contemplation and worship of the divine, which is an end more architectonic than those peculiar to the virtue of chastity? In pursuit of this end of contemplation people in different cultures have adopted chastity in the narrower sense which involves celibacy. This life, the life of contemplating God, was, thought Anscombe, the least likely to become empty. She argued that it was only reasonable to believe that the maker of the essences of things was the source of human language, whose deepest grammar reflects those essences. This source we can see to be in some way rational, as being the source of rationality and the maker of our capacity for speech,[25] God, whose wisdom, the divine logos, enlightens every man coming into this world.[26] He is not ourselves, for we do not invent the essences of natural things as mathematicians do invent the essences discovered in mathematics. By understanding things clearly we are contemplating an aspect of the mind which shows itself in their essences,[27] but if we allow sensuality to rule, we dull our capacity to see the work of this mind. It is consistent with this that both atheism and lasciviousness are very widespread in our time.

Following Aristotle, we can say that the end of contemplating God is one which could be seen as the end of all activity of the noble mind, and the pursuit of which in such a mind causes all the virtues. However, chastity, in the broader sense in which it is the virtue concerned with sex, might be expected to have an end peculiar to itself. This end is to be discovered through the fact mentioned by Anscombe, that sexual actions are always significant; they are never just like a bit of casual eating.[28] This is not surprising, since what supports life is not a single act of eating, but a pattern of consumption more or less maintained in the course of

---

[24] 'Sin', p. 121.
[25] 'Human Essence', *HLAE*, pp. 37–38.
[26] 'On Wisdom', *FHG*, pp. 261–266.
[27] However, the act of creating intelligence, says Anscombe, is shown by logical and mathematical calculae being usefully applicable in exploring phenomena. She refers in this connection to a story of Newton's having felt that he was thinking God's thoughts after him. 'On Wisdom', p. 265.
[28] 'Contraception and Chastity', p. 186.

our existence. A single act of intercourse, on the other hand, may generate a human being. For this reason, I would say, the significance of sex is something one cannot escape by being a kind of sexual Humpty Dumpty: by saying that our sexual actions mean what we intend them to mean, no more, no less. Our sexuality is essentially about generating human beings, as the sexuality of other organisms is about generating organisms of those kinds, and this is why, as Anscombe says, those who try to make sex a matter of mere casual enjoyment become shallow.[29] The same can be said for those who go in for non-conjugal sexual activity in order to obtain some sort of release. For we cannot be profound if we treat with contempt the bodily function by which we ourselves are brought into being. The action of a man who acts merely to placate his sensual nature, while disregarding the ratio of his sexuality, is not an action in which reason is in command, even though the purpose and immediate effect of his action is to enjoy a mental life less troubled by lust.

Now, it might be said that in fact those who make it their end to have as much sexual pleasure as possible, and who conduct their lives on this principle, are not treating the bodily function with contempt, but as something worthwhile in itself. We can object to the generic end of such people not only on the ground that having it is likely to lead to distorted and uncontrolled passion, but also because to treat mere orgasmic pleasure as a final end is to deny the very thing that makes the activity worthy of honour: namely, that it is the kind of activity that generates human beings, and is therefore expressive of the marital relation, which is the proper and natural setting for such generation. Even when there is no possibility of generation, the act expresses the marital bond, so long as the act is of generative kind, expressing a commitment to a shared (and in this case empty) reproductive future.

The end pursued by those who have virtue in these matters is described by Koppelman[30] as being that of making good sexual choices. He sees those whose sexual actions are not of the best as performing them out of what he calls 'neediness', but does not explain the virtue which prevents one from making evil sexual

---

[29] 'Contraception and Chastity', p. 186.
[30] See Koppelman's paper cited in footnote 9 above, p. 30 in the online version.

choices, which are cruel or unjust or irresponsible. If the generic end of the sexually virtuous person is to try to achieve what he calls 'sex at its best', such an end is likely to lead to discontent and promiscuity, with their train of disease and broken families, unless one interprets this expression non-subjectively and not hedonistically. He provides some indication of how to do this when he says that 'sex at its best' is like a conversation in which one loves and values the wholeness of the other. Now, the wholeness of the other includes a history and an intellect and an organic nature, and therefore to relate to the wholeness of the other in sexual matters is through marriage acts which join one organically to a person whose history includes the rationally-chosen commitment to the organic relation which is marriage: I do not see any other way in which one can make a sexual act relevant as such to all these aspects of the person. To relate to another precisely as an organism it is necessary that the relation be of an organic nature in both bodies, as breastfeeding, for example, is an organic event both in the mother and the child. In the case of sexual activity, what is going on organically are events of reproductive kind. To relate to the other organically, it is necessary that one's copulation with them be *qua* copulation an event of organic kind, which it can only be if it is an event of reproductive kind which is one event in the bodies of both parties: one knows that a copulation is as such a sexual event because, under its description as a copulation, it is a part of the biological process by which the seed of the male meets with that of the female, just as breastfeeding is part of the biological process by which the nutrients in the mother pass into the digestive tract of the baby. To relate to the other rationally, in sexual matters, it is necessary that the sexual action be itself a part of a rationally-chosen relationship whose aims are particularly to do with that person and to do with the aforementioned organic relation. To make this rationally-chosen relationship a love which is to do with the life history of the other is to enter the commitment of marriage, where each has in the past entrusted their whole reproductive future to the other person.

To perform any other kind of sexual act is to reduce in oneself a sense of the significance of married life, and therefore of that human dignity from which marriage derives its honourable nature. The mystical core of Anscombe's views on sexuality lies in her seeing the human animal as the bearer of the dignity which belongs to us as rational beings, the dignity of being made for the vision of God. This gives the act by which human beings are generated, and the relation of which that act is the central expression, a dignity commensurate with the dignity of the species.

People who regard sexual activity as something to be used to express love are not completely wide of the mark, since sex is in fact about this lifelong friendship called marriage. The possibility of entering this lifelong relationship is one of the facts specific to humanity which make morality for human beings something peculiar to our species and not the same for all rational beings. I mentioned at the beginning that Anscombe did not regard morality as the same for all rational beings. I take it that the belief that it is the same lies behind the apparent assumption made by those who go in for fantastic imaginings to support their ethical assertions. These people seem to think that the facts about our human nature are mere contingencies in the light of which we as human beings should act, in fulfilment of some species-transcending moral law within whose fundamental generalities the various imaginable material worlds and rational natures are values which its variables may have.[31] But what counts as a good human act is something which is part of the fabric and constitution of our nature. A good human act is one which is not contrary to the virtues specific to humanity, nor to having the ends which a good human being has. One of these ends is the generic end which concerns marriage and the respect which the good man has for this human thing, whether in his own marriage or in another's. What makes it clear that marriage is a part of humanity is the need for this bond, this reality which holds parents together and provides the solid background in which individuals are irreplaceable: persons and not personnel. If we are very unlucky, says Anscombe, we may belong to a society which has wrecked and deformed this human thing.[32]

It is important for the possession of the virtue of chastity that venereal pleasure should never be sought apart from the marriage relation. It might be said that since libido in some way affects our emotions generally, this is an impossible requirement, and would leave us without the bodily drive to do anything. However, it is just because of this influence of our sexuality on passions and

---

[31] This mentality is mentioned by Anscombe when she condemns the 'people seed' argument and suchlike. Opinion 7 in 'Twenty Opinions', p. 67.
[32] 'Contraception and Chastity', p. 185.

motivations which in their turn influence everything that we do[33] that specifically libidinous activity, that is voluntary genital activity, is quite generally corrupting unless it has the specific significance that belongs to such activity. The reason why libido affects our emotions generally is that libidinous activity belongs to a relationship which, in a good man who is married, affects the shape of his entire life. The generic end of the chaste married person is to live a life united with another in such a way that each commits to the other their whole reproductive future, even to the point of accepting that this future is not going to come to fruition. This is a life open to generation in which the parties perform sexual acts only with each other, acts to which that goodness belongs which makes sexual activity a good sort of activity. This goodness lies in the unitive meaning of the marriage act, by which spouses are joined in an act of generative kind which signifies procreation even when it does not procreate.

This act is good if it is indeed of generative kind, but Anscombe remarks that the fact that every single sexual act is significant, as not every act of eating is significant, means that a single sexual act can be bad in itself, not just because of the pattern of which it forms a part or because of the circumstances and likely effects, which is how it is with eating. It is bad, she maintains, if it is not of generative kind, and explains that to be of generative kind it does not have actually to generate, just as an acorn does not have to grow up into an oak tree in order to be the seed of an oak. One could remark at this point that one of the ways of treating with contempt the bodily function by which we are brought into being is to change the sexual act so as to make it not of a kind to generate, and this contempt is shown by those who regard the conjugal act as being just one of the ways in which orgasm is to be obtained.

All sexual actions are related to generation in that they are exercises of the reproductive system. However, I have observed that only in a physically normal copulation is there an event which is a reproductive type of event in the bodies of both members of the couple: the ejaculation of the semen is the same event as the coming of semen into the woman's genital tract. Thus only the

---

[33] And so someone who has attained to the shining virtue of chastity shows this in his whole manner, while someone who is given to sexual behaviour of a sterile kind is apt to show this as well.

copulation of man and woman can, *qua* copulation, be an exercise of the reproductive system: only an act which is such a copulation can join the couple in a coupling which is generative in kind. There is no other way in which a sexual act can be such as to unite the couple specifically as organisms. An intentional sex act which is not a normal copulation embodies the intention to produce orgasm in an individual, or perhaps in more than one individual. The normal copulation of man and woman is a single reproductive-type event which happens in both bodies, and only in performing such a copulation can two people be aiming at a single sexual act.

This biological unification, however, is not enough, according to Anscombe. It should be clear that a biologically normal copulation can take place between people who are too drunk or otherwise mentally subnormal to know what it is that they are doing — that the man is ejaculating into the woman's vagina, and that this is how women come to be pregnant and babies to be born — so there is more to performing a human act which is generative in kind than that the physical copulation be normal.

The act to be conjugal must be an intentional act which, as an intentional act, is of reproductive kind. For this it is not necessary that reproduction be aimed at, only that people aim to perform the kind of act which reproduces. It is inconsistent with this aim, however, that anything be done before, during or after the act to make that act non-reproductive. Anything like this changes the intentional act to a use of one another's bodies, 'no longer to perform a generative-type act, but for one or both to achieve orgasm'.[34] Some contraceptive measures may not prevent the copulation from being a copulation of reproductive kind, but the contracepted copulation is, as a human act, not of generative kind. Lacking generative meaning, it lacks that which makes it a good kind of action, the meaning that signifies and enacts the organic unity of the couple. What makes a copulation unite the couple is that it is a single reproductive-type event occurring in their two bodies, but it loses its meaning as a union of two people if they aim at removing from it the possibility of generation, since then they are not performing a human act of generative kind. Reason is not in command, I would say, when the *ratio* of the human act of copulation has been removed in respect of that particular act. Like an

---

[34] 'You Can Have Sex Without Children', *CPP3*, p. 84.

abnormal act, such as *fellatio,* the sexual aim in such an act can only be orgasm in individuals, rather than a joint act of generative kind, which is the good kind of sexual act which it is reasonable to perform in that it is the expression of that generative relation, human marriage. This is not simply because the couple intends not to generate, but because by acting against generation in this action they have deprived their intentional action itself of the character of being a generative kind of act. It is only *qua* irrational that their desire makes their act a single sexual act: on the level of reason the organic unity is denied by being undone, since what makes the act a single organic event in the bodies of both people is that it is one reproductive event occurring in both bodies. This is why the unitive and procreative meanings of the act are inseparable, so that an attack on one meaning is an attack on the other. A sexual act lacking this meaning is one in which the baser part, the desire for orgasm, is in command. Even if the couple is acting as they think for the sake of their marriage, theirs is like the action of a man who acts merely to placate his sensual nature. I have said, that if he does this while disregarding the *ratio* of his sexuality, his is not an action in which reason is in command, even though the purpose and immediate effect of his action is to enjoy a mental life less troubled by lust. The couple may be aiming at some sort of unity, but are like this man in that they are disregarding the *ratio* of their sexuality.

Anscombe points out that when people temporarily avoid conception by confining their marriage acts to the infertile period, they do nothing to their intentional act of intercourse to make it non-generative, but have non-conception only as a further intention, which they achieve by not performing marriage acts at a later time.[35] Reason, in such a circumstance, can be in control, in that the act is chosen as that good kind of action by which human beings are generated and the marriage bond given expression.

We can connect this with Aristotle's saying that the best way is that which least attends to the irrational part of the soul *qua* irrational, in that the communication between the bodies of the man and his wife is an intentional act chosen as being, on the level of the mind, the kind of act which it is on the level of the body: i.e. a copulation of generative kind. Being this, it does not impede the spirit of contemplation as must actions in which the base motive

---

[35] 'You Can Have Sex Without Children', pp. 86–87.

of sensuality is in command, and as must the generic end of enjoying orgasms without allowing to them the *ratio* of being a part of the marriage act. Whatever be one's motive for making such orgasms one's aim, one is denying the meaning of human sexuality, and hence of human life, by treating one's own sexuality in this way.

It has been objected that the fine distinction between an intentional act and the further intention with which an act is performed is one which most people would find it hard to understand, and so cannot be important to human virtue. Can you say that the generic end of the simple virtuous man is to perform only acts of the generative kind, and those within marriage? This objection can be answered by saying that people can feel a difference which they could not articulate: consider the knowledge of grammar which people have without knowing any grammatical terms. The sense of the difference between contracepting and avoiding fertile times is one which, as Anscombe says, they have by connatural knowledge, because of the virtue that is in them and not because of their understanding of the philosophy of intention. It is when people start talking philosophy, and saying that the intention is the same in both cases, that it is time to show that their philosophy is wrong.

Edward Harcourt

Internalized Others, Joint Attention and the Moral Education of the Child

In 'The Moral Environment of the Child',[1] Elizabeth Anscombe observes that

> a child can be encouraged to have certain ends and concerns by the attitudes of its adults, and sometimes by being associated with the adults in promoting and pursuing them.[2]

The observation may seem not to amount to very much but, as we shall see, there is considerable wisdom in it. This chapter tries to say some more about what's involved in a child's being taught 'ends and concerns [by ...] its adults', and about some philosophical issues that arise when one tries to explain how adult attitudes make the difference to this teaching that they seem to make. It will turn out that the part played in a child's education by being *associated* with adults in promoting and pursuing things proves to be a helpful alternative to a popular rival account of the moral — and not only the moral — education of children.

1

In the same paper, Anscombe continues that there is

> an important sense in which *velle non discitur*: willing is not taught. Suppose, for example, that the adult would like to train the child

---

[1] In *FHG*, pp. 224–233.
[2] 'Moral Environment', p. 226.

> to help people who are poor and wretched. He can do quite a lot...
> But it is not something that can be guaranteed.[3]

Indeed the only sort of action that can be 'pretty well guaranteed [...] by upbringing' is such as is counted absolutely obligatory in a society and whose performance or non performance is quite open and visible: like the prayers at fixed times in a strict Muslim town.[4]

This assessment is both too optimistic and too pessimistic. It's too optimistic because, where bringing up children is concerned, *guaranteed* outcomes are rarer even than Anscombe allows: Muslim children can be trained to pray five times a day in as strict a town as you like, and yet stop doing so as soon as they have the chance.

But it is surely also too pessimistic. Consider the comic passage from *Intention* about the person who 'out of the blue [...] says "I want a pin" and denies wanting it *for* anything'.

> [S]uppose we give it him and see what he does with it. He takes it, let us say, he smiles and says 'Thank you. My want is gratified' — But what does he do with the pin? If he puts it down and forgets about it, in what sense is it true to say that he wanted a pin? He used these words, the effect of which was that he was given one; but what reason have we to say he wanted a pin, rather than: to see if we would take the trouble to give him one?[5]

Asking for something to see if we will take the trouble to give it is quite common in smallish children. But there is an indeterminacy as to whether, at the time of asking, they want the thing or not which it is in our hands to shape one way or another. If we understand that the child is simply testing its efficacy upon us, our very saying that it really *doesn't* want the thing, because (for instance) there's nothing it could do with the thing once it had it, makes the space in the child close over where a desire might otherwise have taken shape.[6] (And the child will have proof enough of its efficacy in eliciting *that* reaction.) On the other hand — though I don't mean

---

[3] 'Moral Environment', p. 227.
[4] 'Moral Environment', p. 227.
[5] *I*, p. 70.
[6] Compare Bernard Williams on responsibility: we help to turn children into responsible agents by blaming them for things for which, first time round at least, they aren't in fact to blame, 'How Free Does the Will Need to Be?', in Bernard Williams, *Making Sense of Humanity* (Cambridge: Cambridge University Press, 1995), p. 16.

to suggest there are only two possible ways in which this case could be further elaborated — a parent may not understand that that's all the child is doing and, anxious that they are not very good at meeting their children's wants, produce a pin on demand. And now the child has been steered into a state of confusion: the validity of its demand has been affirmed by being gratified, so surely (it thinks to itself) I really must want the pin — after all, I asked for it; and yet the pin is (as this child can also see) as little desirable to it as it was to the child who was denied it. This second child has, I suggest, received a little lesson in the formation of counterfeit desires, just as the first child received a lesson in the formation of rational desires. These lessons are cumulative: it is types or patterns of desire that are learnt, not particular desires (e.g. for pins), and there are of course no guarantees of how things will turn out in the long run. Nonetheless, it is a case of the parent's knowledge of the desirable shaping, or alternatively failing to shape, the child's desires — of *velle discere*.

The parent in the first example, unlike the one in the second, is (we may say) authoritative, and this is one of several connections between 'The Moral Environment of the Child' and the discussions of authority in Anscombe's 'Authority in Morals'[7] and elsewhere. Parents need to be authoritative: as Anscombe says, 'not to demand obedience is to inflict a great wrong on the child.'[8] That is partly because the child needs to know things such as not to cross the road without looking[9] which it can't be expected to discover for itself, and will only come to know if those in whose care it finds itself are authoritative. But refusing the child a pin — because, as we might say in anticipation, it doesn't want one — is also an exercise of authority, and as much needed by the child as being told not to cross the road without looking. Just look at the rubbish the second child accumulates: sweets it has no appetite for, knickknacks it will never look at again, pins...

In order to pursue further my question as to what's involved in a child's being taught 'ends and concerns [by ...] its adults', I would like to raise two questions connected with parental

---

[7] 'Authority in Morals', *CPP3*, pp. 43–50.
[8] 'Moral Environment', p. 228.
[9] 'Everyone can see that when what is in question is the avoidance of gross physical dangers', 'Moral Environment', p. 228; cp. 'Authority in Morals', in *CPP3*, p. 45.

authority. First of all, what explains the difference between parents who are authorities for their children and those who are not? Anscombe touches on this question, but parents in Anscombe's writing, when they appear, are on the whole sure of themselves and of what they have to teach and the question is not explored very far.

Secondly there is the question of what comes *after* authoritative teaching. Anscombe touches on this too, though not—if I may put it thus—under that description. For she is interested in what a child comes to do 'by itself and off its own bat',[10] what someone does when he becomes 'autonomous',[11] 'his own pilot'.[12] There's a connection here which Anscombe seems not to draw. In her view, autonomy in the child is 'the time when [it ...] may not maintain its former habits', that is, those its parents have instilled.[13] Insofar as those habits are good habits, I think she sees this as a failure, even though it needn't be 'a failure on your part in the teaching of anything that can be taught'[14]—the *velle non discitur* point again. But it is not—or so I would like to say—a shortcoming of genuinely authoritative teaching that it fails to guarantee compliance with it. Indeed teaching that's 'a mere imposition', that's delivered in 'a situation of stress and tension',[15] is if anything more likely to secure compliance, until the case in which the teaching needs to be applied is too unfamiliar. On the contrary, it is precisely the *success* of authoritative teaching, as distinct from 'mere imposition' or the unself-confident refusal to teach at all, that its graduates are those most able to do things 'by themselves and off their own bats', to 'be their own pilots' or—as I shall put it, in order to make it clear that I have a broad-band capacity in mind, not just the capacity to regulate oneself in the light of *moral* reasons—to be self-regulators. In regulating themselves they may of course make mistakes, but (a) having the power of judgment in themselves, they are less likely to do so than graduates of the 'mere imposition' or 'can't be bothered' schools; and (b) the

---

[10] 'Moral Environment', p. 227.
[11] 'Moral Environment', p. 227.
[12] 'Authority in Morals', pp. 48–49.
[13] 'Moral Environment', p. 227.
[14] 'Moral Environment', p. 227.
[15] 'Moral Environment', p. 228.

teachers may themselves have made mistakes, although their fallibility does not compromise their authority to teach.[16]

It thus looks as if whatever explains the difference between parents who are and parents who are not authorities will *also* explain the difference between children who go on to become successful self-regulators and children who do not. But what is that?

2

It's often said that the developmental history of self-regulation needs to be told in terms of the notion of an *internalized other*: the fact that real external others—such as parents—give way to internal others who are their 'psychic representatives' is what explains the transition from direction by others to self-regulation. But of any such theory we can always ask—and here I adapt some remarks of Anscombe's about legislating for oneself[17]—'Is the internalized other the developing person or not?' If it is, we have self-regulation indeed—but no explanation of it. If it isn't, the purported explanation bargains away the fact it was meant to explain (*self*-regulation), since why, unless much more is said, should the mere internality of another make the difference between self-regulation and regulation by that other? The problem for the theorist of self-regulation is like that of Lodovico Sforza, the fifteenth-century Duke of Milan who invited Charles V of France and his army into Italy to stabilize his own domestic position: once a foreign power has installed itself, how do you get rid of it again?[18] But it needs to be got rid of somehow if—to abandon the simile—self-regulation, as opposed to regulation by another (external or not), is what we are to end up with.

David Velleman has wrestled with this problem in a well-known series of papers which attempt to 'effect a marriage

---

[16] If a child were able to discriminate between the true and the false things his teacher says in every case, he would not need a teacher, so he needs to be *liable* to believe his teacher, and in this resides the fallible teacher's right, that his pupils be prepared to believe him: 'Authority in Morals', p. 45.
[17] 'Modern Moral Philosophy', in *CPP3*, p. 27.
[18] See Francesco Guicciardini, *The History of Italy*, tr. and ed. S. Alexander (New York/London: Macmillan, 1969), pp. 20–21: '[Lodovico] decided to seek protection from foreign armies […] not considering how dangerous it is to use medicine which is stronger than the nature of the disease.'

between Freud and Kant'.[19] Internalization can account for self-regulation, he argues, only if the others internalized are authoritative rather than merely powerful, for if they aren't, to internalize them will simply be to install a tyrant inside one's head. Now I think we can all understand what's being got at by the distinction between having a tyrant inside one's head and having an authority. Someone who founds a society for the preservation of the semi-colon, erupts with fury at anyone—above all himself— who misuses it, but does a bad job of explaining what's so important about it; alternatively, someone who feels so anxious if they fail to comply with some precept ('never be seen without make-up') that they resentfully comply, despite (quite unlike the semi-colon man) explicitly disavowing any outlook that would give the precept a point—we say that they are being bossed around because in some sense (though differently in each case) they have not made the ideas by which they steer their lives fully their own. *That* is not what 'being one's own pilot' is about. But if the external other is an *authority*, there will be no experience of being bossed, so if internalization plays any role in a correct account of the development of self-regulation, it will be the internalization of an authority that turns into willing compliance, the ability to give reasons for compliance, knowing what to do in previously unrehearsed cases, and so on.

So what relation to the external other, if any, would explain the other's authority? Velleman's answer is 'love'. This raises two questions: first, *are* parents who love and are loved by their children more authoritative? And secondly, if that is so, does the fact provide a good explanation of the relation between obedience (in a child) and self-regulation?

To take the second question first, there is a problem in supposing that moving even an *authoritative* external other inwards *on its own* could make the difference between obedience— albeit to a legitimate authority—and self-regulation. For we are still on the second horn of the dilemma I articulated above: of course one doesn't resent the instructions of one whom one recognizes as authoritative but still, even an authoritative internal other isn't me. Velleman's reply to this objection just shifts us onto the

---

[19] David Velleman, *Self to Self* (Cambridge: Cambridge University Press, 2006), p. 131. The papers I have in mind are 'A Rational Superego', 'The Voice of Conscience' and 'Love as a Moral Emotion'.

first horn: love explains why the internal other's authority is *my* authority because I loved the external other from which the internal one is derived, so the external other must have met my own standards of lovability (Velleman adds 'and admirability', but let's forget that). So in regulating my behaviour in the light of the other's standards I am regulating it in the light of my own. My own standards of lovability must therefore predate the internalization, yet it was my very possession of standards *of my own* that internalization was meant to explain.[20]

This problem makes me worry that the answer to the first question should be 'no' too — that really love and authority are unrelated — and (to look ahead) I will end by sounding a note of scepticism on that score. Nonetheless there are reasons for favouring a positive answer. For, plausibly, the *reason* the parent who produces the pin when asked is not authoritative is that there is some *other* defect in its relation to the child. Perhaps what the child really wanted was to talk to or to play a game with the adult, and the reason asking for things it doesn't really want is becoming rather a habit is that it does not often enough get what it *does* want; or, more accurately, what it needs the adult to teach it that it wants. Even if the parent might *say* 'you can have whatever you want!', the child is given only what it asks for, not what it wants. Indeed it's given what it asks for, one might say, because the parent believes they *cannot* give the child what it really wants — themselves — perhaps because they think they have nothing in that department to give. And yet this inability may be the last thing the parent wants to admit to (even to themselves). Perversely, saying 'no' to the demand for the pin *feels like* saying 'you can't have me', so it seems best to say yes. ('I can't deny him anything' euphemizes for 'I can't give him anything'.) Or, if the parent has heard it's not a good idea to give small children pins, its attempts to say no are unlikely to be very effective: the child will howl for what it doesn't really want until it gets it. As Anscombe says, a parent's demand for obedience is unlikely to be met if it feels 'like a mere imposition' when the parent makes it, and it *will* feel like that if 'the adult feels uncertain in giving any moral teaching'.[21] By contrast the parent who *denies* the child the pin may be confident

---

[20] For a fuller discussion, see my 'Velleman on Love and Ideals of Rational Humanity', *Philosophical Quarterly* 59(235) 2009:349–356.
[21] 'Moral Environment', p. 228.

that the child already *has* plenty of him or her, so to deny it the pin is to deny it that and no more, so it's easy to do. Love and authority—and later the capacity to 'be one's own pilot'—seem to go together, as Velleman says. But if that is so, we don't yet have an explanation of it. In the rest of this paper I am going to rule out some more bad explanations, and propose an explanation that dispenses with the idea of an internalized other—whether authoritative or not.

3

It's attractive to say—as a first approximation—that children obey their parents when they do because they seek the parents' approval, and in some sense surely this is right. Take the case of an 18-month-old boy.[22] His parents own a vase and one of the house rules is 'don't touch the vase'. One day he and his mother are in the room where the vase stands on its plinth. Making quite sure she can see him, he approaches the vase. She frowns at him and he can see she is frowning. Then he reaches a finger out towards the vase and, just as he is about to make contact, theatrically withdraws his finger and looks round at the mother (as if to say 'touching the vase is what I'm *not* doing'). She smiles at him and he beams back. This transaction shows that the boy has understood the house rule. It also appears to show that the mother's approval (her smile) and his pleasure in it (his smile back) are motivating him to abide by it. Finally, the specialness of the boy's relationship to his mother surely plays a role: after all, if their relationship were not special, why would *her* approval be so enjoyable to him (or his unforced compliance so enjoyable to her)?

To theorize the role of approval in this type of case, we may find ourselves reaching for what I call the *incentive model*. Approval is good. So getting another's approval either supplies a missing reason for action or adds to an existing one: one acts in a way one thinks will elicit the other's approval in order to get that good thing. The role of *special* others is just this: their approval is especially good. The same goes *mutatis mutandis* for disapproval and disincentives.

---

[22] From R. Emde, W.F. Johnson and M. Easterbrooks, 'The Do's and Don'ts of Early Moral Development', in J. Kagan and S. Lamb (eds.), *The Emergence of Morality in Young Children* (Chicago & London: University of Chicago Press, 1987), p. 267.

However, the incentive model can't be right, at least for all cases. For one thing, empirical work shows that incentives *de*motivate.[23] Parents who offer their children cash to do homework find that, though the children's performance improves while the cash is on offer, it falls back to below its original level once the cash offer is withdrawn. (Presumably because the message sent by the incentive is that homework isn't valuable—what's valuable is cash.) Now think back to the 18-month-old boy. That vignette is a still from a longer moving picture, that is, from a typical developmental narrative. Rewind to an earlier developmental phase and we find compliance in response to explicit *and contemporaneous* parental instructions (contrast the vignette itself, in which the house rule 'don't touch the vase' isn't actually uttered); fast forward and we find, first, compliance in the absence of the parent (though with thoughts of how the parent would react very much to the fore) and, later, compliance in their absence and with thoughts of them playing an increasingly recessive role. That is to say, the vignette is an episode in a typical story of the development for the capacity for self-regulation. It's the process at a certain stage of which the other's instruction becomes one's own mind (and before the continued formation of one's mind perhaps modifies or displaces it). But a step on the way to self-regulation—which contrasts with non-compliance, or grudging compliance, or the need for prods or threats to secure compliance[24]—is just what we do not have in the cash-for-homework case: if the boy was on the way to self-regulation, good performance would outlast the offer of cash. So the incentive model is a poor model for the role approval plays in the case of the 18-month-old boy.[25]

---

[23] I am indebted here to Jules Holroyd, 'A Communicative Theory of Moral Appraisal', *Ethical Theory and Moral Practice* 10(3) 2007:267–278. Just the same goes for disincentives or threats. Holroyd's main sources here are Edward L. Deci and Richard M. Ryan, 'The "What" and "Why" of Good Pursuits', *Psychol. Inquiry* 11, 2000:227–268, esp. 233–4; and Deci, Ryan *et al.*, 'The Support of Autonomy and the Control of Behavior', *J. Pers. Soc. Psychol.* 53(6) 1987:1024–1037.

[24] Some psychologists use the term 'committed compliance': see e.g. G. Kochanska, 'Committed Compliance, Moral Self and Internalization', *Developmental Psychology* 38(3) 2003:339–351.

[25] Holroyd speaks of reinforcement of motivation, and gives internalization a separate treatment, but we don't need to distinguish the two for now.

The disincentivizing effect of incentives is in any case just a useful collateral consideration. Consider the idea that God punishes the wicked and rewards the good. On many fully intelligible religious outlooks, that is not just an interesting fact: the fact that God punishes the wicked and rewards the good helps to explain why people avoid wickedness and do good. But how? On the incentive model, people avoid wickedness out of fear of divine punishment and do good for the sake of divine reward. But that is rather less good than human reasons for action can be: though avoiding wickedness in order to avoid punishment is better than not avoiding it, it's much better to avoid wickedness just because it's wicked, and to do good just because it's good. Much the same goes for parents. At least some parents agree that doing good for the sake of a reward isn't very good. So if the incentive model were correct, First Prize would necessarily go unawarded: no child could ever receive *that* from parents and deserve it. But it at least appears that many parents award the First Prize and award it because it's deserved. So again, the incentive model can't be right.

Perhaps, however, the fault lies not with the incentive model *per se*, but with the fact that in the homework case the incentive on offer is cash—something material—whereas in the 18-month-old's it is something intangible: approval. But the tangible/intangible distinction in fact bears no weight. It's perfectly *possible* for cash—or sweets, or any other tangible good—to function exactly as the mother's approval does in the 18-month-old's case. Of course one can imagine the original nature of the transaction being pulled out of shape if the tangible thing on offer is something for which the child has an immediate and very strong desire (sweets, perhaps): the child comes to see what the mother naïvely continues to regard as his simple expression of commitment to the house rules as a means to getting these highly desirable things, so deceit or at least misunderstanding is introduced into the transaction, which wasn't present to begin with. But though these things *could* happen, they needn't happen: it could just be that instead of turning round and receiving a smile from the mother, the child turns round and receives a sweet, and beams in return. The psychology of the original transaction, whatever that is, is unaltered.

Conversely, words and smiles can be offered as incentives. In a family environment where such things are scarce, enthusiastic—indeed obsequious—compliance could be the child's means of getting those scarce things. Something like this is what we have in mind when we speak of behaviour—and I take it this is always pejorative—as 'approval-seeking'. Or the parent, knowing that the child hungers for his or her scarce expressions of approval, can dangle the promise of words or smiles, thereby exacting the child's compliance.[26]

So I conclude that the incentive model isn't a good model even once we have budgeted for the difference between tangible and intangible incentives. Indeed the incentive model might be said to be a bad model for the 18-month-old case because it's a good model for at least one kind of case where things are not as they should be ('approval-seeking', or exacted compliance, if these are indeed distinct). But for the 18-month-old case itself, if not the incentive model, then what?

4

In pursuit of an alternative answer, I want to look now at a child of around 36 months—that is, where self-regulation in the parent's absence is already happening. The experimental set-up is as follows. The child is with the interviewer. Mother enters with two 'very appealing' toys and tells the child not to play with them as they are 'special', then leaves. The interviewer challenges the child's adherence to the prohibition 'by having a bunny puppet invite the child to play with the prohibited toys'. If the child plays with the toys, the interviewer reminds the child of the prohibition. Then the mother returns and asks the child whether or not he/she has played with them.[27] Here are a couple of examples of what happens. 'When the bunny asks about the prohibited toys, [one child] indignantly says "Couldn't! Couldn't because real special". In response to the next temptation, the child says, "Maybe he could", then agrees to play with the toys but quickly recovers himself: "I couldn't play with her [the doll] now. Mom says I could pretty soon". The child never does play with the […] toys during the mother's absence.' A different child, in response to the first

---

[26] Cf. Ian Suttie on *exacting* expressions of love in his *The Origins of Love and Hate* (Harmondsworth: Penguin, 1960), p. 58—though of course there could be multiple possible explanations for things going wrong, depending on the details of the case.

[27] R. Emde and H. Buchsbaum, '"Didn't You Hear My Mommy?" Autonomy *with* Connectedness in Moral Self Emergence', in D. Cicchetti and M. Beeghly (eds.), *The Self in Transition* (Chicago & London: University of Chicago Press, 1990), p. 50.

temptation, says 'I don't know. What did my mom say? She said not to play with those, didn't she? So I better not play with those.' A third says 'We can't touch these because they're somebody's.'[28]

Attachment theorists emphasize that the need for closeness to certain others is constant across the lifespan. But one might say that maturation poses the 'problem' of how to satisfy this persisting need given that constant physical proximity ceases to be possible, for example as children become more mobile. One 'solution' is to 'stay in touch' by talking rather than by actually touching. This observation suggests a simple theory of the role of love in explaining compliance. Thus in the 36-month-old cases, where the mother leaves the room so touching or speaking to her are impossible, the simple theory says that compliance is a solution to the problem: by keeping the rule mother uttered before she left, the child maintains contact with her. Keeping it is a way of *being with* her while she is not there. Herein also lies a theory of approval that applies beyond just these cases: looking to the mother for approval and receiving it (in the 18-month-old case too) is a case of making contact, like touching but part of an expanded repertoire of intimacy younger children do not have. Compliance is explained by love because compliance manifests love.

This simple theory seems to make sense of a well-known example. In the New Testament, Jesus says: 'He that hath my commandments, and keepeth them, he it is that loveth me.'[29] There at least is the idea that love and compliance go together. But remember when he says it: at the Last Supper, when he knows that he will shortly be leaving his disciples.[30] But this, he is saying, should not be a cause for despair, because they have his commandments: by keeping *them*, they can be with him even across a distance.

But if keeping the relevant 'commandments' is a way of being with another, what is breaking them? One answer is that it is breaking the relationship off, at least temporarily. Similarly, if

---

[28] All three quotations from Emde and Buchsbaum, p. 56.
[29] The first is from John 14:21. See also e.g. John 14:23, 'If a man love me, he will keep my words', John 14:24, 'He that loveth me not keepeth not my sayings', 1 John 5:3, 'For this is the love of God, that we keep his commandments'.
[30] E.g. John 14:18–19 – 'I will not leave you comfortless: I will come to you. Yet a little while, and the world seeth me no more.'

approval is an expression of parental love, disapproval would seem to be the denial or suspension of it. Compare Martin L. Hoffman, who distinguishes three 'methods' of securing compliance: 'induction' (which includes pointing out consequences to the child), 'power-assertion' (which includes yelling at the child), and 'love-withdrawal'—'if you go on doing that I won't love you any more.'[31] Love-withdrawal also features in the work of psychoanalyst Ian Suttie. Because it can be effected unilaterally and therefore inescapably, Suttie argues that it matches the property of conscience—that it's with us all the time, rather than just when an authority-figure is nearby—that Freud looked to explain by appeal to fear, and so is the true explanation of self-regulation. As he puts it, 'only the loved object can wield the separation-anxiety in its true sense.'[32] On this view, the sanction behind parental prohibitions and commands—and what disapproval really is—is the withdrawal of love.

Like the incentive model, Suttie has certainly described a way approval and disapproval *can* function in the context of love-relations, but has not given a general theory of approval and disapproval, and once again it is the defective cases that it fits the best: 'wielding the separation-anxiety' sounds like a description of emotional manipulation.[33] Much the same is true if the parent secures compliance by indicating to the child that they will be *damaged* by the child's non-compliance on the grounds that non-compliance will be interpreted—however unjustly—as love-withdrawal on the child's part. By contrast where love is at its best, it surely won't cross the child's mind that it might suddenly lose the parent's love. So the threat of love-withdrawal can't be what's securing compliance in such cases, because it is not a credible threat. Again, while a loving parent may well be angry with a child if it disobeys, is anger really the withdrawal of love? Quite apart from the fact that love is not something that can be switched on and off from moment to moment—there's a difference between (occurrently) *expressing* love, and loving—the

---

[31] Martin L. Hoffman, *Empathy and Moral Development* (Cambridge: Cambridge University Press, 2000), pp. 146ff.
[32] Suttie, *The Origins of Love and Hate*, p. 102.
[33] To be fair to Suttie, it is possible that he just expressed himself badly in this passage—I can't be sure.

sensible parent's anger will only be directed at what the child has done. So we should forget the love-withdrawal theory.

The simple theory does not, however, imply the love-withdrawal theory of disapproval. 'Harmonious' mother–infant interactions — indeed interactions in any attachment relationship — do not consist of uninterrupted states of mutual attunement, a long waltz in which each is faultlessly sensitive to tiny changes in the other. Harmony has as much to do with the ease with which the members of the dyad can find their way back to one another after a break in mutual adjustment — with cycles of 'rupture and repair' — as it has with the actual persistence of a state of mutual attunement.[34] Rupture and repair is also a much better model of what's going on in compliance in the best case. Disapproval does not mean that love is withdrawn or suspended: it is a further mark of love-relations at their best that the occasion for disapproval can be allowed to arise, that it can be expressed in a non-catastrophic way, and that the pair can find their way back — if necessary via tears, apologies, forgiveness and so on — to mutual attunement with only the fuss or sense of crisis that the character of the disapproved-of act demands.

But if *both* willing compliance plus approval *and* a degree of non-compliance plus disapproval are elaborated forms of being with another across a distance, it can't be the *distinctive* role of approval to maintain the being-with. Consequently, we have so far failed to answer the question how adding love to a child–parent relation renders the parent authoritative. There seems both something right and something wrong with this proposal. To be sure, a love-relation at its best is a stable framework within which willing compliance and non-compliance (meeting with approval or non-catastrophic disapproval) take place, not something which it takes compliance (or the bait of approval) to maintain. At the same time, however, Christ did not say 'He that keepeth my commandments *or breaketh them*, he it is that loveth me', and surely for a reason. Though a love-relation does not depend on uninterrupted staring into one another's eyes, this is not to say there is no difference in value — even difference in value for the

---

[34] 'Empathic ruptures and the capacity to repair them': see Jeremy Holmes, *Exploring in Security* (London: Routledge, 2010), pp. 37ff. and pp. 78ff. It will, for example, be important to 'repair' that the mother doesn't experience the spitting out of the nipple as a rejection.

relationship — between meeting another's gaze and ignoring them. The relation is affirmed when the commandments are kept, even if the relation *exists* also when they are not. The relation is of value, and I am suggesting that the commandments are a token of it, so why would one not want to affirm it (even if one doesn't always)?

5

Nonetheless I am still not satisfied. I hope I've shown at least that there is no tension between love or warmth towards one's children and authority, and it is tragic indeed if children are denied warmth *on the grounds that* they require authority, a fallacy that seems to be betrayed in the double meaning of the word 'spoilt' in connection with children: (i) 'marred', and (ii) 'indulged'. But at least if 'indulgence' means giving lots of what's wanted, indulged is just what the child who gets the pin is not. But though it would be a kind of happy ending if one could say that without warmth there is no genuine authority, perhaps distant parents can nonetheless be good educators. They are just very good at denying things to their children (and no doubt to themselves), without having anything much else to offer. These types of relations are worse because they are less warm, not because they have to be less authoritative. (That was the note of scepticism promised earlier.) I also worry that my 'simple theory' is a better explanation of a person's keeping *divine* commandments than it is of their keeping ordinary ones (or of otherwise behaving as parents have shown them to behave). For — as I understand it — in the case of the divine commandment, one has the curious double *explanandum* 'keep the law because it is the law' and 'keep the law for my sake'.[35] But with human parents (or indeed other loved ones), though one *sometimes* wants to say (e.g.) 'this is our favourite dish so I'm making it while you are away', sometimes one just wants to make the dish because it tastes nice, for all that you showed me how to make it. And when my children in adulthood do what I've taught them to do, it just won't always be for *my* sake, nor do I want it to be: I will regard it as a success if I have faded from view, leaving only what I have taught them. Even a loving Charles V would have got in the way of poor Lodovico Sforza. So I want to make one more attempt.

---

[35] This double *explanandum* is wrestled with admirably by Joseph Shaw, 'The Virtue of Obedience', *Religious Studies* 38, 2002:63–75.

One of the most impressive marks of the securely attached — whether children or adults — and which I didn't mention before is that they are confident explorers of the world.[36] Except in situations of danger, the securely attached have the freedom to look outwards to the world because their base is secure.[37] For the same reason, they are also confidently expressive in the context of the attachment relationship itself (they say what's on their minds). The secure child can rock the boat because it is confident the boat won't sink.[38] By contrast at least one sub-variety of insecure child — the insecure-ambivalent — will focus on the caregiver rather than the environment even when there is nothing in the environment (no threat, for instance) to prompt this, thus inhibiting exploration.[39]

I suggest these facts provide a clue to the problem at hand. A central part of mature self-regulation is the capacity to act for reasons, and to see in one's environment whatever reasons there are going. Now it's not the case that *whenever* another person, or another person's attitude to oneself, or one's relations with

---

[36] Holmes, *Exploring in Security*, p. 32.
[37] For the 'secure base', see John Bowlby, 'The Role of Attachment in Personality Development', in Bowlby, *A Secure Base* (London: Routledge, 1988). 'Higher quality mother–child interactions accompanied secure, confident exploration of the world of learning' (in children starting school), K. Grossmann et al., 'A Wider View of Attachment and Exploration: the Influence of Mothers and Fathers on the Development of Psychological Security from Infant to Young Adulthood', in J. Cassidy and P. Shaver (eds.), *Handbook of Attachment: Theory, Research, and Clinical Applications*, 2nd edn. (New York: The Guilford Press, 2008), pp. 857–879, at p. 870; 'security of attachment representation was significantly associated with attention and participation [at school] at ages 9 and 15', (p. 871).
[38] Cf. D.W. Winnicott: 'Hello object, I destroyed you!', *Playing and Reality* (London: Tavistock, 1971), p. 91.
[39] 'When there is no apparent danger in the environment, some infants with insecure attachment relationships may still direct attachment behaviours to their caregivers, reflecting a constant low-level anxiety about the caregivers' availability', N. Weinfeld et al., 'Individual Differences in Infant–Caregiver Attachment' (in Cassidy & Shaver, *Handbook of Attachment*, pp. 78–101), p. 80. Ditto 'hypervigilance', where the child has suffered harm at the caregiver's hands, J. Simpson and J. Belsky, 'Attachment Theory within a Modern Evolutionary Framework', in Cassidy & Shaver, *Handbook of Attachment*, pp. 131–157, at pp. 138–139.

another person, is one's reason for acting, something is amiss.[40] But theory needs to allow that if—in maturity—I don't touch the vase, the reason I don't may be simply *that it's valuable and fragile*: in other words a reason in which other people, their attitudes to me, etc. are nowhere to be seen. It is therefore a constraint on any theory of the development of self-regulation that it describe the developmental process in such a way that it can, in the most favourable cases, have action on *such* reasons as its terminus. The incentive and the love-withdrawal theories, on the other hand, make loved others or their attitudes *pervasive* among my reasons. They thus look like a special case of what goes wrong in insecure (more properly, insecure-ambivalent) attachment: the learning child's gaze cannot pass beyond the caregiver's attitudes to the world. But if others' attitudes are so pervasive in the early years, it is hard to see how they could become less so thanks merely to the passage of time: they sound like developmental precursors of a 'misdirection of the ethical attention',[41] and thus spectacularly fail to meet the constraint on developmental theories I've just stated. This is just a variant of the problem with internalized-other theories of self-regulation I posed at the beginning: once in the picture, how they are ever to be got out of it again. Putting the point the other way about, where approval or disapproval is implicated *in the right way* in self-regulation, they will play an increasingly recessive role as maturation progresses, gradually giving way to *doing things for reasons*, at most some of which are persons and their attitudes. This is also the problem with the 'simple theory', though somehow it arises there in a more benign way.

---

[40] Some may wish to argue that, in the relevant sense, others' attitudes should *never* be reasons. Thus whenever my primary reason for acting is (say) *in order not to upset so-and-so*, I must in some measure either be humouring so-and-so (and thus not paying them the respect that is their due as the author of reasons) or else be being manipulated by them (and so not paying that same due respect to myself). Conversely, when neither of these problems is present, so-and-so's attitudes are as it were transparent with respect to my reasons for acting: my primary reasons for acting will simply be the reasons we share. (I find something like this view in K. Ebels-Duggan, 'Against Beneficence: A Normative Account of Love', *Ethics* 119, 2008:142–170.) I doubt that this extreme view is correct, but if it is, then that would accentuate the need to avoid the incentive and love-withdrawal models.

[41] The phrase is Bernard Williams', *Ethics and the Limits of Philosophy* (London: Fontana, 1985), p. 11.

Perhaps this is the whole story. But Colwyn Trevarthen also seems right when he says that 'the eagerness with which a toddler turns to a companion to share creations is surely more than an exploration *away from* a secure base.'[42] We have perhaps been making too much in our account so far of the loved and loving parent as a judge and spectator: securely attached children often explore *with* a loved other. This is not to say that we have been making too much of approval and disapproval: it's rather that a correct theory of those attitudes needs to see them not or not only as spectatorial, but as one side of a state in which parent and child both share, that is, as a specialized version of the phenomenon of *joint attention*.[43]

This truth is I think buried in the remark of Anscombe's with which I opened: 'a child can be encouraged to have certain ends and concerns by the attitudes of its adults, and sometimes *by being associated with the adults in promoting and pursuing them*.'[44] It's also there, more explicitly, in Anscombe's paper on transubstantiation, though the point generalizes way beyond this very special example:

> The thing can be taught, and it is best taught at mass at the consecration, the one part when a small child should be got to fix its attention on what is going on. [...] Such a child can be taught then by whispering to it such things as 'Look! Look what the priest is doing...'[45]

The parent teaches by directing the child's attention not onto itself as authority, but onto *something else*.

Parent and baby are said to move swiftly from being absorbed in one another to being mutually absorbed in the world,[46] and part

---

[42] C. Trevarthen, 'Stepping Away from the Mirror: Pride and Shame in Adventures of Companionship', in C.S. Carter *et al.* (eds.), *Attachment and Bonding: A New Synthesis* (Cambridge: MIT Press, 2005), p. 73.

[43] See for example A. Seemann (ed.), *Joint Attention* (Cambridge: MIT Press, 2011) and N. Eilan, C. Hoerl *et al.* (eds.), *Joint Attention: Communication and Other Minds* (Oxford: Oxford University Press, 2005).

[44] 'Moral Environment', p. 226.

[45] 'On Transubstantiation', in *CPP3*, p. 107.

[46] Indeed, as Suttie says, the earliest shared plaything between mother and baby is the baby's body, *The Origins of Love and Hate*, p. 37; cf. also V. Reddy, *How Infants Know Minds* (Cambridge: Harvard University Press, 2008), pp. 100ff. But this is of course a part of the world. So perhaps it isn't a matter of two developmental phases, but of two different ways mother and baby can

of the pleasure for each of attending to whatever it might be is not just knowing that the other is attending to it, but attending to it *with* the other. This shared pleasure is precisely the role of approval in the 'vase' case: the object of joint attention, the thing they both hold in mind, is the rule 'don't touch the vase', the child's compliance is his demonstrating to the mother that he has in mind what she has in mind, and part of what they both enjoy is the fact that they are holding it in mind together. (The child only beams when he sees his mother smiling at him, not when he removes his hand from the vase, despite knowing she is observing him.) The same joint attending is expressed by the first-person plural in 'we don't play with the toys, do we?' Moreover, if approval of the compliance and pride in the approval is a special case of joint attention, it's clear why love at least *can* come into the story: sharing pleasure in objects of joint attention is not something one does so often with strangers. (It might also explain how it comes in with distant parents: if touching, playing and so on are not part of their repertoire, at least there's compliance.)

Now let us fast forward again to the optimal case of which what we are describing is supposed to be the developmental forerunner. An older child seeks approval for an act that he thinks is good, and—*because* he thinks it's good—seeks it because he thinks the parent thinks it's good too. That is, where it isn't about 'approval-seeking', the seeking and bestowal of approval rest on beliefs about the good that are common to the child and parent, and known by each to be common. Parents and their children form a tiny moral community—a community that may of course over the years lose some members, will certainly gain many more, will change with respect to the content of its common beliefs and so on. I want to suggest that the prototype for this already rather sophisticated moral community is the complex structure of shared pleasures present in the 'vase' case. Of course it's the prototype of many other forms of community too: context, gestures, special words used ('we don't do this', 'this would be naughty', etc., as opposed to, say, 'we like flowers') help promote the speciation of this generic shared experience into something more specific (a moral community as opposed to, say, a community of flower-lovers).

---

relate to one another, within the same phase—e.g. playing a game with the baby's body and looking into one another's eyes.

I want to argue, then, that the joint attention model of approval and disapproval can explain compliance in the best case (the kind of compliance that, in the terminology I used earlier, deserves First Prize) because it has the same structure. I also want to claim one further advantage for the model, which adds to the thought that in secure attachment persons are only rarely self-standing reasons. To see the seeking and bestowal of approval (in the best case) as a specialized version of joint attention is to underscore the fact that the focus of both parent and child is on a *third thing* (as it might be, the house rule). Of course it may be that the parent has got rather more of an idea to begin with about what makes the act elicit pleasure than the child does, just as it may be the parent's choice to get the child to focus, with him or her, on flowers rather than on something else. It may also be that what in part recommends the adult's focus to the child is that he or she is already a trusted source of other things. But still, the parent is saying (as it were) 'this is what we think is good', not 'I command this'. It thus holds out some hope of solving Lodovico Sforza's problem: the foreign emperor doesn't need to be got rid of, because he wasn't invited in in the first place. Though loved parents appear in the joint attention story, they don't appear as objects of attention, even in the early years: on the contrary, they function from the start to direct what will become the child's moral attention onto something other than themselves. It is only because in the best case persons needn't *be* reasons, but rather *point to* reasons, that doing things because we're told can give way, in maturity, to doing things for reasons.

John Finnis

Body, Soul and Information: On Anscombe's 'Royal Road' to True Belief

It is a privilege and joy for me to have this opportunity of giving a lecture[1] that is a memorial of Elizabeth Anscombe, just over 50 years since I first went to a lecture of hers, up and across the road in Somerville — and to be giving it under the auspices of the Anscombe Bioethics Centre, which when she and I for many months sat under its auspices on a working party — on the moral questions one faces at the end of one's life[2] — was called the Linacre Centre for Healthcare Ethics, and has been indeed fittingly renamed. Between the two occasions I have just mentioned were the several remarkable meetings I attended of the Catholic philosophers group that she and Peter Geach organized over a number of years to meet annually for a couple of days in Staffordshire at Spode House, Hawkesyard Priory, in those days an expression of the English Dominican life of learning that has since then retrenched to the Blackfriars in Cambridge and here in Oxford, where it provides a home for the Anscombe Centre and a sponsor for this Lecture.

I have three texts, so to call them, from Anscombe, to preside over what I have to say. I will not be using them precisely as

---

[1] The fifth Anscombe Memorial Lecture given at St John's College, Oxford, 21 October 2014.
[2] See *Euthanasia and Clinical Practice: Report of a Working Party* (London: Linacre Centre for Health Care Ethics, 1982); reprinted and supplemented in Luke Gormally (ed.), *Euthanasia, Clinical Practice and the Law* (London: Linacre Centre, 1993).

premises, nor will I be trying to develop the thoughts they articulate as she might have developed them. There is little exegetical about this lecture. But I think I am walking the same road as she did, and carrying a number of the same implements, and sources of formation, as she did. Anyone can, and might do well to.

The first text is from the long essay on Aristotle that comes first in the book *Three Philosophers* that she and Peter Geach published (with Blackwell and Cornell University Press) in 1961; this essay is by her, the essays on Aquinas and Frege by Peter Geach, though they must have taken joint responsibility for everything and certainly for the notable Analytical Table of Contents.[3] This first essay is in large part about substance and substances, and towards the end reaches Aristotle's thought about imperishable substances and the perpetuity, as he thought, of time, for which his main argument (she says) was that the continuity of change demands that the physical universe be equipped with an imperishable clock whose motions are the universe's fundamental time-keeping process, the clock constituted in fact by the visible heavens and the changeless regularity of their motion. And so Anscombe comes to say:

> What should be said on this topic must now be dictated by the present state of scientific knowledge; it is surely a mistake to think that we have effected a separation between science and philosophy such that questions can be firmly labeled 'scientific' or 'philosophical' and discussed by different parties, each ignorant of the other's discipline.[4]

A first text. One might say: philosophy needs to be informed by what natural sciences discover, and the articulation of those discoveries needs to be — and historically has substantially been, at least indirectly — informed by a sound, philosophically adequate understanding of, for example, all the concepts deployed in this sentence.

The second is from the 1979 lecture which Mary Geach and Luke Gormally rightly placed at the head of the first volume of the

---

[3] Early printings of *Three Philosophers*, such as the one I owned for many years (Oxford: Blackwell, 1961), or the one in the Hesburgh Library at Notre Dame (Ithaca and New York: Cornell University Press, 1961), have a Contents page in which there is no indication of individual authorship, such as appears in later printings.

[4] *Three Philosophers*, p. 61.

three that so far they have put together from her (posthumous and other) papers; that is the volume *Human Life, Action and Ethics: Essays by G.E.M. Anscombe* (2005). The lecture is entitled 'Analytical Philosophy and the Spirituality of Man',[5] and opens with remarks about analytical philosophy, as a method or style of thought which she herself employed while not sharing the position so extremely common among analytical philosophers that they often assume it without argument: that the idea of immaterial substance is to be rejected. This text, then, is from the lecture's final paragraphs, where she is talking, as she often did, about homely or elementary events and actions, here the act of pointing to something to indicate, not its shape, but its colour (or, of course, vice versa). Analysing this out and showing that there is no physical difference (e.g. of direction) involved in pointing to colour rather than shape, she comes to the goal or resting-place of the analysis:

> Now if that is so we can say that man *qua* body can't be described as pointing to the colour rather than the shape. For his act of pointing to the colour certainly is a bodily act; but it is not *qua* bodily act that it is determined as pointing to the colour. This does not mean that we have to postulate a different, *another* act of pointing by a *different sort* of substance, an immaterial one — that path to the concept of 'spirit' which Wittgenstein implicitly criticizes. But we can say that this bodily act is an act of a man *qua* spirit.[6]

So, a second text: 'this bodily act is an act of a man *qua* spirit.'

And my third text is from the Introduction to the second of those volumes, *Faith in a Hard Ground: Essays on Religion, Philosophy and Ethics by G.E.M. Anscombe* (2008). There, in the last page of Mary Geach's spirited and informative Introduction, we read her eyewitness report:

> To begin with the Old [Testament], and to see in it the proof of the New, to begin as a Jew and to see in Christ the promised Messiah: this my mother called 'the royal road' to the Catholic faith.[7]

---

[5] That was the title of the lecture as given in the University of Navarre in 1979; its first publication, in a 1982 American volume of essays on Aristotle's doctrine of physical substance, was entitled 'On the Notion of Immaterial Substance'.
[6] *HLAE*, p. 16.
[7] Mary Geach, 'Introduction', in *FHG*, p. xxv.

'Royal road' is an immemorial figure of speech transmitted to us by, fittingly enough, the commentary on Euclid by Proclus, the 5th-century AD Athenian philosopher, reporting that Euclid told Ptolemy the First that to (or into) geometry there is no short and easy way, no *basilikēn atrapon*, royal road.[8] Proclus never travelled the road that Anscombe was referring to (and herself, I suppose, had travelled), and his sort of neo-Platonist pantheism is one of the two main sorts of perennial philosophical opposition to much of what I have to say this evening, the other being the sort of Spinozist materialism that meets pantheism halfway in their shared denial of divine creation—a recent, local, elegant version of this Spinozism is the posthumous *Religion without God* of my late colleague Ronald Dworkin.[9] In either form it is an evasion of truths—information—attained in the first instance without philosophical discipline and method but now appropriated and critically secured by sound philosophy such as Anscombe and Geach sought to illustrate and promote in *Three Philosophers* and their other, many several works.

1

Anscombe's intense, sinewy discussion of Aristotle's conception of matter, in *Three Philosophers*, is followed by a shorter discussion by Geach in the chapter on Aquinas, which concludes:

> It is a serious question how far Aquinas's conception of matter squares with our modern scientific knowledge. To say there is no room for the conception of *the same matter* or *the same stuff* in

---

[8] Proclus, *Commentary on the First Book of Euclid's Elements* 68 (Princeton: Princeton University Press, 1992), p. 57. Euclid perhaps had in mind Darius the Great's road from Babylon to the Aegean. Certain military roads later constructed by the Roman Emperors might be designated royal and were doubtless as fast and direct as roads could be (and more so than the Persian road). The late 2nd-century AD apocryphal *Acts of Paul and Thecla* has Onesiphorus (see 2 *Timothy* 1:16; 4:19) following the 'royal road' (built by Augustus from Antioch to Lystra) from Iconium to Lystra to intercept St Paul. See Bernard Gineste, '*Genomenos en rhômè* (2 *Tm* 1, 17): Onésiphore a-t-il "été à Rome"?', (*Revue Thomiste* 96, 1996:67–106 at p. 78, n. 49) in the course of his powerful argument for a translation of 2 *Tim.* 1:17 that allows the epistle to be dated to 58 from Caesarea, and thus the more easily and securely be historically judged authentic (and so too the other two Pastoral Epistles and indeed *Ephesians* and *Colossians*).

[9] Ronald Dworkin, *Religion without God* (Cambridge: Harvard University Press, 2013).

modern science would indeed be wrong; a scientist [...] might want to know which parts of a man's body were nourished by a given substance, and perhaps use radioactive 'tracers' to show where the ingested stuff went. But the application of such talk to fundamental physics seems out of the question; the identification of parcels of matter seems here to lose its sense [...][10]

And indeed, looking at the question independently of Geach, Anscombe, Aquinas and Aristotle, it is clear that by a revolution in scientific understanding and information in the early to mid-twentieth century, *inanimate* materials and processes — the non-biological though partly organic realm of chemical elements and compounds composed of molecules, atoms and the subatomic realities describable to some extent as particles or clouds and to some extent as waves — all came to be understood as essentially *activity* according to *pattern* or dynamic structure.[11]

A penetrating and informed philosophical account of this revolution of scientific understanding was given in R.G. Collingwood's Oxford lectures[12] posthumously published in 1945 as *The Idea of Nature*. It is a revolution that has not been taken sufficiently into account by anyone who thinks of the world as constituted by tiny particles of *matter* — or *material* particles — and their movements. The concept of matter cannot be eliminated, but whatever reality the concept elusively picks out seems entirely dominated by the patterns of activity which in many kinds of case remain more or less stable, articulable by the same (or same sequences of) mathematical formulae, while the matter[13] or material within, or at

---

[10] *Three Philosophers*, pp. 71–72.
[11] R.G. Collingwood, *The Idea of Nature* (Oxford: Oxford University Press, 1945), pp. 145–152, etc.
[12] Given in 1934 and 1937; Anscombe arrived at Oxford in the autumn of 1937; Geach was here from 1934 to 1938 but afterwards disclaimed attending philosophy lectures outside Balliol.
[13] Here one speaks the language of common sense and much science, rather than the language of a fully rigorous philosophical theory, which in the last analysis will, I think, adopt something very like the Aristotelian and Thomist concept of prime matter as, as it were, the locus of, and sheer potentiality for, some substantial form to be in act as the (form of) a particular, individual being, in particular a three-dimensional (bodily, 'material') thing, subsisting over a span of time (so: four-dimensional). Within the context of such a theory, the proposition in the text might better be expressed by saying that the *material*, or much of the materials, constitutive of the being is being constantly replaced. See Georges Kalinowski, 'L'Homme: Âme et Matière: À propos du "Problème

the place (but scarcely as the subject) of, those patterned activities or active patterns *comes and goes*. And that coming and going leaves undisturbed the identity (or substance) of the being that exists—say, was under observation (direct or indirect) not long ago (whether as moving or at rest) and is under observation now... and will be for a while yet.

Such *domination* of matter by dynamic pattern is found no less pervasively and even more strikingly when we turn our attention to the fields of biochemistry and biology, revolutionized in the mid- to late-twentieth century by advances in scientific understanding that show no sign of slackening off. I will sketch some aspects of this domination by recalling some well-known facts, before considering the character or significance of the shift—or leap?—into the domain of the living, the *bio*-physical and so forth.[14] Of course, the term *domination* must, throughout, be taken with some specificity or adaptation; it is not at all a question of domination from the outside, as one person or group or nation dominates others, but of something as inward as could possibly be, and entirely free from negativity—it is rather the gift, so to speak, of rendering the barely potential into something actual, with three spatial dimensions and some duration: the gift of bodiliness, of being *as body* by virtue of this dynamic pattern— pattern that, as we shall see, has other appropriate names. Incidentally, this bodiliness of the pattern—i.e. as an intrinsic resultant of the pattern—means that, as Baconian, Galilean, Newtonian and all subsequent science triumphantly confirmed, the way to discover and understand the dynamic patterns is through—by inference or induction from—the quantitative, measurable, sense- or machine-observable.

One set of facts that I want to recall has to do with the language, that is, the concepts, in which this rather new scientific understanding, biophysical, biochemical or biological, is universally articulated. The cells and organisms that make up the realm of life, of living beings, are understood and described—their subsisting and their activities are understood and described—as *directed*, at the micro-level, by a series of intra- and inter-molecular realities, activities, relationships and patterns most adequately

---

de l'âme" de Cl. Tresmontant', *Archives de Philosophie* 37, 1974:411–433 at pp. 422–432.

[14] See further at n. 25 below.

describable in terms of *information*: messages and messengers, programmes, sense and non-sense, expressions, transcription, reading, translation, copying and so forth—as aspects of the working of a code with four or five 'letters', the four nucleotide bases in DNA and the slightly different set of four bases in RNA. Of course, all these terms, 'information', 'code', 'programme', 'messengers' and so forth—terms pervasive in all these life-sciences—are being used *by analogy with* their focal or central-case usage in relation to *our* activities as intelligent beings communicating with other intelligent beings by intentional acts of meaning. So I shall call the information spoken of in these modern natural sciences *analogous* information, as distinct from the *central-case* kind of information conveyed by, for example, what scientists tell themselves and others. The structure of the analogy shifts somewhat, we should notice, as one moves from life sciences to so-called information technology. For in the latter the primary issue is transmission and loss or degradation in transmission; the quality and significance of the input is beside the point. But quality of input matters greatly to the survival and flourishing of biological realities, rather as in the case of central-case information, which we distinguish sharply from disinformation—lies, errors, not to mention muddles and nonsense—even when disinformation is transmitted as readily and accurately as is objective information, information *stricto sensu* (central-case).

Among the empirical realities that persuade scientists of the need to use this analogy, this language, these concepts, is the capacity of organisms to repair themselves when damaged, and to work around, and respond ingeniously (and even pro-actively) to, lesions, insults, diseases and threats to their immunity, in ways impossible to machines (however complex) of the pre-information-technology era (and imitated only partially and still somewhat clumsily by even the impressive IT machines of today). That capacity, along with the organism's capacity we call metabolism or nutrition, to ingest and transform external materials into its own organism, and the capacity to reproduce itself by replication without loss to itself, together mark the great advance that the *living* makes over the non-biological, inanimate. And each of these capacities is a potent aspect of the domination of matter by information—indeed, to use Aristotle's language, by form in the strong, central sense in which the term refers to substantial form as that which is the very act, that is, actuality and process, of a body.[15]

Your body, like mine, comprises some sixty to one hundred million million (that is 100 trillion) cells. Each of the cells in your body includes within it a genome, actually or practically unique to that body, a genome that includes (along with thousands of millions of other components) three thousand million pairs of bases from the four kinds of DNA base. That is to say, these billions of pairs are arranged within each cell in your body and in mine, in a way partly unique to each of us but common to all the other cells in the same body, thus enabling your coherent growth and organic functioning, and mine, as the specifically human but very, very individual person you and I each are. But 'a genome', like 'a molecule' or 'an atom' or 'an electron', is to be thought of as essentially an ongoing activity focused by its pattern or (in a dynamic sense) structure. Each of the billions of weak hydrogen bonds helping constitute the strands in a single large, say, DNA molecule is broken and replaced, perhaps scores of billions of times per second,[16] without there ceasing to be something properly called 'that molecule', and without that molecule losing its reality as a bearer of specific information. Nor is this sufficient stability of patterned process subverted, let alone dominated, by the subjection of each of its parts to 'the molecular storm'—the fact that every millisecond an average molecule undergoes ten thousand million collisions, at jet-plane speed, with water molecules (each comprising three atoms). Thus a cell exists and subsists as a maelstrom of molecular activity in which the component molecules and their components, each set unimaginably numerous, are being amended and replaced in a constant stream while retaining their lasting identity by virtue of the more or less constant pattern or structure, the 'information' which unconsciously the cell 'knows how' to read and apply in its activity. And the same goes at the level of the organism. It is an essential if not defining characteristic of the living being that by virtue of its subsisting dynamic pattern or form or structuring information, it subsists even while all its material elements are replaced. So every

---

[15] 'Forma, inquantum forma, est actus': Thomas Aquinas, *Summa theologiae* [*ST*] I, q. 75, a. 2c.
[16] Peter M. Hoffmann, *Life's Ratchet: How Molecular Machines Extract Order from Chaos* (New York: Basic Books, 2012), p. 116.

day of one's life about 500,000 million cells in the make-up of each of us are destroyed and replaced by others functioning to substantially the same pattern. Not one of these cells can any laboratory or network of laboratories engineer; yet one's make-up, dominated as it is by its information both species-specifically human and peculiarly individual, 'knows how to do it'. The analogous 'knowledge' in play here is *that without which* the (analogous) information would not be information.[17]

These and many other facts—remarkable facts it seems to me— I take from their exposition in the books of those scientists who have got to know about, track, report, and partially account for, this analogous information. For them when they discover it, and for us when they report it, it has become or is taken to be central-case information. One such report, out of hundreds and thousands, is the well praised, mainstream 2012 book *Life's Ratchet* by Professor Peter M. Hoffmann. He is a biophysicist, focused therefore on exploring 'the physical underpinnings of living systems and the use of physical methods to explore life',[18] who after his schooling in Germany and university studies in the United States did his post-doctoral work in nano-physics here in Oxford around 2000. Like so many people, I'm afraid, he believes (the book reveals) all sorts of old fables such as that the Gospel of John is 'steeped in Platonic philosophy' and that Christianity 'relegated [the material world] to a corrupted reflection of the spiritual world'. And explicitly following the lead of the old atheist atomists like Democritus he tries, from time to time, to assign everything recounted in his book to either chance or necessity (and sometimes even to chance and necessity at once)—

---

[17] 'Beneath' or 'within' these complexes of intelligibly related molecular realities (things and processes) there is, as we all know, the underlying complex of atoms constitutive of the molecular, these atoms being of exactly 84 naturally occurring stable types defined by the number of protons (1, 2, 3... 84) in the atom's nucleus, and these 84 types, that is, the 84 naturally occurring chemical elements, belonging to one of the eighteen naturally occurring groups, that is, subsets with significantly shared or recurrent features—as is schematically displayed in the periodic table of elements. The scarcely imaginable but thoroughly intelligible complexity of living, organic beings is again, at the molecular level too, a function or resultant of, predominantly, a quite small number of reiterated letters, as it were—analogous to the unimaginable abundance of meaning and information producible with letters, two dozen or so, of our alphabet.

[18] See *Life's Ratchet*, p. 90.

in either case, without remainder.[19] But against that attempted top-down summary of what the science he expounds discloses about the world, there stands the title of his book, *Life's Ratchet*, and its subtitle *How Molecular Machines Extract Order from Chaos*, and equally there stands almost everything in the book's scientific substance — you can open it at random and find statements such as these:

> stability in DNA is also actively achieved by repair enzymes. If for some reason a part of the DNA molecule becomes corrupted, the repair enzymes will fix the mistake, using an adjacent section of the molecule that is undamaged as a chemical template to repair the corrupted part.[20]

So, we should say: besides chance or randomness (which is pervasive but massively dominated by order), there is, not so much necessity, but rather what I have been pointing to, which Hoffmann articulates in his own summary of the subject of his science: 'Life is matter *and program*.'[21] And if we are looking, as we reasonably can, for a better top-down summary of what the science he expounds discloses about the world — for a reflective and explanatory summary, not a research methodology — we can find it, wrapped up in his talk of ratchets and other biophysical machines, and of repairs purposefully achieved by enzymes, and so forth: the special intelligibility of *design*.

This reality pervading and intrinsic to natural reality — this fact of pervasive though far from randomness-free *design* — Hoffmann takes for granted when he is doing and expounding his science, but dismisses when he is doing reflective top-down, philosophically explanatory (or would-be explanatory) summarizing. He dismisses design for two interrelated reasons, it seems. He assimilates design to the idea of 'vital forces', a 17th–18th-century scientific quasi-animism intended as a research programme or

---

[19] Chapter 2, 'Chance and Necessity' has as motto two quotations: Democritus: 'Everything existing in the universe is the fruit of chance and necessity'; *Catechism of the Catholic Church* art. 295: '[...] God created the world according to his wisdom. It is not the product of any necessity whatever, nor of blind fate or chance [...] it proceeds from God's free will.' Hoffmann certainly favours the former, even if he is not unconscious of some strains in the position.
[20] *Life's Ratchet*, p. 117.
[21] *Life's Ratchet*, p. 242 (emphasis added).

hypothesis for investigation by a search for the force within the order of nature, natural causalities and natural events—an inappropriate research hypothesis even in the realm of living (not-inanimate) beings. And he falls the more easily into this confusion because his book knows nothing of the fundamental difference between, on the one hand, causalities *within* Nature (the entire natural universe)—what theologians and philosophers have often called secondary causes—and on the other hand transcendent creative and/or providential causality.

That is a distinction about which (as I shall elaborate further on) Hebrew prophetic and wisdom teaching and then Christian philosophy and doctrine got far clearer than Plato or even Aristotle ever did, for whom the divinities were in the last analysis within Nature. Perhaps the quickest way towards grasping the distinction, or at least its significance, is to recall Thomas Aquinas's critique of a certain scholarly Muslim idea of creation and providence, the doctrine of the *Mutakallimun* who held that the divine designer's transcendent power works its effects by divine decision, moment by moment and independently of natural causalities (which are thus more apparent than real or worthy of investigation). St Thomas's response to this is a reply also to those who imagine that the designer rationally envisaged by Jews and Christians (and by Charles Darwin, in a notable page of his *Autobiography*)[22] initiated everything merely by one tremendous initial creation of natural potentialities which since then have been merely left to their own operations and the independent working out of their initial potentialities. No, says Aquinas to both sides: what we think of as effects of natural causes are indeed precisely that—effects of natural causes, in chains or sequences of causation which can fruitfully be investigated by *natural sciences*. And at the same time all these natural effects and causes are being caused, here and now as much as at the beginning of time, by the power of the intelligent designer. They are, Aquinas goes on, effects *wholly* of their natural causes *and wholly* of the transcendent (beyond-Nature) cause that explains both the creation of Nature from nothing and all the workings of Nature ever since. By reflecting on this 'wholly…wholly'—on the thing or event in question being not

---

[22] See Finnis, 'Darwin, Dewey, Religion, and the Public Domain' in John Finnis, *Collected Essays, Volume V: Religion and Public Reasons* (Oxford: Oxford University Press, 2011) essay 1 at pp. 21–25.

partly attributable to Nature and *partly* to divine power, but rather *in whole* to natural causes and *in whole* to God[23] — we can get some grip on the true meaningfulness of the word 'transcendent'.

That thesis secured and secures the place and integrity of the natural sciences, as they are practised today.[24] And within those natural sciences, there are wide differences of subject matter, as a working *physicist* like Hoffmann emphasizes: the difference between the living and the non-living is vast, so great, he says, more than once, that there is 'no conceptual connection' between them.[25] What is driving Hoffmann's exaggeration (as I take it to be) is that *life* not only, as he says, 'is matter and program',[26] but involves *program* that programs (dynamically patterns) the resilience, homeostatic self-stabilization and self-reparativeness of living beings; and that programs also their responsiveness to stimuli, their self-assembling growth and metabolic capacities, and their reproductivity and signalling capacities. Now it is scarcely possible to refrain from remarking that such reflexively functioning program, brought to light in biophysics, biochemistry and biology, just is what Aristotle called soul, *psychē, anima*: the animation in an animated (not-inanimate) reality (being). To call programs of this kind *soul* (insofar as they are actually in place in or as informing and constituting individual beings) is not to appeal

---

[23] '[...] non sic idem effectus causae naturali et divinae virtuti attribuitur quasi *partim* a Deo, et *partim* a naturali agente fiat, sed totus ab utroque secundum alium modum: sicut idem effectus *totus* attribuitur instrumento, et principali agenti etiam *totus*': *Summa contra Gentiles* [*ScG*] III c. 70 [8] (emphasis added). Thus the Creator, though transcendent, is also present in everything as cause of all existing and operating, and as disposer and ordainer is present to what is disposed and set in order: *Compendium Theologiae* I, c. 135. On the opinion(s) of the Mutakallimun, see *ScG* III, c. 69.

[24] And helping explain the massive superiority of the natural scientific works and discoveries in second-millennium Christendom as compared with the Islamic *ummah*. (Hoffmann, *Life's Ratchet*, p. 15, shows favour for the myth that Islam or Muslims preserved Aristotelian science when Christians had lost it.)

[25] *Life's Ratchet*, p. 240: '[...] there really is no meaningful conceptual connection between a highly complex entity and the most fundamental levels of matter and energy.' (Repeated at p. 241.) Likewise p. 238: 'Complex interactions between parts create new processes, structures and principles that, while based materially on the underlying parts, are conceptually independent of them. This insight is what we call holism [...] Reductionism and holism are two sides of the same coin — they are both parts of what good science ought to be.'

[26] *Life's Ratchet*, p. 242.

to vital forces as an explanatory principle; nor is it to propose either a new research methodology or, for that matter, an old one. It is, rather, to *sum up* the inherent efficacy, substantial effect and mode of reality of molecular and cellular and organic processes — of molecules, cells and organisms — just as they are disclosed to be both in these sciences and in the experience or observation of bodily *life*.[27]

---

[27] *Life's Ratchet*, p. 16, unsurprisingly rejects this move, but in a way both confused and unsatisfying:

'Modern physics, chemistry, and evolution can explain what makes a cell or an organism alive and what gives it "form". Bodies are complex assemblies of interacting cells, operating according to an evolved program written in the cell's DNA. A soul is not needed as the source of form, locomotion, nutrition, or reproduction (in contrast to what Aristotle thought).'

But this is confused because soul in the Aristotelean understanding is not the source of form and activity, but rather it is the form and act of the body as living and acting body. And in other places Hoffmann accepts that the explanations offered by physics, chemistry, natural selection and so forth still leave *mysterious* the realities that the term 'soul' picks out one aspect of, namely the very aspect that Hoffmann accepts is mysterious, e.g.

'The biomolecular world is filled with exquisite structure and a mysterious drive for change and motion.' (p. 90)

His own official final replacement for Aristotelean soul seems to be a regression in clarity and straightforwardness and a move towards the anthropomorphically metaphorical and simply evasive:

'If we were seeking the "life force", the force that animates life, our search has been successful. This animating force is the random force of atoms, the jittering afterglow of the creation of the universe. The molecular *machines*, which *take* this undirected force and *give it direction*, embody the tight *embrace* of chance and necessity and are themselves the product of this embrace. *Sculpted* by evolution, the molecular machines of our bodies tame the molecular storm and *turn it into* the *dance* of life.' (p. 243, emphases added)

Later on the same page we read:

'Life happens on many levels, from colliding atoms to the mind of a genius. The molecular machines are part of who we are, but they do not determine who we are. We are intelligent, creative beings, a natural extension of the creativity of the universe, but we are not determined by nature. While based on machines, we are not machines ourselves.'

Left quite unclear is whether Hoffmann thinks that cows (discussed on pp. 241–242) or mice *are* machines. Aristotle made a more resolute effort to produce an account that describes the facts with categories that properly accommodate them even while leaving much room for further explanations in terms of material and efficient causality.

2

Speaking of soul in this science-led (and not science-leading) way enables us to say a few things about 'body and soul' in animals, leaving aside, just for the moment, the human animal (or treating the human animal in abstraction, for the moment, from any factor that could differentiate it from other kinds of animal). One thing to say is that the animal lives not as a body with a soul, nor as a soul in or with a body, but as body and equally as soul, since the animal's bodily life, its bodiliness, is its ensouledness (as Aquinas says).[28] Or to put it another way, the animal's soul is that in virtue of which the animal has its bodiliness, its corporality. As program dominating (by directing) matter, and as the very act, activity and actuality of the body so actualized, soul dominates (but is thoroughly in service of) body in the life of the unitary being, the organism, the animal.

And much of this domination consists in the animal's responsiveness to what it perceives, via any one or more of its sensory organs. As Anscombe says in the illuminating undated and untitled paper published in the third Geach-Gormally volume, *From Plato to Wittgenstein*, under the title 'Plato, Souls, and the Unity of Apperception': an animal's perceiving a flash and a bang as simultaneous is not a perception of its eye(s) or of its organ of hearing but of sensitive soul. And if the animal is you or me, we can, she goes on to say, consider those perceptions under the aspect of simultaneity, a concept. One's being alive to those perceptions and able to make a judgment about their objects, and to discuss the concept with which one makes that judgment, is what it is to have a soul that is not only vegetative but also animal *and* rational and spiritual.[29]

And to speak more generally, I think Anscombe's many engagements with these issues over the years exemplify a central position some main elements of which are articulated in the Aquinas chapter of *Three Philosophers*, towards the end of a notable

---

[28] As Aquinas puts it: 'Bodiliness (*corporeitas*), since it is the substantial form in a [animal] being, cannot be other than the [...] soul, which—since it is the act of a body—requires that its own matter have three dimensions', *ScG* IV c. 81 n. 7; see John Finnis, *Aquinas: Moral, Political, and Legal Theory* (Oxford: Oxford University Press, 1998) [hereinafter *Aquinas*], p. 178, n. 213.

[29] See the rich and subtle argument in 'Plato, Soul and "the Unity of Apperception"' [undated and untitled ms], in *PtW*, pp. 25–33 at pp. 32–33.

discussion of what it is to perceive and what it is to think about something:

> Here a number of difficulties arise. First, I think we must allow that the traditional way of speaking, in which a man is said to consist of soul *and* body, does not fit in well with Aquinas's thought, and that he creates obscurity by continuing to talk in this way. A man is an animal, and an animal is a body; so a man *is* a body, not a body *plus* something else. Again, for Aquinas, Socrates is a man, and is an animal, and is a body (sc. a *single* body), by virtue of one and the same individualized form, Socrates' soul or individual life; so "Socrates' body" already involves the individualized form that makes it a (single) body, Socrates' soul; so we cannot reckon Socrates' body and soul together as parts of Socrates, in any acceptable sense of 'part'. Again, the body and soul are not parts into which a man can be dissolved: even if the soul can exist disembodied, a dead man not only is not a man, but is not even *a* body (rather, it is now a loose congeries of bodies). What remains after death is not the same *body* but the same *stuff* or *matter*; similarly, we must say that at any given time a man consists of an individual life (the soul) in a certain portion of *materia prima* — not: in a body.
>
> It is easy, however, to rephrase Aquinas's account of what it is that thinks. A man thinks in virtue of his soul — in virtue of having that specific sort of life.[30]

And so on: it is tempting to let Peter Geach carry on to the end of this lecture, but suffice it to say that with this 'in virtue of his soul — in virtue of having that specific sort of life' we reach the point that completed my second text from Anscombe, when she said, about a humble physical act of pointing to something's shape rather than its colour: 'this bodily act is an act of a man *qua* spirit.'

Peter Hoffmann's willingness to affirm that there is *no conceptual connection* between the most fundamental levels of matter and energy and entities so highly complex and mysteriously self-moving as a living cell or organism — no easy matter for a nanophysicist (or any other kind of physicist) to affirm — is significant in various ways. It provides reason, for example, to be open to finding that *within* the general field of 'highly complex' and self-moving, living beings, there is a further discontinuity of type, involving immeasurably more discontinuity than that between the inanimate and the living. For, among animals there are all the

---

[30] *Three Philosophers*, pp. 97–98.

countless kinds each member of which can *deploy* information, dynamic pattern and animal soul, but *only* in dealing with the *here and now* of its own material make-up and the make-up or sensed movement of other bodily realities that impinge upon it, whether directly or by the less direct but still material causalities that we call the senses and animal responsiveness to such stimuli (responsiveness which, as in say sheepdogs, may be wonderfully subtle and supple). And there is one kind of animal that can do *all that* (in some measure) *and also* can consider information as such, search it out, consider it for its accuracy, doubt the truth of claims or other intimations that it exists, subject it to tests of verification and falsification on the conscious hypothesis that if it is confirmed here and now it will hold true at least in all *like* circumstances wherever and whenever, and choose to point out to someone else the colour of a shape on a heat-chart as support for one's opinion that a contrary hypothesis is thereby falsified or at least so far forth disconfirmed or less probable.

3.1

And now we can glimpse Anscombe's royal highway, and at least one lane on it—I will eventually mention four. The world history that natural sciences (in one of their modes) disclose to us is a history dominated by information dominating activity. At this end of a process of increasingly information-rich activity—and correspondingly increasingly complex and self-directing beings (and kinds of beings) over a span of now some 14 billion years since the evidentially-established big-bang empirical beginning—there emerges the kind of being capable of receiving *and assessing and affirming* information. Information thus intelligently received informs no longer exclusively by shaping the being's substance and activity but now, additionally, as a topic of and guidance for the awareness and understanding, the thinking and thoughts, including the deliberations, decisions and choices, of individual beings of this kind. That is to say: with the emergence of this kind of being, there emerges also the logical and it seems empirical possibility of the intentional communication—and, in *that* strong, central sense, the *revealing*—of information, *by* the transcendent source of *all* constitutive information, *to* at least some human persons and, if so, the possibility of those persons transmitting that revelation to others if they so choose.

When we examine this possibility, some notable facts come into view. The Jewish library *we* call the Old Testament displays with impressive consistency a set of claims made over many hundreds of years by self-proclaimed recipients of divine revelation, call them the prophets, and maintained by them against very strenuous opposition and resistance both passive and very active. And when we examine this set of claims, we find that they convey a number of propositions far nearer the truth, as best we can now judge it, than the comparable theses of even the best Greek philosophers.

The thesis which Charles Darwin, even after his famous publication, found so compelling — that reason warrants the judgment that everything in the immense and wonderful universe has a First Cause that is no part of but entirely transcends the universe, of which it is the First Cause by design, decision and activity of its intelligent mind — this is a thesis that surpasses the best in Plato's or Aristotle's philosophizing about the divine causality at work in the world.[31] When articulated more explicitly, the thesis clearly involves the denial that there is or are any divine *being* or beings within the universe. It involves the radical distinguishing of the entirety of Nature from the divine nature, the de-divinizing of Nature and at the same time its de-absolutizing, revealing Nature's (the universe's) thoroughgoing contingency, and its utter lack of any elements which might explain, account for, its existence *as a totality* of intelligible beings and causal interactions. This is the metaphysical reasoning and judgment articulated as a matter of common sense (*our* common sense) handed down — eventually to us (as to Darwin) — from *Genesis* chapter 1, from *Psalm* 19 ('The heavens declare the glory of God'), and from the precision attributed to the mother of the martyred seven brothers in 2 *Maccabee*s 7:28 ('when you see the heavens, the earth, and all

---

[31] See Collingwood, *The Idea of Nature*, pp. 88, etc.; Charles Darwin, *The Autobiography of Charles Darwin, 1809-1882 with original omissions restored*, edited by Nora Barlow (London: Collins, [1882] 1982), p. 92; John Finnis, *Collected Essays, Volume V: Religion and Public Reasons*, pp. 21-26. We can be sure that Darwin had in mind an *efficient*, not (or not merely) a final cause such as Aristotle argued to and Bacon's *Novum Organum Scientiarum* (1620) efficaciously urged must be expelled from natural sciences (an expulsion which, as the present lecture shows, cannot reasonably be anything like complete). On predicating mind (or anything else) of God, see n. 37 below.

that is in it, you know that God made all this *from nothing* [...]),[32] and again from the masterly summation of the Hebrew creation tradition in Rabbi Saul's letter, as Paul, to the Romans: 'God's invisible attributes, his everlasting power and divinity, are made visible to reason by means of his works since the creation of the world' (*Rom.* 1:20).

Applied to the scientific data and inference that I have been recalling, this judgment acknowledges that the transcendent intelligence, will and power has been causing, progressively as well as initially, the existence and content of that vast and expanding, evolving accumulation and transmission of *analogous* information which we call Nature. With the emergence of human beings, and of human intelligence, will and free action, the universe is at last in a position such that it is possible for the transcendent Creator to choose to initiate also a transmission of *central-case* information to members of this newly emerged species of being, humankind.[33] Mind[34] can speak to mind, spirit commune with spirit.

And beyond bare possibilities there are historical facts. The Jewish people and their true prophets *in fact* reached a settled and superior understanding of the universe's origins, and of its natural intelligibility, centuries earlier than Greeks and their philosophers reached their own standard and in substance (result, not method) inferior understanding.[35] This accomplishment of the Jewish

---

[32] *ex ouk ontōn* or *ouk ex ontōn*; the Revised Standard English translation, like some others, adopts the latter reading, as 'did not make them out of things that existed', and scholars who deny that the Old Testament has the concept of creation *ex nihilo* read the passage likewise: Jacques Fantino, 'L'origine de la doctrine de la creation ex nihilo', *Revue des Sciences philosophiques et théologiques* 80, 1996:589–602 at p. 590, n. 9.

[33] The *lex aeterna* is analogously law, in as much as law in its central cases (natural and positive law) is a matter of mind directing mind: ScG III c. 54; Finnis, *Aquinas*, p. 307.

[34] See n. 37 below.

[35] This was explored and expounded in many works by Claude Tresmontant, in at least some respects the most significant French Catholic philosopher contemporary with Anscombe. See perhaps above all his *Le problème de la Révélation* (Paris: Editions du Seuil, 1969), esp. pp. 99–114 against the Spinozist conception of the prophecies of Israel as works of imagination rather than intelligence and knowledge; earlier, Tresmontant, *La doctrine morale des prophètes d'Israel* (Paris: Editions du Seuil, 1958); later, Tresmontant, *Le prophétisme hébreu* (Paris: Gabalda, 1982). With some colouring, Tresmontant,

people seems to have been, *in fact*, an accomplishment both of natural reason (intelligence) reflecting on experienced realities, *and* of the receptivity of that people's prophets and priests to divine communication (in any of the modes they came to call revelation *stricto sensu*). It was reflected and articulated with remarkable consistency and coherence throughout the body of developing and temporally stratified traditions and writings we call the Old Testament.

3.2

The Old Testament conveys a second fundamental truth that was grasped more vividly and fully by the Hebrew people than by the Greek: that we really can, and from time to time do, make free choices—we have 'free will'. Here again it is not a matter simply of proof texts in which the Old Testament articulates this freedom —though such texts can easily be found—but also a matter of the whole narrative of personal and communal responsibility for choices made, of covenants freely entered into and broken and restored by renewed undertaking. *Deuteronomy* encapsulates its presentation/redaction of the Covenant between God and his people in the choice: 'See, I set before you on this day life and good, evil and death [...] Therefore, choose life [...]'(*Deut.* 30:15, 19). Against Hellenistic doctrines of fate, Ben Sirach, writing about 200 BC in the book we call *Ecclesiasticus* or *Sirach* sums up the whole teaching of the Old Testament on human freedom:

The Origins of Christian Philosophy, trans. Mark Pontifex, OSB (New York: Hawthorn, 1963), pp. 17–18 says:

'Here we have an intellectual revolution, a liberation, an act of free thought, a rejection of myth, an effort to use reason, undoubtedly the most important that the human race has known in all its history. On the day when Abram left Ur of the Chaldees, when he ceased to worship the moon and stars, to sacrifice to the idols of his fathers, and when he started for a country which he knew not, called by a God who is not identified with any visible thing, he brought about the greatest, and at the same time the most hidden, of revolutions [...], the most decisive for the human race.

When the prophets of Israel bitterly rebuke pagan idolatry, they are doing something strictly *rational*. When they refuse to sacrifice human children to idols or to myths, they carry their work of the use of reason into practical human conduct.'

Likewise his *Etudes de métaphysique biblique* (Paris: Gabalda, 1953); *A Study of Hebrew Thought*, trans. Michael F. Gibson (New York: Desclee, [1953] 1960).

> When [God] created man in the beginning, he left him free to make his own decisions [or: in the hands of his own counsel/deliberation]. If you wish you can keep the commandments, and it is in your power to remain faithful. He has set fire and water before you; you stretch out your hand to whichever you prefer. Life and death are set before man; whichever a man prefers will be given him. (*Ecclesiasticus/Sirach* 15:11, 14–17)

Like the Church fathers from Justin (the philosopher from Nablus in Samaria, martyred in Rome a century after Peter and Paul) and Irenaeus (from Smyrna, martyred in Lyons forty years later) down to John Damascene (a monk of Jerusalem in the eighth century),[36] Aquinas teaches the radical freedom of the will, one's spiritual capacity to choose and carry out one option in preference to any alternative, such that nothing either outside or inside one's make-up determines one's preference save that act itself of choosing (preferring).

About this I will make just two observations. *Just as* God's causality, though absolutely necessary to explain the existence and the astounding intelligibility and dominant non-randomness and non-necessity of Nature, is so transcendent that (as we saw) it can and should be said to be wholly the cause of natural events which are wholly the effects of natural causes, *so too* God's causality must be the cause of acts of human free choice, acts that truly have no cause other than their making by the human person who makes them, and are wholly the responsibility of that person and not of Nature or of God.[37]

Correspondingly, divine providence, as understood in the Old Testament, is emphatically not the fate, or destiny, in which Greek thought, like that of other civilizations, still encloses and more or

---

[36] See Germain Grisez, *The Way of the Lord Jesus*, Vol. I: *Christian Moral Principles* (Chicago: Franciscan Herald Press, 1983), pp. 61–62 (ch. 2, Appendix 1) (http://twotlj.org/G-1-2-1.html).

[37] As Aquinas explains in his general philosophical teaching about God's existence, nature and action, one cannot predicate anything of God—existence, nature, action, causality, gender or anything else—without a shift in meaning so drastic that it amounts to denying of God any of the usual and humanly central meanings of these terms and predicating them of him only to the extent and in the sense that is necessitated by the need to account for the existence, characteristics and operations of Nature (including human willing and action). See Finnis, *Aquinas*, p. 305 (citing mainly *ScG* I, c. 30, and *ST* I, q. 13); see also Grisez, *Christian Moral Principles*, pp. 43–44, 63–67 esp. 65–66 (ch. 2, Q. B.3 and Appendix 3) (http://twotlj.org/G-1-2-3.html).

less smothers its intimations of human freedom. Providence is emphatically distinct from, and far more true to reality than, the cosmic determinism to which Ronald Dworkin recently gave voice. According to the second of his Einstein lectures in December 2011, there is such an uncountable multiplicity of entire universes (multiverses) — he postulates them 'bubbling out of the landscape' — that the beauty and 'magic' of 'the universe' (including this set [imagined by him] of multiverses) *consist* above all in its *inevitability*. And so, at the climax of the argument, he declared 'It's *inevitable* that I exist!'[38] Such a denial of his own parents' freedom of choice, and equally of his own and yours and mine, is a profound and, I think, inexorable implication of atheistic or pantheistic denials of Creation, when they are clung to against the evidence of the Creator's existence, causality, mind and selection (in Creation) between possibilities. Anscombe chose to make vindicating our freedom the topic of her Inaugural Lecture in the Chair of Philosophy in Cambridge in 1971.[39]

---

[38] Ronald Dworkin, 'Faith and Physics' (the second of his Einstein Lectures given 12–14 December 2011 at the University of Bern, Switzerland), c. minute 22 (http://habermas-rawls.blogspot.co.uk/2011/12/religion-without-god-dworkins-einstein.html) (accessed 14 November 2014). The substance of the first lecture is in 'Religion without God', *New York Review of Books*, 4 April 2013 (http://www.nybooks.com/articles/archives/2013/apr/04/religion-without-god/?pagination=false) (accessed 14 November 2014). While the passage does not appear in the posthumous book *Religion without God* — see the discussion of inevitability in *Religion without God* at pp. 82–104 — the determinism that it celebrated is articulated on those pages. The postulation of multiverses (pp. 94–97) is compelled by resolve to deny any Creative mind (see p. 96), and proceeds more by mathematical assumptions and poetic imagination than in line with evidence.

[39] Anscombe, 'Causality and Determination', in *CPP2*, pp. 134–147; the points made against the 'gobbledygook' or 'unreal[ity]' of soft determinist (compatibilist) freedom are amplified in her 1977 article 'Soft Determinism' in *CPP2*, pp. 163–172, especially the last paragraph and above all its final, clinching sentence. In Finnis, 'Reflections and Responses', in John Keown and Robert George (eds.) *Reason, Morality and Law: The Philosophy of John Finnis* (Oxford: Oxford University Press, 2013), pp. 464–465, I quote that clinching sentence (with its immediate context) at n. 18 but mistakenly say that it concludes the 1971 Inaugural Lecture. Here it is, as I quote it (with its context): '[…] the soft determinist […] does think freedom compatible with physical impossibility […] since, being a determinist, he thinks that everything except what actually happened was always impossible […] I am at liberty to say that a "can of freedom" which holds in face of physical impossibility is pure nonsense.'

3.3

Moreover—second observation—to speak of human free choices is also to speak of deliberations about the merits and demerits of the alternative options between which one must choose. Thus it is also to speak of conscience as one's intelligent reflecting on those merits, whether reflecting in advance and generally (in abstraction from particular circumstances) or concretely in particular circumstances, or reflecting retrospectively on what one could and should (or should not) have chosen. That one has a personal responsibility for one's own character, and that one can and should make the prospective and retrospective judgments about right action (the judgments we call conscience), are truths known more clearly in the prophets of Israel and thus in the Jerusalem of the Old Testament (brought to its full development in the New) than in the Athens of the philosophers. This clarity about freedom and responsibility is new in human history and a third lane on the royal road.

3.4

And the fourth opened up because the Jewish people attained a far-reaching understanding of the requirements of justice centuries earlier than Greece and its great philosophers. Read *Exodus* 21–23, *Leviticus* 19 and 25, and *Amos* and other prophets on the duties owed by all to the poor, widows, new-born children, orphans, strangers, servants, and read—among much else—*Deuteronomy* 4's reflection that the precepts of the Law are themselves *just*, a matter of practical intelligence and wisdom. The far-reaching prophetic insistence on the duties of justice as implications of the rejection of idolatry—that is, as implications of recognizing the transcendence of the one Creator and provident sustainer—is an insistence developed somewhat further by the convert Rabbi Saul in his letter to the Romans, as an implication of that same recognition of the divine nature from God's works 'from the creation of the world'. To shut one's eyes to these works, to refuse to acknowledge, glorify and thank the Creator, is such a failure of reason that passions take its directive place, resulting not only in orientation to and practice of perversions but also in injustices of the many personal kinds that St Paul there lists (*Romans* 1:29–31). For the injustices identified and excluded from conscientious deliberation by the Ten Commandments not only are identified in the revelation of God's will to Israel but equally are in principle identifiable by—accessible to—the natural reason and conscience of anyone anywhere who is open to serving truth and justice: *Romans* 2:8-15. For what could be more clarifying to conscience than an awareness that all that one is and has one owes to the free creative generosity of a transcendent maker and sustainer of everyone like oneself?[40]

The humanism of the prophets who preceded Paul was, at least in its emphasis, more political than his, more centred than his on the misdeeds, the chastisement and the redemption of a whole people led astray in the first instance, though not only, by the misdeeds of their political leaders. It focused, as I said, on the

---

[40] Divine sustaining and providential government involves many acts of creation subsequent to the first; at the very least, these include the creation of each rational human soul (Tresmontant holds there are many other creative acts—that the history of the universe is of increasing information, by ongoing divine creative informing). For: leaving aside the occasional instances of monstrous growths incapable of developing towards human activities (hydatidiform moles and teratomas), and prescinding here from the question explored by Anscombe (and differently by me) of whether ensoulment is or is not contemporaneous with conception, we should conclude that the product of the union of male and female gametes, the conceptus, has the distinctively human form that it has—the information, program, system, dynamic pattern, *soul* and activity it has—by virtue of an initiating act of divine, creative power such that it is a new thing; for this new being's soul, as capacitating it radically for rational, spiritual, personal and freely choosing acts, is not the product or resultant of the biological make-up of either gamete or in any other way of either parent, any more than those spiritual acts, when he or she engages in them, will be products or resultants of his or her biology or brain-states, or parents. Rather, this new person's soul, which from the start will also be the form of his or her body—the source of its being his or her body—is *de novo* something new, and as Aquinas starkly says, *ex nihilo* (*ScG* II, c. 87: the thesis is: 'solus Deus animam humanam producit in esse', and the conclusion of the arguments is: 'relinquitur ergo quod *ex nihilo fiat*. Et sic, *creatur*. Cum igitur creatio sit opus proprium Dei [...] sequitur quod a solo Deo immediate creatur'). An elegant theological formulation of this position we find in the *Catechism of the Catholic Church*:

> 365. The unity of soul and body is so profound that one has to consider the soul to be the 'form' of the body: i.e., it is because of its spiritual soul that the body made of matter becomes a living, human body; spirit and matter, in man, are not two natures united, but rather their union forms a single nature. 366. The Church teaches that every spiritual soul is created immediately by God—it is not 'produced' by the parents [...]

> In brief [...] 382. 'Man [is *corpore et anima unus*, body and soul but truly one]' (*GS* 14 §1). The doctrine of the faith affirms that the spiritual and immortal soul is created immediately by God.

humanity of the exploited, vulnerable, despised and summoned to justice in one's conduct and attitudes towards each and all. It proposes even that all are lovable and, at least as neighbours or companions, to be loved as much as oneself: *Leviticus* 19:18. But in many of those we call the prophets, such as Amos, Hosea, Isaiah himself, and Micah, there is a further humanism and universality —the expectation or prophecy that eventually all nations will go up to Jerusalem to be taught by God his ways and walk in his justice, their disputes settled by him, so that the nations will live in peace with each other, each retaining its identity (even its own religion perhaps distinct from Israel's), while God restores to dignity and a proper place all lame and banished individuals: *Micah* 4:1–6, expanding on *Isaiah* 2:2–4. And with that expectation goes the expectation that the source of this new peace and brotherhood will be a 'ruler in Israel whose coming forth is from old' —a judge of Israel who will be born in Bethlehem Ephrathah, a place too little to be counted among the clans of Judah (*Micah* 5:1–5; *Matt.* 2:6).

Elizabeth and Zechariah's son John, who had ritually dipped Jesus of Bethlehem and Nazareth at Bethany on or near the Jordan's east bank, and had pointed him out to the crowds as messiah, was later locked up—as Josephus records,[41] in Herod Antipas's high palace-prison-fortress of Machaerus five miles east of the Dead Sea. There John heard of Jesus's teaching and wondrous healings in Galilee, and sent two of his followers to ask Jesus 'Are you really the one who is to come? Or will there be another?' Jesus understood that John had conceived a doubt about the form that Jesus's activities had taken—about the difference between those healings and the stern and forceful cleansing of Israel that John had foretold.[42] In words recalling four passages of the prophetic book called Isaiah, Jesus responded: 'Go and tell John what you have seen and heard: the blind receive their sight,

---

[41] Flavius Josephus, *Antiquities* 18.5.2. See M.-J Lagrange, *Évangile selon Saint Matthieu* (Paris: Gabalda, [1922] 4th ed. 1948), pp. 286–289; Christiane Saulnier, 'Herode Antipas et Jean le Baptiste: Quelques remarqes sur les confusions chronologiques de Flavius Josephus', *Revue Biblique* 91, 1984:362–376; Etienne Nodet, 'Machéronte et Jean-Baptiste', *Revue Biblique* 121, 2014:267–282 (discount the lurch in Nodet's final sentences and footnote into the historical rabbit-hole of hypertextual Gospel origins and genre).

[42] See M.-J. Lagrange, *Évangile selon Saint Luc* (Paris: Gabalda, [1919] 4th ed. 1927), pp. 212–214.

the lame walk, lepers are cleansed and the deaf hear, the dead are raised up, and the poor are told good news [...]' (*Matt.* 11:5; *Lk.* 7:22). What was this good news? As everyone knows, especially those in healthcare professions or service, all of us are poor in our illness and disability and the approach of our death. What are these good tidings?

When the diaspora but Jerusalem-educated Jew and rabbi Saul called Paul stood in front of the Athenian elite in 51 AD he spoke to them first about the transcendent creator God, who is maker of the universe in whole and every part, and maker also of all humankind from one stock (though for distinct homelands); and who is author of a universal hope of feeling after him and finding him; and now is mandating an end to times of ignorance so that we all should choose to turn freely towards him and repudiate all that will leave us unworthy in the scrutiny by which the man he has appointed will judge between the just and the unjust, a prospect verified for everyone by the raising of that man from the dead (*Acts* 17:22-31; see also 1 *Cor.* 15:1-20). And indeed the good news—the new or newly sufficient information—as it was preached from the outset by that man, and after he (the Son of Man, Son of God) had left them was preached anew by Peter and the other pillars of the Jerusalem church, and then by Paul after his own conversion and their instruction of him, is always the same information: there is available, on the other side of death (and subject to conditions met or not met on this side of death), resurrection to a new form of bodily spiritual life inaugurated and guaranteed by Jesus's own resurrection, and constituting a new and final stage in the history of divine creation.

That history of creation now lies before us in the set of true beliefs we can and should hold as the rational deliverances of the natural sciences pursued in a historically and experimentally informed and philosophically sound way: the wondrous discontinuity of the Big Bang and emergence of the expanding and always complexifying cosmos, of the emergence of life, of the emergence of spiritual life—each discontinuity an inflooding of information new in kind, and not predictable or even imaginable on the basis of that out of which it emerged. And to that set of true beliefs we can add the true beliefs for which we rely upon the eyewitnesses of the signs and wonders reported to John the Baptist, and of, later, the empty tomb and resurrected life of Jesus the Christ, Greek for Messiah.

The history of Israel is the history of the formation of a people within which the information that is brought to a definitive form in the New Testament could and did emerge and find a cultural vehicle capable of conveying it through immense vicissitudes (occasioning the great Jewish *diaspora* of the Hellenistic age) into the *pax Romana*. With the benefit of both the *diaspora* and the *pax*, and with the courage of witnesses to the empty tomb and risen Lord, the information could be spread even as the Jerusalem and the main institutions of old Israel (and even outposts of it such as Machaerus) were all about to be reduced to desert. That catastrophe of old Israel occurred some five years after the Roman power at its very centre had suddenly turned against Peter and Paul and put them to death there. But not before their preaching had been recorded in its essentials by Matthew, Luke and Mark, as the oldest reports about the formation of those books make clear, and the best recent critically reasonable investigations confirm[43] (against the tide of fashionable opinion to which most Catholic biblical scholarship succumbed after and in plainest defiance of the Second Vatican Council[44]). And the message taught by Peter and Paul (and supplemented by another book-writing eyewitness and Apostle, John) in turn vindicates, just as it is vindicated by, the truthfulness of the prophets of Israel, and thus shows us how to read and understand the Old Testament. This entirely non-vicious circle—or better, upwards spiral—of cumulative presuppositions and mutually reinforcing evidence is, it seems to me, what Elizabeth Anscombe called the royal road to the Catholic faith, the reception and handing on of the good news of the new creation, the promised new life, soul and body.

---

[43] I hope to publish an account and discussion of these before long.
[44] Read *Dei Verbum* (Dogmatic Constitution on Revelation, November 1965), secs. 18 and 19 without omissions.

Index

Abortion, 4, 140, 149 n45, 172ff, 229 n9, 231.
Absolute,
  good, 37.
  imperatives, 2, 48, 80, 198, 206, 244.
  wrongness, 192, 208.
Abstraction, 7, 63, 276, 284.
Action,
  analysis of, 7, 51ff, 113–4, 145–6.
  and consequences, 8, 75, 137, 145–6, 201 n37, 205 n45.
  and motivations, 109ff.
  and obligation, 92–4, 98ff.
  and practical truth, 54ff.
  and rationality, 84 n21, 92.
  descriptions of, 51ff, 135–7, 151–2.
  evaluation of, 12, 34, 51ff, 75ff, 106, 109, 113–4, 233.
  human, 28–9, 53, 146, 280.
  intentional, 54 n10, 137, 225, 241.
  intrinsically bad, 40, 80–1, 93–7.
  military, 172–8.
  morally neutral, 51ff.
  self-interested, 47.
  sexual, 233ff.
  -theory, 7, 51ff.
  virtuous or vicious, 39–40, 47, 82.
  voluntary, 54 n10, 101–3, 113–6.
'Action, Intention, and "Double Effect"', 73, 145–6, 192, 208 n49.
Aesthetics, 31, 41–2.
'Analytical Philosophy and the Spirituality of Man', 11–8, 265.
Anscombe Bioethics Centre, ix, 263.
Anselm, 145 n32.
Appraisal,
  as an aspect of normativity, 105–18.
  moral, 12, 87, 95, 251 n23.
  of character, 12, 102.
Aquinas, Saint Thomas,
  on contraception, 188–9.
  on God's existence, 144.
  on human nature and dignity, 140–1, 174–9, 183–9, 276–7, 285.
  on matter, 266–7, 273.
  on moral evaluation, 7, 113–4, 210, 282.
  on natural law, 91–3, 113.
  on practical knowledge, 52, 55.
  on the 'guise of the good', 28, 66.
  on thought, 13 n10, 16–7.
  on venial sin, 4, 211.

Aristotle,
  influence on Anscombe, 7.
  on chastity, 5, 232–41.
  on God, 48–9, 90–4, 232, 235, 273, 279.
  on human nature, 30, 37–8, 40, 72, 90–1, 174–9, 183–6, 232–3, 264–7, 274–5.
  on moral evaluation, 80, 210, 224.
  on obligation, 85.
  on practical knowledge, 51–61, 70.
  on the 'guise of the good', 28.
  on thought, 13.
Assertion, 23–7.
Attachment, 254, 256, 258–62.
Attention, 9, 104.
  joint, 5, 243ff.
Augustine, 194, 198.
Authority, 92ff, 130–1, 245–50.
  as a virtue, 76–80.
  civil, 138–9.
  divine, 2, 76, 91–7.
  moral, 2, 100.
  parental, 245–60 *passim*.
'Authority in Morals', 94, 245–7.
Autonomy, 5, 72, 141, 246.
Averroes, 27 n21.

Babies, 147–51, 176–81, 212–3, 223, 260.
Belief,
  and assertion, 24–5.
  and thought, 13, 214.
  as faith, 6, 48.
  in God, 48, 95–100, 235, 287.
  reasons for, 218–20, 247.
Biggar, Nigel, 166–70.
Blame, 59, 83, 98ff, 222–9.
Body, 12–3, 31–2, 42, 46, 143, 177–80, 233, 260, 263ff.

Boethius, 174.

Cambridge University, 133, 263, 283.
Carrol, Lewis, 88.
Cartesian, 17, 144, 186.
Catholicism, 6, 117–8, 104, 154, 176, 193–201 *passim*, 265, 285 n40, 288.
Cause,
  and effect, 146, 151–3.
  final, 176–9, 185–6, 279.
  first, 279.
  formal, 178, 185–6.
  natural, 24, 273–4, 282.
Caveman, 20–6.
Celibacy, 230, 235.
Character, 4, 102–3, 217, 220–1, 284.
Chastity, 4–5, 189, 228–39.
Children, 5, 8, 103, 229–34, 243–262 *passim*.
Christ, 221, 232, 256, 265, 287.
Christianity, 7, 43–4, 90–4, 172, 221, 271–4.
Collingwood, R.G., 267, 279 n31.
Combatants, 158–70.
Communication, 18, 20–3, 123–7, 195.
  divine, *see* revelation.
Community, 78, 98, 101, 261.
Concepts,
  general, 16.
  moral, 8, 35–6, 91–3, 100, 141–2, 174–5.
Conscience, 31–2, 42, 78, 82, 255, 284–5.
Consciousness, 17, 25–32, 217–20.
Consequentialism, 39, 41, 53, 85, 193, 201–10.
Contemplation, 42, 52.
  of the divine, 5, 48, 91, 232,

Index

235, 241.
Contraception, 189, 228–42.
'Contraception and Chastity', 31–2, 42–4, 95, 228–42.
'Contraception, Chastity, and the Vocation of Marriage', 228, 232.
Courage, 102, 288.
CPP1, 8, 54.
CPP2, 187, 190, 226, 283.
CPP3, 6, 76, 79, 82, 94, 119, 133, 154–7, 160–3, 172–5, 205–8, 219, 231, 240, 245, 247, 260.
Creation, 275.
  divine, 6, 93, 144–5, 266, 273–4, 280–8.
Creatures, 20, 107, 123–4, 173.
  spiritual, 6.
Criticism,
  moral, 29, 105.
  rational, 33–5, 72, 97–8, 111–15, 234.

Darwin, Charles, 273, 279.
Death, 30, 40–4, 134–7, 145–52, 167–9, 287–8.
Decision, 33–4, 47–9, 99, 161–3, 231.
Democritus, 271–2.
Denyer, Nicholas, 4, 156–70 *passim*.
Descartes, René, 17, 222.
Desire, 54–7, 62–71, 107–8, 230–4, and 241–5.
Dignity,
  human, 1, 3–5, 8, 29–32, 135–45, 169, 191, 237–8, 286.
Disposition, 3, 14, 17, 75, 102, 131, 214–6.
  of sexuality, 229–30.
  virtuous or vicious, 4, 76.
DNA, 173, 269–75.
'Does Oxford Moral Philosophy Corrupt the Youth?', 192.
Domination, 268–9, 276.
Doubt, 176, 187, 200, 213–4, 218–22, 286.
Duty, 35, 76, 79, 98, 103–4, 114, 118, 155.
Dworkin, Ronald, 266, 283.

Education, 31, 229, 243ff.
  moral, *see* moral education.
Embryo, 4, 141, 172ff, 233.
'Embryos and Final Causes', 176–86.
Emotions, 31, 46, 80, 98, 107, 238–9.
Emotivism, 39.
Empirical, 6, 35, 41, 251, 269, 278.
End (*telos*), 62–73, 79, 88–9, 146–53, 196, 223, 234–42.
  human, 2, 28–37, 55–6, 141–5.
  immanent, 141–2.
  ultimate, 2, 5, 7, 28–37, 41, 43–50, 72–3, 90–1, 95–7, 145.
Euclid, 266.
Eudaimonia, 36, 45–6, 67, 90.
Evans, C. Stephen, 94 n59.
Evil, 38, 66, 87–90, 203–9, 231–6.
  necessary, 87–90.
Execution, 6, 80, 133.
Existence,
  of God, 6, 48–9, 95–7, 282–3.
  of law, 77, 100–1, 155.
  of obligation, 95, 100–1.
  of spiritual creatures, 5–6.

Facts, 213, 219, 234, 238, 247–8.
Fact/value distinction, vii, 7, 218 n10, 223–4, 227.
Failure, 3–4, 21–7, 103–5, 114, 219–26, 246–7.
Faith, 6–8, 43–4, 94, 127, 265,

286–8.
'Faith', 6.
Falsehood, 23–7, 53–8, 67–73, 194–7, 219, 224–7.
Family, 38, 40–1, 67, 229–31, 252.
Fear, 98, 252, 255.
FHG, 14, 27, 31, 42, 48, 91, 93, 174–6, 192, 199, 212, 227–43 *passim*, 265.
Fichte, Johann Gottlieb, 198.
Finnis, John, 5–6, 44, 47, 145–53, 263, 276–83 *passim*.
Flannery, Kevin L., 4, 153 n56, 176 n21, 192, 205 n44.
Flourishing, 37–46.
Foot, Philippa, 33–4, 38 n11, 46–9, 75 n1, 84 nn21&23, 93, 205 n45.
Ford, Norman, 181–2.
Framework propositions, 45.
Freedom, 6, 31, 104, 113–4, 141, 258, 281–4.
Frege, Gottlob, 16, 264.
Function,
  appraisive, 105–7, 112.
  directive, 99–105.
  human, 13, 46, 233–9, 270–1.
  logical, 88–9.
Geach, Mary, viii, 4–5, 50 n44, 161 n28, 192 n1, 227, 276.
Geach, Peter, 77, 95–7, 227 n1, 263–6, 277.
Goal, 8, 37, 62, 88, 222, 228.
God,
  and obligation, 2, 35–6, 77, 90–7 *passim*, 100, 117–8.
  and our final end, 8, 43–50 *passim*, 145, 235, 237.
  and revelation, 199 n31, 278–87.
  as creator, 31–2, 141 n25, 272 n19, 273–4, 279–87.
  communion with, 209–11.
  contemplation of, *see* contemplation.
Good,
  architectonic, 1–2, 7–8, 33ff.
  human, 3–8 *passim*, 38–9, 44–5, 87, 132, 136, 166, 226.
  orientation toward, 1–9 *passim*, 11, 29, 32.
  'the guise of the good', 28, 56, 66–73 *passim*.
Goodill, David, 4, 138, 154.
Gormally, Luke, viii, 3–4, 8, 50 n44, 133, 143 n29, 149 n45, 152 n49, 188, 192 n1, 263–4, 276.
Guilt, 31, 37, 134, 138, 158–70, 208, 225.

Harcourt, Edward, 5, 8, 243.
Hare, R.M., 61, 72–3.
Harris, John, 173–4, 188.
'Has Mankind One Soul – An Angel Distributed through Many Bodies', 15–7, 32 n46.
Hering, H.M., 182.
Hiroshima, 45, 148.
History,
  of philosophy, 14, 52.
  personal, 41, 168, 237, 247.
  world, 5–6, 46, 278–88.
HLAE, 11, 13, 15, 29–35 *passim*, 53, 55–6, 73, 84, 86, 95, 100, 133, 136, 143, 145, 173, 176, 180, 192, 205, 208, 227, 233, 235, 265.
Hobbes, Thomas, 125, 128, 131.
Hoffman, Martin L., 255.
Hoffmann, Peter M., 270–7.
Homicide, 3–4, 8, 172, 176, 187–91.
Hominization, 176ff.
Honesty, 4, 45, 135, 203, 207, 211, 229.

Hughes, Gerard, 173.
Human dignity, *see* dignity.
Human life, *see* life.
Human nature, *see* nature.
Hume, David, 3, 37–8, 102–4, 109–14, 119, 128–9, 153 n52, 219, 223, 234.
  neo-Humean, 37–8, 43, 50.
Humpty Dumpty, 193, 211, 236.

Individuation, 16.
Information, 6, 263ff.
  analogous, 269–71, 280.
  central-case, 269ff.
  genetic, 179, 269.
  mis-, 38.
Injustice, 2–4, 39–49 *passim*, 135–9, 162, 166, 168, 172, 284.
Innocent,
  and abortion, 140, 172.
  and judicial condemnation, 6, 39, 80.
  and killing, 3–4, 135–8, 145, 153, 172, 174.
  and lying to protect, 198–209 *passim*.
  and war, 156, 158–65, 170.
Instantiation, 16.
Intellect, 16–7, 141.
Intention, 7, 45, 52–7, 60–3, 66, 77–8, 146–51, 244.
Intentions,
  in action, 3–4, 28–31, 59 n24, 69, 107, 115, 145–53, 166–70, 240–2.
  in communication, 6, 24–6, 122, 125–30, 194–7, 215–20, 225–6, 269, 278.
Intentionality, 17–8.
Interest, 9, 224–5, 229.
  self-, 40–7, 225.

Jesus, 254, 286–7.

Jewish,
  faith, 43, 86, 90, 265, 273.
  people, 172, 280–1, 287–8.
  Scriptures, 6, 279.
Johnson, James Turner, 155–6, 164.
Jones, David Albert, 1, 50 n44, 74 n69, 97 n70, 124, 141, 153 n56, 154 n1, 165 n40, 172, 176–7, 185–9 *passim*, 192 n1.
Judgment, 21–31 *passim*, 89, 142–5, 210, 276, 279–80.
  moral, 52, 57–8, 96, 161–9, 284.
Just war, 4, 154ff.
Justice, 2–6, 39–49 *passim*, 130–1, 135–45, 154–68 *passim*, 189, 227–9, 284–6.
Justification,
  of action, 115–6, 122, 135, 143, 157, 161, 169.
  of belief, 8, 25, 39, 107–8.

Kant, Immanuel, 72, 79, 84–5, 139–40, 198, 248.
Kenny, Anthony, 60 n27, 232 n15.
Killing, vii, 117, 133ff, 209.
  and abortion, 172ff.
  in war, 4, 157–70 *passim*.
  intentional, 3, 133ff.
Knowledge, 25–7, 93–7, 219, 225, 242, 264–6.
  moral, 73, 95.
  practical, 51–68, 147–50.
  theoretical, 52.
Kolodny, Niko, 128–9.
Koppelman, Andrew, 229 n9, 236.
Korsgaard, Christine, 83–4.

Language games, 119, 127–30.
Law,
  divine, 2–3, 8, 39, 44, 48, 86, 91–100, 118, 174.

-giver, 2–3, 8, 77, 94–100.
moral, 35–6, 49, 77, 93–9, 104–5, 113, 118, 140, 154–5, 160, 238.
natural, 91–5, 104–5, 113, 117–8, 155, 160.
Legal,
direction, 99–105, 118.
distinctions, 158–64.
rights, *see* rights.
system, 77–8, 123, 138.
obligations, *see* obligation.
Lejeune, Jerome, 179–82.
Life, 6, 177–8, 268–75.
human, 3, 29–32, 40–7, 56, 67–73, 135–45, 183–6, 191, 233–9.
moral, 31, 92–4.
spiritual, 287–8.
Locke, John, 173–4.
Love, 38, 92, 141–5, 237–8, 248–50, 253–62.
Lying, 4, 192ff.

MacIntyre, Alasdair, 42 n22, 175 n12.
Maritain, Jacques, 182.
Marriage, 5, 189, 233–4, 237–42.
McCormick, Richard, 181.
McLaren, Ann, 182.
Meaning, 14, 18ff, 39–43, 66, 81, 87, 93–4, 151–2, 167, 239–42, 269, 282.
Meditation, 30.
Merit, 109–13, 284.
Metaphor, 36, 42–3, 57, 100, 275.
Metaphysics, 91, 175–6, 279.
Mind, 16–8, 194–211 *passim*, 221, 235, 251–3, 261, 279–83.
corruption of, 5, 73, 80.
'Modern Moral Philosophy', vii, 2, 7, 35, 39–40, 53–4, 83–6, 91–6, 172, 206, 227.
Moore, G.E., 135, 234.
Moral education, 5, 243ff.
Motivation, 101–3, 107–16, 129, 250–1.
Motives, 94, 167–8, 232–3, 241–2.
'Mr Truman's Degree', 154, 161.
Müller, Anselm Winfried, 1–8, 10, 51 n2, 192 n1, 223.
Murder, 4, 38, 40–2, 48, 80, 133ff, 156, 160, 188–9, 205 n45.
'Murder and the Morality of Euthanasia', 30 n38, 133, 136, 140, 145, 173–6.
Mystical, 42, 47, 237.
aspect of virtue, 30–2, 228, 231–2.

Nagasaki, 148.
Nature, 272–3.
human, 1–6, 28–32, 40, 93, 104, 140, 144, 179, 188–9, 227, 238.
rational, 1, 136, 140, 174, 238.
spiritual, 1–3, 10ff.
Nazis, 38.
Normativity, 2, 7, 27–9, 64–5, 79, 83–6, 92–3, 105–16.
Norms, 84–5.
moral, 81, 92–3, 136.
of truth and goodness, 1, 30–1.

Obedience,
in children, 5, 245–50.
to authority, 77, 136, 138, 145.
to God, 50, 92–7.
Obligation,
legal, 78, 99–100, 105, 118.
moral, 2, 7, 35, 76–83, 86, 90–

1, 94–5, 98ff, 112ff, 126, 196.
  practical, 2–3, 48, 65, 75ff, 141.
  social, 78–80, 119ff.
O'Brien, Matthew B., 2–3, 50 n44, 75, 76 n4, 192 n1.
Omission, 98–105, 137–8, 204–6, 212.
'On Being in Good Faith', 4, 212–3, 218–9, 221, 225.
'On Promising and its Justice…', 82, 86–91, 119ff.
'On the Source of the Authority of the State', 79 n11, 133.
'On Transubstantiation', 260.
'On Wisdom', 27, 30 n37, 235 nn26&27.
Orientation,
  to God, 8, 141.
  to truth and goodness, 1–9 *passim*, 11, 29, 31–2.
  wrong, 23, 28, 284.
Oxford, 1, 133, 148, 154, 263, 267.

Pacifism, 156–8.
Pantheism, 266, 283.
Parmenides, 8 n2, 14 n14.
Passion, 98, 110, 155, 229–38, 284.
Paul (St.), 2, 118, 266 n8, 280–8 *passim*.
Perception, 15–7, 23–4, 276–7.
  moral, 30–2, 33–4, 80, 145.
  mystical, 31, 42, 47, 231.
Peter (St.), 282, 287–8.
Pink, Thomas, 2–3, 79 n10, 98.
Plato, 5, 15, 94, 194, 232, 271, 273, 276, 279.
  neo-Platonism, 266.
Pleasure, 231–42, 243–50 *passim*, 260–2.
Pope John Paul II, 178 n27, 188.
Pope Pius XII, 155.
Power,
  and authority, 79, 130–1, 248.
  coercive, 37, 138–9.
  divine, 274, 280–5.
  human, 97, 104, 140, 174 185–6, 233–4.
Practical,
  necessity, 2, 76, 77ff.
  reason, *see* reason.
  syllogism, 54–73, 89, 223.
  truth, *see* truth.
'Practical Inference', 29 n34, 33–7, 54–6, 61–2, 65 n45, 69 n54, 70–2, 86ff, 97.
'Practical Truth', 56, 65, 69, 73.
Practices, 2–3, 21–4, 78, 80–5, 90–1, 96–7, 110–2, 119ff.
  social, 2, 78, 80, 121–32 *passim*.
Prichard, H.A., 83 n20.
Proclus, 266.
Procreation, 5, 239–41.
Promising, vii, 3, 43–8, 86–91, 119ff.
Psychology,
  empirical, 35.
  moral, 130, 234.
  philosophy of, 53–7.
Ptolemy the First, 266.
PtW, 28, n33, 276 n29.
Punishment, 31, 103, 138–42, 159–69, 250–3.
Purpose, 84–94, 148–50, 223–4.

Quinn, Warren, 37–40.

Rawls, John, 120–1, 131.
Raz, Joseph, 83 n18, 107, 120 n2.
Reality, 26–7, 272, 283.
  spiritual, 14.
Reason,

for action, 40–1, 82–97, 126–9, 197–8, 205, 218, 249–50, 258–9, 262.
practical, 2–3, 34–7, 44, 47, 51, 54–74, 76, 79, 88–97, 110–3, 147–50.
reasonable action, 35–8, 44–5, 47–8, 77–9, 107–18, 122–3, 209–11.
the faculty of, 5, 8, 43, 48–9, 82–97, 107–18, 230–41, 279–81.

Reflection,
intrinsic, 199, 211.
philosophical, 6, 8, 179.

Relation,
of marriage, 234–41.
of means to ends, 65–7.
of parents to children, 243ff.
to God, 118, 209–11.

Representation, 15–6.
Respect, 3–4, 30–2, 44, 81, 142–5, 180, 196, 226–9, 238, 259.
Responsibility, 4, 98–100, 108–9, 134–5, 139, 143, 161–70, 204–5, 212, 244, 281–4.
Revelation, 5–6, 94–6, 199 n31, 278–88.
Reward, 43–4, 103, 250–3.
Richter, Duncan, 1–3, 7, 33.

Rights,
basic human, 140, 160–1, 170, 209.
legal, 160.
property, 124–5.

Rodin, Auguste, 12–3.
Rodin, David, 156 n14, 166.
Rousseau, Jean-Jacques, 124–5.
Royal Road, 263ff.

Rules,
logical, 88.
grammatical, 81, 126, 167.
of a game, 48, 91–2.
of right action, 75–6, 92, 217.
social, 144, 250–62.
'Rules, Rights and Promises', 119ff.
Ryle, Gilbert, 88 n35, 214.

Sacred, 8, 31, 91.
Sacrifice, 41, 281.
self-, 42–9.
Sanction, 99–105, 113, 117, 189, 255.
Scanlon, T.M., 107–9, 120–30 *passim*.
Scepticism, 1–3, 6–8, 37, 45, 88, 111–3, 191, 249, 257.
Scholastics, 3, 92, 105, 113–7.
Schüller, Bruno, 193, 201–6.

Science,
ethics as a, 45, 53.
natural, 179, 264, 267–79, 287.

Scotus, 117 n15, 195.
Second World War, 155, 157.
Second Vatican Council, 6, 288.
Secular ethics, 1, 5, 36, 39–50 *passim*, 101.
Sforza, Lodovico, 247, 257, 262.
Shame, 31, 38–41, 80–4.
Sidgwick, Henry, 53 n10, 206.
Sin, 48–50, 91–4, 155, 188, 202–11, 225, 228.
mortal, 196–8, 225.
venial, 4, 196, 209–10.
'Sin', 48–50, 93–4, 234–5.
Sincerity, 4, 212ff.
Socrates, 94, 277.
Soul, 1, 14–7, 29–32, 140, 232–3, 263ff.
of an embryo, 172, 175–9, 184–9.
Spinozism, 266, 280 n25.
Spirit, 10ff, 265, 277–80.
Spiritual nature, *see* nature.

Index

Spirituality, 1, 10ff.
State of nature, 123–5.
Stoics, 44, 86, 90–1.
Student, 9, 161.
Suarez, Francisco, 92 n49, 117–8, 194, 199–201, 211.
Substance,
  immaterial, 5, 17, 174, 178, 183–7, 264ff.
  spiritual, 5, 12, 14.
Suicide, 41, 151–2.
Supernatural, 37, 94.
Suttie, Ian, 253 n26, 255, 260 n46.

Teichmann, Roger, 4, 45–7, 50 n44, 57 n19, 60 n29, 74 n69, 150 n46, 153 n56, 192 n1, 212, 226 n19.
Teleology,
  and action, 148–9, 193 n11, 201–3, 223.
  and human nature, 140, 145, 177.
  of assertion and judgment, 24ff.
Tertullian, 178.
'The Dignity of the Human Being', 31–2, 143 n28.
'The Early Embryo: Theoretical Doubts and Practical Certainties', 176–91, 233 n19.
'The Justice of the Present War Examined', 154–5, 208 n49.
'The Moral Environment of the Child', 5, 243ff.
Theological,
  ethics, 92–6.
  moral theology, 155, 192–3, 204.
  virtues, 94, 209–10.
Thompson, Michael, 46, 52 n8, 120 n2, 131–2.

Thomson, Judith Jarvis, 188.
Thought,
  and behavior, 11–2, 78.
  human, 12ff.
  objects of, 14ff, 107–11, 115–6.
  quasi-, 26–7.
  sincerity in, 212ff.
'Thought and Action in Aristotle: What is "Practical Truth"?', 54–5, 58–61, 72–3.
Three Philosophers, 264–7, 276.
Tolstoy, Leo, 220.
Torralba, José M., 2, 7, 51–2, 63 n42.
Tractatus Logico-Philosophicus, 8 n2, 36.
Transcendent, 6, 141, 273–87 *passim*.
Transubstantiation, 260.
Trevarthen, Colwyn, 260.
Truman, Harry S.,
  honorary degree, 148, 154.
Trust,
  across species, 123–4.
  and faith, 6.
  in God, 41–3.
  violations of, 198.
Truth,
  and goodness, 1, 4–9, 11, 30–2.
  and sincerity, 217–8, 224–7.
  as opposed to lying, 4, 192ff.
  of assertion, 20–8.
  of moral claims, 6.
  practical, 2, 51ff.
Twinning, 179ff.
'Two Moral Theologians', 192–206.

Universal moral principles, 58, 64, 84–5.
Universe, 6, 38, 264, 272–87 *passim*.

Utilitarian,
  aspect of virtue, 42, 228, 231.
  value, 31–2.
  view of ethics, 39, 75, 228.

Validity, 34, 57, 64–72.
Velleman, David, 247–50.
Vermeersch, Arthur, 4, 192–211.
Vice, 40, 102–5, 118, 223–7.
Vigo, Alejandro, 54 n13, 55 n17.
Violence, 125, 138–9, 155–8, 163–4, 170.
Virtue, vii.
  and talent, 109.
  ethics, 39–40, 75ff, 102–4, 227.
  intellectual, 224.
  mystical aspect, 30–2, 228, 231–2.
  theological, 94, 209–10.
  utilitarian aspect, 31–2, 42, 228, 231.
Vogler, Candace, 3, 119, 192 n1.

Voluntary, 54, 101–5, 115–6, 122–3, 142, 212, 215, 225–6.
Voluntarism, 91, 139, 144.

Wallace, R. Jay, 128–9.
War, 4, 124, 138, 205 n45, 220.
  just, 4, 154ff.
'War and Murder', 156, 163, 205 n45.
'Were You a Zygote?', 180–6, 233 n19.
Williams, Bernard, 98ff, 244 n6, 259 n41.
Wittgenstein, Ludwig, 7–8, 11–2, 36–45 *passim*, 53 n10, 88 n35, 119, 175–9, 186, 214 n5, 216 n6, 265.
Worship, 31, 48, 91, 235, 281.
Wright, G.H. von, 52 n6, 61, 70–1.

'You Can Have Sex Without Children', 240–1.

Zygote, 176–91 *passim*.